dunwalkin

by

Paul Barber

Paul Barber

Guide Dogs is a charity close to my heart and very much part of my adventure. I'm hoping to be able to make a further donation to Guide Dogs from sales of this book to continue to support the incredible work they do.

Thank you!

In aid of

Guide Dogs

Published by Publishing Company here Printed by Book Printing UK
www.bookprintinguk.com

Remus House, Coltsfoot Drive, Peterborough, PE2 9BF

Printed in Great Britain

ISBN 978-1-3999-8264-1

Target Audience

Book people and publishers often ask the question, who is your target audience?

Any author surely wants their work to be 'inclusive'. Appealing to all, particularly when you are selling it for charity. However, at risk of putting some off, as a guide, here goes. If you fall anywhere near the following categories, this might be for you.

- Radio Two listeners.
- Enjoy music and are a lyric lover.
- A lifelong 'TOG', one of Terry's Old Gits. Enjoy 'Janet and John' and the phrase, 'Top of the morning'.
- Remember JFK being 'blown away', the Pillsbury doughboy, cheese and pineapple hedgehogs, vol-au-vents, fondue skewers and artic roll.
- Are a former rugby player or sports person.
- If you enjoy wildlife, animals and especially dogs.
- Like walking, camping, adventure and maps.
- If you have seen between 50 and 70 summers. Plus, or minus groups are in no way prohibited.
- Are a Hash House harrier or are intrigued?
- Do not possess an iPhone.
- Have 'a granny who tells you the old songs are the best.'
- Are in any way associated to Guide Dogs for the Blind or the Royal National Lifeboat Institution, but you don't have to be an anorak.
- Remember Green Shield stamps, half crowns, vinyl, and enjoy the BBC archive with Vernon Kay.
- Are happy giving to charity.
- Live in the past but also look to the future. Look back to see forward.
- If you met two around Britain walkers with their dog in 2006/7.
- Are one of the dozens of people who helped us out, put us up, supported, contributed or motivated- thank you, you may get a mention. Hope I haven't forgotten too many, and if I have, please forgive me.
- If you clean your ear with a pen and like inuendo.
- If you are something of a technophobe and prefer to see a sports pitch being marked by a man with a three wheeled push along, rather than a remote handset with a robot roaming at his feet.
- If you have an inquiring mind for all things historical/geographical and a wide-ranging craving for knowledge verging on the compendious.
- Have ever been in/out of love.
- If your views are opinionated and slightly left field.
- If you can accept neurodiversity is 'healthy' and not a disorder.
- If you like to make contact with your inner self.
- If you chase your best self.

If you tick any of the above boxes, I hope you enjoy.

Dedication

For Spud (R.I.P.)

KATHERINE (SPUD) TALBOT-PONSONBY (1967-2010) was the initial inspiration for our walk. We met her originally through her first book “two feet four paws”. She showed us the way. We would meet her again on her farm in Kelso, three years before her passing at the ever too young age of 42 as we followed in her footsteps, albeit following the clock. This is written in her memory and with kind regards to her bereaved husband and family.

Foreword

This is a narrative of a walking odyssey 2006/07. A trio's 11-month continuous trip around Britain's 'outer' coast, a unique beating of the bounds. A journey of discovery; both in the landscape, remote unspoilt corners as well as populated blighted quarters, and themselves. Accounting those they met, dramatic scenery, problems encountered, historical interest, wildlife, necessary endurance. It tells of something very different from everyday life, of a worthwhile and inspiring wandering. To boldly go where others *have* gone before, to consider some of their observations and compare them with random, compelling, quirky left field sightings of the author's own. It is brought up to date by revisits to certain parts of the coast for added contemporary pragmatic descriptions and considers the regenerative capabilities of coastal locations and oneself. Book ended by very honest personal reflection it asks the question 'who is winning at life?' Those who enjoy the call of the sea and the songs of the waves will be entertained by the lyrical references in the 'tracks of my years.' A gripping perambulation not to be missed.

Contents

'Tracks of my Years' Chapter Headings

Preface	Walkin down the street ... don't walk through my words	*Dreadlock Holiday, 10CC, 1978*
Introduction	Music is a world within itself ... You can feel it all over	*Sir Duke, Stevie Wonder, 1976*
Chapter 1	Genesis	*Hebrew beginning, rock band 1967*
Chapter 2	A wee scabby dug as smart as any damn kid	*D.I.V.O.R.C.E, Billy Connolly, 1975*
Chapter 3	Anarchy in the UK	*Sex Pistols, 1976*
Chapter 4	This one's for the children	*New Kids on the Block, 1989*
Chapter 5	Follow you, follow me	*Genesis, 1978*
Chapter 6	Chain keep us together (running in the shadows)	*The Chain, Fleetwood Mac, 1977*
Chapter 7	Kyrie eleison (O Lord have Mercy)	*Mr Mister, 1985*
Chapter 8	Saviour of the universe ...with only 14 hours to save the earth	*Flash's Theme, Queen, 1980*
Chapter 9	Up at eight, you can't be late	*Matthew & Son, Cat Stevens, 1967*
Chapter 10	London calling from the faraway towns	*London Calling, The Clash, 1979*
Chapter 11	Oh Mr Fisherman, home from the sea, have you a lobster you can sell to me?	*The Fisherman Song, Ron & the Rude Boys, 2009*
Chapter 12	You started this fire ...burning out of control	*Don't leave me this way, The Communards, 1986*
Chapter 13	I'm strong to the "finich", 'cause I eats me spinach	*I'm Popeye the Sailor Man, 1934*
Chapter 14	Come hear the music play ...life is a cabaret	*Cabaret, Liza Minnelli, 1972*
Chapter 15	Sun is in the sky, oh why oh why would I wanna be anywhere else?	*LDN, Lily Allen, 2006*
Chapter 16	Round and round The Garden	*Roud Folk Song Index, 19235*
Chapter 17	Will you still need me, will you still feed me	*When I'm 64, The Beatles, 1967*
Chapter 18	All you wanna do is criticize	*Criticize, Alexander O'Neal, 1987*

Chapter 19	Stop pretending, tell me what's in your heart	*If you're lookin' for a way out, Odyssey, 1980*
Chapter 20	Hey there Mr Blue … I'll remember you this way	*Mr Blue Sky, ELO, 1977*
Chapter 21	And the tears rolled into the ocean	*Black and Gold, Sam Sparro, 2008*
Chapter 22	Crying, laughing, loving, lying	*Labi Siffre, 1972*
Chapter 23	I've had my share of sand kicked in my face, but I've come through	*We are the Champions, Queen, 1977*
Chapter 24	She only reveals what she wants you to see	*She's always a woman, Billy Joel, 1977*
Chapter 25	Sad, so sad …. it's getting' more and more absurd	*Sorry Seems to be the Hardest Word, Elton John, 1976*
Chapter 26	Asso Asso Yogoshi	*Max Boyce, 1973*
Chapter 27	Take a black cat and sit in on your shoulder …in the morning you'll know all you know	*Ride a White Swan, T.Rex, 1970*
Chapter 28	But these two …Gumshoes. Picking up the slack	*Chip 'n' Dale Rescue Rangers Theme, The Jets, 1989*
Chapter 29	An invisible force pulling me closer to you …don't stand a snowball's chance in hell	*Moth to a Flame, Oliva Newton John, 1985*
Chapter 30	Open up Your Beach Umbrella	*Hi Ho Silver Lining, Jeff Beck, 1968*
Chapter 31	I see the crystal raindrops fall	*Just the Two of Us Bill Withers, 1980*
Chapter 32	I get up when I want, put on my trousers and have a cup of tea	*Parklife, Blur, 1994*
Chapter 33	You'll Never Walk Alone	*Jerry and the Pacemakers, 1963*
Chapter 34	Past rack and samphire …walking through the tide as rain cuts through the spray	*On Morcambe Bay, Christy Moore, 2011*
Chapter 35	A troubled bridge over swirling waters (*modified*) …I'm on your side	*Bridge Over Troubled Water, Simon & Garfunkel, 1974*
Chapter 36	Fox On The Run	*Sweet, 1974*
Chapter 37	You better start swimmin', if you'll sink like a stone	*Times They Are A-Changin', Bob Dylan, 1964*

Chapter 38	Smiles in the sunshine and tears in the rain	*Mull of Kintyre, Paul McCartney and Wings, 1977*
Chapter 39	Billow and breeze, islands and seas	*Skye Boat Song, Robert Louis Stevenson, 1892*
Chapter 40	You and I must make a pact, we must bring salvation back	*I'll be there, The Jackson 5, 1970*
Chapter 41	Taken my heart, torn it apart	*Where Did I Go Wrong, UB40, 1988*
Chapter 42	Leaves that are green turn to brown, wither with the wind, crumble in your hand	*Leaves That Are Green, Simon & Garfunkel, 1964*
Chapter 43	Feet start to pound ...what you see is what you get	*Going Underground, The Jam, 1980*
Chapter 44	Footprints in the sand ... washed away when the water hit the land	*Live Every Moment, REO Speedwagon, 1984*
Chapter 45	Never forget ...we've looked each day and night in the eye	*Never Forget, Take That, 1995*
Chapter 46	Oh, what about us	*Pink, 2017*
Chapter 47	Beat on the bottom with a Woman's Weekly	*The Ballad of Barry and Freda, Victoria Wood, 1997*
Chapter 48	Can music save your mortal soul?	*American Pie, Don McLean, 1971*
Chapter 49	If I never loved, I never would have cried	*I Am a Rock, Simon & Garfunkel, 1964*
Chapter 50	Brushing off the dust, you hear my voice, I am a champion hear me roar	*Roar, Katy Perry, 2013*
Chapter 51	There are places I'll remember	*In My Life, The Beatles, 1965*
Chapter 52	The only truth I know is you	*Kathy's Song, Simon & Garfunkel, 1964*
Chapter 53	You can go the distance; you can walk straight through hell with a smile	*Hall of Fame, The Script, 2012*
Chapter 54	Thought you were one in a million	*I Wanna Get Lost With You, Stereophonics, 2015*
Chapter 55	Heaven holds a place for those who pray	*Mrs Robinson, Simon & Garfunkel, 1964*

Preface

Walkin down the street...don't walk through my words

"It's a serious business deciding what you want from life."

I WAS GIVEN A copy of an e-book, a new experience for me. I didn't look at it for ages. In fact, it was early September 2020 before I started scanning it. It was an account of a couple's walk around Britain in 2006/07. It took 11 months. I was one half of that couple, one third of a team. I didn't get much editorial and what was there was scathing. (*"Wherever I Hang My Lead."*)

I had kept a diary religiously during the whole time it took to walk 5000 miles - three notebooks, 335 daily entries. I also had five albums of photos as reminders of a unique and colourful story. I had ambitions of writing something to emulate others, my heroes, who had done it before and started tentatively in 2008. Events overwhelmed me and all was put on hold, I thought permanently.

Later in September 2020 I happened to be in Southend for the weekend, the nearest seaside resort from my current home which is about as far from the sea as you can get anywhere in Britain. I had bored many people as I reminisced about our odyssey. After much heartache and discussion, I started writing in earnest in October 2020 - it would be the sequel, the true account, also something of a memoir. Why write it now?

If others can have their say, why can't I have mine? If musicians can do covers, why not amateur authors, especially if they have a unique story to tell. However, this is in no way an attempt to settle a score, sour grapes, be vindictive or vengeful and there is no willingness to discredit. It is more that, having been on the pavement, the time is right to 'take inventory on my investment - look myself in the eye.'

My notebooks held a tale of the country and culture in 2006/07, one of richness and diversity. Walking, although neither of us were fanatics, allowed you to see things not seen from a car. I even think you need to allow yourself time to walk, at a pace which allows absorption; seeing, hearing, smelling, feeling all that is on offer - with time to reflect. Our ignorance of the country was transformed into awareness and knowledge - our curiosity increased.

My observations were random, quirky, and self-absorbing, very often left of field. They reflected the essence of places, history, and trends. The notes held a unique and personal journey, very different from other accounts. There were few lists, little analysis, little pfaffing in the preparatory stages, no van to sleep in, lots of people met who were full of inherent goodness and deserving of a mention. That good will needed to be honoured, the true story told. I wanted my account to be full and wholly accurate with the benefit of contemporaneous diary notes. I also wanted to be honest, including warts and all, but with no intention of seeking self-pity.

"Truth is like a jalapeno, the closer to the root, the hotter it gets." (McConaughey).

There were many times while walking for 11 months you were alone with your thoughts. Ear worms would invade a grey space, those colour this account. Lyrics from across decades. The 'Tracks of my Years.' A varied theme running through the journey, what lyrics can you recognise, how many can you sing along to, are you too a '*Bloody Tourist*'? ('You ain't heard me out yet').

I have read other walkers' ramblings of their experiences and wanted to include some of that by way of comparison. Hence, some of their comments are included and a bibliography provided to enable direction to more scholarly books.

I was aware that 16 years, and counting, have elapsed since this Herculean walk around Britain. That time has seen a stock market plunge in 2008, the coming and going of Obama and Trump, several cycles of summer Olympic Games, a general awakening about the state of the environment, and a widespread call for action on global warming. Brexit, the Covid 19 pandemic with its restrictions and consequences still occurring and, right now, a war in eastern Europe which could still easily escalate. With additional rubble and bodies being piled in Gaza and tensions raised throughout the Middle East, my story was still untold. Somehow global events seemed to prompt me to action.

I felt I needed to bring things up to date. Things will have changed. I wanted to supplement my account of the walk with reflective and contemporary observations since these events. To wander through time. Hence, I have revisited some places, akin to Kevin McCloud in Grand Designs, to see how things are now. Are places 'winning at life?' I needed to check if I was too.

Personally, I am also much older, more decrepit, possibly a tad wiser. I needed to include my feelings and emotions and consider if the process of doing this has in any way been cathartic. This story, although principally about walking Britain's outer coast is also a personal chronical and critique of mid-life years.

Introduction, background, setting the scene

Music is a world within itself... You can feel it all over

"There is a certain romanticism about life on the road."

Inspiration

"I would love to do that."

"We could do it if you wanted."

We were in north Cornwall on the coast path, early days after getting together. Wendy was reading Spud's book, "*two feet, four paws,*" an account of a feisty, young woman walking Britain's coastline with her dog, Tess. Truth beknown, Wendy was full of envy. This book was the real inspiration. My reply was genuine and serious, I fancied it too, but it was also loaded with eagerness to impress.

What was just around the next headland? We had no more time to find out then, but we pledged we would one day. I remembered a story on 'Nationwide' from the late 1970s, about a man John Merrill (JM), who had completed a 7000-mile walking circumnavigation, he was the first. At the time, a young fit PE student in Exeter, I thought, no big deal. I would get to find otherwise. Since JM many have had a go, often sectional walkers, still only around 50 who have completed with continuous walks according to Douglas Legg (*Coastal Walkers*).

Wendy's spirit was straight out of Spud's mould. Determined, strong-willed but also kind and sensitive. She was also very impulsive, which caused its problems. I was determined, strong-willed, less kind, much less sensitive, less impulsive, more impatient and generally pricklier. "*Wherever I Hang My Lead*" describes me as having a 'big, squashed nose and stance' and refers to me as The English Bulldog (TEB). The nose may be right, the stance thick set, dog like, I tend to disagree - more silver back gorilla. 'Lady and the Tramp,' 'Beauty and the Beast,' in both, one was charming, sincere, innocent almost angelic, the other a stunted, cold-hearted rogue.

Educated and Pub dog

In Wendy's account, written under the pseudonym of Havoc, our dog, reference is made to joint working with 'naughty boys and girls,' a happening prior to any walk, background stuff, which needs explanation. Little reference is made to early success she and I shared working just as a couple. That work, with several 'excluded' school children was good, the results exemplary, yet it is conveniently ignored. Also, lots of happy times with tremendous results working together, admittedly before Havoc came along. That I will call the Perkins' era, after a braille machine, also handily bypassed.

It is quoted that I was unable to cope with disruptive behaviour and left the 'Outdoor Education Instructor' work. I think it fair to say I was less tolerant of some of it than Wendy, but had equal success, managing it differently. It also states, I made life miserable for her and Havoc who stayed in their roles culminating in the authorities getting involved and me moving out of a joint home. As with many disagreements there are two sides of a tale, the truth often to be found somewhere in the middle. My reasons for leaving both work and (her) flat had more to do with a new, young, ambitious colleague's arrival, followed by 'whistle blowing,' presented months after alleged events, at a time when we were all being asked to re-apply for our jobs. Any discomfort felt by Wendy and Havoc might be explained as guilt of conscience for displaying little loyalty to me. Any transgressions I may have made were to the controlling/coercive end of a spectrum, rather than the physical/violent end, and the coercion without threat. However, I acknowledge a trait which might show insufficient regard for other people's wishes and now I try to remain vigilant to it.

Homeless, I was able to buy a cottage just up the road. As for 'worming my way' back into anyone's lives, I must have done a good job of that. There was certainly chance for a break and change of direction. It was done with Wendy's full consent, and I feel shows what complete commitment there was from me to trying to make our relationship work. If anyone 'twitched or squeaked' in their sleep subsequently, I apologise. Wendy would move in, leaving her own flat to her teenage children. Time moved on, not always perfect but with many untroubled intervals and we could resume the thoughts of a walk on the wild side.

It would be fair to say I would never have contemplated the walk if it were not for Wendy. I wouldn't have wanted to do it alone, I would have been bored, and couldn't have done it without her. We made a good pairing. We had a certain 'Tsaheylu' (Na'vi word from Avatar meaning bonding.) I was doing it, very willingly, because she wanted to, I wanted her to be happy. Many who have achieved this trek speak of a 'real love of walking,' neither of us could truly be described as belonging to that club.

Character Profile

The third member of our team, making up the dream ticket, was Havoc – a tri coloured mongrel, part Jack Russell, rough collie and German shepherd. It makes you wonder how his biological parents got it together. Scruffy fur, with grey whiskers he stood about knee high. Energetic, with an expressive, characterful face and very cute. From a largish litter in Ilsington, Devon he remembers being the biggest pup, I think of him as the runt of the group. Floppy eared, something of a longish pointed nose, 'eyes as wet as puddles,' and I should say this quite quietly, not the sharpest canine in the pack - minute brained. He was originally named 'Biscuit', a part burned, part underbaked ginger nut, and that suited him well. Wendy, having lost a previous love, Avon, would go to the local animal shelter and walk any abandonee, one was called 'Havoc', she liked the name and re used it when she adopted her new baby. It was appropriate for his mannerisms, though "Chaos" might have been more original. Think cross between Pluto, Huckleberry Hound, Goofy and Gromit and you have a fair image.

He had a bark far worse than his bite. Some running group members (hashers) would get annoyed about it at the start of our runs, excitement causing him to howl continually, he never got trained. Sheep chasing, in fact anything chasing, was an untamable habit. He was quick, never going to outrun a lurcher at a dog show, though he was entered, and fickle, anyone's best friend or orphan if they had food. The barking should not be confused with any sense of bravery. Bravado was very superficial, deep down he was as soft as any down pillow or new baby skin and scared of his own shadow.

He was afflicted by a couple of other negative traits, selective deafness, and wind. The first often got me into trouble as I would say something, he took no notice, ran off chasing something with risk of being shot, for which I got the blame. The second was undeniably all his, easily recognisable, mine were less potent. Wendy adopted him while we were attempting an ill-fated career change, playing at pub workers, and he did sleep in an outbuilding (neither cold nor damp) but was not made to do so by me. As employees you must bow to employer rules and if a new adoptee arrives, you must abide by the boss' wishes. It was unfair to blame me for pet sleeping arrangements. What I do take responsibility for is not fully considering Wendy's reluctance to going to the pub in the first place, her heart was never really in it, and hence it was short lived. There was a good example of that earlier trait of mine.

Owners and their dogs do grow together. They develop strong bonds, but those bonds are not necessarily the same from one individual to another. Havoc was very 'lucky', Wendy was a complete dog 'freak.' It might be said she loved him too much, she said herself she was 'overprotective,' not in an unhealthy way, but in a different way to me. Having the same feelings and emotions as humans, I am not sure of that, however dogs I believe have dog emotions. Dress them up in Vibram shoes that will protect their pads on a marathon trek, I am not convinced, and neither was Havoc, he hated the things, and could not wait to kick them off. For those who go back far enough to 'Watch with Mother' in the late fifties, think 'Woodentops' and 'Spotty Dog'.

I treated him more as a proper dog, he would go to his mum if given the choice, but he also knew I was his dad who loved him in a different way, and I don't think he would have stooped to name calling. He was never deliberately ill-treated by me. That cottage of mine needed to be readied for renting out while we were gone on the walk. While working on it, things needed bringing in from the street, a busy one, so the door was propped open. While baby-sitting, to avoid Havoc running out into the road I used his lead to secure him to a sawing horse. A draught caused the back door to slam, he lurched for the open front door taking the sawing horse with him, which cluttered against a rear leg hock joint. He yelped in pain and fright, but at least he didn't get run over. He did, we subsequently discovered, sustain a small fracture, painful, debilitating for him, a plaster cast, and it ruined my baby-sitting credentials forever.

His role in our venture was significant and settling. As part of a dream ticket when it came to fund raising, a relatively clean-cut heterosexual couple, companioned by a cute mut - he was a conversation piece, who could resist dipping into their purse for such a trio with very good causes? Settling, when things became fractious, he helped to remove many more barriers than he created.

Practicalities

What began as a tingle, became an itch and one which we would have to scratch. Fast forward to late 2005 and the moons were aligning, we were ready for our gap year. Life was finite, 'this' needed ticking off. There was no self-doubt, not for a second, we were fit and had the physicality for anything, mental fortitude not a problem, we were invincible. No alcohol was involved in our final decision to do it. It might not have been shared, but I was certainly too proud and blinkered to accept there might be cracks in our relationship, which could lead to a fall, but it was never really discussed.

This was to be our odyssey, our pilgrimage, our journey of adventure. One of exploration of ourselves as well as the ultimate beating of the bounds. Would we do it again in another seven years, this time in the opposite direction? I was getting ahead of myself; we hadn't started once yet. It would be fun, a quest, we liked taking risks. Having said that we weren't going to a rain forest, abroad, where there might be epidemics, wild animals and bandits - we weren't that brave. We had little to prove, we weren't looking to break records, we would have to dress as a gorn and a phone box, and balance ping pong balls on straws in our mouths for that. We would enjoy glorious isolation, away from habitation (some of the time). We anticipated spectacular and varied scenery, with the odd eyesore. Would we find the cliff carved alphabet spelling out 'Coast' at the opening credits of BBC's TV programme, or was that just clever graphics? 'It' was there, 'it' just had to be done, didn't Bonnington say that about mountains once? Our home islands boundary, the raison d'etre, our reason for being there. If people asked, we would simply say we were taking the dog for a long walk. Perhaps humans retained some primordial migratory imprinting like some of Attenborough's animals? I knew magnetism was to blame!

The distance was arbitrary. I had done the Ridgeway (87 miles) with my nephew when he was only 12. Quite an achievement for a young boy and some say it had been the making of him. Wendy had cycled from St Petersburg to Moscow (nearly 400 miles) on a tandem guiding a blind pillion. What was the problem? We were very naïve, somewhat reckless in our lack of preparedness and as time pressed on did very little research either.

Others might have set rules for their expeditions. We had none except stay as near to the coast as was humanly possible, stay faithful to the sea. An outer coast was attractive, if that meant visiting islands and missing parts of the mainland, so be it. Estuaries: we weren't sure, it depended if there was a boat. MoD land: wave a white flag, if that failed - a white cane. We were determined to make the walk continuous, spreading it over God knows how many years, would result in incompletion and failure, that wasn't our style.

Plans remained sketchy. I had begged a large wall map from Jewsons showing all their depots and usefully a coast outline (I still have it.) A piece of string roughly four inches long matched a hundred miles on the scale. A large blob from a felt pen would mark the start of a week's walking, where the end of the string stretched would see that section done and another pen blob would be added. I reckoned we could do 100 miles a week, roughly 15/20 miles daily with no planned rest days. If we wanted to stop because there was something of interest, we would, we didn't want a route march. Some 'dentists' might have had a schedule like their work diary, that was not for us. JM had said go clockwise, less windy, so that's what we planned. We would give up our jobs and start mid-November (2006), which fitted in with other commitments and periods of notice.

We had enough savings to afford £10 a day spending money, between three, to cover food and lodgings. I saw myself doing the macho, hairy chested heroism bit, an adventure at the limit of human endeavor, (not in the Antarctic and with apologies to The Village People). We would live off the land, eat berries, drink stolen milk off doorsteps, take a fishing rod, forage the foreshore. Use stealth, speed, cunning and raw power to feed ourselves. Who was I trying to kid? A cross between Daniel Boone, pioneering frontiersman and Chuck Noland (Tom Hanks, Castaway) but I had a box of matches. We could rely on finding a dead mouse a day (you will have to read on for that bit.)

We would start at the top of Scotland, John o' Groats, tapping into the end to ender's strap line, I thought it would help publicity. That would also mean we could reach Edinburgh for Christmas and New Year; we fancied seeing it in with style. Starting in Scotland in the winter was not a worry, we would fly down the east coast, hit the busiest tourist spots at the height of summer, easily filling charity collection buckets. 50 weeks, or thereabouts, 5000 miles and back to JoG's.

We chose two charities to support. For Wendy the choice was obvious, Guide Dogs for the Blind (GD). She had years of involvement, would personally rather give to an animal charity than any human one, and GD was a bit of both anyhow. I opted for the Royal National Lifeboat Institution (RNLI). I had long wanted to volunteer as crew but never got around to it, we were going to be by the sea, I naively expected to find old, characterful, stoic, sea dogs who still rowed out to rescue folk and with a station every 25 miles at least we could beg a cup of tea. (We were quickly told at briefing meetings that the Institution had a rule no one could sleep at stations.)

The charities did help with publicity and as a result of articles in their literature we gained contacts and pledges of support, often in the form of places to stay. We were asked for details of a schedule, which hardly existed, and we wished to keep flexible. Asked how much we thought we could raise I brazenly forecast £50,000 to be shared between the two charities. Then I realised that was £1000 a week, for all 50 weeks, over a £100 a day, knowing full well on some days we would not see a soul.

Hence, fund raising commenced long before we started with collections, raffles, auctions of goodies I begged. Devon business folk would spot me coming, turn the lights out, and hold their breath. We even entered and won a prize in the Bovey Tracey carnival, (walking Wizard of Oz) - guess who was Toto! We borrowed the GD 'Penny' suit and took it in turns dressing up as a giant Labrador, rattled tins, entertained children and posed for photos. People were incredibly generous, and we had £12,000 in the pot before we got walking. We had joined Slimming World, coincidentally, and had articles in their releases.

We networked wherever we could and had a good handful of promises of a bed, not evenly spread, but all useful for when we started. To most of these places we posted a 'red cross parcel' prior to leaving containing relevant maps, some food, coffee sachets, spare socks etc. Some nine/ten months later, it was like opening Christmas presents. A courier agreed to deliver them as a complimentary gesture.

The Hash

Incredibly helpful. (H3-Hash House Harriers.) One thing which came out of our ill-fated pub experience was to meet and join a running group. All three of us came to love it.

The curious may be wondering about all this 'hash' activity and references to an organisation akin to the Hell Fire Club or Freemasonry. Hashing isn't a secret organisation, or even an organisation with many secrets. Hashing is basically running, usually cross-country, multi-terrain with participants following a trail most often laid in flour (at least in this country). Originating in Kuala Lumpur in 1938 hashing has spread all over the world. It is very social, but that's not to say all hashers are uncompetitive and never wear lycra. We do have some of those as well. Frequently described as a drinking club with a running problem, it is enjoyed by all ages and socio-economic classes, but it is perhaps the extent to which social activity is enjoyed that distinguishes it from the likes of ParkRun which was founded in 2004 (and now looks like banning dogs!)

The hash network helped and assisted us in too many ways to mention. Offers of sleepovers, fundraising and logistics ad infinitum. Hash kennels (groups) vary somewhat in manner, behaviour and demeanour. I like to explain it by saying that some are better housetrained than others. For example, in Devon Ashburton HHH(H3) would meet on a Tuesday night. They would sit down afterwards to have a meal, enjoy each other's company and eat with a knife and fork. They might even have a special hash menu laid on at the pub after the run. The Old Exeter in Ashburton for example would lay on three hash menu choices: one sausage and chips, two sausage and chips or three sausage and chips. How's your appetite? On Wednesdays, the South Hams Hash would stand up, order and share baskets of cheesy chips. Teign Valley, TVH3 on a Monday would simply order chips which everyone else would then steal and throw around the bar. As for Plympton on a Thursday – well, let's not go there!

The structure of a kennel would include a Grand Master or Grand Mattress (no exclusion on gender grounds, all very pc in 2023). Their roles were self-evident. They headed up a Mismanagement Committee – a Hash Cash collected your subs; the Hash Flash might take your photo and the Hash Haberdasher would order you a t-shirt. The On Sex was the secretary, the Spider or Scribe would write up trail notes. Hares would take it in turns to lay trails using the cheapest flour they could get from Tesco (other supermarkets are available). Hashers and harriet's roughly in equal numbers. Religious Advisors (RA) might well give a short speech after runs usually just by way of satisfying their own egos, and would also assign nicknames, some cruder than others. The best ones included a degree of innuendo, often sexual, for example, Comes Too Late, Forever Blowing, Shirt Lifter. There are thousands more, much cleverer. Some names bore significance to an occurrence on a particular night, for example, what would you call a young boy still growing into his raw paws, the grandchild of a lovely hashing couple who brought him along for the experience, ignored his whereabouts during a five mile run around the forests of the South Hams in Devon, only to realise on finishing, the said child was missing without trace? Obvious – Mowgli! As RA that Wednesday night I was left with only that option. Our names were given to us by TVH3, Bubbles and Soapy. As a collective with Havoc between us that made BHS.

Check Ignition (may God's love be with you.)
A support vehicle for the walk never crossed our minds. We couldn't afford it and the logistics of mustering a small army of reliable volunteers to drive the thing was unimaginable. Well done to those who have managed it, but in some ways, it may have taken away from your experience. We begged and borrowed everything, tent, sleeping bags, boots the lot. We started with far more than necessary or we could reasonably carry and learned the art of shedding spare gear quickly. Havoc might call it moulting.

Training was as and when we could fit anything in, between full time working and fund raising. We would hash three evenings a week carrying rucksacks. A couple of half marathons, the Grizzly run in East Devon, the London Marathon (April), a weekend here and there, Slapton/Beesands (June), something in north Devon (July), Brixham (September). By late October we handed in notices and went to the Inter Hash event in Chang Mai, Thailand. We experienced the inevitable sickness and diarrhoea from being abroad, plus broken ribs for me having fallen down a Thai sewer - some might say the best place for me!

We spent 9/10th November refining plans. Parcels were packed, we drew a little red cross on each, and they were collected by the friendly courier.

On Saturday 11th we were seen off by a couple of friends, Wendy's parents and GD owners and their dogs from Newton Abbot station - 9.03am train to Edinburgh, tickets courtesy of Mr R Branson. Punters were heading for Cheltenham races, as well as Birmingham City verses Barnsley. First sweep on the train raised £160. As we reached a station Wendy would hop off taking Havoc for a wee, my job was to delay the guard long enough for them to get back on. I looked at JM's book to see he did the flat top of Scotland, where we were heading from left to right, 175 miles almost as quickly as it took Havoc to pee. By Bolton I had found a discarded Daily Star. As we passed the Reebok Stadium, (no longer called that) I read they were third in the Premiership that morning, 20 points having played 11, (8 points behind Man Utd and 12 above Charlton, who were bottom.) Who was the manager? (Big Sam - Allardyce.) We collected another £251 before we reached Edinburgh, Waverley station. One well-wisher said, 'you will be better people during and after your adventure'. Clearly, he didn't like the look of us, right now.

We were due to stay with hashers Wick Dipper and Hoggy but needed to wait for them to meet us in a pub. In the rugby, England had lost to Argentina 18-25, that made half of Edinburgh jolly. Scotland had beaten Romania 46-3, that put the other half under the table. Wendy went to the ladies and a very attractive blond nearly stripped the shirt from my back. It must have been the booze! I had to escape to the street, telling Wendy the landlord wouldn't let Havoc in, contesting his GD credentials. (Did I mention jealousy?)

It was back to the station to get the train to Inverness on the Sunday. Wendy had a gold charm bracelet made by a bespoke jeweller in Devon, Ian Hall, valued at £1500 to 'advertise' the walk. We had been told to take bids and not let it go 'cheap.' We received our first interest, £100 but politely declined. Typical Scot. After Tain, it was replacement bus service. We were Simon and Garfunkel (America) not heading for Saginaw but Thurso. Laughing, playing games with faces, there was no man in a gabardine suit, but there was one in Harris Tweed, who might have been a spy. 'Toss me a cigarette,' neither of us smoked, nothing wacky. We found ourselves a cheap B&B, with a toilet off the bedroom, complete with a macerator 'Saniflo' loo. I imagined the shop keeper from TV's 'Mr Benn' (David McKee) appearing, 'As if by magic', inviting me into the changing room for an adventure. That would begin tomorrow, we would start to move. Basie, Miller, Sachmo and Ella might come to our aid, but for now Sir Duke was getting me in the groove.

JOHN O'GROATS 2006
LANDS END 874
PENTLAND SKERRIES 6

Chapter 1 - John o' Groats to Brora
Genesis

"The only impossible journey is the one you never begin."

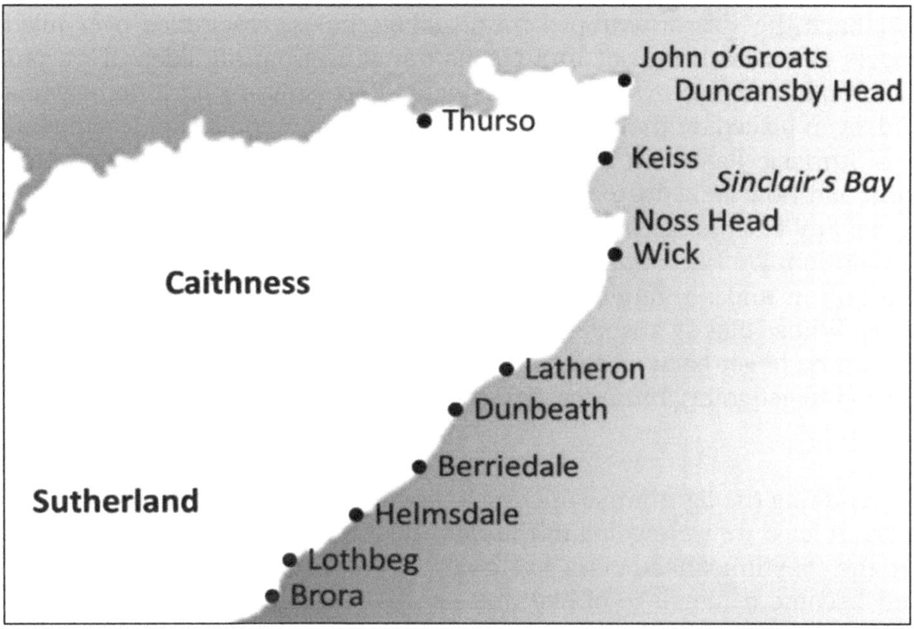

IT WAS MONDAY 13th November 2006. In a cold and wet Thurso I was asked where we were going.

"Edinburgh for starters," I said.

"You'll be needing the station then?"

I interrupted explaining we were going via John o' Groats.

"There's no station there."

I began to think this could be a long day.

If explanations were going to take this long, it could take us to the next millennium to get around the coast. We caught the bus, by noon we were standing outside the First and Last souvenir shop. Hoods up, waterproof over trousers and gloves on, chins and mouths tucked in behind mufflers. If there was a flag the fly edge would have been perfectly perpendicular but any colours were already lost in the North Sea pelted by hail. Staff in the little red kiosk pretended not to be there, not wanting to let any remnants of heat escape and the inn keeper where we went to sign in and record our onset in the log, was most unwelcoming.

“Keep that dog out!”

Our bags the size of wrapped round silage bales, resembled over filled haggis skins, with neepes and tatties dangling from all sides. If we put them on a bench to avoid puddles, one end see-sawed up to the heavens and, even placed on the ground the tarmac shuddered like something out of a Jurassic Park film and ripples appeared in the trinket seller’s tea (who had now locked up and was on her way home). We looked at each other, any enthusiasm had drained from our eyes - now there was only trepidation. We knew nothing of the coast here, hardly which direction to head off in and although nothing was said, we both thought the same thing. Whose bloody stupid idea was this? Havoc looked at both of us and attempted to get back on the departing bus. There was nothing for it, we needed to get going, but after three steps my broken ribs began to tell me otherwise.

On reaching the lighthouse at Duncansby Head anxiety was beginning to ease, at least we were going in the right direction. Turning right we could see the coastline ahead of us stretching out to a point where land blurred and became a marriage of sky and sea. We’re going there, Havoc. Day one, with an injury, I was hardly going to trail blaze. The arch and twin stacks were quite magnificent. Dagger like pinnacles, dark and foreboding against a glistening sea lit by some afternoon sunshine, desperate to make a cameo appearance through ribbons of grey cloud. The sound of the sea was uplifting, especially as a wave rolled back sucking shingle with it.

Quite suddenly there was another sound. We looked at each other with a degree of alarm, people in distress at the base of the cliff. Slipping into first aid/rescue mode we could hardly contemplate how anyone could be down there - the cliffs were sheer. Realisation struck, the sound was coming from a colony of seals, with pups crying, there were 30 at least. Not a bad way to start our adventure, stunning geomorphology and wildlife within hours. Not to go unnoticed, roe deer waved their white bottoms as we approached, perhaps only a dozen of them but by mid-afternoon the light was fading and by Keiss it was quite dark. We learned quickly that days would be short for walking in these parts at this time of year.

A steep slope and wire like grass was our only option for camping at Keiss harbour but a fisherman offered us his cellar for the night. Jammed between chest freezers, piled lobster pots, coiled rope and buoys, Wendy cooked sausages for tea. I lifted a freezer lid to find it full of crabs. All a bit smelly, with rat poison bait boxes around the edges, but on a very windy evening a vaulted ceiling was more preferable than a canvas one. Clear skies, shooting stars and a calm but otherworldly moon were a good way to start proceedings but I went 1-0 down in our backgammon series to the master guru.

In bright sunshine, with sunglasses needed, we headed off around Sinclair's Bay. The shades came in useful as the wind whipped up sand. There was not a soul around and Havoc enjoyed exploring and rolled and wriggled in the softer bits clearly having a great time. The rusting boiler of a shipwrecked steam trawler made a resting spot for two cormorants.

We had already crossed some streams and small rivers by simply wading, just removing boots but the waters running out of the inland Loch Wester were a different proposition. Crossing back at the A99 looked the only option but was a detour I did not want to entertain. With trousers off, the stones of the riverbed were awkward but with a walking pole as a staff I tested the central depth and temperature. Thigh deep and 'cursingly' cold with quite a current. I shuttled over two bags, followed by Havoc and tied him to the rucksacks then returned to piggy-back Wendy. The first such crossing on day two but not the last over the next 300 or so. I was no saint, but it made me feel for the good luck medallion Wendy had given me before leaving.

We had already passed a couple of old castles and after a golf links, we came across Ackergill Tower and then in lesser states of repair, Sinclair and Girnigoe Castles. By Noss Head the path was narrower and muddy and the next mammal we could cross off our spotted list was a hare, actually too quick for Havoc to even notice. He was preoccupied sniffing a seal pup lying amongst seaweed. Having stuck his nose in its bottom he proceeded to cock his leg over it as a sign of affection. Staxigoe was a pleasant little harbour with a mitre shaped rock at the centre, once more active, but now quiet, due to the expansion of Wick.

Reaching there we pitched the tent with permission in a hotel garden, then went for chips and a hot chocolate at Wetherspoons, The Alexander

Bain. (I read later in 2019 it just escaped closure, given a company reprieve after some bad reviews.) We got chatting to a couple and after they left, while spinning out our drinks, the guy returned. He was a local fireman and having checked it out with his superior said we could stay in the fire station. Warm, TV, shower, someone was looking after us. It was more than welcome as Wendy was very tired and Havoc was limping having over done the exploring. All we needed to do was take the tent down in the morning and hope nobody nicked it in the meantime. A seed was also planted in that community buildings might be places to look out for in the next 11 months as places of refuge.

The name Wick is said to be Norse. The river was bridged in 1800 and 11 years later the harbour was completed. It was to become a bustling herring town. A regional newspaper had an office, and we met a reporter from the Caithness Courier who would hopefully put us on the map. In looking around we passed Ebenezer Place which in 2006 earned status as the world's shortest street, just over two metres with one property and one door. John Martin, the lifeboat mechanic, showed us round the RNLB Trent class Roy Barker II and we banked some collection money at the post office. Spud had warned of fundraising overkill in these parts, indifference she called it. End to enders' nose pushing peas on their knees or towing supermarket trolleys with their teeth. We hadn't seen any weird and wonderful antics; folks weren't throwing money at us, but we had still raised £50 and 'Every little helps!'

Consequently, it was nearly lunchtime again before we got going. Peppering the coast were any number of inlets called Geos. Earlier Sclaites, Wife, Ires and now Ashy, indentations along the coastline. Often with sheer sides it was as if they had been cut with a disc cutter or emery wheel. Sometimes scored with more enthusiasm and reaching deeper into our route, sometimes the blades were changed from narrow to wide cut, all took time to round. Barbed wire fences were another obstacle. Often, they seemed to run at right angles to the sea, where there were land slips the fence strands hung limply over the edge with posts still attached and dangling. Each took painstaking negotiation.

Take off rucksack, clamber over, under or through. Wendy would hand over the bags, then Havoc and finally she would follow. Costly in energy, time, patience and kit. One false move and something was ripped. We were conscious that following the coast was one thing but fast falling behind even the loosest of schedules was another. The map showed the A99 and soon the A9 just metres to our right. At some stage we probably needed to pick up speed and join juggernauts heading south.

Slipping between Loch Sarclet and the sea we came to something of an open panorama with an abandoned farm, the Mains of Ulbster nearby. I remembered a postcard sent from a networked acquaintance, Andy. He had said of a possible shelter, maybe more and had given me a grid reference. JM was passing by on 3rd September 1978 and never mentions a crypt or for that matter anything about Ulbster. Light was fading so we checked it out. A six metre square stone rendered building with unusual but elegant ogee shaped roof. Slightly oriental looking, would it be full of 'Eastern Promise?' A raised door reached by steps, a couple of sealed windows, flag floor and a fireplace. Situated in a walled graveyard, we didn't know it at the time, but this was the Sinclair Mausoleum. I lit a fire which gave us some warmth and light and made everything smoky. By 6.30pm we were in our sleeping bags, saw no souls, living or otherwise.

In the morning we could see two offshore oil platforms and, in the distance, the other side of the Moray Firth. Graves were the resting place of Millers, Seymoors, Sutherlands and Sinclairs. The last ones from the 1980s. What was below that stone slab floor, behind ten steps and in the bottom bunk below us last night, one could only guess.

As we hit the road towards Bruan there was gunfire inland but way off. Havoc on his lead was pulling, too nervous to take any notice of the latest RTA, an otter. Every few metres further evidence of human disgraceful ignorance and carefree abandon. Irn-Bru, Coke, Excelsior Bitter, Tennent's Lager, take your pick - we certainly were not excelling in some things. Here in a sparsely populated and well regarded, stunningly beautiful area, miles from the nearest conurbation, litter remained a 21st century plague. On a par if not worse, than fly tipping. Even though everyone I know abhors it, it's still out there. At the time of writing, I see community champion volunteers and countryside pastors daily, combing the same hedgerows. How they sustain their efforts goodness only knows. Inculcate better habits in our young I hear cried. I have seen school fields after students have eaten their summer packed lunches. On the stroke of 1.30pm at the bell, the crows and gulls descend from fences to pick through and fight over crusts and discarded sandwiches. The plastic is left to the PE teacher whose afternoon classroom it is, to sweep through before a lesson can begin.

One national campaign after another all seem to fail. Is there no answer in an age of throw away consumerism? If this pricks just one conscience the space will have been worth it. Just the other day I heard Jeremy Paxman, something of an anti-litter czar, decrying the habit, at the same time advocating harsher punishments for offenders and the use of litter cams to catch them. On the very same day travelling through rural Bedfordshire, I was disgusted by the road verges immediately adjacent to park home properties. It resembled scenes from Slum Dog Millionaire. Can we really have cameras in such rural settings? The authorities seem unable or frankly scared to act against obvious perpetrators. Our beautiful planet deserves better.

We called at a house and asked if we could fill our water bottles from their outside tap. You know what they say about couples growing to look like each other. Mr and Mrs Maclean were like two proverbial peas and insisted on generosity far outstripping water. Embarrassed she didn't have much in, Mrs Maclean opened tinned salmon and made sandwiches, we would still be there now had we not prised ourselves away. Five miles on we reached Lybster. At the harbour a narrow, high single arched bridge over a stream cried out to be abseiled down.

At Latheron we were still 20 miles from Helmsdale and never going to get there in the daylight. While enquiring about somewhere to put up the tent, a couple offered us space with them. Alan and Lynn provided part time B&B, mixing it up with supply teaching and pharmacy work respectively. They had moved up from Wokingham in search of a quieter life and gave us an English perspective of living north of the border. A shower was very welcome after our night in a dusty and smokey tomb and we had liver and kidneys for tea. I joked to Wendy after a night of bones we had moved on to the offal, but she was in no mood suffering from painful blisters on her heels. At least Lynn was able to offer some medication and protection, but discomfort was beginning to get Wendy down.

We had a long day ahead of us and the weather soon deteriorated to add to the challenge. Lorries on the A9 would throw up spray and from Latheronwheel we went on over the cliffs to Dunbeath. We struck out on the road to Berriedale where two rivers converge. Now quiet, small, geometric harbours are a feature of this coast. Flatter crofted land saw abandoned derelict farms often with new bungalows alongside. Clearly it was fashionable and probably cheaper to build new than renovate old. I was surprised at many smart properties with several cars on the drive. Lots of 4x4s but they were most likely essential along with wheel chains. Snow gates on the road hinted things could get impassible in these parts.

Apparently, Scots have 421 words for snow, more than the Inuit. What started as 'freuchter' became 'flindrikin' and soon became 'snaw-powther'. On the hills, conifers and at Badbea the remains of an abandoned 'clearance' village hiding in heather and gorse above precipitous cliffs. Mothers would tether their children in the day to rocks or a stake to avoid them being blown from the cliffs. I pondered whether Social Services would today consider it more of an 'abuse' to restrain or not to restrain?

By the time we reached Helmsdale it was dark. We were drenched through to the last stitch, shivering, and everything ached. Weighed down by bags and exhausted, we had no choice but to check in to a B&B. It was somewhat 'dodgy' and run by a Mrs Overall who would appear out of nowhere and put all three of us on edge. We could at least try to get things dried out, and the backgammon set made another appearance. After wringing out the board I went 4-0 down in the series. I think we got a bit of a reduction, but it was the first, and as it turned out last, accommodation we had to pay for. Just as well because our personal budget would never run to a year of room and board.

At breakfast I was tempted to order 'two soups,' but Wendy, for the purpose of this story aka Miss Babs, wouldn't let me. Instead, we went for two 'full Scottish.' The only difference from 'full English' as far as I could see was white pudding instead of black. In case you are interested, white pudding is just like black pudding but without the blood. Strange when you think of 'Braveheart'.

Our feet were quite precious to us as you might guess. In fact, more so than you might first imagine. A popular hash logo contains feet images. When Wendy and I first got together she had little feet transfer stickers on the dashboard of her Vauxhall Astra estate, one of the things I liked about her. She also was blessed with very 'sexy' real life ones. Right now, however, she wanted to trade them in for an up-grade. Blisters, one might think, are a bit of an insignificance for a round Britain walker - a not unexpected occupational hazard. Several days of pain and increasing rawness, with the thought of only 50 weeks or so to go, was taking its toll. Starting boots had been 'broken in' but despite this and having emptied all of Caithness chemist's shelves of 'Compeed', witch hazel and moleskin it was time to call in international rescue.

We bundled ourselves through a narrow shoe shop doorway, knocking over stands of polish and bootlaces. Ignoring the gold slippers, sling backs and stilettos Wendy picked out some more forgiving boots and tried them on. The next bit of the story is right up there in the coincidence stakes. Our assistant was a true Essex girl called Vera Andrews who it turned out was a round Britain coastal walker herself. In 1984 she had clocked up 3524 miles over 223 days from Clacton. Known as Granny Vera, a book "*I've Seen Granny Vera*" followed, and she gained a Guinness World Record for the longest continuous walk by a woman. She showed us poster memorabilia of her walk and posed for our photos. In some ways it was a bit of a take down. How many round Britain coastal walkers are out there, for goodness' sake, are we going to find one in every corner we visit?

Snow had settled on the hills above Helmsdale. In the Kildonan Burn in 1869 Robert Gilchrist a prospector found a nugget which triggered a gold rush. We took the road towards Portgowe, crossed a railway line and stayed on the beach or grass bank just above it. We were accompanied by seals swimming alongside us as we came upon a colony of seabirds similar to the cormorants we had seen earlier at Sinclaires Bay. With their dark plumage, thin hooked bill, they demonstrated their wing drying skills like fashion models. They might have been shags, but we needed Bill Oddie to authenticate. By afternoon there was some warm sunshine for them but when that faded, we were set for a cold night. Coming across a deserted caravan site at Lothbeg Point we sought some grass between vans to pitch tent. I just happened to try a van door and it was open. We decided to 'squat' with heat from the stove warming us. I got a game back in the backgammon world cup, but then lost another as I pushed my luck. We left everything as we found it and as Havoc hoped 'the owners wouldn't have mind us staying!'

Just a half day walking, all across beach, with exciting little footprints in the sand - otter, we suspected but they were all tucked up in their holts. A golf links led us to Brora which had been our target for the first week. At the Sutherland Arms just up from the Clock Tower War Memorial, we were met with great interest and generosity. The clientele in the bottom bar were thoroughly welcoming and gave the impression they never left the place. It was a bar where you might have found Lord Lucan and Shergar at a corner table playing dominos or cards and we were told about days when Brora produced salt for fish curing. One regular, Terry, insisted that a £20 note was for us to have a meal, while another was for the charity tin. Havoc had already used sad, longing eyes to procure roast beef from Sunday lunch diners and the landlord promptly offered us a room for the night.

We decided to be pious and went to an evening church service. We sat at the back of a full Clyne Church of Scotland. The congregation were all in their Sunday best, not a woman without a hat, a male without a suit and tie. The children were immaculate with manners to match, it was really like travelling back in time. We shrank down into our pew, walking clothes out of place and nodded politely as clergy turned to view the imposters. We stood to pray and sat to sing, no music but psalms led by an elder who turned to guide. I did my best to mouth words, more like John Redwood attempting 'Mae Hen Wlad Fy Nhadau', than Susan Boyle doing 'Great is the Lord'. Later, everyone came to see who we were and chat, Havoc was mobbed by inquisitive children who really should not have got dog hair on their finest accoutrements.

We had made our beginning. I couldn't help but think of public schoolboys in shorts at Charterhouse in Surrey. Gabriel, Banks and Rutherford to be joined by Collins and produced by a King. What would their house parents have said? What 'Revelations' still beheld us?

Chapter 2 – Brora to Inverness

A wee scabby dug as smart as any damn kid

"The core of a man's spirit comes from new experiences."

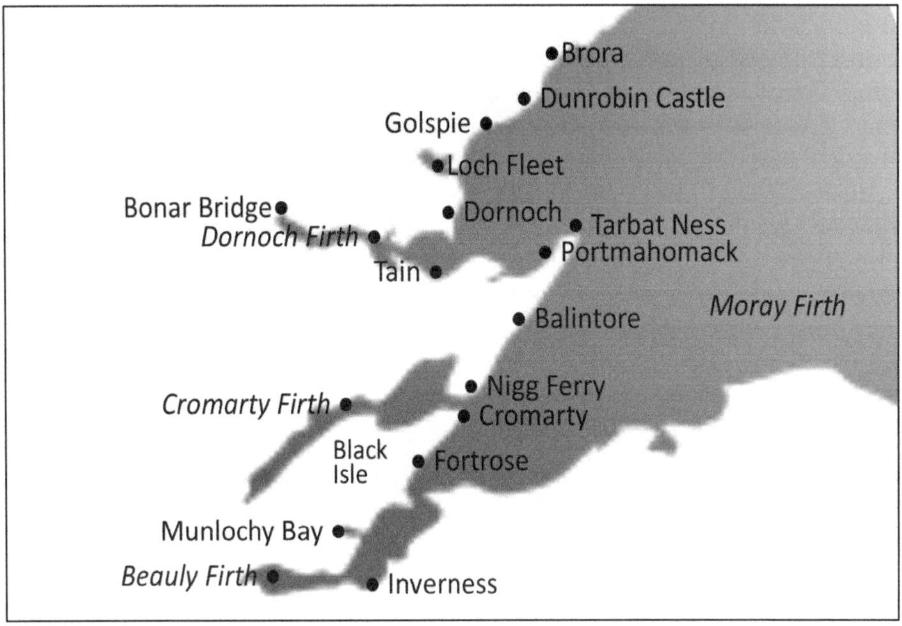

LEAVING BRORA, Havoc was dressed in a little red number. A K9 topcoat that reminded me of a tomato. A stretchy one piece, with his paws popping out from four corners and a gap at the rear for his tail. Think doggy baby grow and you have the image. Blue panniers to accessorise, though he never carried a great deal, he absolutely hated it, and a couple of working sheep dogs could hardly contain themselves. It was turning out to be a Kennel Club sort of day as we also passed some huskies training in the forest.

"Think this is cold, you want to try Siberia."

Given the option of being left cold, or endure the taunting from other dogs, we all know what he would have chosen.

The next mile marker was Dunrobin Castle, seat of Clan Sutherland. It came into view around a sweeping bay, white horses stampeding against pontoons of seaweed and gulls in flight enjoying a frenzied jamboree. It had been around for centuries but had seen many upgrades. Multiple turrets, and a pyramidal high point peeking over beech woods which hid a carpet of ferns to trudge through. French chateau style, it was a majestic hybrid of Colditz, Neuschwanstein and Cinderella.

A falconer was exercising his birds. Displays can be seen up to October as the house and gardens are open to the public, bit of a change as when JM was passing in 1978 it was a boarding school.

"Got any rooms?" I joked.

"Just the 189," came the reply.

A lodge keeper was preparing winter logs and when we said what we were doing his expression said it all, mad fools! Call me old but the lyrics, with some allowance for inaccuracy, of a Kenneth McKellar song came into my head.

"Roamin' in the gloaming with my lassie by my side". Dunrobin ticked off.

We moved on to Golspie to find Mitchells the chemists. I had met Val on the train a week or so earlier as we journeyed up and she had said to pop in. Her colleagues opened their purses for our collection, and we headed around Loch Fleet to The Mound. An early 19th century causeway, designed by, you guessed it, Telford, and constructed by over 600 labourers. It ran over time and budget, like every engineering project before and since, setting a precedent for the likes of HS2 and of course instantly made Littleferry redundant. The Loch itself provided sightings of grey heron, seals and oyster catchers and place names like Skelbo and Embo revealing Viking influence, made me think of who had sailed, explored, traded, pillaged or plundered right here.

Dornoch has a cathedral. Perhaps no longer the seat of a bishop but it retains its historic grandeur. Madonna had her son christened here in 2000 and was married to Guy Ritchie nearby at Skibo Castle. Golfer Sam Torrance did likewise, perhaps after a round at the Royal Golf Course. Word clearly travelled because Elon Musk followed suit in 2010. It was also the last place in the British Isles where a witch was legally executed, burned in the 1720s.

We followed the north shore of the Dornoch Firth coming close to Loch Evelix and the river running from it. This is one of a very few places in northeast Scotland where Margaritifera margaritifera produce fresh-water pearls. Unlike JM we were not heading for Bonar Bridge, we crossed to Tain on the A9 road bridge. The Dornoch or sometimes known as the Meikel Bridge, wasn't opened until 1991. In doing so we said goodbye to

Sutherland and hello to Ross and Cromarty. Enjoying a dram at the Glenmorangie distillery as we passed, a Highland Whisky, light medium bodied, I'm sure the Baldwin sisters in The Waltons would have liked the 'recipe'.

We split up in Tain. Wendy went to find a vet as Havoc now had a prominent limp from overdoing things. I was charged with finding us somewhere to stay and we agreed to meet up in the pub, the St Duthus Hotel. By the time Wendy showed up I was on my third drink and had met a local guitarist who had gifted us one of his CDs entitled Evelix, after the waters the other side of Meikel. I would have preferred some of the fresh-water pearls, even a mussel or two, but never look a gift horse in the mouth, even if it meant more ballast in the bag.

"What's the verdict?" I said.

"He needs five days rest and he's got these anti-inflammatories to go in his food."

We sat pondering the predicament. Stay put for a week, where would we stay? Try to transport him. He had been carried in a rucksack while cycling back in Devon on the Exe towpath, but to carry him and all our own gear was a non-starter. A wheelbarrow, even better a shopping trolley! We wouldn't have to buy one of those but how would that perform off - road and either would be a hindrance at stiles and kissing-gates.

We explored all Heath Robinson options before Wendy reached for her little black book. In it she had a number for a Guide Dog activist in Forres, Chris Bonnie, who we had never met but were due to stay with when we reached the Moray Firth. She gave him a call and he volunteered to drive across the Black Isle tomorrow to collect Havoc for rest and recuperation, while we walked to meet him the other side of Inverness. Hesitant about entrusting a complete stranger, we had few other options.

St Duthac (Duthus) was an 11th century Saint, who died at Tain. He too must have been keeping an eye open for us, as I had secured digs at the Catholic church hall. We just could not show up until after aerobics had finished and had to be gone before Play Group arrived the next morning. Wendy washed some smalls to help ease her misgivings and had them stretched on a string by the heater, while I had a complete all body strip wash in the kitchen sink. If Play Group arrived early, they were in for a shock.

Waiting for Chris to drive the 60 miles to meet us we did some collecting. I went into a hotel and came out with a life size Labrador and puppy in the form of a fiberglass Guide Dog collecting container under one arm and a bar size tin half full of loose change in the other hand. The manager said he was unable to contact anyone who had placed them there years ago and would we please take them. With the natural demise of volunteers in local groups I imagine tracking and tracing collecting tins does sometimes go a miss. In addition, we banked £166 before Chris pulled in from Forres. The spitting image of Noel Edmonds, he seemed very caring and animal friendly, passed Wendy's interrogation and listened to all the care instructions given. He left with Havoc and a kennel of moulded dogs while we headed off in the direction of Inver.

Over dunes and by mid-afternoon in twilight all we could make out were dark boulders on the beach which looked like an army of headless, melting snowmen that didn't seem worried by the accompanying smell of rotting seaweed. The lack of light and the stench really did provide the 'gloamin'. We passed the Tain Air Weapons Range and overhead the lights of jets flashed across the sky. In the dark what seemed like two squadrons of geese, took off as if to engage them. We could just hear their honking, the sound of flapping wings and the screech of fighter planes playing out their war games.

We were making better time without Havoc and reached Portmahomack. At the Caledonian Hotel Phil and Irene offered us their ironing room to throw down our sleeping bags. We explained we wanted to leave our bags and go on in darkness to the lighthouse at Tarbet Ness. With a tower of 41 metres and a light 53 metres in the air it wasn't hard to find on a clear night. To one side the night lights of Dornoch and Golspie where we had come from, on the other those of Lossiemouth where we were heading. More jets racing around the sky, and we jogged back to get news on Havoc. He was up on the sofa in front of the fire having had two helpings of fresh chicken and feeling quite at home we were told. We were also upgraded by our hosts and given a complimentary room, without 'pressing' duties.

Wendy was digging deep, still suffering with sore feet enhanced by separation anxiety from her true love. My ribs were not troubling me, in fact I can recommend wearing a rucksack with all the straps to hold the torso together. Coughing was to be avoided at all costs, and sneezing was surely a pain on a par with child labour. I had no real blisters, some painful and swollen lower shins but nothing to moan about and no one was listening anyway. I tried cheering her up with a few lines from the Supremes, walking 'barefoot through lives gravel' with deeper undertones than just the current toe tenderness, but all to no avail. I had 'no doubt we would work it out', but even at this stage I am not sure my optimism was shared.

Always keen to try local cuisine we had scotch pancakes from a shop for breakfast and made for Rockfield. Pictish heir looms are common on this peninsula, the museum was closed but we did come across several ornately carved large stones, some in protective cases. Depicting interlocking circles and all manner of creatures, real and mythical, they made for stimulating finds. Picts were Celtic speaking, and it is thought were so named by Romans, 'painted ones' because of the fashion to tattoo and colour the skin. I contemplated the current fashion of tattoos and thought about getting one after the walk. That fashion has surely escalated today but as yet, I still haven't summoned up the courage. It's my observation that the fashion is addictive, once one, it is often followed by a full epidermis of others, and I'm certainly not brave enough for that.

Elsewhere we came across what seemed to be a scrapyard for rusting anchors, and 30 foot high poles with a pulley at the top, I guessed something to do with drying fishing nets. Also, as we passed Seaboard villages, Hilton and Balintore, I could not help noticing the proliferation of loft extensions as signaled by Dorma windows, often with flat roofs. It was either all keep up with the Mac Jones' or the local window company had a great sales executive and a closing down sale on.

We knew the Nigg ferry would not be running at this time of year and were quite expecting to be walking to Invergordon and on down the Cromarty Firth to cross nearer Dingwall. At the rickety jetty on the Nigg side we were met by Dan, RNLI Coxswain from Invergordon, and two guys in a rib. Unbeknown to us, a hasher from Devon, who had been looking after our 'JustGiving' page and other online stuff, had arranged for us to grab a lift across to Cromarty and the Black Isle. It was quite a short cut, saving according to JM some 50 miles of walking, but it would have been rude not to accept.

Our hash IT wizard incidentally was called 'Flowery', short for 'Flowery Twats'. So named because his parents had a small hotel in Torquay. Still not there yet? You need to think anagrams and visit back episodes of Fawlty Towers.

It was very often our first visit to many of the places we were ticking off and we knew nothing about them. Cromarty was no exception, in fact the sole thing I knew was that I had heard it mentioned on the shipping forecast. Flowery had also sorted us out with accommodation at the Royal Hotel and there in front of a fire drying off we met the distant character cousins of those in Brora, including 'Santa Claus' (we never discovered his real name and he bore no presents), and Dave the baker who promised us oatcakes if we called by in the morning. This was the opportunity to find out the history, present and future aspirations of such towns. Tomorrow we could also look around a bit as Flowery had saved us at least two days walking both sides of Cromarty Firth.

The estuary was, we could see, a natural harbour used as a naval base in both World Wars. HMS Natal had been blown up here in 1915 killing over 400. Metal netting was placed across the entrance as a deterrent for German submarines. We had already seen the remnants of gun emplacements on North Sutor. Two hills, one either side of the inlet, Sutors, were natural defences. Sutor, a Scottish word for shoemaker, legend has it two giant cobblers would work either side of the water and throw tools at one another, more in a sharing sense than in anger. By now I was hooked and couldn't wait to look around tomorrow. I felt almost obligated to find out more, natural inquisitiveness, some might say nerdism. The enthusiasm to widen one's knowledge was not always mirrored and on reflection, was a source of frustration.

The seasonal ferry was sometimes called the Kings Ferry on account of James IV and Robert the Bruce travelling these waters on pilgrimage to St Duthac's Shrine in Tain. From our inflatable coming in the opposite direction, we had seen to our right evidence of the oil industry. Platforms undergoing repair and moored up towards Invergordon. The oil boom of the 1970s had brought prosperity to the Firth, and from what we had already seen, Cromarty had seen some of it.

Next morning, we found the small lighthouse and George Ross's Courthouse, though it wasn't open. The Georgian town from the late 18th century is largely credited to him. Another noteworthy inhabitant from the mid17th century Laird, Sir Thomas Urquhart. Inventor of a language, indulged in incomprehensible mathematics and claimed to be directly descended from Adam and Eve, come to think of it there were a few eccentrics in the bar last night like that. We found crow stepped gables, the vennels (passageways) of Fishertown and the interesting East Church with a T plan and lofts or galleries requiring three staircases.

MacFarquhar and Miller had a certain posh feoffee sound to them and I imagined them ordering shoes from one of the Sutors. In fact, it was all my creation, MacFarquahar gave his name to caves and natural arches where we were heading and Hugh Miller, who lived in the only remaining thatched property in the town, was a self-taught geologist who no doubt spent time in MacFarquahar's bed.

We picked up Dave's oatcakes as well as some shortbread and headed for South Sutor and on down the coast. Over Gallow Hill, so named because it was the site of public hangings, and the route became frustrating. Nearing Navity we had the same problem as JM experienced 18 years earlier, 'hopelessly overgrown and making progress proved a nightmare'. A tidal shore route might leave us scrambling up sheer cliffs caught out by advancing waters, staying on a higher route took us away from our coast. It wasn't the last time we met such dilemmas. We floundered around, through wooded valleys, waterfalls, over broken bridges to a sign saying, 'Fairy Glen'. Wherever they were, they must have been laughing their wings off.

Eventually we reached Rosemarkie and found something of the Black Isles agricultural base. Potatoes washed out from fields which we foraged for supper. We carried on to Fortrose and thanks to Father Stone found lodgings in the Catholic Church kitchen, opposite the ruined cathedral.

Some irony in the good priest's name, the stone from the cathedral had been pinched by Cromwell's troops to build a fort at Inverness.

I could see no reason why the Black Isle was so named. Shally Hunt (SH) described the interior as 'very English' and the coast as having a 'Mediterranean richness'. Jannina Tredwell (JT) found no 'trolls or Alan Titchmarsh' and found everything in 'technicolor', but then it was gone Easter when she arrived. The best I could manage from a local was that it was once covered in dark, dense woodland. It wasn't even an island, although it was the filling in a triple decker sandwich of Beauly, Moray and Cromarty Firths with just a narrow neck of connection at Muir of Ord.

We were receiving daily evening updates from convalescence HQ in Forres but when we reached the harbour village of Avoch, Wendy was prompted to make a daytime call. Havoc had had a bit of a lie in, late breakfast and then gone to the beach for a gentle stroll and some sea wave hydrotherapy for his muscle strain. Returning for sirloin steak, several Bonios and was now watching re-runs of Lassie and Beethoven, resting peacefully and grazing on Good Boy choc drops.

Just before starting and for time context only, (October 2006), Jeremy Clarkson, one of my favourites, was expounding the merits of pets. Apparently, dog ownership in Britain was down to fewer than one in five households. After Havoc breaking his leg, I was all for walking with two fish in a plastic bag, but Wendy made me reconsider.

'*Jezza's*' latest addition then was a hybrid with quanta of poodle in a mix, a hellhound costing more than a 1991 BMW. Havoc wasn't from this litter, he may have cost more than 40p, he was micro-chipped, but could be fed on half a tin of diced horse once a day, if you hid the ingredients list from Wendy. He wasn't the collie in the news who, when a Scottish hill farmer suffered a stroke in the glens saved the chap from certain death by snuggling up and guiding the search helicopter to affect a rescue. Havoc would have chased it off, not allowing it to land for a zillion miles. He was however, our faithful, cute, hound at least until someone else came along with something tastier to eat - Chris Bonnie, rather than Billy Connolly. Havoc, loyal and intelligent, we should have renamed him Baldrick, he always had a cunning plan.

Avoch by contrast, was busier with small boats coming and going. Legend suggests it was founded by survivors of the Spanish Armada in 1588, perhaps supporting SH's comment about the coast being Mediterranean. Soon we were scrambling up steep wooded slopes, over fallen trees and fell into a field of swedes. Not Bjorn Borg and Zlatan Ibrahimovic but the kind Scots put with potatoes and call neeps. A pheasant fell at my feet, soon retrieved by a spaniel and we were overrun by Land Rovers, tweed caps and hip flasks. We were in the middle of a shoot and although we weren't beaten, nobody reached for their money clips either, not a penny, in sharp contrast with the bottom bar at Brora.

Sunshine on Munlochy Bay and we passed a clootie well. Ancient springs were places of pilgrimage, particularly in Celtic areas, where waters were often thought to have healing and other special powers. Rags and strips of cloth are often hung from nearby trees. My initial thought was they were sanitary towels, but then I was an ignorant sassenach, my palliating water purchased from the Peckham Spring. (Thanks Del, 25th December 1992).

The cable stayed Kessock Bridge led to the capital of The Highlands, Inverness. This type of bridge has wires which run directly from towers to the deck often forming a fan. It wasn't completed until 1982, the reason why JM had to go via Beauly. Budgeted at £17.5 million in 1975, around £150 million in today's money, it has transformed road transport in the Highlands and is a key factor in the growth of Inverness. The population of greater Inverness was around 43,000 when it was built, 55,000 in 2007, and by 2018 had reached 64,000. In 2012 the bridge was estimated to be used by 30,000 vehicles per day.

We followed the A9 for over a kilometre, seeing the river Ness enter the Moray Firth, over the RNLI inshore lifeboat station and the Caledonian Stadium, home of Inverness Caledonian Thistle Football Club (ICT). We passed a sign reading 'Pedestrians on Dual Carriageway ahead', and for a moment, full of self-importance, thought it was for us. Flowery must have told them we were coming! We had not twigged it was a Saturday, and ICT were at home to Hearts. I thought it might be a great opportunity to collect, but the Police warned of trouble and since the crowd had suffered a boring goalless draw, we moved on. The bridge features on a Bank of Scotland £100 note, has done since 2007, but we were never offered one and to be honest I've never seen one either.

We stayed in the Back Packers Hostel near the bus station and met any number of younger internationals all on their own gap years. Some female company for Wendy who I could not prise away to do some evening collecting. The fast-flowing river had numerous bridges and I tried shaking a tin on both sides of the Greig Street Bridge in Huntly and Bank Streets. There was quite a lot of nightlife but there was something unsettling about a city, after the places we had been for the last two weeks. Without a four-legged fury companion, and Wendy less than enthusiastic too, I gave up early and retired to a narrow bunk bed.

Chapter 3 – Inverness to Rosehearty

Anarchy in the UK

"Dogs do speak, but only to those who know how to listen."

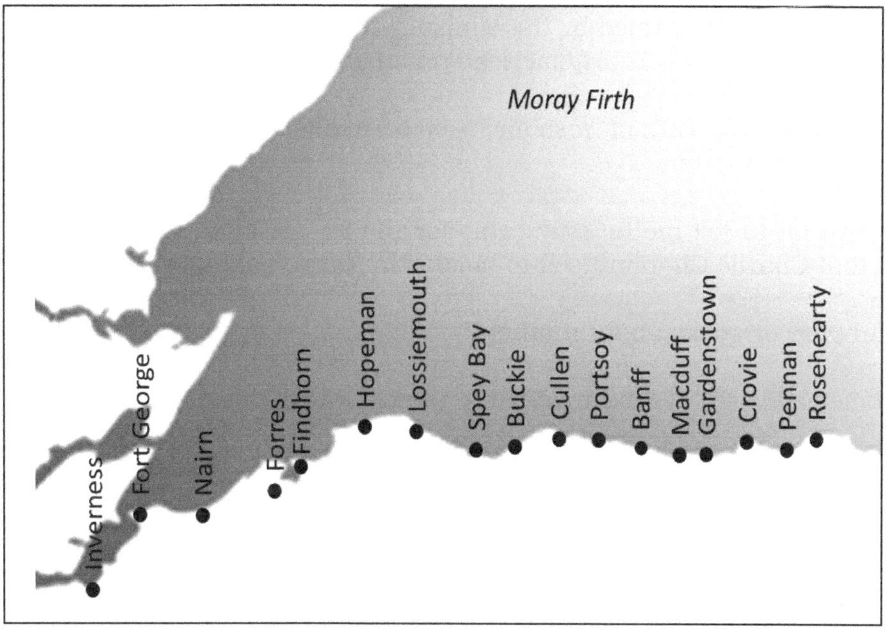

ON LEAVING INVERNESS in 1978 JM 'committed to reach London on 8th November, at one o'clock' (57 days to cover the east coast). We couldn't commit to reaching anywhere with such precision, nor would we have wanted to. (As it turned out fast forward 57 days for us and we were in the Alma pub at Scarborough ready for lunchtime service.)

Longman Point and at Milton, signs for Moor. Here in 1746 Bonnie Prince Charlie had his bottom firmly kicked by William, Duke of Cumberland. Nick-named the 'Butcher', the English named a flower, Sweet William, after him, at least that's one tale. It goes down in history as the last battle fought on British soil, if you turn a blind eye to the likes of the Peterloo Massacre and Maggie dealing with the miners strikes in the 1980s. We followed the old military road from Castle Stuart to Ardersier and on to Fort George. Still an active military base, the 18th century architecture robust and impressive. We enjoyed tea on the drawbridge, played soldiers in the sentry boxes and by mid-afternoon the sun was setting spectacularly over where we had come from. There was something particularly satisfying at looking back and reflecting on the experiences of the past couple of weeks.

Arriving in Nairn it was dark and an accident on the A96 meant traffic was diverted on to smaller roads, which made for some precarious episodes dodging frustrated drivers. A large congregation was gathering at the Free Church for a Sunday evening service, and we were ushered inside. We were welcomed by the Minister, Bill Evans, who if my memory serves me correctly was an American on an exchange.

“He’s brought a breath of fresh air,” said an old boy next to me, “all these families, down to him”.

He went on to tell me he only came for the free biscuits, ‘nairn’s’ own, and that Charlie Chaplin used to holiday in Nairn, adding,

“But he never spoke about it much!”

A homemade sign had been added to the reading podium,

“Lean on the Lord, not this Lectern”

People retired to the hall for refreshments, and we were told, ‘come on, this is the best bit!’ What followed was quite bizarre. A children’s game of baseball, using a blow-up globe (a prop from the sermon) as a ball and a hymn book or it could have been a bible, as a bat. With cheering excitement, we thanked God Havoc wasn’t with us, we would never have stopped him barking. Fielders sliding between our legs and home runs being tallied, parents exchanging niceties while juggling teacups and saucers and Bill, bless him, donated £50 on behalf of everyone to our collection and offered us floor space for the night. We even had the leftover biscuits thrown in, stem ginger oats, the choc chip ones had all gone. If this is how to boost flailing congregations, Church authorities take note and God Bless America.

We banked £196 as we went to the harbour, Fishertown. It was built in 1820 by Telford, born 1757 and raised in poverty in Dumfriesshire. It seemed you could put a pin in a map of Britain blindfolded and somewhere nearby was a project Telford had a hand in. Due to his command for all types of civil engineering, particularly highways and bridges, he was named The Colossus of Roads, and although we didn't know it at the time, we were to trudge on many of his early 19th century designs in the next ten months.

Crossing the river, we headed out for the Culbin Forest which stretches all the way to Findhorn. An area of moving sand dunes until the 1920s, pine trees were planted to stabilise the area. There were still lots of salt marsh, marram dunes and mud flats.

We should have been treated to all sorts of wildlife, excited by the prospect of pine martens and capercaillies, but to be truthful we saw none and indeed very few signs of life at all. The wood grouse had all done their kamikaze bit for JT, there were supposed to be humans on bikes, but they all must have had punctures, and apart from insects for company whenever we stopped for a breather and bag rest, we were as alone as Hansel and Gretel.

Almost hourly, we needed to take the weight off our shoulders. Not necessarily take the rucksack off completely, it was too much trouble putting it back on again, just rest the bottom of it on a gate, tree stump or old shrew for a few seconds relief. With no wildlife to admire, there was nothing to do but contemplate all the pallets, chipboard, fencing and construction timber all the trees would end up as.

On other parts we strode out across flat sands, Wendy close enough to photograph me like Lawrence of Arabia, not with a keffiyeh but the motif of Guide Dogs on a pennant dangling from a rucksack.

We met up with Chris Bonnie in Forres and to Wendy's comfort and contentment - a fully recovered Havoc. It was like the reunion of the prodigal son, no killing of the fatted calf, but we did have shepherd's pie, a real fire and, for Wendy, the best night's sleep in a week. Our good shepherd had done a great job of looking after our lamb.

After a hilltop view of where we had come from, we left Sueno's Stone, a six metre high Pictish stone with interwoven knotwork. We would always be linked to Chris, thankful for his support and we left him those cast guide dogs to empty and pay into the Association. Havoc wasn't too keen to get walking again, his expression said, 'do I have to?' and he froze to the pavement considering a mutiny. Given an off-lead option I think he might have joined the SNP.

Findhorn is the site of an experimental living community. Set up by Eileen and Peter Caddy, with a friend Dorothy Maclean in 1962, it offers a spiritual experience and awakening. A place to go if you are into ecological buildings, organic food, renewable energy. Famously talking to brassica led to a 40lb cabbage, something I would willingly have swapped for my 70lb bag. I gave myself a good talking to while sitting on a giant washed up log on the beach of Burghead Bay.

Spiritual enlightenment came from a bag of Wotsits, of which Havoc pinched half. Second World War pill boxes were to be found what seemed like every 400 metres and between anti-landing blocks like ice cubes, with a loop on the top, every metre apart. Some of the concrete hexagonal guard posts, each with doorway and weapon firing windows, expensive to demolish, were now giving way to the sea. Partially submerged, I wondered how estate agents might market them. 'Desirable sea front residence, 180-degree uninterrupted ocean views, bomb proof construction, buy of the week- needs some modernisation, but with huge renewable energy potential'. If there had been a dry one, we might have stopped for the night but carried on to Burghead, and the smell of a brewery or maltings wafting through the streets.

A cut down barrel called a 'clavie' is set alight at New Year's Eve celebrations, usually on 11th January! For this bit of ceremonial tradition, they use the old Julian calendar, they are really not so far behind the times this north of the border. We were clearly too early but imagined something akin to the pyrotechnics which happen back in Devon on 5th November at Ottery St Mary, though not so psychopathic. You might be lucky enough to spot locally a Burghead Bull, etched into a stone slab from Pictish times, one has grazed on to Edinburgh and another even reached the British Museum in London. No doubt if Nicola Sturgeon gets her way, she will be wanting that back.

Our destination for the day was the Railway Hotel at Hopeman, where we were to meet an old college friend of mine. We followed an old railway line and at 6pm met Chris Barton who was to take us back to his house at Cummingstown. We had walked right past it a little earlier. I had only seen him once since our days at St Luke's in Exeter where, as freshmen, we had shared a room. How many under graduates would contemplate shared rooming today? I had been up to Gordonstoun School, where he was a teacher, once while I was working for the Amateur Swimming Association, to lead a short swim course. Then he was a boarding house master, now he had moved up to a Deputy Head role. Some of the class of 1977-81, flourished in education.

Gordonstoun of course is a prestigious place, established by Kurt Hahn, renowned for a spartan something, life expanding curriculum with a strong service element. I was at least doing my bit there. Former students included the Duke of Edinburgh and the Prince of Wales, (now King Charles III) - The Crown (series 2, episode 9) sheds more light. Its prominence even extends to fictional alumna, Lady Lara Croft (Tomb Raider). My only claim to fame was being asked to address the whole school, staff and students, at assembly in the chapel, close to the Round Square back in 1986. We reminisced over smoked salmon, chicken casserole, cheese board and Belgian chocolate, not so spartan. Chris was a wonderful host, nearly as good as he was a cricketer, and we were made to feel very welcome, as long as I promised not to spill the beans on some of his student antics, which included getting a First. (I could be jealous too.)

We re-traced our steps back to Hopeman, which brought us a little closer to JM's total, with Chris's parents address in Kent, for a room when we reached the southeast. That is often how logistical accessibility panned out.

Nessie is not Scotland's only under water beastie. Hopeman's Grin Iron Wife is a legend of a witch who will grab child bathers if they stray out too far. I did wonder if the plaque had been sponsored by ROSPA. Jaws is not the only thing to scare kids from going back in the water, instead the council had built a posh skateboard/BMX park. Apparently, ROSPA thought wheels were okay. The harbour crane looked a bit worse for wear. I later read it is now completely restored. If we needed tracks, we could have followed the large reptile/lizard like footprints found nearby when a quarry was reopened, only 250 million years old, but Wendy was sceptical, and if honest, a bit dismissive. A golf course and caves had to be admired and on sandy beach bits the wind blew willow-the-wisp ribbons of grains seaward.

Speaking of skateboarding, I flicked through JM's book. In 1978, walking through Greenwich, he noted the 'craze' (p17) ten months later, on returning to London, it was 'over'. I couldn't help thinking he was a bit premature with his comment. The concrete creations in nearly every town and village in the country seemed to disprove his observation. Fast forward 2020, Tokyo Olympics, the sport would make its debut. Sky Brown might have something to say about the antecedental remark.

Lossiemouth lighthouse towered above us, jets from the RAF base had accompanied us most of the day and there were more golf balls to dodge at another golf course, this one we collected at - fore! Known simply as 'Lossie' to locals, James Ramsey MacDonald, first British Labour PM, was a Lossie-ite, born 1866 the illegitimate son of a farm labourer. An impressively long footbridge took us over the river to the east beach with more stabilising forest and war defences and by mid-afternoon, rain and Moray Firth Way signs took us to Garmouth.

Situated near the mouth of the River Spey, Speyside whiskies are either light and grassy for lunchtime or rich, sweet and sherried for either side of that, according to one local who might have had quite a few by the time we arrived. A pub meal and a keyholder for the village hall found, again we would need to be gone before playgroup arrived next morning. We developed our now emerging hall star rating system, a comfortable stellar '3'.

We crossed an old iron girder railway bridge (one that had escaped the manufacture of a certain 'other Scottish' drink) some 280 metres long I reckoned, with a bowstring central section. Then we became frustratingly lost, land which is now partly the Scottish Dolphin Centre, eventually finding our way to Portgordon and on to Buckie. If anyone said just keep "*the sea on our left*" SH, I would have breached them with a can of rusty coloured soft drink.

There were no fewer than five lifeboats, two in the water, three more in the boat yard, it is a service centre for vessels. What can be gleaned on a flying visit? Other than noting the twin spires of St Peter's RC Church from the harbour and being told Isla St Clair, late 1970s co-host of the Generation Game and a bit of a student pin up, once hailed from here, it was time to move on.

Portnockie and the Bow Fiddle Rock, so named for its resemblance to something orchestral, though you might need to have been a maestro or first violinist to spot it straight off. Arriving across a lovely beach, umbrellaed by a series of viaducts, past a famous ice cream shop, we were searching for an address given to Wendy for a stay over in Cullen. Shadows were being cast by the aforementioned arches, but we spotted three post-it notes stuck to the inside of a small window at number 37, somewhere? Welcome 'Paul, Wendy and Havoc'. I am not sure how she

had found the Pinkertons, Rob and Evelyn, perhaps through a detective agency, but our rest for the night was assured.

We were to learn we were now 60 miles from the nearest KFC and 50 from McDonalds. The pie and veg was more appetising anyway, the Skink too repeating to be served, and a soak in a bath very welcome. Though not lit yet, the Christmas lights, Cullen's own Coca Cola Express, were mounted on the viaduct brickwork. We had 24 days to reach Edinburgh. Havoc, clearly not suffering leg strain hangover, wrestled with Skye, the house collie in the yard until we had to tell them both to come in for bed. Good night Rob, good night Evelyn, good night Skye, good night Jim Bob!

Next morning, we were all intrigued by the coloured pebbles and headstones of the pet cemetery. Benji, Max, Felix and Hoover all still eternally, plus hundreds of other loyal pets, a splendid final resting spot for anyone. Off his lead Havoc charged around like a greyhound and scratched rodent-like in the sand, gloriously content. Burying bones was in his genes, he had never seen it done but as a puppy would bury the like of a pig's ear in a houseplant pot. Store thy bounty for a rainy day. He had not picked up any goodies from the animal hallowed ground but wanted to make his mark of remembrance.

A feature known as the Giants Steps led to Logie Head. Built apparently single handedly in the late 1980s by a local, Tony Hetherington. He unfortunately died quite young in 1993, I could only think of a hernia. Sunnyside brought tales of Charlie the Hermit. Reputed to be a French navy deserter, he built a shack and lived a self-sufficient lifestyle in the 1920s, but sadly ended up in an internment camp in southern England and died in 1937.

Rocky promontories dominated this stretch, like the teeth of a saw, and perching on one were the ruins of Findlater Castle. An aura of history hung over the rubble and a similar one of risk for ancient attackers and modern-day explorers. Sheer drops sufficient for anyone to lose their head. Mary Queen of Scots besieged the place in 1562 and Sir John Gordon lost his. In land an ancient 'doo cot', which over the centuries had probably seen more strife than peace.

At Sandend Bay we stopped for lunch and watched two surfers attempting their stuff even though it was December. We had promised ourselves a short day, perhaps only going to Portsoy, but I was conscious of the miles left to reach Edinburgh and suggested we push on for Banff. That proved to be a mistake.

"Well which way is it?"

I was asked, and I knew I had touched a nerve. I tried helping both Wendy and Havoc over a narrow cattle grid, where there was also a swing gate at Redhythe, but Havoc slipped, temporarily losing one leg down between the bars, and all hell broke loose. The first real domestic of the walk. In an instant, she knew which way to go and stormed off. My fault, probably mirroring sentiments re his injury pre-starting.

I didn't catch up till we reached Portsoy, it was still only 2.30pm. We should have stayed put, enjoyed a dram, it was later the principal location for the 2016 remake of Whisky Galore. No sooner had I arrived Wendy was off again.

A number of wind turbines at Inverboyndie, you either love them or hate them, some carrots in a field to forage and the Castle Inn at Banff. I left Havoc and Wendy to warm up and rest a bit and went off to find somewhere to stay. The Boys Brigade Hall on Seafield Street offered us floor space.

On the juke box back at the pub, Proclaimers, 'I could walk 500 miles' something of an uplift, but I still had thousands to roll to be forgiven.

In the hall, sausage casserole and local carrots for tea. Wayfayrer foil wrapped meals were good, only needed heating and were quicker than dried food which had to be reconstituted and took more burner meths. However, they were heavier to carry which was a serious downfall. There were large landing mattresses to use as beds, but it was a mistake as you sank into the foam, becoming a frankfurter in a giant blue roll. It required an exercise in contortion on a par with Harry Houdini just to get up. We also needed to be out by 8am as a jumble sale was setting up from then. The conversation shifted to the extent to which we were fundraising which would rumble on for the next ten months. Once again none was done, I just about had the energy and drive for it, Wendy was less enthusiastic. It was a continual cause of argument. Consequently, the backgammon world series also stuttered.

Smeaton's bridge over the Deveron took us eastwards. We had heard of him, think lighthouse on the Hoe back in Plymouth. Seven arches and completed in 1779, at double the estimated cost, confirming my belief about engineering projects. Whoever makes these costings?

Macduff started out in life simply as Doune. The second Earl James Duff built the harbour in 1783 and renamed the spot after his supposed ancestor, Lord Duff, Thane of Fife, from Shakespeare's Macbeth. We were told the inshore lifeboat was bringing in the body of a man, but when it approached the harbour we could see it was a large wooden log in tow, recovered by four volunteers. This B class Atlantic is unique within the RNLI being stored, launched and recovered from an LGV, fitted with its own crane. It means launch and recovery can be made from different locations. (LGV - large goods vehicle, thankyou EU, this acronym thing was addictive, when I could just have said, lorry!) The old disused Tarlair lido pool looked very sad, suffering from vandalism, but I did read in 2013 some £300,000 was thrown at it for refurbishment. Who knows if armbands and woggles are now in use?

On the golf course, golfers who told us there were more courses in Scotland than there were sheep in New Zealand and even in the last three weeks, we could probably confirm it true. We stumbled onto St John's Church and Kirkyard a roofless rectangle, about 28m x 5m. We were told it was once known as the Kirk of Skulls, with three skulls of Danes inside. Down a steep valley, between interlocking spurs, the path twisting and turning, over a stream and along the beach to Gardenstown.

As if by way of welcome, a seal on a rock just 15 metres away. Earlier in the day we had seen newborn lambs, surprising this far north this early. Between the Garden Arms Hotel and the Spar shop we bumped into Barbs and Clog. They had a houseful, a son Adam visiting from Newcastle, as carers they looked after Frankie, the house was in the middle of a rebuild and Kevin the cat liked lots of space. Despite this, we were made very welcome, just three more for curry, totally relaxed, generous beyond measure. Two houses had been washed away in 1953 and the road, a sea defence on top of a sea wall was controversial due to uncertainty as to who was responsible for maintenance. I read the arguments were still rumbling in 2014.

Shortly after we were there Malcolm McLaren, godfather of British Punk and former manager of the Sex Pistols caused a stir. After a blasphemous pitch to become Laird, as part of The Baron reality TV show he was run out of town. We were told of strong religious convictions held in the community, leading to many conscientious objectors to The Great War. For McLaren to call 'Jesus a sausage' was no basis to make many friends and further his ambition.

We jumped waves to Crovie. A single row of houses, a sliver of land between shore and cliffs soaring over 100 metres. Once a local schoolmaster compared the cottages to a brood of young sea birds with their tails in the sea and their heads nesting under a bank. Peter Hill (PH) admired its traditional styling, while bemoaning Gardenstown's drab modern architecture with pebbledash finish. Scots might call it 'harling'. We climbed out over Troup Head the wind blowing us sideways, we needed walking poles to stabilise ourselves. I particularly found them very useful aids. Something to push off going up hills, balance security coming down, rhythm/cadence metronome, all in all perhaps the most useful bit of kit I bought but totally unexpected.

Hell's Lum was an ominous sight, a collapsed sea cave and tunnel. I loved seeing dramatic coastal features. Soon afterwards I had a bit of banter with a farmer. On his pond were three plastic ducks, and nearby two peacocks.

"Good layers?" I said.

Fortunately, he saw the funny side, and instead of escorting us to his gate, led us to see his hens and cows. Spud recalls an old farm near Pennan and pictured herself with a smallholding and a few animals living the 'good life'. Perhaps this was it? She describes the village itself as 'precipitous', like coins in a fairground game, never quite toppling. She was right, it did resemble something from Tipping Point.

'Probably the most picturesque fishing village on the east coast of Scotland!' according to the man from Carlsburg. PH spent an age here, but not at the fair, perhaps in the red phone box! (Reference - Local Hero film.) Months after we were there the village was hit by landslips and again, but more seriously, in 2009. You gamble if you live this close to the North Sea.

Mounthooly Doocot inland, perched on a hilltop and looking like a rook on a chess board came into view. Rosehearty, was about as far as we were going to make on a Sunday evening, and we looked around for somewhere to stay. Quite a large square, an old house named 'The Jam' dating from 1573, a new school due to be fully open in 2007, a couple of hotels and a post office. At the Spar shop Sandra was very helpful, put us onto Harry who held the keys to the church hall and Bob's your uncle. Havoc's recollection is a bit confused; it wasn't here that he joined in with children marching and barking, that was at St Combs the other side of Fraserburgh. Rosehearty was a quiet, restful night after being buffeted by winds. It was here Spud had her Spudtruck violated, burglary of cash, credit cards, cheque books and cameras. For us it marked the end of spectacular Moray Firth cliffs, to the east we would find sweeping sands, rocky beaches and prayers from children, but that was still to come.

Malcolm McLaren, The Jam, Spud's misfortune and reflections on life in the 1970s all led me to consider disorder and non-regulation in this corner of the country. If that meant using a swing gate rather than treading over a cattle grid it might help me 'dodge the flak'.

Chapter 4 – Rosehearty to Stonehaven

This one's for the children

"Plagiarism before Stovies"

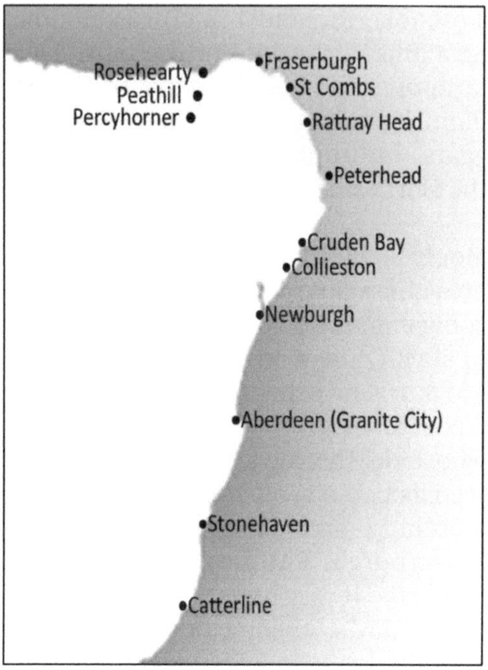

I HAVE ALWAYS enjoyed maps. At school, I would be looking through the atlas, when I was supposed to be concentrating on something else, usually French, what a waste of time!

I would imagine the outline of Britain to be a naughty Scooby-Doo, scampering away from a scary janitor. This bit of Scotland was therefore the top of his muzzle, Peterhead his black nose, an eye at Inverness, everything above floppy ears, Fife a big slobbery tongue. To some I found out, it is called the knuckle of Scotland, with Pitsligo Castle one of nine to be besieged. I found it just inland, neighbours with Peathill (Pete Hill) and Percyhorner (Percy Horner) and just up the road lived (Fraser Burgh.) You can tell what sort of mood I was in. We were hitting the Phingask shore, Aberdeenshire, and the tide and wind were at odds. The latter was from the southwest blowing the tops off incoming waves, spilling spray, so they looked like porcupines on surf boards.

Our route was not straightforward, at one point I leaned against a large red sign reading 'Coastal Path Closed.' The last thing we needed was a 'Sally Traffic' diversion, they are usually about 80 miles in Scotland. The industrial sights of Fraserburgh came into view; fish processing factories, waste ground, scrap steel yards, demolition sites and the Scottish Museum of Lighthouses at Kinnaides Head. I imagined if your surname was Stevenson, you got in for free, I think they built 97 in Scotland over two centuries.

We found the lifeboat station in a porta cabin, a temporary affair while a new one was being built. Outside a major commercial harbour, white fish port with many large boats, inside a gang of five guys hanging out, sharing a dram and dialect which was totally incomprehensible. 'Och aye the noo.' We took that to mean, come in! 'foos yer doos'- hello! and 'fit like', I guessed that was not aimed at me! Doric is spoken in this corner of the country, but I think I would have coped better with Klingon. The town has lost three lifeboats in disasters, 1919,1953 and 1970. The ill-informed might say 'careless' or 'too many drams'.

After coffee, I headed for the shops while Wendy stayed put. I needed to post used maps home, check bank account, find 20p to use a public toilet and do some collecting if possible. I met a lady with a dog, Piper, who turned out to be a failed guide dog. 'Guide Dogs' generally selectively bred these days to ensure greater success in their programme. A gene pool is used where health, behaviour, trainability is more guaranteed, rather than rely on potluck.

Wendy had a history of puppy walking, successfully preparing three puppies for formal training, which went on to be guides for blind owners. Her last puppy, a huge German shepherd, Avon, failed his formal training, and Wendy had him back as family pet before he unfortunately developed a tumour on his spine. Despite his size and a wolf like appearance he was the softest thing since Andrex, scared of bangs and loud noises, which probably resulted in his unsuitability as a guide. All this while Havoc was still a glint in her eye. I outlined our tale to my new acquaintance, who spoke similarly about Piper, while helping me with my fundraising.

Back at the porta cabin we packed up, said our goodbyes and headed across the sand towards Inverallochy. The Water of Philorth had to be crossed. Trousers off, it came just above the knee, and I carried Wendy and Havoc over (feeling like 'St Chump') to view a stricken ship, The Sovereign, left to break up near Cairnbulg Point. She had gone aground just under a year earlier, 18th December 2005 due to the watch keeper being on his phone rather than concentrating on navigation, he may well of had a dram or three as well. Sovereign would never make it back to Banff, even for a coronation of Queen Nicola. (2023 – with that ambition scotched, watch this space and look out UN!)

I had read Cairnbulg and Inverallochy were lawless places in the early 19th century, full of heavy drinking brawlers and piled high rubbish which led to cholera epidemics. My source said St Combs was nearly as 'evil', but that was certainly not our greeting. True, some wartime defences were evident among the low dunes, but we met John at the Assembly of God and 18 children of various ages who were at the modest building for a get together. Singing, marching - Havoc being an exhibitionist allowed all of them to smooth him, take turns at leading him around in return for a lick of their faces. Excitement, barking, chocolate eclairs and marshmallows it was all completely overwhelming. To cap it all in a tear-jerking moment one of the boys said a prayer, asking God to look out for us. Had he been primed or did his dad own a copy of the Merry Christmas album from 1989? It seemed very spontaneous and was a lovely welcome. They all departed to do their homework and we had the hall to ourselves, Irish Stew and ready for bed by 9pm. John returned as we were retiring and brought chocolate bars and crisps. If this was 'evil' bring on Hannibal Lecter.

After all the petting of yesterday evening Havoc was keen to roll. A slithering action, a bit like Baloo with an itch, only horizontally. Followed by forward rolls and head stands, he was rehearsing his own floor programme, more ear and elbow than formal 'Olympic' but nevertheless impressive. Then came flight in the vault as he leapt a six foot wide cattle grid while wearing his panniers, no sign of any leg strain here. We entered Richard Adams' the sequel territory, the return of Bigwig and silflay, and our Max

Witlock didn't know which way to chase first. Rabbits dispersed in all directions like seeds from a squirting cucumber plant.

We needed to cross the Waters of Strathbeg, and I used binoculars to try and locate a bridge. Eventually, we came upon three deserted houses at Seatown. The landscape was positively Saharan, and very slow going. A dinky offshore lighthouse at Rattray Head, waves breaking at the base of dunes, foamy surf washing our boot laces, which evaporated as the waves died on the beach. It certainly crossed my mind that we could get cut off, soft sand preventing any escape at the mercy of the North Sea. From that sea, gas comes ashore. Flares, twin security fences, CCTV, mile upon mile of regular pipework. By the time we reached the small track that led inland to the A90 near St Fergus, we had done some 14 miles taking us nearly seven hours. We struggled on to Peterhead, where we had an address to stay, and Havoc found a dead sea bird to chew upon and ease his appetite.

Dennis was a pest controller and was finagled into putting us up by our man in Aberdeen, hasher Olymprick. We were nevertheless made very welcome by his wife Svetlana and new baby Maria, donning boxing glove scratch mittens. The cat, Charlie, was not quite so receptive to Havoc. Over fish and mash, the healthy option in this part of Scotland, we learned of his spot of bother with the authorities. I still had images of exploding plants in my head, when he explained about using bird scarer pyrotechnics to keep intruders out of his garden, earning him the nick name the 'Peterhead Bomber' in the press.

Peterhead was a sizeable town, the largest in Aberdeenshire, a population of over 18,000 and many social issues and high levels of deprivation. Dennis warned us to look out for drug dealers and gave us a giant catering size bar of chocolate he had acquired from somewhere, the size of a A4 ream of paper. Just what we wanted to lighten our load, but at least we would have something to fight muggers off with. This was more mountainous than your giant Toblerone, six times larger than your biggest Yorkie on any lorry dashboard and may just about have silenced JM's chocolate habit. How we would get into it without catering cutlery, or a jack hammer was another matter.

The town still had important fishing industries and was an oil service centre. We passed the prison, with a reputation as one of Scotland's toughest, and the thought that youngsters here are more than ten times likely to end up behind those walls than those from more rural spots just down the road.

Andy, the mechanic at the lifeboat station showed us over his pride and joy, a Tamar, built back in Devonport. £2.5m worth of high tech, dual diesel engines, individual computer screens for each seat, watertight-bulkhead, self-righting capability, virtually unsinkable, dram proofed. All very different from the row boats I had naively imagined seeing prior to setting off. This one, The Misses Robertson of Kintail came into service just a few months earlier.

We journeyed on around Sandford Bay, past a power station, dubbed Scotland's worst air polluter in 2020. At Boddam I treated myself to a hot pie, still not having worked out how to get into our 20 quires of Dairy Milk. Near Murdoch Head a granite memorial to a couple of climbers, James Paterson and Alexander Hamilton, two strong Scottish names, who came to grief on the cliffs in 1967. It reminded me of a near accident on Haytor in Devon when protection Wendy had placed while leading, pinged free and her head ended up millimetres from my feet belaying her. As we walked in a south westerly direction a setting sun coloured the coast ahead, tangerine and terracotta, with outlined shadows of buildings.

One was that of New Slains Castle. In darkness by now it made for an eerie sight. Roofless, round and rectangular stone towers and regular window reveals disclosing nothing but blackness. It had quite a history, a 16th century core, many later additions, once a Clan Hay fortress, visited by Dr Johnson who wrote of it.

"Built on margin of the sea, one must enjoy the terrific grandeur of the tempestuous ocean".

A shipping tycoon, Sir John Ellman, was a later owner but in 1925 the roof was removed to avoid taxes, and no doubt the lead was flogged off too. The 7 reception rooms and 14 bedrooms soon fell into disrepair, no one visited to play tennis or croquet, and a place said to be the inspiration of Bram Stockers 'Dracula' became a gothic horror in its own right. By now we had managed, using a rock, to snap off jagged dagger like bits of chocolate to gnaw upon, in fact melting it by sucking was more effective than teeth, but we were now armed if any vamp came a calling.

It was now ebony black, a full moon was to follow, but had not risen yet and our pitiful head torches did not stop us tripping over another memorial stone. This one read,

'These Cliffs are very dangerous - Nicholas French, our son, fell to his death near Sugar Loaf Rock, 1991, aged 7 years.'

Although we had not covered a great distance, (JM managed from Peterhead to Newburgh in a day, it would take us two) light had run out on us and at Cruden Bay we were glad to find a friendly post mistress just about to close. She gave us a donation, food from the shelves and showed us to a church hall where I could study tomorrow's map and read what some of those whose footsteps we were following had written. On a bookshelf, a 1972 edition of the AA Book of the Seaside. Flicking through its hard cover I couldn't help noticing its similarity to JM's 1979 account of his 7000 mile walk! The enlightening facts in the latter, nuggets of knowledge, had always impressed me, but now I felt as if I might be carrying the wrong book. The hall came out with three stars.

The morning greeted us with a fresh cold start, fine drizzle and wind in our faces. If last nights' red sky was anything to go by, it should have been delightful, but the shepherds got it wrong I am afraid. Mourners at a funeral sheltered under umbrellas and we knew it was time to make haste. Muddy tracks and just a single ruined corner at Old Castle Slains. By Collieston the sea was at its angriest, low grey clouds and pelting winds smashing waves over the break water, rising spray and foam way into the air. All the small boats were pulled way up the shore, the shop was closed, and we saw no one. A rare occasion at lunch time we tucked in behind a wall, lit the Trangia and made a cup of soup.

The modest remains of Forvie Church did little to inspire. Archaeologists may keep a watching brief, but Wendy was nonplussed, and Havoc showed his contempt in traditional canine fashion. Paths improved over the nature reserve, and we cut back to cross the river Ythan. Said to have the largest eider duck colony in the world, there were plenty of piebald males and I imagined the baby soft down used by Icelandics, Inuits and duvet makers to tog up warm. These birds were the subject of one of the world's first ever protection orders, set up by St Cuthbert in Northumberland, 676 AD and are therefore sometimes known as St Cuthbert or Cuddy ducks. My warped, weary mind soon transported me to John Denver's Grandma's Feather Bed. Who was going to be pedantic about the difference between ducks and geese, if you were tucked up with hound dogs, a pig and homemade butter on the bread?

In Newburgh we found the old lifeboat station by the river. The first station in Scotland to be set up by the RNLI was established here in 1828. Service would become consolidated at Peterhead and the station finally closed in 1965. We were fortunate to be passing The Udny Arms Hotel just as Guy and Susie were tangling themselves in their Christmas lights, having far too much fun. In return for a hand with the tree, we were offered a room, number 8. On the dining room walls, old photos of lifeboats and at breakfast Pearl, a maid, brought in family treasured memorabilia, cuttings and gallantry medals of relatives who had been involved in rescues from the Imperial Prince, 1923. You could see the resemblance to John and James Innes in her face.

As we left, across the links golf course I was surprised the club emblem was a Sandwich tern, not an eider but it didn't seem to bother the seals near the beach. Wendy uploaded our Christmas message, to hashers

back in Devon, scratched into the sand, 18 years on from 'annus horribilis', the Queen recorded hers at Southwark Cathedral.

More golf links at Balmedie, somewhat more modest than those seen earlier, but the frequency begged the question, how many bunkers and fairways in Scotland? Michael Forbes, a local farmer, would famously refuse to sell lands and the following year plans put forward for a Trump golf course would be rejected. Alex Salmond and the SNP would later lend their support and some of the future President's Men would mark their cards after 2012 when the Trump International Balmedie opened. I read that it has lost money ever since.

The skyline of Scotland's Granite City came into view. The spires not quite up to Oxford, silhouetted in late afternoon sunshine, beneath mottled ruddy grey clouds which matched the buildings' stonework. Lord Byron was raised here, but we needed to find a later son, Graham Thain, aka Olymprick, our man in Scotland's third city. We crossed the arches of the Bridge of Don and past Pittodrie. In the 1980s Alex Ferguson had put The Dons firmly on the European map. The harbour dating from 1136, now a support centre for offshore oil and gas, with new buildings - tower, pilots office, traffic control centre included the Victoria Dock where we found the lifeboat station, opened 1998. I read the very first lifeboat, a ten-oar rowboat, was established in response to storms in 1800 which saw 30 shipwrecks and 80 seamen lost in one week. The RNLI took over in 1925 and at our visit the second mechanic was a lady, Zandra.

Olymprick met us on foot and led us through a shopping precinct, 'No Dogs allowed' to George Street. We put Havoc's yellow handmade tabard on him, mentioning Guide Dogs and ignored the glances from security guards.

“He’s a new experimental breed,”

I told one of them, as we hurried on through, on arrival ready for a Mealy Pie. Olymprick ran several shops, fancy dress, bakers, and pies were a specialty rivaling Wallace, Gromit and Mrs Tweedy. Mealy ones contained oatmeal, so a Scottish delicacy which had to be tried. Pizza or Stovies were also available 24/7. (Stovies - meat and potato leftovers, served in a polystyrene cup, a favourite with clubbers going home at 4am.) We met his brother Alan and partner Ruby, who, although we didn’t know it at the time, we would see a good deal more of ten months later. The Thains had ancestry in Balmedie where we had come through, and a clear hostility and mistrust of all things Trump. Mention of the name caused Graham to spit, fast forward a decade and a half, and the bucket would be overflowing.

After a short ride in Olymprick’s bread van, in time I would get to drive it, we continued to Battery Head. We looked back to see large ships, fish processing buildings and dolphins breeching near the harbour entrance.

It was a cold Saturday, we kept going around Nigg Bay, past Cove Rangers football ground before stopping for a break at the Neuk Pub in Portlethen. Over a free cuppa I was to realise this part of the world had a long history in angling, probably made even more popular by the likes of Mortimer, Whitehouse, Wade and Green. On display was the sea angling Douglas cup from 1896 which may have been won by Downies or Cove but had come to rest at Portlethen.

We hugged the coast as best we could, before being forced onto a path beside the dual carriageway A90 to Stonehaven. The railway is squeezed here too, 14 years on, a short distance to the southwest, a train hit a landslip killing three people. Through hash contacts we had secured a static caravan stop-over at Cloak, but it turned out to be further south near Catterline. A misunderstanding meant we were picked up and taken there, forcing us to retrace and walk the five or six miles the next day if we were to stay honest to our cause. OS map number 38 was behind us, now we needed to borrow number 45.

It was day 28, a Sunday and we needed some exercise so went hashing with Aberdeen H3. I thought they said we were going to Balmoral, but it turned out to be Banchory, same direction just not quite so far. We left Havoc in the caravan, resting, I couldn’t help thinking we had been duped. A couple of hours trail and ‘on-downs’ in a forest car park, we were dropped back to Stonehaven. We did some food shopping, walked to Dunnottar Castle as the weather deteriorated. The ruined fortress had a rocky headland to itself with a narrow strip of land leading to the gatehouse. The Honours of Scotland, the Scottish Crown Jewels, were apparently hidden here from Oliver Cromwell's army in the 17th century. It was also used as one of the film settings for the 1990 film version of Hamlet.

Our shopping and OS map 45 that we had loaned from harriet 'Trouser Shredder', (don't ask!) were now becoming completely sodden as we made our way back to Catterline. Wind directly at us, a flashing blue light from a Police car insisted they drop us back to the caravan. I was not so keen, but Wendy did not want to leave Havoc alone any longer and we jumped in, the Police adamant they would not tell a soul we had yielded to a short lift. Havoc was spread eagled on the sofa, his autobiographical account, somewhat inaccurate in detail. We had a large fry up and watched Zara Phillips win Sports Personality of the Year. The backgammon set made a reappearance, and I got a game back in the series, 2-5 down while wondering if you can ever trust a Policeman.

Chapter 5 – Stonehaven to Elie

Follow me, follow you

"South to the Tay and on to the Kingdom."

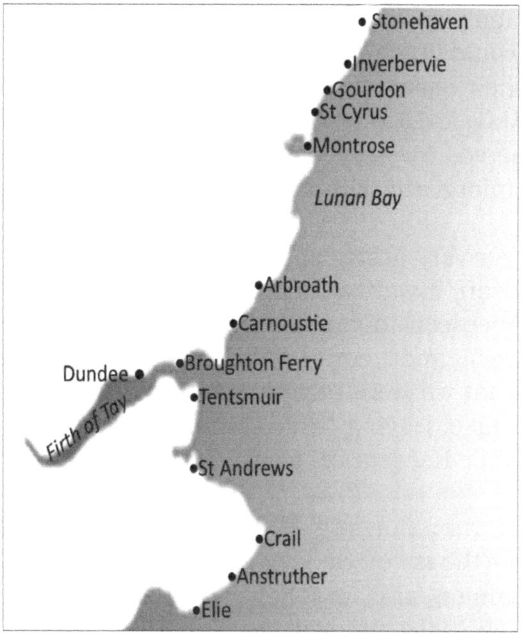

LEAVING A THANK you note and the key under the mat we trotted off for Todhead lighthouse. Soon afterwards we came upon two barns full of pigs. They were clean with fresh straw, but the noise and smell were quite bewildering especially for Havoc. I lifted him up to get a better view, there were too many to count, you could hardly get a scratching between them, and they all raced to the gate, keen to drag him in with them. I had to hold on and quickly reverse to save his bacon. Wendy was all for giving them their freedom, rather than a trip to see 'Corporal Jones' in shop hours, but I scotched that idea, not so much on animal welfare grounds, more for self-preservation. If we had opened that gate, it was us who would have been scoffed.

Our timing of arrival at Inverbervie could not have been better. Some farmers had gathered at a pub for lunch and contrary to what is often said about farmers, especially frugal Scottish ones, they were in generous mood. Perhaps they had all done especially well at market that morning, but our collection tin was stuffed with notes, and I didn't tell them we had let their pigs out. At one end of the Jubilee Bridge, a memorial to Hercules Linton who designed the Cutty Sark, born here 1837. It took the form of a figurehead from the Clipper, supposedly a scale model, and that of a scantily clad maiden. However, I could not help noticing she was only revealing one breast, her right, and I being a stickler for detail on all things nautical, researched the lady on the bow at Greenwich to find she was fully topless. (Arrival in London would necessitate double checking!) Perhaps it was felt pietistic coastal townsfolk were not quite up to the voyeurism lavished on ocean racing tea boys. The research also uncovered the model was based on 'Nannie' from Robert Burns poem Tam o'Shanter. He always gave good value for money, its 20 verses long and some of those have 32 lines, thank goodness translations are available. Just to fully embellish the Scottish theme, Mitchells of Glasgow once marketed a favourite dark flake pipe tobacco under the name Tam o'Shanter, 11d an ounce.

Gourdon had an attractive harbour and I read at one time tens of boats would line up across it enabling walking from one side to the other across their decks. It also had one of the first inshore lifeboats from 1890. The Maggie Law remains as a museum piece, once rowed by six men she served for 40 years, saving 36 lives. A fitting reminder that this coast is unforgiving, three generations could be wiped out in a single incident.

Our very first responders to pleas of help and shelter were a couple from Usan. Ewan and Jilly met us at St Cyrus. Jilly was on her way to Aberdeen to catch a flight to Luton, she commuted to Hertfordshire for work, and I could not help but think how totally different that was from what we were currently up to. Ewan dropped us back to their beautiful house, leaving three complete strangers with a cottage pie in their home, while he went off to play squash, a terrific 'boast' of trust.

In the morning Ewan took us back to Woodston Fishing Station, northeast of St Cyrus, now a luxury B&B, but once donkeys hauled salmon, and we followed in their hoof prints. An impressive viaduct from 1865 took us over the North Esk at Kinnaber. Beeching closed the line up the coast, an insult to the workers who laboured on its many arches.

The links golf course, one of the oldest in the world, led us into Montrose with a chance to explore and try our luck at collecting in the town centre. The steeple of Old and St Andrews Church dominated the skyline, and we were told of 'Big Peter', one of its bells cast in Rotterdam in 1676. An historic trading connection with the Low Countries had influenced some of the house architecture. The Basin, a large tidal lagoon inland and we learned GlaxoSmithKline were still to be around a while providing jobs for many of the 12k population. At one stage just, months earlier its future in the town was in doubt.

At the harbour a life size bronze of a Norwegian St Bernard, Bamse, a lifesaving hero who died here in 1944. It was only unveiled in October and Havoc was really taken by it. Perhaps Scotland's greatest sculptor, William Lamb was born in Montrose. Trained as a right hander, he lost the use of this at Passchendaele, and had to learn to become a southpaw. Until a biography in 2013, he was hardly known outside of Scotland.

For me however, it was Links Park in Wellington Street that captured my interest. Home of semi-pro football club, Montrose FC, proud since 1879, they won the Cup in 1921/22 season. I remembered all these 'smaller' Scottish clubs from the footy results on a Saturday afternoon. How they all got a mention on 'English' TV only John McGovern knows. (He was born in town and went to a rugby playing school.) By the time the announcers got to the end of Queen of the South, East Fife and Stenhousemuir it was time for bed, that's if Zebedee hadn't already declared it, boing! The nick name of Montrose is 'Gable Endies' after humble houses that were built gable on to the street on 12 ft plots. The year after our visit they put down an artificial pitch. Synthetic surfaces have generally found more favour north of the border than in England, which might be indicative of rainfall. We scurried on over the South Esk Bridge, wet and windy, to Scurdie Ness lighthouse, puddles lapping the kerbs both side of the path, for a second night in Usan. Thank you, Clan McCulloch.

The House on the Rock was the one those piggies back at Todhead would have opted for, elsewhere in the old Fishertown a dilapidated tower and row of cottages abandoned as if built of straw. When we were first told of digs here, we were grateful, but both said, 'Where's that?' Now we knew and would always remember, a warm welcome just north of Lunan Bay.

Fields to the south led to Elephants Rock. It was just like a leathery thick-skinned matriarch pachyderm; Saint-Saens must have visited to inspire him to pen his carnival. The picturesque remnants of Red Castle were perched above Lunan Water. I could have easily stopped to explore but fine drizzle which had been around all day meant Wendy was head down, in no mood for antiquity.

In a blink we were at Auchmithie, and she warned me be careful where to tread. There seemed to be dog poo everywhere. There is only one thing worse than dog poo and that is owners who pick it up only to throw the bag in the hedge. Why? You will have seen them too, plastic nappy sacks dangling from branches. It is not pretty. Here endeth the lesson on dog shit.

We tried to grab some shelter at a pub, which turned out to be a restaurant and we were asked 'have you booked?' The church was padlocked, nearby vegetables in the fields and poly tunnels, would have made terrific shelter, except the 'poly' had gone, just metal frames. The day was 'dreich' and so was Auchmithie, not very welcoming.

The wild Seaton Cliffs lead to Arbroath. Now you are just as likely to see adrenaline junkies leaping off the sandstone sculpted precipices framed by features like Needle E'e. In his day and own way another risk taker Robert the Bruce in 1320 would proclaim Scotland's Independence at the country's richest abbey, Arbroath. Now a shell, for years sailors would look for the navigational light that burned from the 'O', a large circular window. With the aid of binoculars, you could just about make out Inchcape reef and Bellrock Lighthouse, 11 miles off the coast. Local Guide Dog supporters billeted us, helped us raise the profile in the local press and along with lifeboat crew, made us very welcome. The Arbroath Lifeboat has a history dating back to 1803. The current Mersey class boat is called 'Inchcape'. A predecessor in 1953, The Robert Lindsay, was lost along with six crew members. Including the Irish Republic, Isle of Man and the Channel Isles a list reveals the loss of 54 lifeboats since 1810, with over 600 lives lost.

With the smell of smoldering oak in our nostrils the local delicacy had to be tasted. Smokies, generally haddock, are hot smoked, a bit like a kipper but they are herring and cold smoked. If you don't like bones, best to leave it to Rick Stein and blue blistering barnacles, Captain Archibald himself made Scottish by Steven Spielberg. Legend has it Smokies originated in Auchmithie when a store caught on fire, destroying barrels, by accident an industry was born.

Arbroath Abbey altar is where the Stone of Scone turned up eventually in 1951. It had done more miles than we were planning to which was not bad for a 150 kg oblong of red sandstone, also known as the Coronation Stone. Mined in Iona it went to Scone near Perth before Edward I, took it as a spoil of war, and it found its way to Westminster Abbey. Students pinched it in 1950 and it turned up at Arbroath only to be returned for the Queen's coronation in 1953. (The film Stone of Destiny 2008 tells the tale.) In 1996 John Major returned it in the face of Scottish dissatisfaction, a symbolic response, and it now rests in Edinburgh, ready for the coronation of Queen Nicola (United Nations).

The shoreline took us past Gayfield Park, home of Arbroath FC and on to East Haven. Synonymous with golf, Carnoustie. The Open was due to be played here the following year and even in late 2006 some house owners were preparing to make a killing. Property lets for the duration of the Championships were at a premium, and if you played it right one might earn enough to see you through to the next rotation. (Padraig Harington went on to win in 2007, the circus returned in 2018 and no doubt the gravy train pulled in once more.) We crossed Barry Links, sometimes shared with the MoD, but my thoughts were with the like of Player and Watson, both Open winners here, rather than of red firing warning flags. As we entered the Firth of Tay, Monifieth and Broughty Ferry were in our periscope.

Until the construction of the Tay Rail Bridge at Dundee, this point, 'Broughty', opposite Tayport was a busy one. Now the ferry is somewhat redundant, but the castle stood proud. We visited the lifeboat station, one of Scotland's busiest and not just because of the Dook, an annual New Year's Day fancy dress swim. They had seen some 25 lifeboats here over the years and lost the Mona in tragic circumstances in 1959. We were told not to miss out on the award-winning fish and chips, but frankly these awards seem to be two a penny, everywhere has one. In the 1950s you could easily buy chips by the penny worth, six penn'oth of chips and 'cheap as chips' came into the vocabulary. We looked at the price list but decided we could not afford it.

Our budget was really only £10 a day, food and shelter for two adults, plus a dog. Havoc did have his own sponsorship from 'Eukanuba' but let's just call that a bonus. £300 a month, £3600 for the year, with a £400 contingency. We had joint savings of £4K. B&Bs were out of the question, but we had not factored in people's generosity, who commonly fed us. Hence, our kitty did not get overstretched. The parcels we sent out containing some meals were also donated and our bonus. Ask me why we didn't have a support vehicle, the price of diesel was around 80p-£1 a litre in 2006/7, and you have your answer.

At Dundee the local RNLI stole our thunder with a Saturday collection, but we lent a hand anyway, our tabards and large bags being talking points. It was a pity events like this could not have been coordinated with our arrival, making more planned and widely received publicity and bigger contributions, but alas we could hardly influence that while walking. An organisational overseeing was necessary. We stood under the Christmas lights, next to a giant statue of Desperate Dan. Said to be built on Jute, Jam and Journalism, there was little evidence of the first, save the Cox's Stack chimney, but marmalade and DC Thomson media moguls still seemed to be doing a bit.

The best way of seeing it seemed to be from Law Hill. Tower blocks, the river, road and rail bridges and the masts of Scott's Discovery and back-to-back Dens and Tannadice Parks. I bet the police love it on derby days. Mandy Burk and her family were kind enough to offer us a room for the night, her own children tossed from their beds, in a flat near Ninewells Hospital. Very humble, but extremely welcoming, chicken dinner (the curry roasted vegetables were good too).

One Dundonian was thrilled we would be walking over 'his bridge, it's all uphill from here to Tayport.' He claimed to be a descendant of William McGonagall, also from Dundee, known as the 'world's worst poet!', although his name was Campbell, which might explain a continuance of poetic mediocrity. He was full of the rail disaster of 1879 which saw the collapse of the bridge but assured us the road one carrying the A92, since 1966, would not let us down. That optimism has been matched in recent years. Dundee is now termed 'One city, many discoveries' and new research and technology industries have set up, one in seven of the population is a student, which might explain the growth of video game production. A regeneration has seen it being awarded UNESCO first UK Design City status in 2014, named 'coolest little city in Britain' 2015, 'hottest destination to visit' 2018, the same year the V&A arrived. The TV crime thriller Traces, 2021, was even set here.

We crossed on the central walkway between railings, a mile and a half, over the Tay. I read later that natives had voted for it to be named 'Steve', surely, Mr Campbell's christian name. We turned right to have a look around Newport, but Havoc instinctively knew that was wrong, sniffing the air to the left above Tentsmuir. This beach walk with dunes and forest inland was amazing, the first bit of Fife. Seals in the water were inquisitive, a frost had frozen the top layers of sand so as you trod on it, it cracked like biting into a choc ice. Seashells left after an ebbing tide had seen the sand wind-blown from under them, leaving them perched like on a jardiniere, a frozen sand pillar. Sun on ice crystals made blue patches behind grassy tussocks, which stayed with us reflecting off calm gleaming waters all the way to Guardbridge and on to St Andrews.

At the New Inn we shared a meal with Dean, a former pupil from the school I taught at back in Exeter, himself partially sighted. On the entire walk it was unusual for us to meet up with people we knew, most were strangers and fleeting acquaintances. He was a staff member for most of our contact, helping in boarding houses or acting as a teaching assistant. He was very much into sport, active and enthusiastic and was forging a new life for himself with his partner Rhona, running an outdoor and adventure business. It was good to reminisce and see him thriving. We chatted long into the evening before going just inland to Balmungo near Brownhills where Guide Dog supporters Zoe and Ian were to put us up. Their dogs Hovis, Cassie and Scribbles were given hot buttered toast at bedtime and Havoc was not missed out. Zoe also volunteered to take our bags on the next day to Crail, leaving them at the Golf Hotel.

We could not move on before having a look around St Andrews which had a majestic look and air of grandeur, popular with tourists. The Kinness Burn trail, smart shops and expensive houses, ruins of cathedral and castle, university buildings, Madras College, and everything golf - museum, club makers, six courses with another opening the next year. The saltire cross of St Andrew, adopted as a national flag was everywhere and the coast itself was special, West Sands beach was used in the opening scenes of Chariots of Fire and also featured in the 2012 Olympic opening ceremony. Not to be out done I read that in 1864 a Bootlace worm (Lineus longissimus) was washed up measuring 180 ft long (55 metres) on East Sands. It has a toxic mucus, and I thought no wonder they built a leisure centre and pool nearby.

We shared a rocky, undulating path with another couple which was a first in 36 days. We had quite a bit in common, Margaret was from Branscombe in East Devon, but was now living in Cupar. They stopped for lunch and without bags we pressed on at pace not seeing them again. The path became flatter and easier as we got to the East Neuk. One of

Scotland's James's described Fife as 'a beggar's mantle fringed with gold'. A beggar's hand stretching out to the sea, a ragged coastline a fringed cloak, gold lining the fishing villages. He should have worked for the tourist board. From Fife Ness we could get a good look at the route ahead, across the Isle of May which had a coal fired lighthouse in 1635, to Bass Rock and the Dunbar coast.

That was to come after Edinburgh. Later that afternoon we collected our bags from the Golf Hotel, half hoping they might offer a room or at least a trolley but in Crail we found the British Legion Hall. The lovely old lady who held the keys was certainly golden. Chicken casserole for tea and a good three stars for facilities at the Legion. I was given good luck mementoes as we left which I posted home at the first opportunity.

On the way to Anstruther we passed Caiplie Caves, once a site of early Christian worship, later the home of a hermit and place where farmers housed cattle, pigeons and doves. At Kilrenny a remembrance service, the trawler Meridian had been lost with four lives earlier in the year and a local skipper John Bowman had also been lost off Weymouth recently. There were mutters of government not helping fishermen enough, meaning they must go out regardless of weather, travelling further to make a living. That brought it home that places like the Scottish Fisheries museum and the Mersey class lifeboat on a mooring at Anstruther are not just tourist visitor locations, behind them lie an industry upon which families depend. Another award-winning fish and chip shop here, but somehow the prices didn't seem quite so high.

As we continued south, we came to Pittenween and the iron gate to St Fillan's cave. An Irish seventh century missionary is said to have lived here and legend has it, God gave him a glowing left arm to see by in the dark interior. A bit further and the St Monans salt pans were said to have taken eight tons of coal from the nearby Coal Farm to produce one ton of salt. The unusual windmill provided the power to put salt water into the pans. To me it seemed it was just waiting for Don Quixote to arrive. Between Newark Castle and Lady's Tower we stumbled on a dead grey seal. Gulls had made a meal of its eyes, the remainder of the decaying carcass at the mercy of nature's other scavengers and recycling agents. The Lady Tower dated from 1770. It had been built for Lady Janet Anstruther so she could watch the world go by. Apparently, she was fond of skinny dips and would send a servant around ringing a hand bell to warn off local 'Toms' when she was about to take the waters. Rumour has it, she was also very beautiful and something of a flirt, so perhaps the bell was only to advertise her bathing. Grandstanding and voyeurism nothing new in these parts. Ruby Bay led to the Elie lighthouse. Here, if lucky, one could pick up a ruby-coloured gemstone among volcanic sands. Garnets, known as pyrope are the deceiving nuggets. We found sanctuary in a small hall at Toll Green. A brightly lit Christmas tree on the grass outside was as if it was erected just for us. I didn't care who did the following, the infatuation was all mine. 'Stay with you, if you stay with me' the 1978 ear worm that was charmed to the surface.

Chapter 6 – Elie to Edinburgh

Chain keep us together (running in the shadow)

"Every mountain is within reach if you just keep climbing."

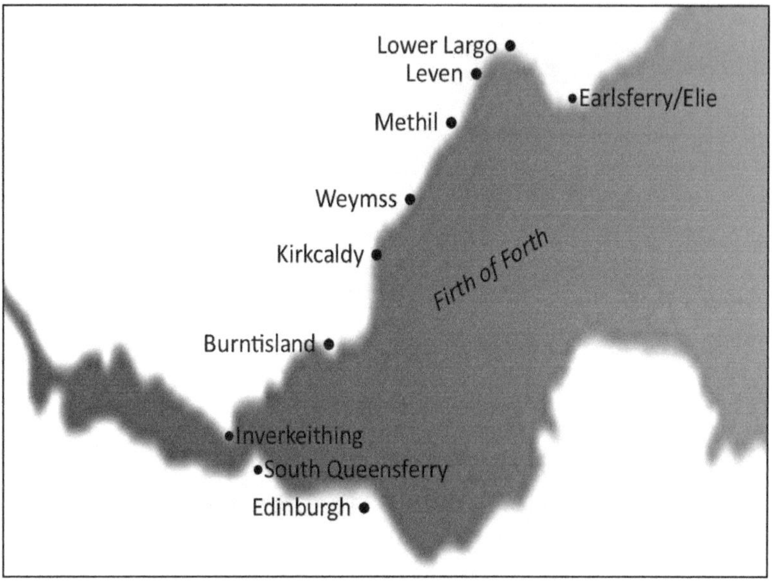

NEXT MORNING AS we deposited collection money at the Post Office, we were given cloth Fife Coast path badges. Completed in 2002 this path ran from Newport to North Queensferry, some 87 miles. It was extended in 2011 and again in 2012 to reach Kincardine and Newburgh on the South and North coasts of Fife, extending it to 116 miles.

Elie and Earlsferry are linked villages. Legend has it that Macduff, Earl of Fife, fleeing from King Macbeth crossed the Forth from here in 1054 after hiding in a cave near Kincraig Point. A route was established allowing pilgrims to traffic in the opposite direction from North Berwick heading for St Andrews and between the two stories Earlsferry was born. The etymology of Elie is less clear. We met a lady who asked us how we could manage to look at the sea each day? She had lost her son 14 years earlier at sea and could still not look at the ocean. It was hard to know how to respond, and we made an uncomfortable exit.

We were told to check out the graves in the parish church, looking for the grave of 'Charles Fox Cattanach, wife of James Smith.' It seemed the grave belonged to a lady who died 25th March 1872, aged 67. Given a man's name mistakenly at christening, her superstitious family continued to use it. It wasn't the only bit of trivia to be had. The floral clock, admired by me previously, in Edinburgh Princes Street gardens was originally constructed in 1903 using a mechanism salvaged from Elie. I collected at The Ship Inn on The Toft to be told the village cricket team who frequent the pub are the only team in the world to play their matches between tides on the beach, 'Howzat!'

We crossed yet another Scottish golf course, passed old gun emplacements along with a group of schoolboys who were clearly late for the morning bell. They muttered something about missing the bus and detention and disappeared in the opposite direction. Coming across the Elie Chainwalk, 'unique coastal, hazardous scramble' our adventurous spirits were aroused. Havoc had been up the Tree Root back in Devon at Chudleigh Rocks many times, 'squeezed under my arm' and had 'trusted' me lots of times, contrary to others' opinion. However, we did not know what to expect so left him tied to our bags, while we ran on over the top, to the other end of the feature. We then negotiated the eight vertical and horizontal chains that allow passage over the half kilometre of cliffs and basalt formations back to where we left him. The 'jukebox' flipped to

Fleetwood Mac for 'Rumours' between the rocks. It was great fun, one needed two hands free to haul ourselves up the crags and it would have been foolhardy to try it again with ruck sacks and canine, so after a posed photo, we went over the top again, on to Lower Largo.

While Havoc chased an old, discarded football around the beach I went off collecting. In the Railway Inn I bumped into Nigel Smith, a New Zealander but perhaps Largo's most notable, if temporary, current day resident. He was to help publicise our efforts with calls to radio stations and paid for a future stay for us at a hotel in Inverkeithing.

Largo's most noteworthy ancient inhabitant was Alexander Selkirk born here in 1676. By all accounts he was rather like me, quarrelsome and unruly. In 1704 he would find himself on a ship called Cinque Ports bound for the South Seas. He asked to be put ashore on an uninhabited island off Juan Fernandez, 400 miles from Chile. Here he stayed in solitude four years and four months, no volleyball called Wilson or Tom Hanks double, though he 'may' have had toothache and danced frantically with pyromania when he achieved friction combustion, who knows? He did however know something about the sea worthiness of ships, hence his request, because the Cinque Ports was to sink off South America and survivors were imprisoned in Peru.

Selkirk would be the inspiration for Daniel Defoe's Robinson Crusoe, though he may have embellished the island solitude to 28 years. Selkirk would return to Largo, before going back to sea, contracting yellow fever off the Gold Coast, West Africa and was buried in the ocean aged 45. His statue in Largo, musket, pistol and goat skins could not escape the deposits of sea birds. We trekked onto Leven, with thoughts of cannibalistic natives in mind but were relieved to remember it was only Wednesday. The Church of Scotland was very accommodating, letting us stay in the vacant Manse House before shopping at Lidl's and having a Vesta beef risotto for tea. (Other supermarkets and other risottos are available.)

Thursday 21st December, day 39 of our adventure, was an uninspiring one. We made our way to Methil, the Proclaimers summed it up in their anthem, 'No more!' Past tired docks and a brief respite in the form of East Fife FC. A trio of Wemyss's, former coal towns, the West one at least had a continental looking clock tower and we sat on a bench eating 'ice creams and lollipops', waiting for the 'child catcher' to arrive. Dystart, although it doesn't sound like it, was a little less depressing, Ravenscraig woods offered Havoc a few grey squirrels to chase, and we arrived at Kirkcaldy. Social philosopher and economist Adam Smith was born here in 1723. David Danskin (1863-1948) grew up in the town, a principal founder of Dial Square FC, which became Royal Arsenal and now simply Arsenal FC, 'the gunners'.

If you ever wondered where Raith Rovers stem from, it is here in Kirkcaldy, population around 50k, though they do well to get a couple of thousand at Stark's Park. One of them might be Gordon Brown MP for the town, Chancellor and made PM in June 2007. (Since our walk had 'visual impairment' connections it is worth noting a little-known fact that Brown is 'blind' in his left eye, following a retinal detachment incurred while at school.) We made a short day of it as St Bryce Kirk offered us their hall to stay in overnight.

It meant we had a long day ahead, some 18/20 miles to Inverkeithing. Fortunately, it was dry and fine and helped on our way at Kinghorn lifeboat station by Operations Manager, Charles Tulloch MBE, with tea and biscuits. Charles had given 40 years' service having volunteered at the station since the boat was introduced. The remainder of the day offered sharp contrasts. Magnificent views over the Forth to islands like Inchkeith and Inchcolm. The seasonally closed attractions, fairground rides and crazy golf of Burntisland, and depressed housing hemmed in by railway lines. A cheeky robin posed for his Christmas card photo, and we shared a sandwich crust with him.

We lost the path here and ended up climbing fences and scrabbling over tracks to rejoin a westward route. We were Freewheelin' and Bob Dylan's 'how many roads must a man walk down' was in my head, supplemented by my own lyrics, 'before he admits he's lost!' Pleasant, wooded areas at Hawkcraig Point, Aberdour too was attractive, other areas were industrial with gas terminals, big ships, working boats and docks. Massive, luxurious 'upper-class' houses with manicured gardens approaching Donibristle, "middle class" residencies near St David's Harbour, contrasting sharply with the "working class" rentals seen at the backend of Burntisland. I couldn't help thinking of the Two Ronnies sketch with John Cleese, (The class system 1966).

It was almost dark when we reached Inverkeithing, the Forth Rail Bridge beckoned us as the sun set, but that would have to wait until tomorrow.

True to his generous word, New Zealand Nigel had booked us a room (no 8 again) at the Queens Hotel, it was uphill to reach it, but a complimentary lasagna soon helped us forget that. I collected in town in the evening and one donation was a 50 Euro note, some munificent souls in Fife. That Chinese lucky number has become mine ever since.

The Forth Road Bridge crossing certainly gave us the feeling we were well on our way and a passerby stopped his car and asked to take our photo. It ran alongside the iconic rail bridge with its cantilever arms and central truss. The Queensberry Crossing carrying the M90 was added in 2017. A window cleaner, who turned out to be a RNLI fundraiser, was having a few drinks with lifeboat crew from Kinghorn and a Forth ship pilot in the pleasant little town, officially South Queensberry. It was a fine day, but one thing was for sure, not many windows were being cleaned.

Rounding Peatdraught Bay, pleasant woods led to Barnbougle Castle and the impressive Dalmeny House and golf course. We cut up to Cramond Brig to cross the River Almond. It was something of a detour, but the former ferry was no longer running. An information board said a former ferryman, Robert Graham, had found a gold Roman lioness in the water, perhaps it gave him the security to be able to retire? I belief there has been lots of proposals to reinstate a ferry, even build a bridge, but as far as I can find out, the Cramond Brig detour is still the only option. Back to the coast at Granton harbour, the walk seemed popular with dog owners and parents/ children on bikes, then we turned right to cut up through Edinburgh, past the Royal Botanic gardens to the city centre.

Chapter 7 – Edinburgh, time to chill!

Kyrie eleison

"An advent journey re-enacted."

WE COULD FEEL quietly pleased with ourselves. The first stage of our not uneventful journey completed and exactly on schedule. We had planned to reach the Scottish capital for Christmas, take a few days to recuperate, see in the New Year with Hogmanay up close and personal, that was part of starting at John o' Groats - 41 days, covering what Spud reckoned was 523 miles, an introduction at a modest average of 12.7 miles a day. Easy some might say, sure enough on day one, even perhaps day two, but try it carrying a sack of potatoes for another 39 days. JM did it in 26 days - but then who's racing?

The city was decorated for someone's arrival, we felt very special. George Street and the tree at The Dome pub a cross between a rainbow, Joseph's coat and a chameleon. We had chips while others rode the ferris wheel, helter-skelter, or did Torvil and Dean impressions at the Winter Wonderland. Street stalls were manned by Edinburgh's own Delboy and Rodney and Wendy treated herself to a pair of 'silver' earrings - £5. She had done remarkably well finding us three hosts for the ten or so nights we planned to stop. Unfortunately, the first of these did not materialise but even better, Olymprick, the Aberdeen hash/baker made available his flat on The Mound, overlooking everything, The Royal Mile at the back door. We were to have five restful nights here made slightly less peaceful by Havoc's experience of the lift. In/out, in/out, tail shut in the door, shake it all about. He couldn't quite get it when the doors re-opened, he was in a completely different place than he had been a few seconds earlier. It was all too much for him and a call of nature usually ensued.

Christmas Eve was spent hashing with Edinburgh H3 at Bonaly Country Park with pre-Christmas drinks at a hasher's house. We borrowed a telly and did the Christmas shop. Here is a tip, Sunday evening, five minutes to closing, Tesco turkey crown, £1.50 with all the trimmings, paid for by donated Club Card vouchers. It felt like someone was looking out for us, so we went to the Watchnight service at St Giles Cathedral. Had we walked into Bethlehem? I was no carpenter, Wendy certainly wasn't pregnant, and we had a dog instead of a donkey. Somehow, we seemed very blessed. We were receiving God's mercy, Kyrie eleison, a road we must travel, a highway in the night. Our stable, very near luxury. Thank you.

Christmas Day was a lazy day. A traditional lunch, crackers with a paper hat for Havoc, a bottle of Cava and the backgammon world series continued. Boxing Day was much the same. Lots of text messages with best wishes and come 27th we were ready to do some fundraising. Havoc now sporting a blue all in one suit easily gained the 'Ballon d'Or' most appealing to punters. More hashing in the evening with TNT H3 (The New Town) around the streets and a chance for him to bark himself hoarse, especially when he saw a full-size plastic cow, carol singers had no chance.

Three nights were spent courtesy of Anne Robinson, definitely not 'the weakest link' at Liberton. She was a teacher, who had spent considerable time abroad in China and the Middle East. She also made us do our 'homework' loaning us maps of the West Coast and Islands, sowing the seeds of Island hopping and introducing us to Calmac ferries. Her help was invaluable in firming up a northwest passage, something we had not properly considered, and Anne clearly saw we were flying by the seat of our pants. We banked nearly £450, walked the coast from Seton Sands through Prestonpans and Musselburgh to Portobello and the Leith docks passing The Royal Yacht Britannia. We were walking the wrong way; the sea was on our right, but we were being honest to our objective.

Events were building ahead of New Year's Eve, costume, extravagant eye make-up and outrageous headwear in George Street as continental celebrations mixed with Scottish. (No wonder Scotland voted not to leave!) Wendy was keen to take Havoc to see Grey Friars Bobby, they might have shared the loyalty that John Grey had with his trusted Skye terrier. We hashed again on Sunday 31st along the river Leith before meeting our final Edinburgh host.

Roz was a blind lady, with guide dog Lillie, who lived in a tenement flat. She was an extraordinary person having travelled extensively; she was to tell us how she had been abandoned by her guide while visiting Prague. She could not have been more welcoming, giving up her own bed and insisting she would sleep on the sofa. The house was full of German shepherd ornaments, dog pictures, printed dog cushions and the micro centimeters that were not taken up by these were filled with catholic religious effigies and memorabilia. I was fearful if I turned around too quickly with my rucksack the Virgin Mary might lose her head. The big shock was still to come, as she said to us,

"You're not faint hearted, are you?"

Opening a cupboard, she revealed the stuffed heads of two previous trusted and loved companions, German shepherds who were remembered via the taxidermist.

We had wrist bands to enjoy the Hogmanay city centre and left Havoc with Roz as we headed off in the wind and rain. Fireworks were being let off from all corners and Havoc was certainly not one to relish bangs. As the evening progressed, we had an anti-climactical experience as Hogmanay 2006 was cancelled due to high winds and stormy weather.

The street party never happened, and Princess Street was void of all other humans. The mobile rang and it was Roz who was summoning us back to rescue Havoc from a wall he had attempted to climb into. If there was a space between the skirting and the brickwork, he would have found it. Much needed K9 'magicalm' or diazepam was absent, he was still quaking well into the New Year.

It started with yet another Hash. This one from Carlton Hill, we could get a good view of where we had been and where we still had to go. Rory Bremner would vote this his best view in Britain. He should know, impressionism is supposed to be the greatest flattery, to misquote Oscar Wilde. The hare for the trail, Charlie Tuck had done 1000 runs. At an average of 50 a year, 20 years of hashing. The 'on down' was at the Cask Inn, and we contemplated our four Edinburgh runs and the thought of getting back on the horse tomorrow and resuming walking. We said our goodbyes to Roz, an independent character we would never forget, she wished us well in Gaelic and we departed to catch the bus humbled and grateful to have met her.

Chapter 8 – Edinburgh to Eyemouth

Saviour of the universe with only 14 hours to save the earth

"Here's one I made earlier."

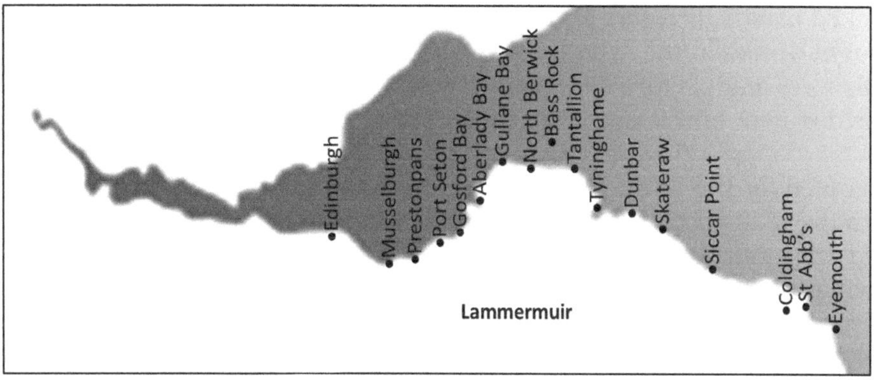

ON A FINE BUT cold Tuesday (2nd January 2007) we started off again. On the bus we bumped into an Edinburgh harriet, 'Oral Sex', origins of her hash name unknown. She gets a mention only because she gave us the two quid to pay for the bus fare. We passed Easter Road, Hibs football ground, where she worked, and the Meadow Bank athletic stadium where a few summers earlier Wendy and I had brought visually impaired athletes to take part in the National Schools Championships. (On that occasion we had run up Arthur's Seat.)

Heading for Seton Sands again, now it was time to push on eastwards to Longniddry, through stunted trees the impressive neoclassical frontage of Gosford House. Once occupied by the army as a World War II mess, now more used as a film or TV set (Outlander), and as a wedding venue, the interior apparently exceeding the expectation of the elegant exterior. The joints were aching, and I was tempted to grab a handful and munch on the bright orange Sea Buckthorn berries (hippophae) which I believe have medicinal and anti-aging properties, abundant, free and not £20 for around 60 capsules.

The smells of a BBQ and alcohol hit us at Gullane Bay, not golf balls from the Muirfield Links, a regular Open Championship venue. An additional Bank Holiday in Scotland meant locals were enjoying the beach and we were not forgotten with burgers and sausages. Behind us a sunset over Edinburgh and ahead a full moon over Lamb Island and the two Dog

Skerries. Bass Rock and North Berwick Law came into sight. In the town a church key holder was locking up but hurried away before we had chance to plead sanctuary. Instead, we were spotted by Gordon Stephens, the huge ruck sacks had their benefits.

'Flash' (Gordon) was connected to the local RNLI, his family had collectively amassed 118 years of service, and we were ushered to the lifeboat station. We got to meet crew, see the Blue Peter III, minus sticky backed plastic, (inshore D class, since 2013 the Evelyn M) and were then bought drinks in the Auld Hoose pub, unpretentious like us, while phone calls were made. Our collection tin was filled and one contribution of £50 was donated, 'put it in the tin if you like or buy yourselves B&B.'

We opted for the former. 'Flash', organised us to stay in Melbourne Place with two of his friends Ailie and Russel. Ailie was a chef, with a very heavy cold who had just finished many long 'Christmas' shifts, so I am sure having us thrust upon her was just what she needed. Russel was a bin man and they shared a tiny flat with Bumble and Basil, two cats, and Sheba a big German shepherd. Three additional bodies made the place very sardine can like, the cats forced to stay in the kitchen to avoid Havoc's attentions. In a cupboard off the entrance corridor was a shower, you needed to undress outside, leave your clothes, cover your modesty with a towel and throw that out after entering, as you stepped immediately into the shower tray. There was a 'Rizla' between the shower door and that of the cupboard. Modest it was, but we could not have been made more welcome. Homemade game pie made the whole North Berwick experience unforgettable and delightful in one. 'Flash' had been a saviour, he was a miracle. Ailie (aka Dale Arden) Queen of the kitchen, and Russel (aka Hans Zarkov) King of the impossible, to get a shower in that

cupboard, will always be remembered. Dum, dum, dum, dum, dum, a-ah, Freddie provided the rhythms.

There was just time to bank over £200, look around the Scottish Seabird Centre, the long High Street, and see the 'Law' close-up. To be honest it was more impressive from a distance. The former volcano, a conical hill (613ft), now resembled an unfinished sandcastle on a flat beach. Dunbar beckoned, or was it Mongo?

Bass Rock looked like a giant ice cube, ancient volcano with perpendicular cliffs, home to thousands of gannets, just sitting off Tantallion, with the Isle of May in the background. At the castle Havoc had his second breakfast. In his autobiography he records this as the venue of the first 'big row' of the walk. Arguments and differences of opinion had raised their heads already over the last six weeks and I do not recall this being so 'big'. My recollection of events also differs from his somewhat. I wanted to have a look around the stronghold poised on sheer cliffs and use my cheek to ask for complimentary entry. Wendy was opposed to both, the difference had little to do with me wishing to take an 'illegal' route.

With shoes and socks off I carried the two of them over the Peffer Burn. At the Tyninghame estate there was an old bridge where it might have been possible to cross the Tyne, but like JM we found it gated, guarded by spikes and barbed wire. JM scaled it, we decided not to, eventually crossing at the A198 road bridge. We made our way to Dunbar, the John Muir trail being part of our route, where we had been given permission to stay at the lifeboat station. The lifeboat was moored at Skateraw further east. The atmosphere remained 'thick' but that was something to do with having a frustrating day with navigational issues. Seven hours of walking, and we had only covered approximately 15/16 miles. We were both tired and tomorrow we needed to get beyond Cove having been told the coast was virtually impossible to follow and tough going.

Navigation was never as simple as keeping 'the sea on your left'. Wendy was better at it than me, particularly the micro stuff, head into the map, looking at details. I was more a head up guy, look what was there in front and in the distance, try and make sense of the picture drawn on the paper. Both have merits, the two in combination where not a bad mix. Today I was 'in charge', Havoc gave me a 'Grommet' look, head tilted to one side and had his first roll of the day on the beach. Wendy was keeping well away from anything marked OS. The wind was from the north-west, behind us fortunately, as we experienced our first sandstorm. Pebbles and rocks covered with sand were as if they had been sprayed with mortar, like part of a Disney theme park set. Dunbar's lifeboat moored at Skateraw harbour came into view along with a cement works inland and Torness power station. The angular constructions looked like two brothers competing. I imagined them as Lego builds in my 'Thunderbirds' set, certainly not out of place in 'Lost in Space'. 'Flash' had triggered a Sci-fi gene, all we needed now was Darth Vadar, Yoda and Chewbacca to walk in. In contrast, tiny snowdrops just in flower dodged our weary feet.

Beyond Pease Bay we reached Siccar point. The twisted and contorted rock formations along this bit of Berwickshire are amazing. James Hutton, sometimes known as 'the father of geology' spoke here of his 'classic unconformity', (1788). In essence, he formulated that the world was a lot older than the time held biblical view dating it to about 6000 years. The compressed and folded vertical and horizontal strata looked like God when making the earth had a bit of modelling clay left over and put it to one side waiting for ideas on how to finish this bit. The terrain did make for tough going and the wind continued to howl. A farmer on a quad bike herding his sheep was taking them off the coastal hills and warned us we could be blown from the cliffs around Telegraph Hill and Wheat Stack, so we headed inland over Coldringham Moor to the village similarly named.

We stayed in the village hall. Not a great one this, only two stars. Rather dilapidated, a clock that clanged what seemed like every minute for the whole night, no microwave and no loo roll. We had to put a £1 in the meter, described in Havoc's book as 'greasy and sweaty'. On the bright side, a new one was in the planning. We did get given some chilli and rice and with half a swede I had collected off the road and some sprouts scrumped from a field the day earlier, we had a filling supper. (The hall might have only got one star, but a good kitchen knife, enough to hack through the swede saved its bacon.) Collecting in The Anchor was successful, but I was sent packing from The New Inn, can't win them all.

We were due to meet Spud (the inspiration for the walk) the next day in Eyemouth. Wendy had managed to secure some contact details for her through the publishers. She had now set up home in The Scottish Borders. That wasn't far off so in the morning we had time to back track, leaving our bags at the hall and visit St Abb's Head. We headed across country from Northfield. The physical topography was something else, rounded grass topped hills swallowed you up, between them gullies and in one low lying valley the man-made freshwater lake, Mire Loch. Sea stacks were home to numerous species of nesting birds. A monastery once stood at The Head set up by St Aebble. David Bellamy did his bit for establishing things with a Marine Reserve in 1984. The area is popular with scuba divers, Wuddy Rocks, a favourite dive, marked on our map along with Starney Bay, as we headed back to St Abbs village. A gated archway leading to Northfield House carried a stone carved image, a face looking down at us, presumably the good Saint, but it was something of a reminder of 'Tellytubbies' as if saying 'Eh-Oh!' and welcome to St Abbs.

At the lifeboat station in the centre of the harbour, repair work was taking place on the roof. Two men, one big guy in a boiler suit, were concreting the slipway. He had given 41 years' service to the lifeboat, and it resonated with other stories we had heard of extended volunteering. Could anyone possibly put a figure on the total number of volunteer hours given freely to the lifeboats? As it happened, as part of a reorganisation in 2015, the RNLI withdrew from St Abbs. A year later an independent service was resumed, the boat now carrying the name 'Thomas Tunnock' - the main sponsor, Tunnock's bakery from Uddington, Glasgow. Now every time I treat myself to a delicious 'Caramel' wafer, bearing the label that says 6,000,000 are made and sold every week, I like to think I am contributing to the service in St Abbs. I did write to them in 2007, asking for a contribution, perhaps that spark resonated deeper prompting their huge contribution. Much of our fund-raising efforts were about awareness raising and ballyhooing as about hard cash.

More recently a Harry Styles video for 'Adore You' was shot in St Abbs (His Isle of Eroda.) Twelve years earlier there was nothing more for us to do but take 'one direction!' up the Creel path a mile and a half back to Coldringham to collect our bags. A 'creel' was a basket for carrying fish. For centuries fisherfolk and holy men would have walked this, the Great Priory of Coldringham dates from 1098. I imagined King Edgar sending the abbot and his Benedictine monks off from Durham to establish it, and I wondered how scenes would have changed from then to now. Carrying a small sack of gold coins, I hoped they were tempted to pop in The Anchor rather than The New Inn! Their priory was destroyed and rebuilt, destroyed and rebuilt, destroyed again by Cromwell's artillery in the 1650s and rebuilt largely as it is now in the 1850s.

We headed back to the sea and Eyemouth. With artillery thoughts still in my head, we came across cannon at the old fort. The lifeboat station was locked, and I hoped another great storm was not brewing. In October 1881, a fishing disaster here saw 20 boats and 129 lives lost in bad weather. In the 1860s this village was described with 'wonderful filth scattered about' as 'rough, uncultivated and drunken'. The sheltered river harbour we found, with foot bridges, trawlers and yachts berthed alongside one another was quite eye pleasing. One fishing boat was just returning, followed by masses of gulls, a bit like flies on a cowpat, to harp back to the 'filth'. Two resident seals in the harbour seemed to like the resort, flippers, not thumbs, up on the water quality. More sea birds and indeed those two pinnipeds waited for scraps to be tossed over boat gunnels while we waited with a cup of tea for Spud's arrival. A quick look around the vennels, imagining centuries of pirate activity, smuggling and the like and we came across a cemetery watchhouse built to guard against body snatchers. Resurrectionists were apparently very active in Scotland, and we were of course not far from Burke and Hare's nighttime playgrounds.

Spud collected us and took us inland to near Kelso. There with her doctor husband Rob, two boys and a host of other animals we were to spend two nights in their comfortable converted barn. Her walk dog, Tess, was no longer alive but two others, sheep, a ram, pig, cat and heavy horse (Ben) who had guided her over the Scottish drove roads ("*Small Steps with Heavy Hooves*") were company. I was in awe, having met very few authors and asked for advicc. She offered at least six adjectives describing what a good walking book might be like, this book probably resembles none of them. I had something of a heavy cold, but got little sympathy from Wendy or GP Rob, who roped me in to wrestle his ram to the straw in order to treat the creature's feet. He did suggest we contact GPs all over Britain who he felt sure would put us up if we approached them. It was a nice thought, but somehow, I don't think Messrs. Findlay, Cameron or even Hilary Jones would be too pleased to get a phone call. Spud and Rob's homelives were a bit like that of Barbara and Tom. Home reared ham, bacon, lamb chops, redcurrant and quince jelly, Hugh Fearnly-Whittingstall look out.

Spud was clearly a confident, strong willed, independent person probably qualities she possessed prior to 1993/4 when she did her walk, but I also wondered how the whole experience also contributed to her shaping. A brief trip into the confluence town of Kelso, astride the Tweed and Teviot, let us see a bit of the 12th century abbey, and the prosperous farmland around it. I was hoping we might bump into rugby commentator Bill McLaren on a day out shopping trip from his home in Hawick, just down the road, but alas that never happened. (In his day he would always give St Luke's a mention!)

Chapter 9 – Eyemouth to Seaham

Up at eight, you can't be late

"The fishing boats go out across the evening water...the wind whips up the waves so loud...the ghost moon sails among the clouds... turning riffles into silver on the border."

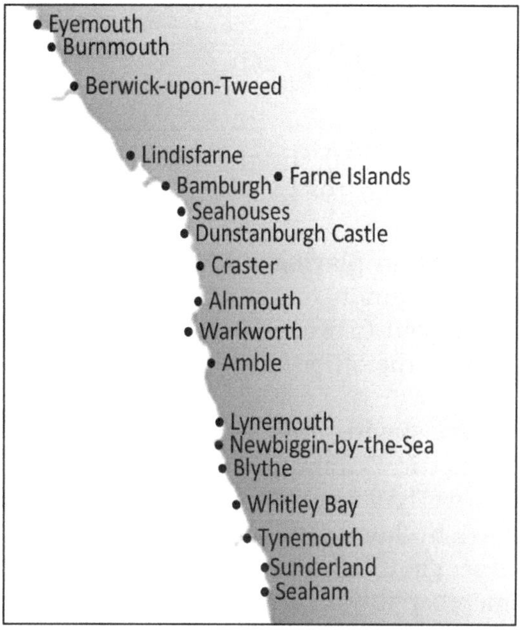

APPROPRIATELY, WE had porridge on our last day in Scotland (for a while) before Rob dropped us back to Eyemouth. Sandstone cliffs dominate sculpted by North Sea storms. Burnmouth is about the only break in the cliffs on the ten miles from Eyemouth to Berwick-on-Tweed. Part of the village is known as Partanhall, a string of cottages at the foot of the cliff. Partan, we were told was Scottish for crab. There was just time to read that the harbour was improved in 1879 and the inner basin only added as recently as 1959. We climbed the cliffs out, hard going with my chest feeling tight and wheezing heavily. Even with Scots porridge in me, I could hardly lift a shot put.

We reached the border squeezed between the ocean, east coast railway line and the A1, and did cross on the seaward side. We were totally alone, just the 'Across the Border, British Railways' sign announcing we were leaving Scotland, for the time being, and back in England. Unlike JM there was no piper, airs, crowd or cheque for £4.5k. Somehow, I think our fundraising efforts, minus raffle, and unsupported by other agencies (Rotary Club), were harder earned.

Berwick is a medieval town with fantastic surviving walls. Much dates from Elizabethan times, as additional fortifications were added then. It was felt necessary to guard against threats from the Scots while at war with Spain.

Four bridges clamber for attention. The oldest dates from 1611, I counted 15 arches, but it was strengthened in the 1760s. The Royal Tweed Bridge was added to keep it company in 1925. The Royal Border Bridge, that man Robert Stephenson again, carries the railway although he did have 3000 others to help him get it opened in 1850. In thc distance, the A1 bypass bridge, a whipper snapper, from 1984.

I was still in playing soldiers mode from Eyemouth and came across a Russian cannon, extremely elegant if things of destruction can be elegant, pointing out to sea, a spoil of war from the Crimean. Apparently, it is one of a pair, the other has found its way to Dartmouth in Devon.

We were staying in Palace Street, with a lady named Frances Ord who we had met in Edinburgh. Along with her teenage daughter, Issi, and dog Lilly, we had sausages, baked potato and vegetables for tea and were joined by her friend Susan for after dinner conversation. I am afraid Havoc got this completely wrong. We did not camp, and he cannot remember the military like erection of any tent at Berwick. In fact, we only put it up once on the whole of the east coast, at Wick, and even then, we didn't sleep in it. It wasn't used properly until Swanage. I remember it distinctly as it was a good chunk of weight to add to the packs. 'Insurance' perhaps should we have needed it, we thought we would, but as it transpired other indoor options emerged. Shame we didn't know in advance, we could have picked it up from somewhere on the south coast. I mention this because it does illustrate a certain inaccuracy about Havoc's account. If you read it, you might also notice, I 'TEB', get something of a continual slating. If you can find one positive mention in relation to me, please let me know! This fallaciousness might also be held in mind when considering my 'grumpiness', prior to meeting Spud and other references to 'shouting' and mistreatment of both him and Wendy throughout '*Wherever I hang my Lead*'. Faults, I have many, but cut me a bit of slack mate.

In fact, the conversation with Frances and Susan was very revealing about the town's past. A political and economic 'tug of war' had gone on for centuries over the town between the Scots and English. The flag had changed at least 13 times, with St George coming out top, although for example the local footie team play in the Scottish League. Who knows it might change again, particularly if Ms Sturgeon gets her way, and ends up with St Andrew? They saw themselves as neither one nor the other with a unique identity as Berwickers! If we had been in the tent, we would never have had intellectual fun with flags on a par with Sheldon Cooper, and..... we slept on the lounge floor.

Back in England we continued following the Northumberland coast. I read it stretches 62 miles to Cresswell south of Amble and we reckoned we could almost 'fly' down this as there seemed few major rivers to negotiate. I remembered Richard and Shally Hunt (*'the sea on our left'*) telling us when we met them at their home prior to starting our walk, you can make good time down the east coast. All very well for the 'man in the lead with a woman in his wake', and when you read their quest, no sooner had they heard their first Geordie tones, and they stepped into quick sands.

That was on my mind as we considered hacking over the sands from Goswick to reach Holy Island (Lindisfarne) and further reason for caution a sign warning of both quick sands and explosive hazard (former military target area). Instead, we took the causeway, there was always a refuge box if we needed it. This is basically a shed on stilts for anyone cut off by tides. Apparently, I told Wendy couples have been known to spend four hours in there. (Waiting for the sea to ebb, some excuse!) She adopted a Queen Victoria pose and strode off.

I had always wanted to visit Lindisfarne. 'The cradle of Christianity in England', all that about St Aidan and St Cuthbert, the Viking raid of 793 or was it the band from my student days, 'Run for Home'? I admit I've 'made my share of mistakes' but going there was not one of them. To have missed it out would have been. The missionary impact of the Island was certainly hugely significant in contributing to the spread of Christianity in England. How could we miss it out? We checked out the site of the old Priory and went into St Mary's Church. We helped the vicar move some furniture, ahead of his builders arriving the next day and admired the fantastic wooden carving of St Cuthbert's coffin being carried by monks. Outside we knew camping on the Island was forbidden and the only likely spot was already taken by a huge flock of Pale Bellied Brent Geese anyway. (Black heads, neck, grey body, white rear and underside - I knew this because of the wildlife information board.) Two small shops, one was closed, as was the pub, but we did manage to buy bread, milk and cheese. The whole place looked as if it was in hibernation. We did get seen by Sister Tina, who described herself as the Catholic presence on the Island and she made available a room in the Catholic hostel, which we had to ourselves. All mod cons, a full kitchen, we knocked up a tuna bake, there was a TV... and beds.

I had found a prayer and it seemed only appropriate to read it aloud.

"Grant to me, Lord Christ, for this pilgrim journey through Life your ready hand to guide me, your light to go before me, your protection to guard me from evil, your peace to rest within me, your love to sustain me. That through all the joys and sorrows that meet me, I may know the promise of your abiding strength, until I reach my final homecoming with you forever, Amen."

In the middle of a very windy night, the windowpanes rattling, I was woken by Wendy saying the front door is open. In the pitch black I was instantly awake, was it evil, Vikings, the Lord coming to get me to ask me to answer for my mistakes or was it time to 'run for home, run as fast, as I can?' In fact, it was just St Cuthbert's heavy breathing having been chasing Sister Tina!

In the morning it was just as windy. We passed a house with a bird box barely clinging to the pebble dashed wall. Bra Cottage - (underneath) 'Tits Only!' It made us chuckle as we headed back across the causeway, the wind in our faces, very tough going, hardly making any progress - what was the line in that prayer, the promise of strength to battle this infernal wind?

Living at Fenham Mill was Jilly Banyard, a GD supporter who had contacted us after seeing something in the GD magazine. She and her architect husband kindly provided crusty bread sandwiches for lunch, and she joined us for part of the walk in the afternoon. A very nice house, as one might expect, with wonderful views back to Holy Island. Havoc chased a young roe deer, and then came upon a group of six who did not run but stood up to him as if in a Dodge City gunfight. Our brave companion was completely taken aback, stopped in his tracks, until he thought it time to make his way back to us for security, tail slightly between his legs.

Bamburgh, a small village dominated by the massive edifice of its castle, perched on a 40-metre-high block of basalt, looking out to sea, majestic and mighty. Undoubtedly its most famous female, Grace Darling, who's museum was closed. I remembered the tale well from Blue Peter, a lighthouse keeper's daughter, the Farne Islands which we could clearly see, the troubled 'Forfarshire' in 1838, and a rescue saving nine crew members. She was awarded a Silver Medal for bravery by the forerunner organisation of the RNLI but died aged only 26 of tuberculosis, an impressive monument to her stands in St Aidan's church.

We continued to Seahouses and met John Hanvey, mechanic, at the lifeboat station. The Mersey class boat was appropriately called 'The Grace Darling'. (She was retired in 2020, a Shannon class boat replaced her.)

The station was very proud of their own four gallantry medals.

We were collected by Anna Baker-Cresswell, a friend of Spud's, and taken to the village of Preston near Ellingham for the night. Our company for the evening, David her partner, a Devonian and two dogs. 'Ruin,' a big black lab and 'Puppy,' a terrier cross, but who was he trying to kid, he had more grey hairs than I did. The house interior was a 'country' one, sports at least, very much hunting, fishing and shooting memorabilia. We didn't get to see the outside as it was too dark on arrival. I remember my cold was at its worst as I tried to darn socks and sew my trainers back together. Anna was full of remedies, 'feed a cold' and fed me leftover Christmas pudding. In truth, I think she was emptying the fridge ahead of a new year diet. She was launching a Horticulture Therapy project, (as seen on BBC Coutryfile, 14th November 2021). I had heard of Occupational Therapy, but something of this kind was new at the time, now of course it is much more publicised with more contemporary thinking towards things like mental health and PTSD. Cynics might call the two of these, basket making and growing stuff in order to feel better, why make them all grandiose adding 'therapy'!

We woke to find we were staying on an 'estate'. The Pele Tower, one of a number along the border, had great history, built as a 'confirmation of status and prestige' they stood guard against raiders and cattle rustlers.

Back at the sea we headed for Beadnell. Havoc was in his element, chasing everything that looked like it needed chasing, meeting walkers and other dogs. I was in my element smirking at the map names, Lady's Hole, Long Nanny, Snook Point and Football Hole. We attempted to put Wendy in her element, with lunch at The Ship, Newton-by-the-Sea, soup and stottie cake, a Northumberland bread.

The ruins of Dunstanburgh Castle came into view. Built on the mound of an iron age hill fort it has been slowly decaying since 1538 but was still impressive. At its feet, sea horses raced in, their white manes of spray perfectly forming the base of a photo we took to remind of this precarious pile of masonry defying gravity. Moving on to Craster and then Boulmer, Havoc once again was flush with ambition and chased a group of bullocks. They stood their ground, testing his resolve and rather like with the deer, he was quickly engaging reverse gear. That's my boy, brave for all of 15 seconds. In all the excitement Wendy dropped his lead and realising this, we were forced to recover our steps and retrieve it. WW2 anti-tank defences still guard Alnmouth's north beach and with an absence of fording opportunities, we crossed the Aln on the Duchess's Bridge before heading south again to Warkworth.

Squally showers being driven towards the sea became more constant rain. JMW Turner painted the castle here (1799) and two amateur artists were attempting to copy him. Their water colours, very washed out, were certainly not masterpieces. We were soaked, at least on our right-hand side, by the time we found the lifeboat shed at Amble. There we met a crew member, another John, and we listened intently as he told us of fishermen dredging up bombs and depth charges in their nets, when landed leading to road closures and house evacuations. At least I think that's what he said, Northumberland accents can be hard to grab.

Shelly Stuart and her son were a bit easier to understand. They collected us and offered bed and spaghetti bolognaise. In a galaxy far, far away, Cornwall, Shelly's dad was a lifeboat man, who in time we would meet. Shelly was a childminder; you can always tell by the presence of painful plastic Star Wars figures under the sofa cushions. If I remember correctly, we had 'networked' her via Slimming World, but it was okay the spag bol was a sin free version.

A stunted clock tower and town square sundial led us out of Amble, past a primary school. The smell of roasting meat made me feel hungry - Slimming World recipes go empty on you quickly. Coquet Island reminded me of a Yorkshire pudding, floating in gravy, but the sand being blown into my face by Hauxley was enough to awaken me from a food delusion.

At Lynemouth an industrial landscape. A coal fired power station (converted to biomass 2012), chimneys of the aluminum smelter (closed 2012), ash lagoons, and power lines, 36 of them, on three sets of pylons. My mind went to Fantasia, broomsticks carrying buckets, conducted by sorcerer Micky. I think the weight of the bag, the need for some magic, was beginning to make my imagination more peculiar than ever. The Bewick drift conveyor that used to go out under the sea had gone, the

Ellington colliery known locally as 'The Big E' closed in 2006 and was in the process of being developed for housing. For now, travellers' piebald horses grazed while tethered.

The 13th century St Bartholomew's, 'church on the point' has a dramatic headland site, a landmark through the centuries for mariners and for January 2007 walkers. Newbiggin had cobles, high bowed, shallow sterned, boats developed in the Northeast. We were collected and taken to Ashington where a blind lady, Jo, and her black lab Grace, were our hosts. It was even more meaningful to be collecting for individuals when you could share the lives you were influencing. After their hospitality it was inland walking to cross the Wansbeck and Sleekburn to arrive at Blyth.

Royal Navy ships were scrapped here after WW2, contradicting the slogan 'Born in Blyth, made in the Royal Navy'. Two landmarks the 'High Light' lighthouse, now some way from the quayside and the easily forgettable 'Spirit of Staithes' sculpture, opened in 2003 by Princess Anne but I bet she doesn't remember it. Seaton Sluice, although it didn't sound it, was a pleasant enough place but with a force eight against us, progress was definitely impeded. We took some respite in one of many pubs and chatted to locals about a hidden industrial past. Then it was on to St Mary's Island to photograph the lighthouse, causeway and rocky foreshore before staggering into Whitley Bay to meet new acquaintances Roger and Dawn Matthewman. I don't recall how we got their number but as well as providing digs they were also keen to join us doing some miles.

They were a lovely couple, brimming over with support. We talked about the Northeast, discussions confirming my belief that many folks in these parts were something of wage slaves. That and their surname fostered an ear worm, 'Mathew and son' Cat Stevens, 1967, Yusaf if you prefer. Roger also looked a bit like the song writer, or at least the 2007 version. There was no cold coffee, and we did have cake. They very much energized us and were true friends.

Whitley Bay was a seaside resort, once popular with Glaswegians. 'Spanish City' once an amusement centre but in 2007 derelict. (It did see a refurbishment, with the addition of a dome and re-opened 2018.) Cullercoats lifeboat station had just received a new rib and the crew were there in force - big kids and their new toys. Tynemouth was showing off its old Priory and divers were asked via a yellow sign not to show off their bits, 'Use discretion when undressing'. The long breakwater, with its twin at South Shields like two antennas reaching for Amsterdam. Collingwood looked down from his monument on the river, Nelson's second in command at Trafalgar, for some a forgotten hero. Pairs of High and Low

Lights at North Shields helping mariners avoid the submerged Midden rocks. In 1864, five ships floundered in just three days.

As we said goodbye to the Matthewmans it wasn't Cat Stevens who was in my ear but Gazza, 'The Fog on the Tyne is all mine all mine', the day bright and sunny without a haar in sight. Roger stuck to his word and would ring us regularly to check on progress and give an encouraging word. We caught the ferry to South Shields and found the 1833 lifeboat 'Tyne', in a 60 year service her crew would save over 1000 lives.

Souter Point and The Leas and I was soon looking for Roker Park footie stadium, but it had gone ten years earlier swallowed by development. Just the ghosts of Ian Porterfield, Jim Montgomery and Bob Stokoe and memories of the 1973 FA Cup Final. The Wear bridge was impressive and as we headed for Sunderland Docks, we needed a drink. We stepped into a social club to find the place packed and noisy. The moment we crossed the threshold the place fell silent, and all eyes left the big screens to gaze our way. I swallowed and without thinking turned to Wendy and said aloud,

"Have I grown a second head?"

The place erupted and the ice was broken. We stayed for several drinks; I don't think we bought any. Our collection tins were passed around and filled, Mackems knew how to welcome folk, and we were Marras for life.

Chapter 10 – Seaham to Filey

London calling to the faraway towns

"Ha'way the lads."

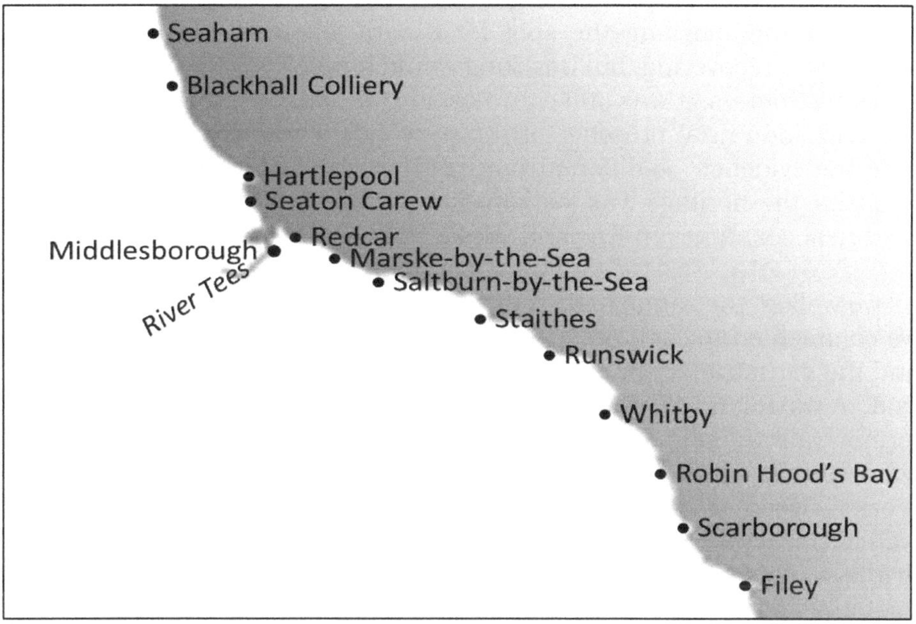

SEAHAM IS A former coal port. In 1880, 164 people and even more pit ponies were killed in a mine explosion, the latter fact upset Wendy more than the former.

"At least they had a choice", she said.

Byron had married the lord of the manor's daughter here in 1815, (I do not know if she had a choice) and even in the year of Waterloo, he described the coast as 'dreary'. We paid our respects to those lost in the town's lifeboat capsize when in 1962 the George Elmy floundered. In 1978, JM was appalled at the tipping of coal waste, a hideous sight, a bit further south at Easington. For Spud in 1993, 'every visible thing was black' and a fisherman even caught her a 'coal fish'. The Clash from 1979 filled my ear space. The mid 1980s of course saw the miners' strikes, the beginning of the end for Durham collieries, and scenes from this area and those times were immortalised in films like Billy Elliot (2000) showing the industrial decline. In the late 1990s and early 2000s great efforts were put in place to regenerate this coast. Turning the Tide Project awards were collected, it even gained 'Heritage' status. 'Chemical and Blast Beaches' remained.

Our experience was of something of the 'new green'. A deep ravine at the Hawthorn Burn meant we crossed on the railway line. At Dene Mouth near the former Blackhall Colliery we sank up to our ankles in black coal sludge and ended up interning a broken walking pole, adding to the pollution and marking the spot for others following in our footsteps. Nature was recovering, but how long would it take? For PH in 2014, seven years on from us, it was still convalescing, 'it hadn't completely obscured the grim industrial presence of the past, but it was trying very hard to hide the evidence'. A different nature than was originally there, and he remarks 'the heritage was lost' on him. Online it is described as 'one of the finest coastlincs in England' Make your own minds up!

As we walked the sands to the north of Hartlepool and arrived at Steetley, we commented to each other that overnight WW3 must have broken out and the industrial carnage we saw was all that remained after a bombing raid. A wasteland of broken concrete, rubble, twisted metal, barbed wire, former railway sidings, a chimney, circular settling pits with exposed concrete rib cages. This was what was left of the Steetley Magnesite Works, closed in 2005, the giant tanks once held eight million gallons of water. Hartlepool got its name from a place where stags once came to drink, whatever water to be found here now one certainly would not put past any lips. It was a staggering sight, a blight on any environment and evidence that mankind cares very little about his beautiful planet. The chimney eventually went in 2012 and I saw a tweet from 2017 that said it was 'all gone', ten years on.

Turning right at St Hilda's church on The Headland and a different side of Hartlepool beckoned. A new marina with shops and café culture, embracing the marine past that in 1900 saw this place as one of the four busiest ports in the country. Peter Mandelson had done his bit up to 2004 and Ian Wright, not the footballer, took over as Labour MP keeping his seat until 2017. Then of course, the place went shockingly Tory in 2021. We could see that changes were a foot. The Tall Ships event was to come to town in 2010, visitors could see HMS Trincomalee, the last of Nelson's Frigates, the oldest war ship afloat in the UK or take a day trip on the Princess Royal Lifeboat. She had been around in 1939, left in 1968 but returned in 2000 her brilliant white gunwale loops like skipping ropes along her sides.

We stayed at the Marina office, courtesy of Allan Henderson. I was up early as it was Wendy's birthday. I wanted to get her something. I soon bumped into the Hartlepool monkey. As the story goes in the Napoleonic Wars, locals hung a ship's monkey as a French spy! Even worse it could have been a young French boy, a 'powder monkey' who armed the guns. I read after the Black Lives Matter protests (2020) an explanatory sign had to be attached to the statue to avoid causing any offence. The town football team are nicknamed the 'monkey hangers' and their mascot was H'angus, although perhaps for similar reasons of political correctness, I think he was retired at about the same time. Not the only sporting team to invite criticism with their name and mascot.

Back in Devon, Exeter Chiefs, debated changing their name and indeed their mascot, Big Chief, was similarly retired. The controversy continues as other topflight rugby teams threaten banning Exeter supporters wearing native North American headwear. It would seem it is all too easy to cause offence.

Back to mid-January 2007, Wendy had to make do with a card, a box of Maltesers and Jaffa Cakes. There was no way she could carry flowers. Hopefully she was not too offended.

Following the promenade, we arrived at Seaton Carew. Locals were collecting coal, particles virtually rather than lumps, from the beach and said they got £8 a ton from the power station down the road. An information board informed us this spot was once a popular seaside resort. Changing cubicles for bathing provided the wheels then for beach tracks, rather than the makeshift carts the men were using for hauling coal now. Coaches and later trains brought folk from all around, particularly a wealthy Quaker community from Darlington, who adopted Seaton Carew as their own resort. I remembered in around 2002 a former teacher/prison officer, John Darwin, left a canoe here. It was the start of a fraudulent insurance scam where £250,000 was claimed for his death. Five years later, in December 2007 he was discovered alive. He and his wife went to prison. Latest I read was that he is now living with a much younger wife in the Philippines. (Look out for Eddie Marsan in the role, The Thief, His Wife and the Canoe, ITV, 2022.)

The golf course took us to the A178, seals at what is known as Seal Sands Bay seemed unphased by the multi-sensory onslaught that greeted us. The stench of a landfill site, blended with chemicals from nearby works, not only made us reach to cover mouths and noses but made our eyes sting too. The sight of ghost ships waiting to be broken up and billowing grey smoke from Teeside factories. You could taste the pollution. The noise and vibration from lorries rushing past completed the experience and I thought John Darwin had got it right, move to Manilla or somewhere just outside.

The Tees Transporter Bridge, opened in 1911, became a very visible landmark at 69 metres high and 259 metres long, the world's longest. Around 20 were constructed worldwide between 1893-1916, we were to find another in South Wales. Effectively it was two almost independent structures, one on each riverbank, joined in the centre by a gondola, suspended by steel cables. It was our means of crossing the Tees and on the south shore in a café, close to the former Swan Hunter Yard, we enjoyed a proper brew, chips and curry sauce. We just had time to wave to the Riverside Stadium, home of The Boro, before heading off up the Teesdale Way to Redcar. Sandwiched between miles of pipework, industrial paraphernalia and debris, behind endless security railings some eight miles of unloved man-made wilderness was not a highlight for Wendy's birthday. We didn't hang around, there was little to enjoy. PH described it as 'imposing' and made him feel 'uncomfortable and unsafe'. With time to kill in Redcar we peered through the museum windows looking at what was billed as The Oldest 'Life-Boat' in the World, the Zetland, (1802.)

Bamburgh Castle claims the first ever lifeboat (1786), a converted coble, but Formby in Lancashire (1777) may contest this. The 'Original' (1790) Gateshead is often quoted as the first specialised boat.

We also did some collecting before being picked up by the Eccles family, who were to host us inland a bit at Nunthorpe. A bath and jacuzzi, a TV larger than my lounge, lasagna, wine and all the trimmings was a better way for Wendy to celebrate.

We banked a further £187 in Redcar before rattling off locations to the south. Marske-by-the-Sea, Saltburn and its pier, Skinningrove with former ironstone workings, Boulby and its potash mine. We were even told that somewhere beneath us was a laboratory searching for Dark Matter. That is the complete limit of my astrophysical knowledge, and my attentions were clearly focused on above ground matters.

The crumbling cliffs rise to 666 ft here so there was plenty of huffing and puffing as we found our way to Staithes. Guidebooks describe it as quaint with a rugged aspect and storm battered. Hail stones and strong winds greeted us into Captain Cook country. He was born in Marton near Middlesbrough, went to school at Great Ayton and in 1745 was apprenticed to a grocer/haberdasher in Staithes. Looking out to sea, as we did, may have inspired him to a naval career but he could hardly have imagined three great voyages of discovery and an early death in Hawaii at 50, disembowelment and his bones baked.

With the help of an 84-year-old local gentleman, Clem James MBE, we were introduced to Patricia, partner of RNLI man Sean Baxter who was himself away in Africa. She put us up, in a somewhat cluttered cottage (compared with last night), introduced us to boys Luke and Thomas and collie Tiffy. Pasta with pesto and cheese sauce for tea. What a great welcome, and I tried to get a ringing from a Buddha bowl while Havoc petted with Tiffy. We were shown around the lifeboat house where training night consisted of map/chart work. We were warned of the cliffs, better late than never, and told of a boy who had fallen all 666ft (203m), only losing two front teeth.

Staithes, a traditional fishing port could boast few boats in 2007. By the 2020s tourism had proliferated with many drawn to eco pursuits. Whale watching, often Minkes along with sea bird spotting. 2021 would see a widespread die off of shellfish, particularly crabs, along 70kms (44 miles) of coast here. That impacted on the food chain and marine life more widely, with seals being affected. As for explanation, theories were expounded. Pyridine, a chemical released through dredging in the river

Tees versus other novel pathogens found more naturally occurring. The science at present not providing the answers.

Patricia offered to take our bags on to Whitby and we briefly watched surfers out first thing in the morning before climbing the cliffs out over Old Nab to Port Mulgrave. To avoid the climbs and the risk of being blown from the cliffs, I was keen to take advantage of a low tide and scramble around the base of the cliffs to Runswick, Wendy less so. It turned out to be very tough going, impossible with bags, but we were free from those and that fed my invincibility gene. We broke two further walking poles and very nearly three ankles to say nothing of getting separated as I went ahead, keen to find a route and with one eye on the suspicion of being cut off by rising water. We may have needed Runswick Bay's privately funded rescue boat. It all led to something of an atmosphere as we tucked into free prawn sandwiches and chips at the Hotel Royal. Not for the first time my sense of immortality, infallibility, unyielding and slightly reckless attitude got me into trouble.

I picked up the Baywatch newsletter to change the subject.

"According to Mike Sewell" I said, "wildlife in the bay is thriving, seals, eels, pipefish, Manx shearwaters and all manner of birds. In fact, back on 19th October last year a humpback whale weighing six tons and measuring 30ft was washed up here!"

"Pity it wasn't you," came back the reply!

A rope handrail helped us climb up a gully. Thank goodness it was secured; I might have been lynched. Alongside the steps a stream cascaded down, the muddy waterfalls often covering our boots. Kettle Ness disused quarries were another scar on the landscape, where shales were once mined to make alum, used in the dying industry. (BBC Villages by the Sea, 15th November 2021 - Ben Robinson can shed more light on the importance of pee!) At Sandsend we met Dingbats, one of the Scarborough Hash who was to help us over the Yorkshire coast. In fact, the hash kennel there couldn't do enough for us. We were almost credited with celebrity status. Various individuals, Swampy and Dolittle/Talking Pussy almost competed to do more for us and outdo one another.

It was as if Yorkshire had suddenly dropped into the sea. Seeing huge waves hit the cliffs and roll along the rock line it was easy to imagine how a headland village at Kettle Ness was simply washed away in 1829. We had an appointment at Whitby, not a synod, but a publicity thing with a photographer at the temporary lifeboat station in the marina. (A new station did not open until September 2007.) Then we were whisked off to

'Bats and Broomsticks' B&B where it had been arranged for us to stay. En route, a stunning act of kindness, as a lady pensioner outside a warden-controlled bungalow gave us a can of 'Chum' for Havoc's tea. This sort of act was so nice and appreciated, but also humbling and slightly embarrassing in a way.

The 'Horror/Dracula' themed accommodation was fun, Kevin the owner had bought right into the Bram Stocker thing, right down to coffin wardrobes and ghostly salt and peppers. The Abbey looked moody and in itself might have been literary inspiration.

The Esk and harbour, normally picturesque with houses coming down to the water's edge, was even more so as a result of majestic tall ships tied up as we climbed the 199 steps up to St Mary the Virgin Church beside the Abbey. A crowded churchyard, Norman exterior with Georgian windows, and inside box pews, galleries, a triple decker pulpit, heated by a large central stove that was being stoked and all lit by candles. I said a little prayer of thanks before we headed off on the Cleveland Way accompanied by goats, for Robin Hood's Bay.

The old town nestles at the mouth of Mill beck, now the eastern end of Wainwright's Coast to Coast. In January 1881 'The Visiter' got into trouble and the Whitby lifeboat was hauled six miles over land by horses, through snowdrifts, to enable a launch and rescue from here.

At the Victoria Hotel we were introduced to a guy called 'Phil', who we were told was also walking the coast of Britain. Apparently, a former marine, dressed and kitted out immaculately, also raising money for the RNLI. His appearance immediately caused suspicion, unlike us who had endured the coast path, covered in mud, with holes in all our clothes. He also was very vague when we attempted to discuss and compare routes and we were to hear later he was a fraudster and had been arrested.

I am certain our new coastal circumnavigator acquaintance had not been to Ravenscar, although that was apparently the direction he had come from. The Romans had; they built a fort here in the fifth century. The present day hotel was dramatically situated 600ft above the sea, a popular wedding venue with battlements, rose garden and a llama, which bemused Havoc. We met up with two other 'helpers'. These were GD ones, Anne and Clive Townsend. They were to arrange a reception for us at Scarborough and organise volunteers to help with a collection. We even had time for a swim in the pool. Ahead the sea at the twin bays of Scarborough in January was not going to be so inviting. The grey North Sea was where in the 18th century naked gentlefolk ventured to do themselves 'good'. The bathing machine was invented at Scarborough (places in Kent and Devon may contest this) and the craze swept the country. It is interesting to note the current popularity of open water/wild swimming - regardless of season, but I was not that tough.

The path signed 11 miles to Scarborough, dropped down into Hayburn Wyke, a beautiful National Trust oak wooded valley. Natural stone steps looked less imported, less clinical than wood or slabs, but because they were irregular in height and width made for difficult descents. Through trees a seaweed bobbing sea. Waves looked like bishops' mitres, each with a fairy light on the crest, as sunlight hit waxy leaves, which would short circuit as the celestial warmer went behind a cloud. Cliffs at Cloughton Wyke were as perpendicular as a plumb line and the path became a muddy slide as we got to Sailors Grave. Hashers joined us, on into Scalby Mills and a GD posse swelled numbers with collecting buckets. It was a fantastic welcome and reception at the lifeboat station, tea and cakes and although it was mid-January, so one could assume not too many people about, we raised over £300 in no time. It was to turn out to be the best supported, coordinated collection of the walk. If similar things could have been put together at other locations, it would have greatly aided the money raised. Thanks particularly to Anne.

We stayed with hashers, Havoc needing to sleep in the porch, with minimal fuss. (Fast forward 63 days to Poole, where similar doggy out-turning would be met with pulpable contempt.) We joined the hash for a run on Sunday morning with Monkey Hanger laying the trail and 'on downs 'at the Alma Inn. By 2pm we were walking again, leaving behind sand sculptures, ice cream, chips, seagulls and friends heading for Filey. Thirty plus surfers, evidence of land slips and caravans perhaps destined to be joining them and by Filey Brigg the hashers were there to join us again. Dolittle, TP, and Doctor Ruth who would put us up with a Sunday roast at Primrose Valley. Conversation with her farmer friend Derick even stretched to rape and oil seed. Little did I know that just over ten years later I would be earning a living from it. (Chiltern Cold Pressed Rapeseed Oil.)

Chapter 11 – Filey to Skegness

Oh Mr Fisherman, home from the sea, have you a lobster you can sell to me?

"What can tha do when thi boots let watter?"

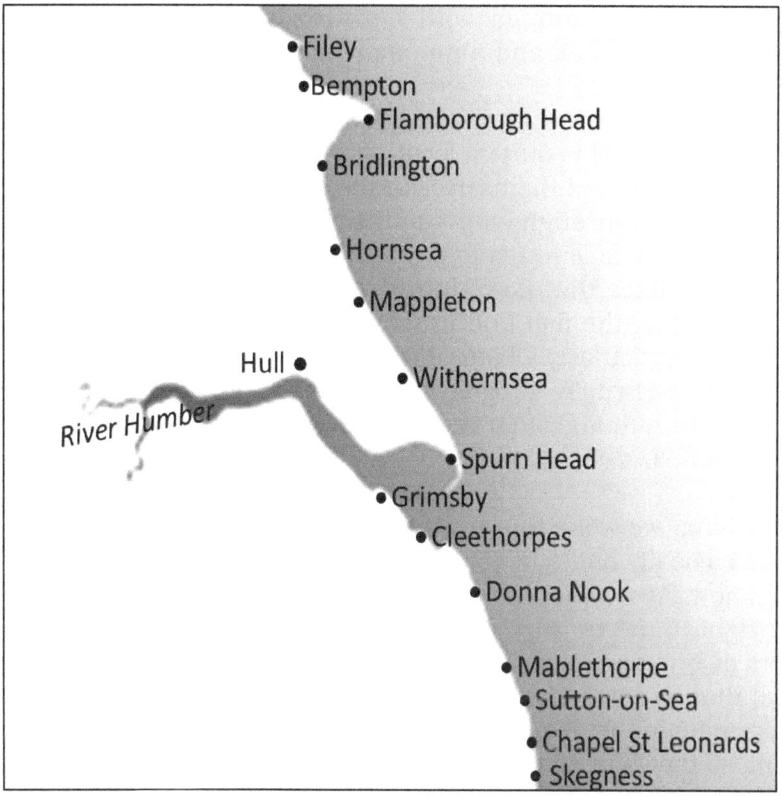

WE HEADED OFF around Filey Bay to Reighton Sands. With the tide out there was enough spume on the beach to supply all the world's Turkish barbers. Waves were turbulent, not angry and Havoc was very lively chasing birds and scavenging in the rocks for pipe fish particularly. The high chalky white cliffs at Bempton provided ledges for all manner of sea birds. Up until the early 1950s climbers used to use ropes to swing down and gather eggs. Stopped by legislation in 1954, now the RSPB has a shop and we stopped for coffee and a postcard. Havoc paid in full, by regurgitating those pipe fish and we snuck off quickly climbing down a ravine at Thornwick Nap.

We were to see Swampy again at North Landing, who gave us a £50 voucher to use for B&B at Spinnaker House Hotel, Bridlington and an extra £5 for the charity tin. (You see what I mean about one hasher wanting to outdo another in generosity.) Passing Flanborough lighthouse I noticed the topo scope commemorating the sea battle here of the American Revolutionary War (1779) when Captain John Paul Jones captured two Royal Navy ships. His name would pop up again, on the west coast, when we got there. Ben Robinson would visit in series 3 to stride around Flamborough with enthusiasm, talking about geology, 'hard' East Riding chalk and a unique equally resilient village identity.

One could hardly visit Yorkshire without some mention of cricket. The Sewerby Hall ground is quite a location butting onto the cliffs, some well struck sixes might find themselves in the sea. The last few miles of a long day seemed to be through empty amusement arcades that simply could not have been taking enough to pay for the light show. We made our way to the Gypsey Race that flows into the harbour and could not have left without sampling the fish and mushy peas. Bridlington is really known for shellfish, particularly lobster, but that was out of our price range. (The day of the bawdy rugby song seems also to have gone the same way as the club bath, although Ron and the Rude Boys may have made a bob out of it, 2009?)

Next morning, we woke to a dusting of snow. It was a cold day, and we knew we basically had a beach walk some 14 miles to Hornsea. Hail and further snow flurries accompanied us with clay cliffs from three to 40 ft on our right. Sand to walk on with occasional pebble dashed rendering and bits of broken concrete where World War II defences or sections of sea wall that had succumbed to the twice daily ravishes of an industrial washing machine with no delicate setting. We could see and hear bits breaking off the cliffs. In places above cracked clay, precariously balanced caravans, abandoned bungalows and then great mass slumped sections. At the base some huge clay boulders, mud loaves resembling seeded bloomers and small balls looking like they should be hung from a bird table. Some might say a 'shrinking' coastline, to me it seemed like Yorkshire's East Riding was in full retreat, the battle with tide, sea, storms and all of nature's erosive elements lost. Lines of ever optimistic groynes, turbines harnessing what was to be had from the wind and ever so rarely a cockle/winkle picker searching for something chewy. There has been a managed withdrawal here for centuries, settlements too numerous to mention now left for Neptune as the coast erodes at five feet a year.

We arrived at Hornsea, much to Wendy's delight. She was tired, it had been the first day for ages we had needed to carry our own bags, and she feared we were still only at Atwick, evidence that at times one merely switched to auto pilot. The railway had heralded Hornsea's growth as a seaside town (1864). Bettison's Folly overlooks the town. We were recounted the tale that a servant of a Hull businessman could see his return home after work from the tower and would run back to have his tea ready for him on arrival home. Yorkshire's largest freshwater lake, Hornsea Mere lies just inland, and the perpendicular styled church of St Nicholas was impressive and provided us with an ecclesiastical mini break.

The townhall once housed the lifeboat, pulled by horses to and from the sea and in 1949 the Rawson brothers started their pottery. In its heyday it employed up to 700 people but went into receivership in 2000. Quite collectable by some auction going types, the town museum holds over 2000 pieces, the V&A in London, one or two less, but highly 'selected' exhibits. We had to get our own tea, not served from Rawson tableware, but we did have our own tower, that of the United Reform Church where we stayed in the hall. I needed a farrier, re shoeing imperative.

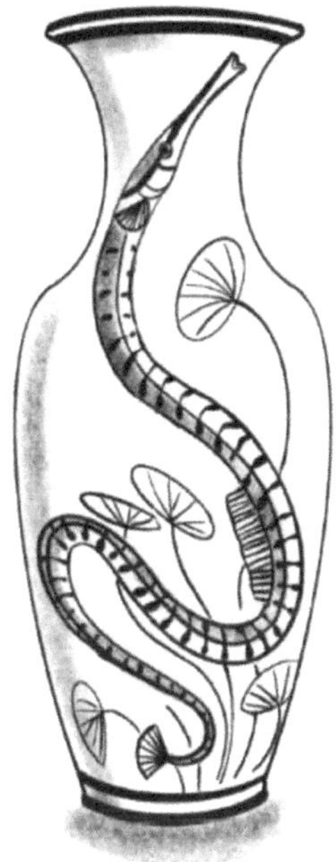

We were now only a day and a bit from the great gash, halfway down England's east coast, the terrible tear that was the Humber. It still stands out for me on the weather map. It meant a 120mile detour via Hull to Goole, if we followed JM's footprints that would take us a week. Even the Humber Bridge at Hessle didn't seem very inviting. The likes of Spud and PH crossed here on one of the largest single-span suspension bridges in the world opened in 1981. That prospect lay ahead as we encountered a flat green landscape with more crumbly clay cliffs through Mappleton, its church spire visible for miles, and south to Withernsea. Clusters of caravans and dilapidated chalets at the ends of lanes which had often undergone amputation in the wake of North Sea breakers. A beach comber warned us of debris and signs reading 'Danger' - cliffs subject to coastal erosion and others warning of 'Ordnance' were enough to see Havoc tethered to his lead. This was no place for random leg cocking.

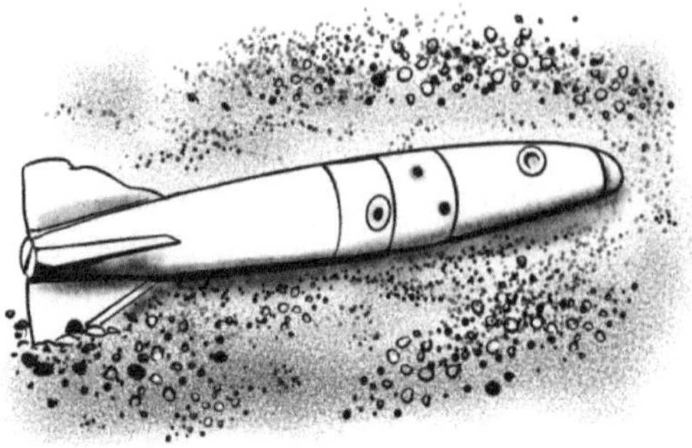

There was plenty of evidence of former military activity. Old riffle ranges, control towers and just lying there on the sand, UXOs. That stands for unexploded ordnance, rusting bombs in the shape of mini rockets. My thoughts on seeing the shape went back to Bleep and Booster, a 1960s cartoon, first shown on Blue Peter. If you are not that old think Leicester Rocket Sculptures, 2021. The disposal boys would have their work cut out and just to confuse them near Great Cowden someone had collected, and half buried all East Yorkshire's old caravans, cars and tractors and created a vehicle burial ground. If the explosives didn't raise the adrenalin the landslides did. Terraces created, some 15ft (4.5m) wide, where great chunks of land had just slumped to beat the Germans to the beach.

Withernsea was a welcome break at the lifeboat station where Ops manager Martin Woodhouse introduced us to Captain Phil Pannett of Associated British Ports. How we would negotiate the Humber was an obvious topic of conversation and a solution to our river detour was offered. It was arranged we would get a lift via a Humber pilot boat from Spurn Head across to Grimsby. We would not get to see Spud's cigarette end, any of Salt Ends chemical works or need to negotiate Hull's working docks, but who cared. The Vikings could have the Humber and the Ouse on their way to York, we were headed for Lincolnshire.

The Humber became visible through the Easington gas terminal. Mason Williams, 1968, Classical Gas, was in the ear, with time for a bit of air guitar thrown in. Eric Clapton would follow suit a year later. After Kilnsea we entered the Nature Reserve and were waved through, even though dogs were not normally allowed - touché Havoc!

Spurn was a narrow spit in 2007 but became more of a tidal island after a 2013 storm. The lifeboat station is a full time one, crew members have RNLI houses, there are Port Authority offices, a disused lighthouse, which in 2016 was reopened as a Yorkshire Wildlife Trust Visitor Centre. Sue, our river pilot met us, and Havoc was allowed the front seat for our short trip across to Grimsby. He sat gazing, bemused at the ship's instruments with an expression familiar to all exam invigilators. When told to turn over their papers, students would have dread etched into their faces when they hadn't done enough revision. Havoc's face replicated it perfectly, no competent crew award for you mate.

We were dropped right in the docks, next to the 309ft (29m) high tower, a landmark for miles and resembling a Muslim minaret. Built in the mid-19th century it used to hold pressurised storage reservoirs and Sue reckoned it was built on cotton wool foundations. The likely basis for this bit of local folklore is that the impetus for the docks and tower was the import of cotton through the town. We walked through areas clearly not open to the public, but how many 'visitors' arrive here by boat and find themselves on the wrong side of dock gates? Past fish boxes and all manner of piscine artifacts, I even popped into 'Youngs' in a vain attempt to pick up some sponsorship then found a gap in the fence and turned for Cleethorpes.

Thanks to two kindly folk, Margaret and Derick who looked after St Andrews Methodist Church we found some digs. It turned out to be for two nights as we took the opportunity to rest up a bit and do some much-needed self-maintenance. Wendy was suffering big time with her feet so we were in search of more 'Compeed', witch hazel and some of Mercury's plates of meat wings if we could find them. I managed a free and much needed hair cut from Polly at A1 Barbers and we both did a Nick Kamen impression at the Dolly Tub launderette. Some rest! We seemed to trek miles around pier, promenade, statue of a Boy with a Leaking Boot and the Greenwich Meridian zero degrees longitude marker. That read South Pole 9919 miles, North Pole 2517miles, and London where we were headed 143miles. (JM - quotes some different figures; global warming seems not only to have warmed the planet up but swollen it too.) Time spent 'resting' meant we fundraised and banked a further £500.

We collected a free packed lunch from 'Deli-licious' and headed mainly over grassy bank tops passing the caravans of Humberston Fitties to Horse Shoe Point. By the time we got to 'Tasty Treats' mobile caravan Wendy was in trainers and Havoc a shivering wreck. We had seen the 'Danger' boards for Donna Nook firing range and the targets on distant sandbanks, but the sound of firing had completely phased him, and beagles being worked were more than he could bare. I ended up carrying him. Seals were much more accustomed to the military presence. It was a Saturday, and an FA Cup tie was on the telly at The Crown in Saltfleet. (Man Utd beat Portsmouth 2-1, Rooney got both goals.) We found the village hall key holder, and somewhere to stay near a sail-less stump of a windmill for Vesta paella with the sea way off across sand, mud, dunes and marsh.

We were still a good 40 miles from Boston, but Wendy's phone started to steam with calls from Mary, a resident there. She was a GD owner herself, had offered us accommodation when we reached town and was going over and beyond by rallying friends and acquaintances of hers to help as we approached, if needed or not. At Mablethorpe the lifeboat crew, just back from an exercise could not have been more welcoming. A very lifelike model of the station complete with two ribs, launching trailers and personnel was entertaining and someone's labour of love/appreciation.

It was a bright Sunday, lots of folk around walking dogs, some even collecting coal off the beach for their narrow boat. Havoc was saying hello to everyone and a beach hut walkway all the way to Sutton on Sea made it easy to shake a collecting tin. We crossed the drain at Anderby Creek and carried on to Chapel St Leonards where we stayed with a contact via Mary, Bruce and Margaret Chapman. Bruce was one of those dual trade sorts, being a joiner and undertaker. The association still exists in many places, particularly Cornwall I understand. He amusingly remarked that they made,

"Coffins in the better weather and when the bad weather killed off the sick and lame the boxes were ready for the corpses. If you weren't very good at carpentry you made bird boxes which you traded for coffins so you could still get in on lucrative cemetery rates".

Chapter 12 – Skegness to Kings Lynn

You started this fire…burning out of control

"Wading through the Idaho of England, not one giant step, just lots of little ones."

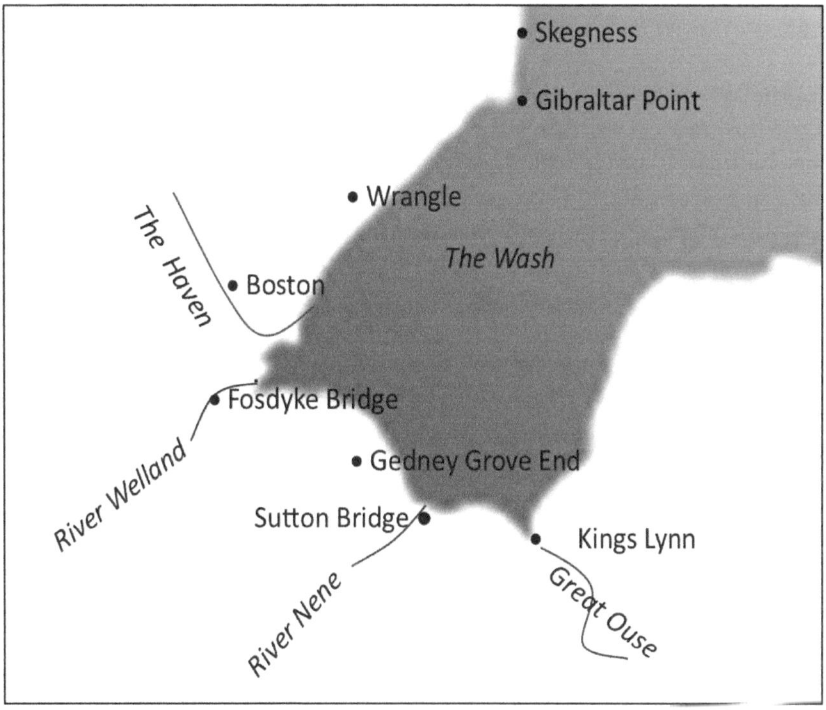

WE WERE ABOUT to reach what is called the 'Fun Coast'. A combination of beach and promenade led us through Ingoldmells to Skegness. Past Butlins, Fantasy Island, amusements and chalets all products of the town's tourist appeal. East Midlanders particularly were drawn to this seaside, ever since the railway provided the link in 1863. There was a Derbyshire Miners convalescent home (closed 2018), and a Derbyshire Holiday Camp from 1939 to the late 1990s showing the links between East Midlanders and Skegness, and the lifeboat also has received great support from Leicester and Nottingham. At the station there was something of a reception with a photographer who Havoc wrestled to the floor and proceeded to lick the poor guy's face with abandon - I think he confused him for Paul O'Grady. Coxswain/Mechanic John Irving took us onto the boat, the Lincolnshire

Poacher, along with several rather better behaved golden retrievers, who were also there to greet us.

For me architecturally, the highlights were the clock tower and the Jolly Fisherman Fountain. The latter has come to symbolise Skeggy, appearing in mascot form and on retro posters of the Great Northern Railway with the annotation 'Skegness is so bracing'. Later, the image would focus some controversy as it was used with the logo 'is so Brexit'. (Bill Bryson would bag the frolicking fisherman for his *Little Dribbling* cover.)

Complimentary bacon and egg rolls from 'Windy's' helped us on our way - we passed on the beans. It was bad enough sharing sleeping quarters with Havoc, without two extra trumpeters. ('Chappie' resulted in the most offensive stink!) Kent may be the 'Garden of England,' but Lincolnshire should be named the 'allotment' or at least the 'veg patch'. Fields were full of every sort of brassica, sometimes rotting and that ponged too. Sprouts on the stalk had escaped a Christmas boiling and looked like haemorrhoids. Wendy may have scrumped a few for tea, too many and we may as well of had the beans.

We skipped over Seacroft golf course to Gibraltar Point. Havoc was right, we didn't see any Barbary Apes but had to scamper like them to cross the Steeping River. We found a sluice, guarded by a six-foot fence, but at the bottom a hole, a bit like a cat flap could be used and we passed through bags, dog, and followed, scurrying on all fours. I think Spud found the same hole and perhaps Tess even excavated it a bit for us.

Much of the land around The Wash has been reclaimed for agriculture. From the grassy seawalls over steep sided water filled trenches one could see cultivation for miles. Not too many animals, except for geese, after the nature reserve, just kale, cauliflowers, and savoys. There didn't seem much to 'poach' in Lincolnshire, more veg than venison. Tractors and trailers bore the name 'Staples' and we watched a gang harvesting. A driver, four cutters, a conveyor lifted the cabbages on to two others who were packing at the rear. Many workers were, of course, Eastern Europeans, their numbers in this corner of the country would give rise to calls for immigrant limitations.

We hardly saw the sea all day, but near Wainfleet and Friskney there was new visual interest. Red warning flags and in the distance, what looked like 'Dyno Rod' vans. The bright orange objects turned out to be MOD bombing and strafing targets not 'bog' cleaners. We hadn't planned to stop at Wrangle, but Boston Mary, who we were yet to meet, arranged for us to stay at the Angel Inn with Sue and Eddy. We were only about ten miles from Boston, but hospitality was not to be sniffed at. We visited St Mary and St Nicholas Church which seemed huge but probably points to Wrangle once being a large harbour on this coast, now it is two miles from the sea.

It was as if we had wings, certainly no halo in my case, as we made off to Boston. At Freiston we met other pub owners who coincidentally also knew Mary. We began to think, who is this lady? A character known all over the manor. Rabbit pie was on offer at the Kings Head but although Havoc and I were keen, we passed, succumbing to Wendy's expressions of horror. It was the last day of January but on the way, we saw catkins, pussy willow, crocus and snow drops. With time on our hands, we headed for 'The Stump', St Botolph's Church, dating from 1309, and not easy to miss at 272ft (83m). It was an architectural gem, a landmark for miles around, and whether built to honour God or as a navigational aid for The Wash it must be admired. The octagonal lantern style top reminded me of Colyton church in East Devon, where I had started my teaching career and where I was married in 1982.

We met a young Richard Coles, a youthful curate and former Communard. (How poignant would their title from 1986 prove to be?) We had no idea he would go on to celebrity status as a broadcaster and Strictly contestant. Whenever you see him on TV or hear him on the radio, he seems so nice - he was just the same in 2007. We were given free tea and cake and a pass to the tower. I seem to remember being told it was a calendar tower, 365 steps to the first stage landing (145ft up), 7 doors, 52 windows, 12 supporting pillars - but never counted for verification. We climbed eagerly for the surrounding view, spotting the five sail Maud Foster windmill, something of a rarity. I couldn't help but reminisce of going up the John Hancock Tower in Massachusetts years earlier soon after it was opened. In 1620 citizens from here landed in New England, founding a colony they 'imaginatively' called Boston. The Lincolnshire parent remains a draw for visiting Americans. Back in the nave a carved choir stall from 1390 showed the humour of the carver. (A school master birching a boy, who protected himself with a book.) Was it an image of his own youth and was the book a Bible, who knows?

We couldn't put it off any longer and went to meet Mary and her husband Alf. We were treated to steak and chips which came with mushrooms and onions before sleeping on her lounge floor. She was quite a character, bold and brassy, and a complete chatterbox. Alf nor the both us could get a word in, but she was lovely - very kind and generous and I wondered if the talking masked a degree of insecurity. Heidi, her current Guide Dog had the company of Pedro and Ben, two former GDs and Havoc managed to boss all three around. Alf was ex RAF, and the little house was lined with model aeroplanes, china dogs and pictures of both. We were made very welcome; Mary was clearly very appreciative of GDs and all who raised funds for them and felt involved by being able to help us out.

It was a new experience to observe Mary working Heidi the next morning. They accompanied us to cross The Witham, the top end of The Haven, the tidal arm of The Wash. We said our goodbyes, headed off and soon got lost. We needed a visually impaired guide! Near Wyberton a white van man went around a corner too fast, and a boxed core drill set flew out of a door. He drove off unaware, so I picked up the tools and later sold them for £20 to another van driver boosting our fundraising. Ever entrepreneurial, resource investigation! More by luck than judgement we found our way to Fosdyke to cross The Welland. A man stopped his van and for a moment I thought it was 'The Stig' wanting his core drills back. Fortunately, this guy just said hello and gave us a donation of his own - another £20 and lighter to carry than a tool kit.

We turned left and made our way in the dark to Holbeach St Marks. The New Inn gave us supper and Tony Holland, the caretaker of the village hall, gave us his keys in return for a future phone call to tell him how we were getting on. Goodwill just seemed to rain down on us. It was a foggy night as the murk rolled in off The Wash. Over 300 square miles of muddy water, silted from the Fens with 12% of England draining into it via four or more rivers. It is internationally important for nature conservation and one of the top ten bird watching sites in the world. Land reclamation began in the 17th century, now what exists are a series of seawalls protecting farmland, which give way to marshes and a sea that seems miles away.

There was no shop at St Marks so early next morning we reconstituted our last three dried meals having noodles for breakfast and taking the rest to have with us for the day ahead. Havoc had dry 'Bonio's' mixed with marmite - he obviously was a lover!

From the embankment paths the morning sky seemed huge. White, turquoise, pale blue and grey streaked with bright rising sunshine. You will need to take Wendy's word for that, because I am colour blind. I do not see quite like an English Bulldog; I could make out the pure white of more snowdrops and a brilliant yellow of wild anemones. I pondered how

Havoc saw things knowing that dogs' vision is quite different from humans. Near Cox's Creek more loud bangs and he leapt higher than Fosbury and left his fur coat on the turf. From then, on his lead he pulled tearing one's arm out of socket, fortified by yeast extract. Another bombing range and 'Dyno Rod' were back, this time with pink, fluorescent outline.

On reaching the western lighthouse at the mouth of the Nene outfall, there are two, one on the opposite bank also, we turned right to Sutton Bridge. JM encountered restless cows here in 1978, arriving at the Bridge Hotel in the dark and staying there after a 33-mile hike from Boston (20th October 1978). We arrived in daylight, having taken two days, negotiated the cranes, girders and cables of the docks and were offered similar accommodation via its owner Chris Boyall, for what came to be an interesting evening.

Chris was a fish and chip tycoon from Wisbech and told of his family business, operating for over 70 years. Backed up by framed newspaper cutting of how publicity events to celebrate longevity turned back the clock, offering 1936 prices of cod 2d and chips 1d. On the menu was samphire, we were told a local delicacy, harvested from the salt marshes and in these parts called 'poor man's asparagus'. A previous visitor was someone who could afford the real thing, Prince Phillip, Duke of Edinburgh, who's close friend Peter Scott rented the east lighthouse at the end of the Nene in the 1930s for £5 a year.

Sir Peter: ornithologist, conservationist, painter - son of Robert Falcon of the Antarctic, lived in said lighthouse for six years, and as a result got a 'walk' named after him. We had seen his dad's ship back in Dundee, The RRS Discovery, and would in time discover Slimbridge and The Welsh National Wetland Centre, two places Peter was associated with. I opened his book, *'Observations of Wildlife'* and thumbed to chapter three, 'Concerns for the Planet'. It was ironic that in the news that day were reports of new evidence of world heating and rising sea levels. I also read an old Portuguese proverb which amused. 'Architects cover their mistakes with creepers, cooks with sauces and doctors with earth'. I couldn't help but thinking man covers the earth with his mistakes! Some of Scott's paintings could be seen on the hotel walls, including a self-portrait, with him holding a gun. More irony perhaps that both Scott and HRH, both known for wildlife conservation, at least for part of their lives were also keen hunters and field sportsmen. The hotel would suffer in succeeding years. It was left empty, became run down, endured a fire in 2016 and as far as I can reveal in 2021 is derelict, dangerous and scheduled for demolition.

With a retreating tide, wildfowl both ducks and geese, landed in formation on the Nene, turned to face up stream and found shelter by the riverbanks. It was a frosty, sunny morning and in a municipal car park joy riders had left stolen and abandoned vehicles, broken car parts littering the surface and a Community Police support car arrived. All, it seemed, were signs of the time, anarchy, criminality, litter and law enforcement.

We reached Scott's rental and began his ten-mile trail over wet Terrington Marsh to The Ouse. Wendy had opted for trainers and had wet feet within metres - somewhere nearby, King John in 1216 may also have got his feet wet. It is recorded that his baggage train and the crown jewels were lost in marsh after the indignation of Magna Carta. Modern archaeologists have even tried looking for it, but Tony Robinson had them focus their attentions on the Nene nearer to Wisbech as land reclamation since then means the sea has been pushed back. Even so, I told Havoc to keep his eyes peeled for anything shiny.

Needless to say, he was too busy cocking his leg on gateposts to sniff out any silver and at West Lynn we caught the ferry to the other one, King's. Our map was almost so old it could have been labelled 'Bishops', but Henry Vlll was having none of that. The ferry was as historic as the town having run since 1285. Early rent on arrival was then one dove. By 1649 it would cost you two well fatted swans. I think that was annually. Now (2007) it was 60p an adult, but we were not charged, in fact we were given a £10 donation. It remains a bargain trip at £1.20, and I think dogs are free! We were now in Norfolk, Nelson's birth county. King's Lynn was once one of England's most important trading ports. The much-treasured

Custom House from the 1680s was our meeting point for Rob and Denise Hunt, who would be our next hosts and Stuart Knight, postman, who had previously done the coast himself, back in 2000. It was a Saturday; he had the day off and was wearing long trousers. Jonny Wilkinson was in the shorts; England beat Scotland 42-20 and Jonny scored 27 points.

Chapter 13 – Kings Lynn to Great Yarmouth

I'm strong to the "finich", 'cause I eats me spinach

Spoken to me by a mermaid. "*Beauty comes from within, live so deeply, sea treasures in simple things, share life's joyful song, be the calm in a storm, take time to shellebrate, play on waves, have no fear of depths, believe in magic.*"

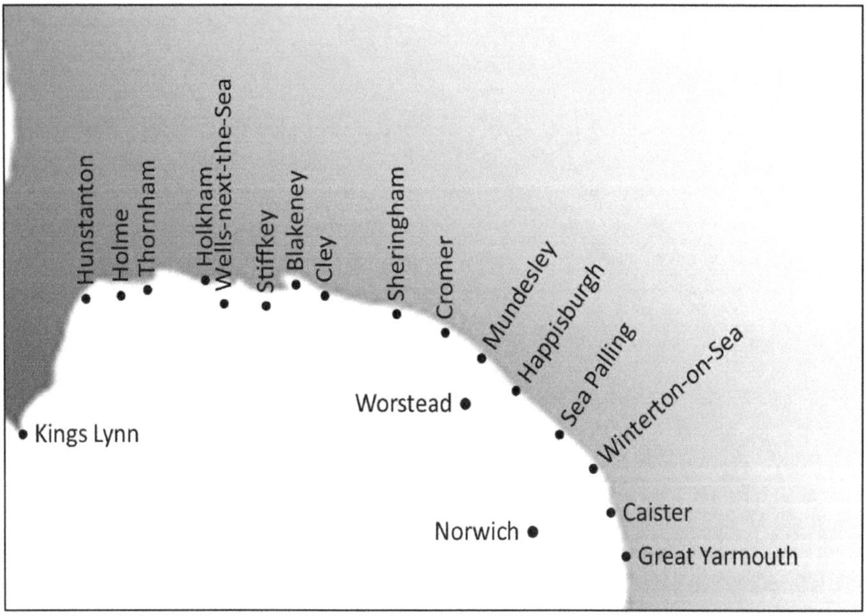

WELL PRESERVED AND elegant Georgian buildings grace Kings Lynn, along with fine medieval merchant houses and cobbled lanes. Once the fourth most important port in England and remaining well up the league table until around 1784. Captain George Vancouver was born here (1857) who helped map 4,000miles of America and gave his name to an island, a couple of cities and at least two mountains. We headed north up the third side of The Wash.

My wandering, curious, gypsy spirit provided the energy. New places and new faces were in themselves a motivation, but early February was again seeing a widening rift between Wendy and me. Words of affection and compassion were greeted with contempt and physical attempts at closeness, either a kiss or a hug, were almost always shunned. We were approaching some of the beaches where HRH Princess Diana had previously reflected and sobbed when escaping from Sandringham. I mainly noted factual stuff in my diary, but here I recorded comments and emotions. Like Diana, Wendy must have been extremely sad, I was too, but try as I might to improve things, I was often getting it wrong or not consistently seeing the problem. We tip toed around the estate and each other with heather fields inland and scruffy boathouses and banks of gulls, thousands of them, out to our left. Place names intrigued. Dog Sand, Vinegar Middle, Snettisham Scalp - as we made for 'Hunston' (Hunstanton) an East Coast town facing west. As for energy, 'Together in electric dreams' (Moroder and Oakley 1985) was in my ear, but I may have been over optimistic.

In 2021 the BBC Autumn Watch programme would come partly from Wild Ken Hill nearby at Heacham. Those heather fields, if anything like the giant plant in my garden would make glorious playgrounds for bees. Interestingly, Michaela Strachan and crew would eulogise about local farming practices stepping away from intensive cultivation in favour of more environmentally friendly pursuits. Herbage ley, carbon sequestration, nitrogen fixing and greater biodiversity all part of our 'every day is a school day' experience.

The Hunts (Rob and Denise) were lovely hosts, and if they saw through our thinly veiled attempts to hide relationship friction, they never showed it. Their two golden retrievers, Misty and Herbie ruled the house, at least until Havoc arrived and bossed them shamelessly - the terrier terrorising tyrannically. He took over the sofa, colour supplement, remote and mopped up their bowls for them while they submitted without resistance. We were introduced to more Norfolk Guide Dog support workers and lifeboat crew keen to show off their weaponry which at this junction included an eight metre hovercraft. For the first time for days, we heard the sea as the tide came in at 5.30pm. This is one area of coast where land is defeating water. Dunes and marshes, broken by shallow creeks extend from here eastwards to Stiffkey. Shingle and sand swept down from Yorkshire and Lincolnshire arrives as we did and is deposited - hence the need for air cushioned, amphibious rescue craft.

Vertical cliffs are stunning, 60ft high. Red/orange limestone called Carstone, a bit like gingerbread, is topped by white chalk forming a cake Mary Berry would be proud of. Reflected in shallow pools, broken by rounded boulders themselves like pastry cobbler at the cliff base gave this resort a 'Bake Off' appearance three years before Hollywood et al rose from the oven. Ancient tracks, the Peddars and Icknield Ways terminated at Holme next the Sea. It is thought the Romans ran a ferry service across The Wash to Lincolnshire from here, giving travelers no chance to burn off calories if they bought a ticket rather than trudge around the UK's largest estuary system. Had it been running from Skegness I might have been tempted to stow away.

The terrain became a bit more undulating than the sea wall of the last week. Boardwalks with compacted stone and wooden edging, railway sleepers topped with anti-slip chicken wire made the North Norfolk Heritage Coast less wilderness more superhighway. I was in something of a dilemma, improved access means more visitors but how do authorities maintain the wildness of places? I had felt similarly about locations back home on Dartmoor. Fast forward to 2019 and the Glover Report (Review of Landscapes) was published but further ongoing years would see no government response to it. It makes interesting reading if you share my dilemma.

Those upgraded access ways led us to a small army of zoom lenses, accompanied by camera clicks. Near Thornham twitchers descended on a solitary American yellow leg (genus Tringa) who I am sure was just

seeking a bit of peace. One of them, not Bill Oddie, but he spoke with the same authority, told me the grey/brown streaked wader with a long bill was a sandpiper, quite like a curlew or a greenshank. I was really none the wiser. With the aid of his lens, I could see its tail bobbing, something which apparently Aristotle had noted. Suddenly I felt intellectual. 'It should be in the snow forests of Canada or Alaska, it is very rare' I was told. It was also very lost I thought, and those yellow stockings - very last season.

Grey seals were to be seen along the coast here. Overhead huge numbers of geese did several fly pasts. Havoc would normally bark frantically at anything like this. A noise of a helicopter for example would be drowned out like a penny whistle on a battlefield. Today however, not a peep until we came across a scarecrow and then all hell was unleashed on a par with the opening scenes of Gladiator. Worzel Gummidge would have peed his pants!

Whelks used to be an industry here too, now only a few boats make a living from taking tourists to see the seals. We were told a few velvet and brown crab were to be had but whelks had now gone north to Grimsby, caught by larger boats and shipped abroad for the Japanese market. We passed The Victoria Hotel Holkham, which JM had stayed at, 22nd October 1978, we hadn't done 39 miles that day, 5th February 2007, so kept on going.

Wells-next-the-Sea was the next tick off. A glance at the map one might expect a river running through it, but there isn't one. Old maltings and granary buildings, now converted to apartments, point to something of the town's past. Notorious floods all along the East coast in 1953 seriously affected Wells. 1978 saw more, but the town was better prepared. The last serious storm surge was in 2013 but the worst of its action was offset by a tidal barrier built in 1980. Sea walls defend caravan sites, coloured beach huts brew cuppas and since 2018 a three-metre-high steel horse sculpture stands proud on the harbour sands. It is in fact a tribute to the horses that once pulled the lifeboat.

Alan Frary was Mr Lifeboat, coxswain since 1997 with forearms which the eyes were instantly drawn to, bulging and tattooed. He must have done some sweating on sheets I thought. Fortified by tins of spinach his Olive Oil was Bridget who made us very welcome in a home full of cats, fish, guinea pigs, a parrot, a brown lab called Bourneville, not to mention three live in adults with learning difficulties. Just what she wanted I am sure, an additional three mouths to feed. (Alan would retire I think in 2018 after 21 years' service, but I see another Frary on the current crew list and a new lifeboat station due in 2022.) Lifeboats seem to be in the blood.

Alan pointed out the memorial marking the 1880 lifeboat disaster which saw 11 crew drown leaving widows and 27 children fatherless. He still coordinated memorial services - Lest We Forget, and I think had quite a bit to do with buying Black Beauty also. At the lifeboat station in the smallest room a carved wooden and jointed old sailor figure riding a mono cycle. It was actually only about ten centimetres tall and provided smoother, ironed, easily distributed toilet paper acting to brake the over rapid rotation of the roll. The caricature was the spitting image of a hasher back in

Devon, 'Broken Man.' I hope the little figure isn't broken and finds his way into the new boatshed.

Wells - two good, two bad. Start with the bad. Sharing a room with that parrot made my chest drum-like. I was wheezy and every expiration was accompanied by a tiny whistle. The other bad, actually I couldn't think of anything, but there were far more than two goods. Meeting the mum of a man who was fast becoming my idol. Who had given birth to someone, who when acting as mechanic, could unbolt boat engine parts without the need for a spanner. I was very jealous of those carpi radialis and pronator teres.

In a very pleasant High Street, we were recognised by 'Norfolk' who had seen us in the local paper. Donations followed and I soon banked another £150. I bought a new A5 hardback notebook - volume two of the diary. Georgian houses on the Buttlands - so called because Henry VIII designated it an area for longbow practice. A Frary fry up the size of the county had everything from Norfolk's larder (except canned spinach) and we were out on the Peddars Way again headed eastwards, taking with us very fond memories of a town and a man.

Bumping into a guy whose job was to maintain and keep clear the coast path I had an interesting discussion about that dilemma re superhighways or wilderness. He was quite scathing of the public who dropped litter and showed little respect to the countryside they were visiting. He was doing a great job but admitted if the council paid him to keep the area wilderness, he would hang up his chainsaw and croppers.

We were treated to seeing reed being cut for local thatch. Attractive houses at Blakeney boasting knapped flint construction and one of the county's finest windmills at Cley, built in the early 1800s (some say 1713?) and now a very fine B&B - such are the number of folks on wheat free diets. What is for sure, it wasn't around in 1612 when a fire destroyed 117 homes, accordingly to archaeologist, Ben Robinson. He explored to explain why Cley is no longer 'Next-to-the-Sea' and how French and Fleming protestant 'strangers' came to settle in the 16th century.

Havoc met a beautiful GD puppy called Ellie and promptly tried to mount her! Forced to move swiftly on we soon reached Salthouse where the pub was closed but banked another £56.50 at the Post Office. Then it was on to Sheringham with a bit of a mix of shingle and sand. A dead seal and headless porpoise were obstacles to hurdle. Perhaps they were victims of a Yow Yows? - a brief but violent storm in these parts (themselves the cries of drowned fishermen!). I read the selenium (Se) rich soil locally means there are more centurions here than in anywhere else in the UK. It wasn't doing much for the marine life.

From 63m (206ft) at Beeston Bump, (formed from a 'kame,'- glacial deposit) you could get a good view along the north Norfolk coast. Almost back to the site of the ancient sea henge at Holme, through Stiffkey pronounced 'Stewkey' and onto the church (160ft – 49m)) dominating Cromer, Norfolk's tallest tower. If you now want to see the timbers of the Bronze Age henge you need to visit Lynn Museum. I reflected on all the places of interest, hidden gems squirrelled away that punctuate this coast, many towns and villages with churches which seemed to 'pepper' the landscape. I use the verb since they looked like pepper mills spread across tables in an Italian restaurant.

(For those calling for consistency when using imperial or metric units, I have done a few conversions for you. The variance is something, surely Bill Bryson must have picked up on, a peculiarity that makes us Brits unique. Personally, I like the freedom to use both. I once taught a 'remedial' maths lesson, topic money matters, where I briefly varied from the script to expound about pre-1971 LSD and the arrival of decimalisation. Prescription from a syllabus, the likes of the national curriculum, allows for little individuality and freedom. I, like Boris Johnson, am not one for sticking to the rules or script. The hierarchy observing thought it a deviation too far, I didn't get the job.)

Our stay over in Cromer, a second home, courtesy of Len Boyd. We had never met him and haven't since. 'Collect the keys from a neighbour.' How is that for Christian trust and generosity. Wendy was doing the evening reading. Apparently, Norfolk had more than its fair share of ghosts and weird and wonderful stories. I was glad it wasn't Halloween. Dartmoor does too, I put it down to the fact people don't have much to do of an evening, so they sat by the fire, told stories and scared the crap out of one another. (Except in Cromer, it might be crab!)

"The church here is haunted" she said, "And can we go to Upper Sheringham; All Saints has a carved pew end, something about a mermaid dragging herself from the sea to the village. There is also a White Witches house".

I explained we had already bypassed Upper Sheringham, needless to say we didn't retrace our steps. That would need to wait for another time.

Instead, we went to the pier and the current lifeboat station where we were given a very nice wall plaque. Something else to weigh down the rucksack until we could post it back home, not that we were ungrateful. 'From here you can see the sun rise and set' we were told. I think because it was at something of a turn in the coast.

We looked around the West Runton Elephant, in the museum, Britain's oldest and most complete elephant fossil. 'Cromer is renowned for its geological importance' we were told. 'Must tell my son' I replied. Wendy was getting a bit 'museum-ed out' sulking a bit for that mermaid and I was seeing lots of the white witch emerging. That said we could hardly do a RNLI road trip without paying homage to Henry Blogg, the greatest lifeboat man of all time. Since 1824 the RNLI have saved something like 137,000 lives. Henry joined up in 1894 aged 18, retired at 71 giving 53 years of service, 37 as Coxswain at Cromer. In 387 services he helped save 873 lives along with his lifesaving apprentice Monty, his dog. A fact I had to point out to Havoc. Highly decorated for his gallantry he would have floundered if he fell in weighed down by medals, especially since he couldn't swim. We signed the visitors' book; Wendy was out of the door in a shake of your sou'ester and we were on towards Trimingham.

More southerly parts had reported snow showers and as we were going that way, heading into it. My mind was elsewhere, an ear worm I could not extinguish, 'Don't Speak' by No Doubt, a somber anthem from 1995. Selected lyrics repeated, 'Losing my best friend... don't speak...you and me, we used to be together...looks as though you're lettin' go...don't tell me cause it hurts... hush, hush darlin.'

What we needed to do was to speak - to each other, turns out we ended up speaking to a ladies' luncheon club. At Mundesley Royal Hotel we took shelter from a blizzard and over a cup of tea got talking to hotel staff. They had a group gathered ready for lunch and a guest speaker but the latter had not showed, unable to travel due to bad weather further south. Were we interested in stepping in? Anything for a free meal, so after poached haddock and a crumble desert we took turns at expanding stories from our first 88 days. £100 was raised for our charity pot from the impromptu mutterings. We were well received, and it made us both feel better, at least for a while. We could make a living out of this.

Our celebrity lunch hour however meant we were now late, or at least pushed to make a rendezvous down the coast. The weather had improved a bit after the last custard, and we bashed on for Bacton on the beach, past a gas terminal, Keswick, Walcott and Ostend. Wait a minute, were we lost? I didn't recall walking on water, and the 550 of Walcott and Ostend combined looked crumblike against an imagined 70 odd thousand of a same name cousin over the sea in Belgium. If nothing else all this walking improved one's geography. If you have clocked Ostend Norfolk before it is probably because a rare beaked whale became stranded on the beach, in 2002.

At Happisburgh (pronounced Hazeborough/Haisboro) we came up from the beach in the dark by the lifeboat station. Little did we know at the time the slipway had been washed away. We were due to meet Dillis (a primary teacher) and Nick (offshore technician supervisor) Lewis, our hosts in the pub and we were late. On meeting, we were even more embarrassed since they actually lived a little way inland at Worstead. This was the place that gave its name to the fine specialised yarn used for expensive suits (Worsted), its wealth dating from the 12th century when Flemish weavers settled there with the King's blessing. The industry now long gone still left a legacy in the form of a grade one listed church.

The Lewis' barn conversion was also more Savile Row than Primark. Havoc chewed a toy belonging to Laura the cat and Milli the dog was politely ushered into another room; Havoc's reputation preceding him and doubled our embarrassment as guests. I think we got away with it however, as Dillis dropped us back to the sea next morning, she promised to organise a 'mufti' day at her school to help raise a bit more charity cash. In less than 24 hours we could see she was one of those people, like many primary teachers, who just oozed energy - and this morning a bit annoyingly so, since I was feeling far from dynamic.

The coast here is literally falling into the sea. Evidence of erosion and man's efforts to stall it. Spud - (p27) describes it insightfully. From dunes to marram grass and old Christmas trees, groynes to Russian boulders, bottomless pits of money are thrown at slowing what seems, with climate warming, to be an unsolvable problem. What did seem to be evident was that our coast was increasingly concrete. A wave shaped parapet facing outwards, terraces below, rocks at the water edge and offshore reef - just a cross-section at one point, and all failing, as about as much use as King Cnut. Rather dilapidated chalets, that reminded me of the 1950s, snuggle for shelter while retaining a glimpse of ocean. At one, named 'Tring Tot' we were offered tea and discussed the dilemma. Make the most of romantically named places like Eccles-on-Sea, (soon to be Eccles-in-the-Sea,) and Sea Palling (as seen on the calendar, Coastlines 2021, October) since if climate experts have it right, old names might be all that remain. Like the ships lost along this coast; Invincible, Hunter, Peggy, Young England, to name but a few, the sea will claim its fare.

Havoc chased stones, scared of getting his feet wet so decided to alarm two horses being exercised one of which reared, even more alarming its rider. He then moved on to rabbits which prompted a 'debate' between Wendy and me. Should he be restricted via lead or allowed to do what dogs do? The bunnies were only taunting him, and if one was slow getting in its sand warren, he wouldn't know what to do with it anyway. The former won so the canine was shackled, reduced to self-throttling by continuing the instinct and giving Wendy a subluxated shoulder in the process. Still, 15/love!

We swept down the coast as currents do bringing wreck wood to Winterton-on-Sea. Locals once used it for building their winter houses where they eked a living for a few months off the sea before going inland to summer dwellings to work on the fields (East/West Somerton). Daniel Defoe wrote that 200 coal ships were wrecked in one winter night. Valerie and Michael along with their very strong yellow Labrador Prince were to billet us here. Valerie had walked GD puppies and was a bit of an amateur artist. She joined us walking the following day behind sand dunes, but I never found out if we made it to one of her canvases.

Hemsby independent lifeboat crew made us a tea in between cleaning their old former RNLI caterpillar track launching tractor (PLA 698). Caister, also had its own independent lifeboats. Their moto 'Never Turn Back' which also happened to be the name of the pub where they drank. Bernard Matthews and Jim Davidson were among sponsors of boats, and they had gone for jet engine designs. Despite the fact we were raising money for 'big brother' (RNLI) they were still very welcoming, and we had more tea - a turkey sandwich would have gone down well, but that never happened, not so 'bootiful'.

In the rain by early afternoon, we were in Great Yarmouth to meet up with a young girl with her GD, and Brian and Kay, old acquaintances, with their GD Kim, a Leonberger, a large German breed. That meant we took over the entire bar at Wetherspoons. By 5.30pm we were picked up by Tina, this time a Slimming World contact, and whisked back to Norwich for an evening with her friends - Delia Smith and Nicholas Parsons. (Actually, they weren't there, but I was so tired I couldn't tell the difference.)

Most people when fatigued rest, have a lie in, it was a Sunday even the Lord advised it. We were off hashing with the local kennel, taking Tina with us for an introduction. (I hope she's stayed the course?) We had attended Nash Hash at Norwich in 2005, woad compulsory, met a fair few folks who still remembered us mainly from the 'shiggy' run! (Get as muddy as possible.) Invited back to a hasher's house for a combined birthday/on down bash, with lots of shenanigans, shaving foam and mixed alcoholic cocktails. I think Havoc did quite well hoovering up BBQ bits as well.

We confirmed accommodation for Caernarfon, a hash couple, JJ and Mo, were moving to north Wales, 'Turn up when you get there!' France beat Ireland 20-17 in the rugby on the telly and it was off to Dexter's for the night at Blundeston, Suffolk, only three miles from Lowestoft. More drinks at the Plough Inn, connections to Charles Dickens who wrote about it in David Copperfield, and we needed to be up early.

Chapter 14 – Great Yarmouth to Burnham-On-Crouch

Come hear the music play... life is a cabaret

"To succeed you must believe in something with such a passion it becomes a reality. Through Suffolk, a hint of wilderness in its tamed beauty and the tang of the North Sea never far away, rural England pulling at the heart strings."

AT 6.15AM DEXTER DROPPED us back to Yarmouth throwing a piece of paper at us saying,

"She might be able to help?"

On it was a phone number. With that he was gone. It would have been even earlier if Dexter hadn't overslept, I had provided the early morning call. What to do in Yarmouth at a quarter past six on a February morning - HAVE SEX! I jest, that was long removed from the agenda, replaced by invitations to join the monks at Buckfastleigh. One of the brothers there once told me it's not so bad. We get a choice of breakfast cereal and your turn to go to the bookies on a Saturday with the collective bets comes around quite quickly.

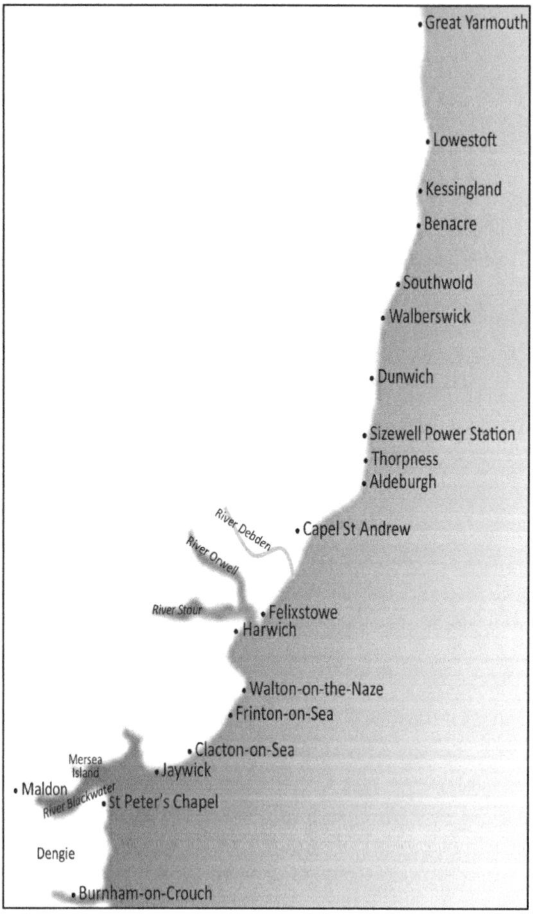

We looked around, the fast-moving River Yare, and closed-up pleasure beach. The Golden Mile looked more tarnished tape measure, two piers, a few old buildings, the odd bit of wrecked city wall - what the Luftwaffe left in 1941. The council and town youth had done their best to ruin even that, I speak of flat roofed blocks of flats and industrial units adorned with graffiti. All the 'trappings of a popular resort!' Dickens, in David Copperfield had called it 'the finest place in the universe'. I must run that past Tim Peake. It was a very strange mix. At South Denes the Britannia Monument (41m – do you own conversion!) globe, olive branch, trident, a tribute to Britain's finest navel hero Nelson, a son of Norfolk born at Burham Thorpe, stuck in an industrial estate. Visitors like us could choose to look at it or the gas power station. Yarmouth suffered a lot from the 1953 flood and subsequent flooding too. Only in September 2006, five months earlier, 90 properties were flooded. I was beginning to think pity it wasn't a bit more extensive. We crossed the Haven Bridge, past docks to Gorleston. The lifeboat station was closed, they had more sense and had stayed in bed. I began to think of those brothers (monks) back on Dartmoor's southern edge, surely Matins can't be that bad.

I am not sure if we were lost but our path took us across a ravine and into a further gully under a massive gorse bush. Then we were on a golf course with signs saying 'Private, No Right of Way and Danger of Fatal Flying Golf Balls!' We ignored them but became very squeamish and tried to appear invisible when we met several greenkeepers laying turf. One kept uttering 'green side up', they didn't tell us off, in fact they donated and wished us well.

At some point we must have crossed into Suffolk. The wind turbine at Ness Point known locally as Gulliver came into view. At 126 metres in 2005 when it was completed it was the largest in the country. The renewable energy industry in Lowestoft has taken off. It was perhaps only in its infancy in 2007 but there was still lots to see in the form of turbine construction and plenty of 'windows in fields' as I've heard solar panels described. Gulliver dwarfed the lighthouse, and we made our way through Suffolk's second town, crossing the inner harbour/Lake Lothing which to our right became the river Waveney leading to the Broads. I did call into Birdseye and asked to have a word with the 'Captain' to see if they might like to sponsor us. Unfortunately, I was frozen out.

Feeling more like le petit pois than a fish finger I followed Wendy as we came up from the beach at Pakefield to meet Brian, Kay and Kim again at the Jolly Sailors. This was where we had first run into them in 2005 when the idea of the walk was merely an embryo. It was kind of them to give of their time to encourage us, and buy us a carvery, the pub had run out of peas, but we had to push on. The information board at Kessingland said it was once more important for fishing than Lowestoft having to pay 22,000 herring to their Lords in rent. I couldn't help thinking that was a lot of fish fingers.

We phoned that number from Dexter.

"We don't know who you are, but we were given this number by an acquaintance who said you might be able to help us!"

To cut a long story, Joan Oddy turned out to be an 'assistant' vicar who with some persuasion, managed to arrange for us to kip down at the village hall. The inducement came solely from Havoc, Joan was to make a complete fuss of him, and I am certain without his coercion we would have never got the gig. He was quite irrepressible, this encounter all down to his initiation. The photo of him that night reveals a completely exhausted canine laid out on a bare communal kitchen floor, eyes closed, motionless, corpse-like, sleeping like a beauty.

We gave thanks outside the church, St Edmund's, unusual since it had a thatched section in the middle of the nave. Joan and her dog Bracken saw us off, Bracken's sentiments to Havoc, 'and don't come back!' Jealousy isn't only a human failing. I reflected on Joan's likeness to Geraldine Granger (Vicar of Dibley) not in physical appearance but in manner - bit of a rebel in the community, but very well meaning, she certainly pulled out the stops for us and we returned to the 'denes'.

We soon found ourselves on top of low mustard-coloured cliffs that were falling into the sea. A farmer had planted winter corn which was now sprouting right on the edge. There was no field margin, that had disappeared and quite rapidly. There was no way he could have ploughed/cultivated and planted right to the edge. What was more was that halfway down the cliff face on a narrow terrace corn was still growing. It made me think erosion here was occurring faster than anywhere else we had witnessed it. Spud had seen similar in 1993, how much of eastern England had disappeared in the interim?

Benacre was quite beautiful. February winter sunshine, a fresh south westerly wind, fantastic sand; you could have been on a Pacific or Caribbean Island. Some trees had lost their battle to stay erect as the sea had washed out their anchorage. One huge root stump had been smoothed and worn by the elements leaving it almost fossilised, a 'stumpery,' with jagged prongs pointing upwards and outwards. It would carry a several £100 price tag in a garden centre, but you would have needed a JCB to get it there. Now on the beach we could see a thin green carpet from the fields above hanging over like artificial grass on a greengrocer's market stall. In one spot the remains of a dung heap/clamp hung precariously over the soft mustard rock, decaying layers glistening in the sunshine, a cornice you would not want to find yourself under.

Southwold's curiosities on the pier became the next point of interest. Unlike many piers this one was not in decline. It was popular, packed, as was the town. Half term and sun had brought out the crowds. The coin operated novelty machines by inventor Tim Hunkin, in the style of Heath Robinson, were amusing. The Mobility Masterclass zimmer frame was just what I needed, and Rent a Dog provided an instant companion, Havoc watch out. Five years earlier, 2002, it was named Pier of the Year. The lighthouse location in the centre of the town a further curiosity, a sailors' reading room full of naval/ship memorabilia. One photo took my eye a picture of pier keeper, a certain Mr Barber. One occupant, an old guy who didn't speak or move, he may have been a wax model or peacefully passed away without notice?

Colourful beach huts with wacky names, 'Lovely Jubbly' and 'Gin n it' to name just two fetch up to £60,000 and a whiff of malt around the town courtesy of Adnams Brewery. The town sign depicts two galleons from the Battle of Sole Bay (1672) jousting. England (with a bit of help from France) were at odds with the Dutch, a very early Jeux Sans Frontiers contest. Eagle eyed visitors might notice the home ship flying a Union Flag, minus the red diagonal cross. That wasn't added until 1801 when the Irish got on board. At Gunhill Cliff six cannons given to the town in 1746 by the

Royal Armories may have replaced even earlier ones used to deter privateers. The Blyth's swirling channel was a hive of wooden jetties, boats, net mending, and those half termers crabbing. We had planned to get to Dunwich but that would have to wait and instead sought sanctuary at Walberswick.

Rest came in the form of a village hall annex. With few facilities, not much more than a kettle and a loo, it hardly registered on our star chart for communal 'hostels'. It did have a lit make-up mirror, surrounded by bulbs, Hollywood style, and I wondered what celebrities had graced the stage. On the walls, photos of amdram productions. (2006 – 'Peter Pan,' 1990 – 'Wats up the Beanstalk,' and 1952 – 'As other's see us' put on by a Review Company. I half expected Windsor Davies and Don Estelle to come through the door renditioning Whispering Grass – 'Sing Lofty!') Why is it that people go out of their comfort zone just to make fools of themselves? Liza Minnelli was in my ear. In the pub we met a guy who claimed to have gone around Britain, he said 3,500 miles, on a horse. I thought to myself if it was only that far it wasn't Champion, more Mr Ed, amazing!

In the drizzle and mist Dunwich bordered by marshes and heathland was now a mere village of around 200 people. Once an international harbour/port the size of 14th century London, what could still be found were the remains of Greyfriars Priory. It survived the Dissolution of the Monasteries but has since fallen into ruin. Over time churches, more numerous than Henry's wives, have fallen into the sea. Legend has it you can still hear church bells tolling below the waves. Evidence of leprosy, endemic in Britain for centuries, exists at Dunwich in the form of architecture from a leper hospital. The last victim of the disease was apparently buried in 1536. Woods sharing the name of the Priory provided a carpet of snowdrops and in places daffodils just showing colour.

Minsmere led us to Sizewell. We imagined ourselves on Bond film, Star Trek and Dr Who sets. Built in 1958 it still seemed futuristic, what must locals have felt when it first emerged? Davros might well have risen from the huge, white tiled sphere which we observed through some shimmering steam somehow worryingly escaping. Two workmen attempted to slow its escape with a polythene sheet and gaff tape - worryingly non-high tech! Another engineer in a bright yellow suit seemed to have a glowing halo above his PPE hood causing Havoc to wee on what surely was already radioactive grass. At the aptly named Vulcan Arms it was time for tea and chips and a quick rub down with a Geiger counter.

Keeping on a theatrical theme the curtain went up on Thorpness. The observable features, a large lake known as the Meare, the House in the Clouds, windmill, timber clad houses and no promenade. This was a man-made stage set of a village, built in 1911 by Edwardian GS Ogilvie as a tourist destination, to include activities for children but only those whose parents could afford a nanny. (Featured 'Villages by the sea' BBC, 22nd November 2021). We took our final bows and exited front stage left for Aldeburgh.

Our arrival was marked by the somewhat controversial beach sculpture 'Scallop' (2003). Visitors are encouraged to sit on it to get a textual sense, while others not so keen have daubed it with paint. Havoc provided a different liquid by way of raising a hind leg but there was no sense this summed up his artistic judgement of the piece. Fortunately, there was no one around to 'voice' Benjamin Britten words of reprimand and the sound of shingle being thrust and counter thrust on the shore would have 'drowned' them out anyway. We needed to find a fisherman, (Peter Grimes?) or similar, to help us across the river Alde and were guided by Steve Saint (tentative link to our earlier Bond set via Roger Moore!) at the lifeboat station. (I think he is still the Coxswain, just a little less hair, expecting delivery of a new boat 2021- a Shannon Class, with 'Freddie Cooper' sidelined. Not sure if it ever arrived?)

The lifeboat station itself seems to hang from several 'A' frame scaffold poles and contrasted with a finely preserved Tudor 'Moot Hall', and towards Slaughdon a unique quatrefoil Martello Tower from the early 19th century. This was the first and most northerly of many; only another 102 or so to find, 'sandcastles' albeit made from bricks, dotted along the southeast coast. All, I imagined hanging sheets from the windows with the words 'Keep Out Napoleon' painted on them 200 years ago.

Steve sorted us out with a roof over our heads for the night and we were left to explore. From the lack of house lights, it seemed there were a lot of second homes. The mermaid figurehead above the chip shop used her arm pose to promote her cleavage and Snooks the dog was just as motionless - a memorial to a local GP (and wife) who tended to Aldeburgh's acne, ulcers and piles for 28+ years. We met a very cute real pocket-sized terrier, complete with diamanté collar, a template for all barking, somersaulting, flipping child's toys.

We shook our tins in the lobby of the cinema helping us bank a further £330 and were joined by two hashers from Rendlesham (Rambo, not the TVH3 one, and Hotstuff) for a pub quiz at the Mill Inn. It was good to get their encouragement, but we didn't win. Bedtime reading would reveal Aldeburgh had the first British female Mayor (1908), John Gummer was the MP - he would remain in post for 31 years until 2010, and the year before our arrival (2006) a local lad, Sam Wright, became the world's youngest town crier at 15 - Oyez! My crystal ball showed Roy Keane moving in (2009) when he managed Ipswich Town F.C. 25 miles down the A12. (He would only last 18 months.)

Thanks to 'The Saint' we were given a free breakfast back at the Mill Inn and an introduction to John who would get us across the Alde. We found Upsons boatyard, and I had to do a double take. John was a spitting image of a Teign Valley hasher, 'Forest Stump'. It was a very fresh morning, photos show us all looking frozen, a choppy swell, me with a massive ruck sack about to unbalance a grimy rowboat, John doing his best to steady it with an oar and Havoc with his own panniers looking thoroughly panicked, despite being picked up his paws doing air doggie paddle. In the confusion Wendy left behind a telescopic walking stick but we never went back for it.

We followed the inner sea wall with Sudbourne marshes on our right and Orford Ness across to our left. We counted 11 transmitting masts, one belonging to Radio Caroline. There was also a lighthouse on the narrow spit and we arrived at Orford quay. The well-preserved 12th century castle keep looked down on us with suspicion. We had hoped to get a boat ride across the River Butley, but despite putting soundings out on

Radio Suffolk, local mariners it seemed were suspicious of us too. Inland instead to Chillesford, Butley Mills and Capel St Andrew where we came across the pietist - wrestling with a fish and an eel - in statue form.

We were definitely taking an indirect route. We found our way to Boyton and could still smell the smokehouse we had left hours ago back at Orford. Hares were doing their 'mad hatter' thing, it was only just past St Valentines, at least two weeks to March. Hen harriers, according to a couple of bird watchers, seemed unphased by bangs from bird scarers but Havoc was having a meltdown. He was the same colour as a green woodpecker that was intermittently dipping into a side order of ants while laughing at our boy.

At Hollesley we had our own meltdown. We were used to having a cuppa offered perhaps accompanied by a 'Kit-Kat', but Judith Andrews went one better, take away cheese on toast. She also pointed us in the direction of a local vicar, Geoff, who was to put us up, but he lived at Shottisham, more miles we could really have done without.

He turned out to be a very interesting pastor. He had spent time abroad, was into science fiction, looked after seven churches and rode a motor bike. Not at all like my stereotypical image of a holy man. We discovered he had been married and chatting I think like me he carried some guilt at not having made it work. I was reminded of meeting the vicar who married my former wife and me, his words expanding permanence, which I had not achieved. However, Geoff was a very different man.

"Make yourselves at home, I have to pop out", and he was off burning up the lanes of Suffolk.

We discovered a pool table, remote control for a fart machine and behind a door, which turned out to be a cupboard, a wood axe and an air rifle. Havoc curled up on Geoff's favourite cassock and was promptly sick. We didn't see Geoff again that night, just dreamt about being chased by a guy on a motor bike wearing a dog collar, brandishing a gun and quartering us with a hatchet.

He was around at breakfast, and we watched the visitors on his bird table – blue tits, finches, blackbirds and a spotted woodpecker. There was more wildlife than in Snow White's Garden. After a quick lesson in method bell ringing where I couldn't tell my 'Plain Hunt' from my 'Grandsire Doubles', we headed for Alderton, Bawdsey and a ferry over the Deben.

We now came across 'Restricted Zone' signs warning of control measures for Avian Influenza. (In Suffolk large numbers of turkeys were culled

2006/7 and Bernard Matthews was reputed to have lost £20million in lost sales and costs.) I did say to Wendy we should perhaps head north to Woodbridge and take in the Sutton Hoo treasure, dress up in chicken suits for publicity en route, but was immediately told to 'get stuffed'. She had arranged a special 'off-season' crossing with John (I was beginning to think all boat owners were called John) and we clambered on his clinker vessel.

It seemed like we had been on the Deben peninsula for an odyssean age, and we scampered away over a golf course towards Felixstowe before we were enticed back by bell ringing sirens. We were met by puppy walkers. Wendy liked these welcomes particularly, having done the job herself, and we were grateful to volunteers for giving of their time to offer words of encouragement. Havoc perhaps less so, since all the welcoming party were either cool Labradors or cute retriever cross breeds; he had something of an inferiority complex and came over as a bit of a militant mongrel.

Generally, things were sleeping. In fields giant irrigation sprinklers lay dormant, a few cabbages were being cut, gardeners on an allotment were digging in manure and feeding a smoky bonfire and in Felixstowe itself the pier looked very forlorn. (Ten years on £3million would be thrown at refurbishment.) Gardens were trying, with violets, miniature iris and crocuses showing us Spring was just around the corner. We had been blessed weather wise, the winter 2006/7 had not thrown us too many curve balls.

With Felixstowe being the UK's largest container port, one might have expected security to be high. We walked straight in unchallenged and caught a pilot boat to the jetty of the lifeboat station at Harwich. We could look out over the harbour to Shotley Gate and HMS Ganges now decommissioned. The mast which 160,000 boys climbed at the Royal Navy training establishment prompted me to make a prank phone call (alike Noel Edmonds) to Goolie, a hasher in SHH3, who was someone who passed through the base. I claimed that in clearing sheds a pair of underpants bearing his name tag had been found and would he like them returned to him? For a few minutes I had him going until I couldn't restrain myself any further and burst into laughter.

To the left the river Stour leading to Manningtree, and ahead the Orwell with Ipswich at its head. In October 1978 JM would take a good day and a half at breakneck speed to reach Harwich from Felixstowe, no short cutting for him. Spud was up early to get a commuter ferry from Harwich to Felixstowe in August 1993. Our boat ride along the outer coast saved us time and miles but it didn't seem as if we were cheating. We were following our own rules. That night we slept next to the 'Duke of Kent' in Essex - the RNLB tied up on the jetty. (In 2021 Harwich would appoint the first female coxswain.) JT (p43) would have it Essex has England's longest coastline, undulating for over 400 miles. However, I think she is mistaken. Cornwall holds that record, followed by Essex and then Devon. Need to check, buy a pedometer and book some holiday.

To reach Walton-on-the-Naze we needed to skirt around Hamford Water which we did via the Oakleys and Kirby le Soken. A busy promenade through Frinton and Holland-on-Sea collecting all the way. Havoc set the pace with his little tabard advertising what we were up to, by the time we caught up punters had their purses open. Wendy was suffering again with her feet and was holding back debilitating pain and tears. In Clacton, Pat and John Scott were our hosts, a puppy walking family, with dogs Jasper and Quade. Also, allotment holders with a few chickens and geese, we enjoyed Shepherd's Pie and a crumble which Pat was apologetic about – it really wasn't soggy. We couldn't have cared less before sleeping soundly in a caravan on their drive.

Another meeting with GD volunteers and their pooches at the lifeboat station meant we were late getting going to Jaywick. A collection of rather dilapidated prefabricated bungalows, potholed streets and alleys, some unadopted, and boarded up public loos. Wendy was desperate and fortunately a kindly local resident opened their house. It might have been Prue Leith! (An image of the town was actually used in 2018 as an attack ad by an American politician which received angry criticism from residents and a subsequent apology.) I was taken by street names – odonomy was my new science - Austin, Morris, Rover, Vauxhall Avenues; there was even a Bentley and Daimler, but they might have been a little misplaced.

We had put out some feelers to see if we could get help around the river Colne and the harbour master from Brightlingsea picked us up. Not sure where we were being taken, an RNLB rib appeared and we were boarded and kidnaped only to be taken at high speed to Mersea Island. People were competing for our company. I didn't know there was such a place, but it nicely fitted our outer coast and there was celebratory cake at the lifeboat station too. Peldon, Tollesbury, Heybridge Basin and the north bank wall of the river Blackwater took us to Maldon.

The muddy banks and marshy creeks of Essex resembled chocolate cake mix with the tide out. Maldon, although a long way from the open sea had a definite nautical feel. Scores of small boats crammed in like sardines, some tethered to moorings others lay helpless in sticky mud. We were a bit early for the springtime charity mud race across the

Blackwater but made a note to return. Larger Thames barges, we were told they could be crewed by just two, and Smacks showed off their red ochre sails and the ribs of one lay dinosaur like in one muddy graveyard. Cooks Yard revealed barge blocks for boats to be marooned upon at low water and crossing the Chelmer to the Hythe and Queens Head we met Essex hasher 'Vicky Vomit' and his wife 'Dr Dolittle' who were to be our hosts. Over lasagna and the world's best garlic bread we were to hear about Brent geese, teal and wigeon to look out for with an invite to return and visit inland Abberton Reservoir a haven for bird watchers. When he wasn't hashing it seemed he liked nothing better than to 'Dolittle' (taking his wife's hash name) and grab the binoculars.

One of Havoc's back scratching log rolls became more of a head over heels which surprised him and brought on a sneeze. The causeway to Northey Island was just visible and we saw the statue of Byrhtnoth, the slain Saxon warrior marking the site of the Battle of Maldon 991, one nil to the Vikings. At Bramble Farm near Steeple, we came upon a site where old petrol pumps came to die - the sort of place American Pickers would now love to visit.

The Dengie peninsula is very remote, one reason why a Magnox nuclear power station was built there which started producing electricity in 1962. It was now in the process of being decommissioned but plans were a foot for a new next generation station. We saw a sign advertising Bull's Eggs, which got me wondering what fallout from the reactor did to local bulls? That evening we would find out there was little to be wary of. At the Othona religious community, set up by Norman Motley in 1946, we were treated to pancakes as it was Shrove Tuesday and the Bulls, Ruth and David, turned out to be local hen keepers, less evil than Mr and Mrs Tweedy.

Ash Wednesday began with an 8am service at St Peter's Chapel with our foreheads crossed. The austere simplicity of the building, one of the oldest places of worship in England, dating from St Cedd's time, AD 654, made the experience very poignant. Stone from a former Roman fortress here was used in its construction. Then it was back to Othona for a Lent breakfast of porridge before heading off south on St Peters Way. Dengie is a large flat peninsula with muddy marshes, but I reflected the welcome received at Bradwell was neither flat nor muddy.

Fields here are used for growing animal feeds, and we passed three donkeys which fascinated Havoc. Plaster render decoration, pargeting, adorns many buildings. Some regular geometric patterning, elsewhere with more artistic flare. One exuberant hunting scene we saw was Constable 'esque'. To finally get to Burnham and the River Crouch we had to crawl on hands and knees beneath fallen bushes over the path. The image, complete with large ruck sacks would have been a good one for Constable or a pargeting craftsman to capture. Burnham is known as the 'Cowes of the East Coast' all masts and chinking halyards. If you don't like crowds avoid it the first week in September, regatta week. There was far more elbow room in mid-February.

Chapter 15 - Burnham-On-Crouch to Whitstable

Sun is in the sky, oh why oh why would I wanna be anywhere else?

"Trying to make a difference and facilitate somebody in their journey to whatever - but the eyes were not smiling."

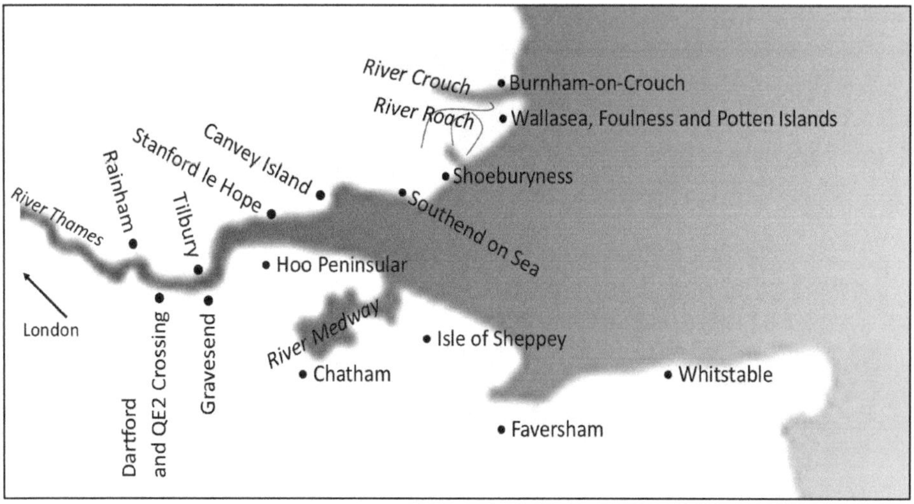

IT WAS THE 22ND FEBRUARY 2007. A glance at any map shows the land south of the river Crouch to be a mass of streams, river-lets and channels separating islands like Potton, Wallasea and Foulness. JM had headed west from here to ford the Crouch at Hullbridge. PH would in time, 14th November 2014, cross at Battlesbridge even further west. It seemed to me Spud playing the role of damsel in distress had it right, a boat. JM a purist, would have certainly poured scorn on the idea of hitching a boat ride; outrageous! PH in 2014 also had his rules. We were a little more laissez-faire and allowed short-hop ferries. Hashers might call me a 'SCB' (short cutting bastard) but frankly I didn't care. The rule of hashing that I held on to, was 'there are no rules!' JT would report she used a boat only travelling in the opposite direction to us in 2006. All we needed to do was find Spud's 'knight-turned-ferryman', instead we found a damsel with her own Arthur as a page.

We had met Lizzie the night before. She and her son, Arthur, gave us a lift across the Crouch. What is more, this young attendant brought with him bacon sandwiches, so Havoc was happy. Two bungs were missing from the small boat which meant four inches of water was soon sloshing about in the bottom of the vessel around our ankles and not far from where Havoc's testicles should have been, now he wasn't so happy. However, I sensed there was no real cause for concern, even if we sank, we could all manage a bit of doggy paddle.

Southend or 'Sowfend', as my dad would have mimicked, beckoned. We passed signs for the airport and Southend United Football Club and headed for the pier. Alas, entry was for assistance dogs only. Wendy tried profusely to claim Havoc was indeed such a dog.

"He is supporting Guide Dogs for the Blind". It all fell on deaf ears. The desk officer was having none of it.

"He doesn't look like a guide dog to me!" There was nothing wrong with his eyesight.

I also do not like taking no for an answer, a trait which has got me into trouble on many occasions before and since, but it was no use. Short of actually getting arrested, not a good advertisement for the RNLI wearing one of their tabards, flung over the side or swimming to the end of the world's longest pleasure pier, we weren't going to see the far end of it, not that day at least.

Wendy extremely offended, consoled herself by getting a haircut, perhaps as we had an important meeting coming up with a VIP. Havoc and I collected along the seafront and walked as far as Shoeburyness. I couldn't help noticing the pier seemed to have a bit of a kink in it. I wondered if that was where the tanker, the King's Abbey, had crashed into it in 1986 which I remembered. The mind wanders when you have time to stop. Did tanker drivers have to do a driving test? Were they subjected to regular eye tests? How could anyone run into something that was 1.33 miles long, extending into the Thames estuary almost like a fence saying to shipping tankers and jet skiers alike, 'give me a wide berth?'

Behind us some 1,300 miles of coastline from John o 'Groats. As we were leaving the last town on the east coast before our journey into London, I looked across the river to the views of the Kent coast which lay ahead. However far was it to go, what would be waiting for us?

We eventually met up with 'Windsock' and 'Tops', hashers from Essex HHH who were the people we were to put upon for the night. We had met them in 2005 at Norwich Nash Hash, covered in woad to meet the theme of Ancient Britons. We couldn't run with them as it was a Thursday and this kennel exercise on Tuesday nights. Nevertheless, it was not a blue night. Windsock, a tall electronics engineer in ordinary life but with a hairstyle and appearance that made him look like a bit of a rock star, or at least one of a band's road crew, and his teaching partner, Tops were excellent hosts.

Tops dropped us at the pier, and we hardly had time to say thank you and goodbye. Was she that desperate to get rid of us? Kids might do their homework on the bus going to school, teachers go in early to mark it if they have been entertaining the night before. We finished getting dressed on the kerbside and put on our boots. A muddy path took us past the remains of Hadleigh Castle at the bottom of the Benfleet Downs. Somewhere near here JM had ceremoniously buried his 32nd pair of socks. Right, I thought, Havoc get that nose of yours working and find them. Alas, he failed miserably. For some reason he was anosmic for John's old socks (who knows, perhaps the Corona Virus was floating around in the canine population a decade or more ago.)

We decided Canvey was one of the islands of our 'outer coast'. We briefly crossed onto the island at a flood barrier and asked four Environment Agency workers if there was any way off to the west. The answer was a firm 'no!' Below sea level many drowned in the 1953 floods, even with its many defences, the 40,000+ who live there must keep one eye on global warming, rising sea level threat and further flooding.

We did get to see a massive landfill site and, more pleasingly, one of two 17th century octagonal Dutch cottages preserved on the island. Havoc quite fancied it for a kennel, but it had already been spoken for by a museum curator and his pooch. These were probably a throwback to Dutch settlers who remained after helping build Canvey's sea defences. Let's face it, the Dutch should be good and holding back water, as evidenced by the story of the little Dutch boy who remained all night with his finger in a dyke! (Am I still allowed to say that?)

Near Pitsea ten coloured horses took an extreme interest in our little pup. 'Are you the dog walking around Britain?' 'Think you're a bit special, do you? 'Got any carrots little canine?'

I was just waiting for them to break into song like the crows mocking Dumbo in the film. Havoc had his tail between his legs, and we hurried off to Vange for a baguette from a sandwich van.

Wat Tyler, the leader of the Peasants' Revolt (1381) started his uprising at nearby Fobbing and a country park is named after him in remembrance, either that or they couldn't think of a better name. Due south the London gateway cranes, container ships, storage tanks. An industrial landscape leads to Tilbury and a short hop passenger ferry crossing point to Kent. Very handy for some round Britain walkers, but we wanted to go into London, if for no other reason than to try and collect for our charities and get more publicity.

We stayed overnight in Grays with two more hashers. An easy-going Irishman known as 'Digger' (Fergus) and his wife 'The Duchess' (Christina). I noted in my diary that after a day of almost entirely very muddy underfoot conditions, a relaxed welcome and a hot Jameson's were just what the doctor ordered. Havoc didn't know quite what to make of Christina's golly collection. 'First horses, now these, I'm going to Parliament to petition for Reform!'

Leaving Grays we walked the river wall path to the Queen Elizabeth II Bridge at Dartford. Digger took our bags on to Greenwich. Yippee, shoulders – you're on holiday! The cabled-stayed bridge above and the two tunnels below are the only fixed road crossing of the Thames east of Greater London. Overhead literally hundreds of vehicles would have passed in the time it took us to pass underneath and admire the 130-metre-high concrete monster, or masterpiece, depending on your judgement. Below, we could only imagine the congested tunnels although you could see the ventilation shafts. Havoc had his smell back and could sense the fumes causing his top lip to pucker.

The whole length of the river wall was decorated with graffiti. Four boys, perhaps part of a community youth scheme, were in full flow. There were holdalls full of spray paints, more colours than Dulux, plastic paint trays, aerosol tops and empty cans. Rembrandt eat your heart out. I'm not a big fan of graffiti or at least tagging, Banksie I can live with. However, my mind remembered scratching my initials in a desktop when I was at school – yes, even me, and I went on to be Head Boy. I also thought of the beautiful Hertfordshire village of Ashwell, near Baldock, and its Church of St Mary. Known for its graffiti from medieval times, much in Latin, with the help of a friendly vicar you can find and decode it all. 'Barbara (might have been) a vixen' who knows? All this just goes to show there is nothing new in immortalising oneself on property somewhere. (Ashwell although nowhere near the sea, is worth a visit. Look out for the exceptional embroideries too, and if fallen on hard times, help yourself from the village community food bank 2020.)

We crossed Rainham marshes, now a nature reserve, formerly a rifle range. It gave me quite a thrill because due to firing in 1978 JM couldn't cross these and had to use the A13 instead -15 love! After this it was Limehouse, south on the Isle of Dogs to cross under the Thames using the Greenwich foot tunnel. We did some collecting and escorted a group of pirates (birthday, stag or hen do, not sure?) around a few pubs. Havoc got terribly excited by a wristwatch reflection on the ceiling. I like calling these 'Tinkerbells', Wendy preferred the term 'Noddies'. We wouldn't even agree on that.

We found the tidy, well decorated house of our next hosts, where our bags had been deposited, the home of John and Margaret Foster. I am not quite sure how we came to know this couple, probably GD supporters but our networking attempts before leaving, had thrown up a good number of offers of shelter. What's more, we were ahead of schedule. Our appointment beckoned on the 28th February, Wednesday, and since it was only the Sunday before we all rested, never even leaving the house. I wrote some begging letters and made some phone calls to try and promote the walk, but we all needed to take in a deep breath. The next 48 hours were spent sightseeing and making more effort to publicise our walk. ITV (Loose Women), Elton John (I was once a Watford FC schoolboy), Bruce Fogle (the author and vet) – all without much success.

We were staying with 'Call Girl' (Nicki), yet another harriet, this time in Twickenham. Hugh, my next-door neighbour in Devon, who also had a house in London, brought us some kit changes and took back unwanted stuff. He stayed a good while, perhaps any chance to give himself a break from his wife.

We visited Tower Lifeboat Station at Waterloo Bridge and Havoc and I were photographed in the rib. While there, CCTV security cameras caught an attractive female, who must have been desperate for a pee, drop her knickers while she thought she was out of sight on the gangway. (It wasn't Paula Radcliffe.) Right at that moment Lily Allen came over the radio. I didn't want to be anywhere else, but I bet that lassie caught short wished the ground could swallow her up.

My ego had to be satisfied with a photo of myself at Queenhithe leaning on a sign saying, 'Pauls Walk EC4'. In the middle of The Strand a man stopped us and said,

"I saw you about two weeks ago in Aldeburgh when I was on holiday."

It was only 12 days earlier that we were there. It did bring it home to us what we were doing. We hashed with City HHH on the Tuesday evening in Stockwell, the on down at The Priory Arms and members were generous with their donations. I get by 'With a little help from my friends' (Joe Cocker 1969) was in my head, a little later March 2007 his 'Hymn for My Soul' album was released.

Our VIP appointment was at Portcullis House, Westminster. Wendy had written to and got an appointment to meet David Blunket, MP, former Home Secretary under Tony Blair. Photos and a bit of video with the Press Association as memories. I was taken by his genuine interest in what we were doing, his ease of conversation and a very sharp mind. His fifth guide dog Sadie was known as a bit of a character in the Commons. Asked what his guide dogs gave him, he replied 'independence, friendship, companionship and dignity'. Wendy was handed his personal cheque book and wrote out one for £50 (I might be wrong) which he signed. On leaving he remarked 'these two people should be sainted!' I think it might have been the unintentional omission of Havoc that caused him to have a go at Sadie. "*Wherever I hang my lead*" covers it nicely. Of course, the Right Honourable Gentleman might have been referring to Wendy and Havoc!

Time to get going again, and now heading east to Cutty Sark. Definitely two breasts exposed! 'Nanny' in very short dress, gives the ship her name 'Cutty Sark'. Next, The O2, Thames Barrier and exhausted to Erith. We were now in Kent. We got talking to a vicar at Christ Church, Victoria Road, Erith. We asked if he knew of anywhere we could pitch out tent. He was very concerned for our welfare and suggested not doing that in this area. Somewhat showing a lack of confidence in his parishioners, I thought. Instead, he offered us bed and supper (Erith not Gillingham Havoc – you might be getting ahead of yourself!)

Like many vicarages, the house was large and rambling, a lot to look after. Inside plain, tired decoration, carpets rather worn, outside gardens left to resemble a biblical wilderness. Two big English bull terriers welcomed Havoc. Not very cute, bit smelly, 'thick horny toenails' – you are right Havoc, especially if they stand on your foot, only in socks, just as you were asked to say Grace. John and Pamela (I think?) did tell us that if requested, Church of England clergy were obligated to offer shelter/sanctuary. This was very interesting. Could be useful on the remainder of the walk. I remembered Quasimodo crying 'sanctuary, sanctuary'. Not that I had ever read Victor Hugo, but I have seen Disney. I didn't really understand, and still don't, the meaning/extent of this 'obligation'. I wasn't a criminal and haven't been threatened with deportation (yet!) so could a couple of average Joes who just needed a bed to lay their heads for the night use this opportunity? I am certainly not suggesting you go up to the nearest church, knock on the door and exercise your right. However, it could be useful to remember that with just a little subtlety you might just be in luck.

It was Thursday, St David's Day, the 1st March. My earworm was giving me Hymns and Arias. I reminisced about seeing Max Boyce with Wendy. We both liked him, even if it was a bit of a 'press rewind' but we had had a nice, argument free evening in Ilfracombe (16th November 2002.) When would we be arriving there this time? With imagined leek and daffodil hanging from our rucksacks we were on tarmac. Hashers call 'petrol' to warn one another about cars and traffic but there seemed to be fewer of these about in these parts. (Virtually silent electric ones, cause quite a bit of anxiety.) We later found out that Tesco's and Morrisons had sold petrol in the area, presumably unwittingly, with a mixture that meant cars conked out. The equivalent of corporate sugar in the tank brings whole new meaning to the slogan 'Every little helps!'. (Apparently it is a bit of a fallacy that sugar kills cars any more than anything else stuffed in the tank – water is just as effective.)

We walked, rather than rolled, along towards Dartford to cross the river Darent. We weren't stoned but I knew Mick Jagger was born here and started an impression. Lips puckered, hand clapping, 'Jumping Jack Flash It's a Gas' with an air tambourine for accompaniment. A dead ringer for Len Goodman gave me a 'SEVEN'. I later found out there is a Goodman Dance Academy in town. Could he have been the real 'Mr Fleckle'? I don't think so but to get a seven from a Len lookalike had me 'strictly made up' all the way to Stone and Greenhithe. (RIP - Len).

It was here (not on Grain Havoc), that a stray brown and white collie cross followed us for about a mile. Very nervous, marks around his neck as if he had broken free from a tether. He very nearly got himself run over several times. He eventually disappeared. Havoc may have been sad not to have got a walking buddy, I was quietly quite pleased. Our £10 daily budget to feed two adults and a dog would hardly stretch to an addition and I certainly did not want to carry any extra cans of 'Kennomeat.'

Swanscombe was next – a name familiar to all anthropologists and historians interested in Neanderthals. Former gravel quarries line the way. In one of these in the 1930s skull fragments were discovered about 400,000 years old. Swanscombe Man was later found to be a woman. A bus passed us, and I felt like getting on but it was signed for Bluewater, a huge shopping complex, built in one of the old quarries. We marched on, first Northfleet and then Gravesend. The name is disputed probably not where graves ended after the Great Plague or the Black Death or something like that, but I liked this misnomer. Another explanation is a meaning of 'a place at the end of a grove' but I certainly hadn't seen any trees. SH recalls all manner of river traffic - tugs, a ferry, container ships. I cannot say I noted any in my diary, but fast forward a few years and I can vouch for people messing around on boats.

Spud didn't much like Gravesend! 'It was how it sounded', a series of rat-infested foreboding alleyways. SH said it was a lot better than it sounded. She mentions the statue of Pocahontas, (Gravesend is where the poor Princess died) but there were several landmarks. A statue of Queen Victoria, covered in pigeon poo, graffiti and wearing a traffic cone. One of Major General Gordon who was stationed in the town and contributed to social work by caring for homeless boys, providing education through a ragged school and donating large sums of his salary to charity. The clock tower from the 1880s was based on a design of the Elizabeth Tower, Westminster, better known for housing 'Big Ben', where we had not long come from.

The Port of London Authority station looked out on the river. I imagined historic activity, smugglers and the like, little did I know that I would have a lot more to do here in a few years' time. In fact, I would get to know Gravesend quite well.

The old 15th century pub The Three Daws (not doors) wasn't far away from the Tilbury ferry landing point where SH/RH would cross the Thames from Essex. I could only imagine the press gangs operating in places like this coercing locals into government service. I read the town used to have a football team, nicknamed the 'Shrimpers', what is more you could buy 'Shrimper' beer. Pilgrims would use the river crossing on route to Canterbury. The Cornish chough was associated with St Thomas Becket, murdered in the cathedral in 1170. It is thought choughs have been corrupted to jackdaws (daws) and hence the pub got its name. (It is also interesting to note Bovey Tracey, where we were from, has a church dedicated to St Thomas and it is suggested it was built by the de Tracy family as a penance, for it was William de Tracy who was one of the four knights responsible for the murder.)

Two boys who looked like they should have been at school stopped us and gave Wendy some pennies. A lady who had heard a radio interview of our trudge also opened her purse. By the oldest cast iron pier in the world (1834) we found the lifeboat station. First thoughts were 'this is a bit of a poor relation' - two portacabins, one on top of the other. Turns out it was only temporary. The station is one of the RNLI's newest, covering the river rather than estuarial waters or the sea, set up after the

Marchioness disaster (1989). We received a very nice welcome, homemade chicken soup (with some to takeaway), sandwiches and a jet boat ride to the Hoo Peninsula and Cliffe Fort. Old fortifications from all ages lined both sides of the river – torpedo launching points, gun emplacements. Across the water Elizabeth I saw the fleet sail to repel the Spanish in 1588.

"I may have the body of a weak and feeble woman, but I have the heart and stomach of a concrete elephant", and now go forth and 'unleash hell!' or words to that effect.

In a suburban semi at Chalk, a village just outside of Gravesend, a mother of four went about her daily chores. Loading the washing machine, making packed lunches, doing her own day at work, picking children up from school, dying her hair, and gazing out to the river, we sped straight past. Little did I know that Chalk and that mum would feature in a future chapter of my life.

The Hoo/Grain peninsula was like a handle on a joystick as we studied the map. We just had to get around it and back to Rochester. Cliff itself had many timber clad buildings, they hadn't learned the lesson of 1520 which saw a fire destroy much of it. Cement was produced near here for over a hundred years until 1970 and remnants of the industry remained but you couldn't see a lot of it in the buildings. Cooling Castle was more robust. We posed for photos in front of the outer gatehouse and waited for resident Jools Holland to appear - he never did, too busy 'Squeeze (d)' in and jamming on his keyboard. My stomach was less robust, as a result of Gravesend RNLI chicken soup, and a dose of Grain belly left me changing my underwear which had Wendy in fits. I read an explosive storage factory used to be on the coast supplying ordnance for the Great War. The explosion in my pants was just as concerning. A former giant BP refinery and the remains of the SS Richard Montgomery off Sheerness on Sheppey, 1,500 tonnes of UXBs just sitting there contrasted strongly with what we saw elsewhere. Fruit canes, orchards, rhubarb under straw blankets, bees busy on blossom, a warm day fortunately because I was just in shorts by now.

At Lower Upnor we came upon the figurehead from the Crimean ship, Arethusa. Wendy had stayed at the training centre set up there as a teenager and cadet. (The centre finally closed in 2019, and the lady of the ship, now having undergone a makeover, with one breast still exposed, remains.)

There was no pedestrian access to the Medway Tunnel, so we thumbed a lift in the back of a white van man's vehicle before walking to the dockyards at Chatham. We were to stay in Strood with cyclists we had met while on their holiday in Southwold.

Resuming the walk from Rochester we passed through Gillingham and onto Upchurch. It was a Saturday and we briefly stopped as the village was in festival mood with a marching band present. Lower Halstow had an interesting village sign.

I loved these as they shed light in the character and history of the place. In the background is the church of St Margaret of Antioch alongside a Thames Barge, the Edith May, which could be seen on the creek. (I would see her again in 2012 on the Thames forming part of the Queen's Diamond Jubilee Pageant.) It also shows a brick maker as Eastwoods once plied trade here. We stood by the bridge on the A249 leading to Sheppey before following the Swale, to bypass Sittingbourne and onto Faversham.

A winding creek leads to Kent's oldest market town, home of Shepherd Neame, Britain's oldest brewery. We bumped into a couple, Tony and Cherrie, who offered to put us up, partly secured by Havoc as they were dog lovers. It had been a long day, we were all exhausted and I think they felt sorry for our mutt. Bailey was their miniature Yorkie, think toy Chinese dragon, and Bisto (aah!) an elderly senior citizen who had suffered meningitis making him as wobbly as any Weeble.

Chapter 16 – Whitstable to Eastbourne

Round and round The Garden

"Keep calm and Harry on!"

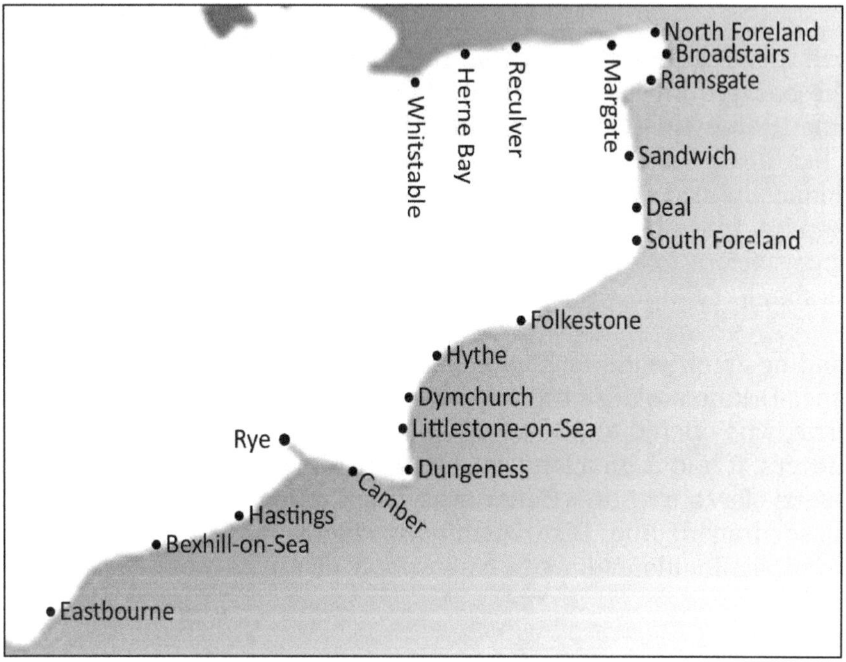

WE SAUNTERED PAST coloured beach huts at Seasalter and waltzed into Whitstable. JM didn't consider this the 'coast proper', that wasn't achieved until he reached Herne Bay. I think there were one or two locals who might have agreed to differ with him. Anywhere as synonymous with oysters and shellfish as this must be proper coast. Admittedly, the Tarmac plant made the place more Macadam metalled but the heaps of discarded shells along the shingle beach and attractive homes said seaside to me. One might once have been owned by Peter Cushing, actor in the Hammer Horror films, who once lived here, now the Wetherspoons is named after him. Out to sea some nine miles off the Maunsell Sea forts, built as WW2 defences, still looking like they had arrived out of War of the Worlds.

Other celebrity residents, Alan Davies alias Jonathan Creek and QI regular. We would need his wit to negotiate Squeeze Gut Alley especially if we ran into Harry Hill, another local, who might be heading in the opposite direction, 'fight!' #YBF. We needed Creek's detective skills to help three children we came across who had lost two golden retrievers and a black rabbit, careless! Who left the gate open Jonathan? With the livestock rounded up the phone rang. It was my son, who had been on Dartmoor Ten Tors training in heavy rain. That same day, 4th March 2007, Charlotte Shaw aged 14, from a Bideford college, would lose her life, drowned when river crossing. It was poignant because I had been involved for many years in preparing youngsters for moorland expeditions.

We met up with Dick and Joan Barton, parents of my old college mate Chris, who had put us up on the Moray Firth, 97 days ago. Made very comfortable in Chestfield, Dick had moved his own dog out so as not to disturb Havoc, with roast beef for supper. Our mutt had achieved celebrity status.

Swalescliffe Beach, if you can call it that, more tussocky, stony, wilderness really, was at least by the sea. Two signs 'Beware Soft Mud' and 'Naturism is not condoned', only the later had been changed to read 'not condomed'. All that was missing was a photo of a naked couple emerging from the dunes, one wearing wellies, the other something else in rubber.

Herne Bay wasn't a bay. I was dumbfounded. The pier on our 1947 map was in bits. A fire in 1970 and a storm in 1978 had left a near end and an abandoned far end, the filling had gone. Tea beckoned, and a sign outside the Divers Arms reminded us it was only 2675 miles to the North Pole. Time to nip there and get back before a dunking ginger nut had softened.

Reculver's twin towers at St Mary's church came into view. On reaching them, stonework from a Roman fort nearby and bored school pupils on a field trip. I imagined this was a popular venue for enthusiastic academics, less so with their apathetic charges. Six years on I would be proved right.

A long concrete path was the 'shade' after the 'light' of Whitstable through Birchington and Westgate to Margate. Here in the 1960s Mods and Rockers would clash, I could just remember it. There had been some friction in Faversham; I was hoping for a clash free passage around Britain's southeast corner as we turned right for Land's End. The three Cs, essential in a relationship; communication, compromise and commitment - I knew the theory.

I was quite looking forward to going back to Margate. It had been a family holiday destination decades earlier when we would bundle into a chrome embellished Austin A30, run the gauntlet of the London South Circular and head across north Kent for a week by the seaside with buckets and spades. (The M25 was still a glint in the eye of anyone in the Department of Transport, at best 'dotted aspiration' in an AA atlas.) I reminisced about staying in a dodgy B&B, sharing a bed with my brother and while both tugging at a threadbare cover sheet, managed to clean tear it down the middle to the embarrassment of my mother having to explain it to the landlady. It had been on the bed since Margate first became a tourist destination, back in the 18th century, at least that was our reasoning.

Once folk had flocked to this horn on the pommel topping Kent's saddle, for sand, sunshine and 99s for a week. Now it seemed they at best might visit for a day and if lucky, escape by elevenses. It really was disappointing and depressing, the decline endemic and attempts to revitalise futile. The monster tower block of Arlington House built in 1964 cast an ugly 58 metre shadow literally and metaphorically over the sea front.

Margate boasted many firsts. A namesake Thomas Barber, a carpenter, had set up the first commercial sea bathing in 1736. Half a century later the Royal Sea Bathing Infirmary was treating poor souls suffering from scrofula. About the same time the first donkey rides were offered, and bathing machines became very popular just after the turn of the century (1805). Contrast these firsts with more recent events - the pier, shown on our map, had gone in a 1978 storm. Dreamland amusements had closed in 2006, the old Winter Gardens were all boarded up and it seemed the mayor hardly needed his marked parking space.

We popped into a Wetherspoons intriguingly named the Mechanical Elephant. It turned out an attraction once graced the prom. A very early one from 1881 and in 1949/50 Frank Stuart developed a tusker offering children's rides, powered by an 8HP Ford engine. I read up about the town lifeboat and the heroics of coxswain Edward D Parker who rescued 600 men from Dunkirk in May 1940 and summoned my own courage to ask the current Operations Manager if we might sleep overnight in the boat shed. We got a refusal but were rescued by the yacht club who found us a space to throw down sleeping bags and a somewhat 'embarrassed' RNLI crew member turned up with two plates of spaghetti bolognaise by way of restitution.

Still with memories of childhood holidays lingering we continued to Cliftonville, Foreness Point and Kingsgate. An old folly, Neptune Towers resembled an elephant's foot, and I wondered if that was all that remained of Margate's mechanical pachyderm. Across the bay a bigger more impressive Kingsgate Castle, now it seemed private homes, all perched above chalk cliffs with a sea arch and Botany Bay to lure visiting Australians. (Little did I know I would return in September 2018 to attend a 90th birthday party for a matriarch, Botany Bay Hotel, fearing for my life as the camper van I was in might take off in high winds. It just stayed grounded, which was more than could be said for a couple of portaloos which were auditioning for bit parts in The Wizard of Oz).

I think I counted seven small bays in Broadstairs, contrasting with its neighbour around the corner because it had a look and feel of a place people would stay well beyond coffee at eleven. Fairy lights, gift shops, flower beds, a flint fronted little cinema; the jewel in Thanet's crown was shining bright. For about 20 years Charles Dickens visited, staying it would seem according to signs, in every house in town. Bleak House, even marked on our 1945 map, was where David Copperfield rose from the page.

Ramsgate is generally regarded as a bit rough. The mainstays of the economy were fishing and tourism - both it seemed were in decline. The harbour was massive with berths for 700 and in 2005, 12,000 visiting boats, so we were told, but things seemed quiet which was exactly what it was like at the lifeboat station which we eventually found for a brew. The hoverport which I remembered as a kid with its heyday in the 1970s was long gone, we hardly saw a soul, just gulls and pigeons squatting on roofs, nets to deter them in places and the occasional plastic owl which they took little notice of. It needed a boost but had to wait till 2017 when Historic England would make it a HAZ (Heritage Action Zone) in order to stimulate the economy. You would have to ask the birds to find out if it worked. Highlights were the purple petals of dog violets and Hugin, a Viking longship at Pegwell Bay, a gift from Denmark commemorating Hengist and Horsa (449AD) floating on a sea of brilliant yellow daffs. Van Gogh liked the place in 1876 when he visited, had those blooms been there then, who knows, perhaps sunflowers wouldn't have got such a look in? We also looked out for Lizard Orchids around Sandwich Bay. It is an IPA (Important Plant Area) with the largest population of Himantoglossum hircinum in the country - but we were about three months early and I couldn't cope with any more acronyms.

When Thanet was an island, Sandwich dipped its feet in the sea more than it does today. We still needed to cross the river Stour and feeling peckish our route took us into the Kent town. One of the original Cinque Ports (old French, meaning 'five harbours', a confederation for trade and defensive purposes, with the term in use by the early 1100s). The continental connection prompted my choice of lunch, cheese and mange tout between two bits of bread. Never tried this combination. The 'eat all' pea goes well with a bit of cheddar in a sarnie. John Montagu the fourth Earl of Sandwich invented the sandwich, allegedly, around the mid-1700s but I am not sure he tried this foody marriage and for that matter Del Boy and Rodney definitely didn't. If it ever appears in a Nigel Slater cookbook I will sue for plagiarism! Back to the Flats we wandered over golf courses, Prince's and Royal St George's, host to the Open, which would return in 2011 and 2021. I also ventured into the reception of Pfizer, keen to secure a giant pharmaceutical sponsor but left with my tail between my legs. They cut things in Kent considerably thereafter.

Deal seemed quaint, its streets crisscrossing like a grid iron, in the absence of any urban planning. Pepys called it 'pitiful', Cobbett 'villainous' to show that the fortunes of places can change. By 2020 Kent Life said it was the town everyone wanted to move to. Sitting on the pier we reflected on where we were in 1989 when the IRA bombed the Royal Marine School of Music in the town. In the pub Havoc met a young cream Staffy wearing a pink jacket with a fur collar about a hundred times longer than its smooth coat. It was instant attraction and he pined for her all evening. That night, our pillow, on the floor in St. Georges church, courtesy of vicar, Chris Spencer. It also scored quite well on the BHS accommodation guide gaining 3 stars! (Bubbles, Havoc and Soapy - our hash names.)

Next morning, we banked a further £60 and I attempted to count the inner and outer bastions on Henry VIII's castle making it look like a Camellia bloom. No sooner had I imagined dodging fire from its many cannons, and we were at Walmer. Another Tudor castle, more artillery pieces and allegedly the landing spot of Julius Caesar, 55BC. (Some now say it was more likely to be back at Pegwell Bay.)

By St Margaret's Bay we were on white cliffs and could see France across the channel. It soon disappeared however as an offshore wind blew black clouds out to sea. South Foreland lighthouse greeted us along with heavy showers which made the coast path drab and Dover ferries emerged through the gloom. The medieval castle looked down on us from its vantage point, the cliffs more mixed grain than premium white in the cloud and bluebirds long gone at least until tomorrow. In their place, a few gulls, one of which pooed on my sleeve. The noisy constant, the drone of lorries arriving and departing.

By Samphire Hoe we could look down on the warehouses and ventilation fans of the Channel Tunnel. The ground disturbance accredited for aiding the rare Early Spider orchid (Ophrys Sphegodes). We were told to look out for green/yellow petals with dark red lips, but it was still only 7th March. The sexually deceptive flowers might appear in March and April, but it was too early for any Itsy Bitsies to be 'sirened'.

A muddy steep climb up Abbots Cliff led us to the site of the Battle of Britain memorial where a stone figure of a young, seated pilot poignantly centres a space where the names of nearly 3000 air crew are displayed who took part in the 1940 battle.

Where the southern edge of the North Downs escarpment meets the sea lies Folkestone. The white cliffs of Dover have become green by here. On a personal level we reached the Leas Lift funicular railway.

One of my many faults it would seem is that I am incapable of reading minds. A scan of "*Wherever I Hang My Lead*" suggests I marched right by when others fancied a ride. Perhaps someone wanted to get Grandpa a souvenir ticket for his collection? I certainly had no conscious desire to give it a miss.

Wendy would find us digs with Alan and Annette Mills in their spare room and conversations occurred where I suggested we retrace steps in order to see if the Leas Lift was open the next day and if dogs were permitted. That was rejected but the Folkestone fracas serves to highlight the importance of communication - the write up, evidence I was fast becoming a whipping boy. Sorry Havoc, you should have barked louder! (The Lift painted brown and cream, hardly 'bright', the only thing missing was the masking tape on the lite windows and it would have been straight out of wartime Britain. It went on to have its own problems. Closed in 2009, funds were raised for a refurbishment, closed again 2017 and at the time of writing, 2022, listed as 'Permanently Closed'.)

As we left Folkestone I was filled with a sense that the town needed something to trigger regeneration. We were again just too early. 2008 would see the first Triennial, a three-year cycle of cultural festivals which would see quirky new works of public art appear around the town. 'Baby Things' (Tracey Emin) would have intrigued visitors looking to prise up teddy or a shoe from the environs, placed there in bronze to call attention to the town's place as having the highest level of teenage pregnancy in the country.

Day 116 was a lovely sunny day as we headed for Hythe. I wanted to see the rare ossuary at St Leonard's church, some 2,000 skulls and 8,000 thigh bones in the chancel but everything was locked up. (Seemingly in those days people had four legs!) Dogs were being walked, babies perambulated, and we did well collecting. Sidestepping the army ranges and repair work to the sea wall we often found ourselves on the A259. Anyone bagging Martellos was in the right place, number 24 in Dymchurch is regarded as one of the best surviving examples.

We stepped into a pub hoping to get a cup of tea and ran into a gentlemen's drinking group, one of whom was Fred Housego, cabby and 1980 Mastermind Champion. I recognised him in an instant and joked was he available to take a fare to Rye. Although he was still driving in 2007, he said he was on an afternoon off and well over the limit by 3pm. We had a good natter, 'I've started so I'll finish' and by the time I got around to trying the tea, it was cold. Fred must be in his late 70s now. We banked the day's takings, £140, and continued to Littlestone where Charlie Davies, lifeboat operations manager found space for us beside the Gore-Tex dry suits.

Next morning started well with bacon rolls. Thanks Charlie! We walked on east facing sands for an hour to Dungeness. My head was full of confused lyrics to the sailor's song Spanish Ladies; 'farewell and adieu' (told you I was confused, we were only arriving) pom, pom, pom, 'thirty-five leagues' pom, pom, 'Fairlight and Dungeness' pom, pom, Steve Wright would have been proud of me.

The first very obvious sight was the shingle beneath our feet. Then the awareness of Spud's semaphore waving pylons carrying electricity from the power stations. Lighthouses old and new, wooden dwellings of fishermen and reclusive bohemian arty types nestled alongside old railway carriage homes. I noted the Britannia pub, the narrow-gauge light railway, but the stark almost desolate landscape is most memorable. Not barren or a desert, but a microclimate where many species thrive, particularly plants, if you have the time find them.

The Kent coast was behind us. We had rounded it and the garden of England. It had taken us more than one or two steps, but we were quite tickled with our achievement. We should have had a picnic, bought ourselves a stuffed toy and called it Theodore, only Havoc would have ripped its eyes out.

To the west firing ranges, littered with old, armoured cars and tanks, targets on another day but with no flags flying we could kick stones all the way to Jury's Gap and on to Camber. I hadn't been there since I was a small child. Then, on a week's holiday, probably at the holiday camp, I would spend the entire week on the beach, bright sunshine, plastic tools, refusing to remove a cardigan. I have rusty memories of anxiety of turning black skinned ('negro') if I uncovered. Not intended as a racist term or in any way offensive, just a naïve infant misunderstanding sundrenched in heliophobia. 2007 and a resting spot for a rusting Pontin's tram car, green and yellow, with no sign of any powered element, we were relying on worn boots.

Now in East Sussex and the Rother led us to Rye. Cobbled streets, half-timbered houses now two miles from the sea. JMW Turner painted here a lot. A charming tourist destination with hotels, guest houses and restaurants.

We headed for the lifeboat shed for pot noddle. On a November morning in 1928, 17 crew members lost their lives, practically the whole male fishing population of the village. Launched to rescue the 'Alice', the 'Mary Stanford' capsized in a gale. News that the crew of the 'Alice' had been rescued never reached the lifeboat which would ironically perish with father and two sons, two sets of three brothers, the entire open boat crew, oldest 47 the youngest just 17. R.I.P. It is impossible to imagine the level of grief felt by loved ones.

That evening on the TV - EastEnders! And the Britannia pub from Dungeness, used as a set for a special edition (9th March 2007).

Walking to Winchelsea I thought I was stepping in the footsteps of Spike Milligan who used to live in the area. He might have called me a 'little groveling bastard' like he did a future King, but he still got a Knighthood! Furthermore, he may well have demanded 7/6 for preparing the ground as well. The comedian, writer, Goon, one of my dad's favourites, is buried at St Thomas's church, the grave marked by a modest Celtic cross. The epitaph is partly in Gaelic reading 'I told you I was ill', but the diocese refused the wording in English. Of fellow Goon, Harry Secombe, Spike apparently joked he was glad Secombe died before him, he didn't want him singing at his funeral.

In the year of our visit, I read Ofsted reported Milligan's children's poem, Ning Nang Nong was among the ten most taught poems in UK primary schools. Even in death he taught more than I ever did in a career.

Cliff End and Fairlight and the best examples so far of a shrinking island. A bungalow with its foundations undermined and red doored garage at

45 degrees, still largely intact but five metres below amidst rubble and debris, tobogganing to the sea. It might still have had a car in it so sudden it seemed was the land slip.

We arrived in Hastings, Saturday 10th March, a day before the half marathon. All Saints Street, an original thoroughfare in the Old Town was a delight and we passed the yellow Piece of Cheese triangular cottage, once a summer residence of Michael Mouse, according to the blue circular sign. The town was lively, punters seemed well sloshed, and we collected with good success. Stopped by a couple, one half Frank Howard, once of Hennock, Devon who had heard of our endeavours on Kent radio opened his wallet. It felt good that someone from very near our home was alerted and efforts to publicise the walk were reaching people.

The Saxon Shore Way, what we had found of it, was behind us - 163 miles back to Gravesend. East and West Cliff Lifts looked down on black long, tall sally fishing huts and I suggested we take one or the other to make up for Folkestone but was rebuffed. Actor, Harry H Corbett (Steptoe and Son) lived nearby and died in Hastings in 1982. He stared in a film, The Bargee, made at my childhood home in the 1960s.

Sunday (11th) was going to be a day to take in the Hastings Half Marathon, (won by Philemon Gitia Baaru in 1:03:22) do more fundraising, meet up with locals Richard and Shally Hunt (*the sea on our left*) and later end up as far as Bexhill. It was good to see the Hunts, as past participants they knew the score and were very encouraging. We were joined by a small army of children and dogs, together with Steven and Avril, who were to be our hosts in Bexhill. There, Havoc stuck his head through the molded balusters on the art deco De La Warr Pavilion and looked out to sea, a bit put out by curly coat retrievers and German shepherds who had Crufts credentials. Later he would have his birthday cake, single candle and a few other treats. (Whichever day was his birthday, 10th or 11th, that was what happened, the devil is in the detail, and if it is lacking perhaps that draws into question other comments!) We would bank £400 as a result of fundraising efforts.

Chapter 17 – Eastbourne to Lymington

Will you still need me, will you still feed me

"Where others fear to go, that's where you will find us."

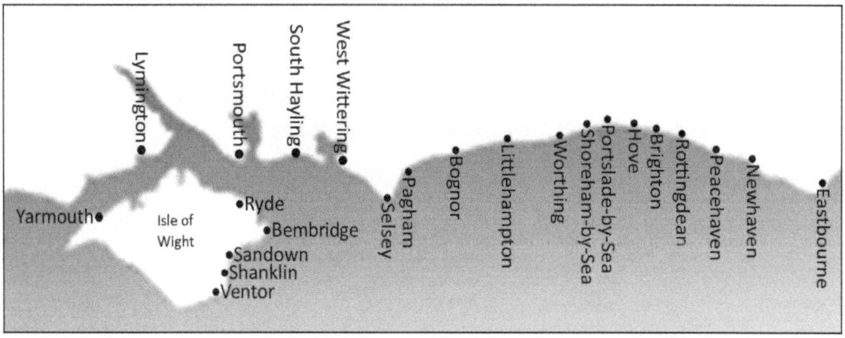

TWO CHARITY DONATIONS memorably punctuated our walk to Eastbourne, not in terms of their size, but the givers. One a traffic warden, not often you get money from one, more usually a ticket. Even less often you have cause to thank one. The second from a guy fixing his TV aerial who wanted someone to foot his ladder. Whatever it took.

Somewhere along this stretch, perhaps at Pevensey, William the Conqueror came ashore on 28th September 1066. For me it was a must to close my eyes and imagine a force of some 8,000, many mounted knights striding up the beach. Much of the area to the east of Eastbourne was known as the 'Crumbles', now changed considerably with the development of apartments and a new marina. (The rifle range shown on our map was consigned to history.) In the 1920s two unconnected deaths took place here, known as the Crumbles murders. Three perpetrators were subsequently hanged at Wandsworth prison.

The lifeboat is stationed at Sovereign Harbour. Eastbourne's first was provided by John 'Mad Jack' Fuller in 1822. Inspired by the loss of the 'Thames', the MP, philanthropist, slave owner and folly builder, endowed Eastbourne with a rescue boat and in 2007 the Mersey class boat was intriguingly named, the 'Royal Thames'. (Replaced 2012 by the Tamar 'Diamond Jubilee'.) Squire 'Honest John' Fuller was buried in the hamlet of Brightling, Sussex 1834 - in a pyramid!

Eastbourne wasn't all retirement and tennis. It was busy with coaches, and it seemed had become the rollerblading capital of the world. Knee and elbow protection whizzed past on inline wheels and we had to be watchful for miniature traffic cones or were they giant thimbles? The very attractive pier was getting a coat of paint. (Seven years later it would be badly damaged in a fire.) A group of four well-wishers met us with at least as many dogs. There were photos for the local paper, radio interviews. Coffee in a hotel lounge, while under the table a small army of canines dozed peacefully. Derick in yellow oilskins, a massive supporter of the RNLI, gave us a very sizeable donation (£100) and walked with us as we climbed Beachy Head (162m), the highest chalk sea cliff in Britain. This is now patrolled by clergy looking out for potential suicide jumpers and Samaritan's phone numbers were prominent.

The current red and white striped lighthouse sits at the base of the cliff built in 1902. The first one at Eastbourne appeared in 1828, greatly assisted by 'Mad Jack' Fuller's patronage. Belle Tout replaced it, at the top of the cliff but sea mists meant it was often obscured, hence a location nearer the water. Belle Tout had to be moved away from the cliff edge in 1999 as it was feared it would end up in bits on the rocks below. It was used in many film and TV productions including the 1986 BBC creation, The Life and Loves of a She Devil. Wendy posed for a photo, and I joked did she want to audition. It didn't go down too well.

The grassy downs are well trodden and nibbled by sheep and rabbits. Birling Gap and onto Seven Sisters, the south coast's roller coaster. At Cuckmere Haven the tide was just about wade-able. I carried bags, Havoc and Wendy in that order to avoid a detour via Exceat Bridge. Past the coast guard cottages and we turned to look back, chimneys in the foreground, white dentures behind, Des Lynam would pick this as his favourite view in Britain.

A row of brightly coloured 'plastic' beach huts and a recently renovated Martello tower, complete with top mounted cannon (no 74), led us on to Newhaven and the river Ouse. On its west bank, dwarfed by cross channel ferries, we found repose at the lifeboat station. Our host was someone who we had met before. A coxswain now returned in his own back yard, previously met when he was providing relief at Harwich (16th February 2007). I read through some RNLI literature - 2006 was the charity's busiest year ever - 8,377 call outs rescuing 8,015 people.

We took in Palmerston's Fort as we headed through Peacehaven to Rottingdean. A black wooden windmill on Beacon Hill keeps watch. The village had a reputation as a smuggling hot spot in the 18th century. Wool was smuggled out, tea and tobacco among other things in. It is rumoured a certain vicar, Dr Thomas Hooker, also did some watching, acting as a lookout. He also founded schools in the village. Today Roedean Girls School collects fees. Rottingdean may sit in a 'dry' valley, but a natural pond and a green lie at the centre, The Elms, a property which Rudyard Kipling rented for five years is nearby where he wrote his poem, Sussex. Just to keep Havoc happy, dogs were not allowed in the garden. My lasting memory of the village is one of pomposity, rather overfull of smartly dressed, wealthy ladies too posh to smile, at least to three somewhat disheveled foot sloggers who no doubt needed a shower and some 'bare necessities'.

We took the Undercliff Walk to Brighton. Not far away the modernist architecture of St Dunstan's built in the 1930s for 'blind' care (now Blind Veterans UK) at Ovingdean. Each discovery like this connected to our story, working as we had done with visually impaired people, currently raising funds for Guide Dogs. (The centre is scheduled to close in 2024.) For now, it reminded me of an explanation given to me as child. Watching two dogs having coitus I asked what they were doing. I was told the one in front had gone blind and the one behind was pushing them to St Dunstan's to be looked after.

An angular skyline came into view. London-by-the-Sea, trendy, cosmopolitan, diverse, the 'hippest' city in Britain? Certainly, on the south coast. In 2001, 2.6% of those surveyed stated their religion was 'Jedi Knight'. Welcome to Brighton. All of London had taken a midweek day trip to the seaside - the place was humming. Fine weather, we were in shorts, Cliff Beach was Britain's first 'naturist beach' but we didn't feel like getting all our kit off. We moved through swiftly forfeiting fund raising opportunities, Wendy was not in the mood. Hove was clearly more upmarket, the regency sea front buildings, tranquil.

A southwest coast path acquaintance, Jean Blemming was our host at Portslade and over pizza and wine I asked her what she got from walking, a question we had been asked a million times. Visual stimulation from a dramatic coast, self-gratification from achievement and being able to see and measure that on a map, came the reply – and I was expecting the same answer as I had given a million times, blisters!

Shoreham harbour proved to be another place where we got hopelessly lost. Who was it who said just 'keep the sea on the left'? The lifeboat house was due to be knocked down and replaced but the boat, the Hermione Lady Colwyn, looked shiny and polished. (New boathouse opened 2011, Tamar class lifeboat in 2010, Enid Collett.) At Lancing an equally polished glass hearse, with a pair of magnificent jet-black horses pulling the carriage. Wendy asked a spectator if it was for a celebrity, the on-looker's reply was that it was for a 'gypsy'.

Worthing pier rivalled Eastbourne for gold and silver medals in our league of top south coast piers, Brighton had already been confined to bronze place. At Ferring we recalled the car breaking down years before and our relay recovery ride back to Bovey Tracey via Salisbury. We met another keen long-distance walker, Andy, who had given us the coordinates for that mausoleum stopover in Ulbster, Scotland, and he was just as keen to tell us how to cross the Erme down in south Devon. I rather switched off since how could anyone tell us about our own patch - told you I was arrogant! A GD puppy walker, Yvonne Woodcock, showed off Scramble, a black lab, and Wendy was all ears and gushing, having walked in her shoes. Havoc was more interested in a passerby throwing away an apple core.

On the outskirts of Littlehampton a BMW convertible pulled up alongside us having seen my flag. Just as we were speaking a golf ball came over the hedge and hit her car. Moments later a second ball shot across the road, this one bouncing off the collapsed car roof. I was beginning to think this encounter might end up with a claim against me. With that, two embarrassed 'golfers' emerged, and it turned out they knew the car driver, small world. In total the out of bounds experience earned me £16 in donations, no 'handicaps', and I just wished 'fore' golfers had come along.

We walked to the Spotted Cow at Littlehampton and were picked up by Steve Rickman. I had networked him prior to walk when he ventured into Devon to fit a kitchen. On site over a workman's shared sandwich, I had tapped him up, an address for a swig from a flask, and this was time for him to pay up. Inland at Barnham, we met his family, Isobel and young children, Joseph and Tara. They would be teenagers by now and breaking hearts, causing Steve parental nightmares - I wonder if he is still fitting 'excellent' kitchens?

Back at the Spotted Cow it was Red Nose Day and I sensed donations to us would be lean and slow running. Past a quaint clock tower and on to cross a footbridge over the Arun. A sign read a boat built here at the local yard was the first to take sheep to the Falklands. What a load of 'Trossach'. (That was the name of the ship, built in Harvey's yard, today half a million of the fleecy buggers share grass with the penguins, 153 for every Falkland human inhabitant.)

Butlins had got its best red coat on and looked classy, you could catch Toyah Wilcox, if you hung around a bit. In shorts, seats in a flint wall gave some protection, apart for the legs, from a wind coming straight off the sea as we took a bag break. Bognor it seemed was home to the top mobility scooter salesman in the world. The riders were holding their own grand prix, racing along pavements, taking no prisoners, pedestrians leapt into bushes for cover, small children and dogs terrorised by the antics. Little exercise seems to make large bodies even larger, crushing the power batteries below.

This was the southern end of Bill Bryson's *Little Dribbling* 'Bryson Line' dividing the country in half on its way to Cape Wrath. He waxes lyrical about discovering Branston pickle and having a hair cut in Oxford from a vet (Yvette) as he describes the peculiarities of a small isle. We were discovering our own.

At Aldwick a hotelier offered us a bed for the night, but we declined settling for tea, wanting to get a bit further by nightfall. A local journalist gave us a map, convinced we were going to get lost, our old one still in rods and chains.

From Pagham beach it appeared the harbour was about 50 metres wide at the mouth. The tide seemed out and onlookers watched astonished and alarmed as I took my boots off to wade and carry everybody and everything across. From the other side we could look back to Arundel Castle and a sweep of coastline where we had come from. Selsey East Beach had railway carriages converted to bungalows and we found the lifeboat station at the end of a jetty, home for the night and 'Wayfayrer' chicken casserole for tea. (Boathouse demolished 2016, the end of slipway launches.)

I have returned to Selsey several times since. Its exposed position linked only by the B2145 to Chichester makes it quiet and still, somehow timeless and unchanging. Sit at the Bill long enough and it is easy to imagine smugglers hanging in chains from a gibbet, 1749, to deter others from wrongdoing. The heritage trail Blue Plaque is worth finding as is The Lifeboat pub after a swim or cycle to explore Chichester Harbour and Bosham. You might also find the Blue Plaque dedicated to Eric Coates who was inspired by the view across to Bognor to compose 'By the Sleepy Lagoon' (1930) which became the BBC signature tune for 'Desert Island Discs'. Sit on the bench and play the tune on your iPhone.

It was mid-March in 2007, St Patrick's Day as we headed for Bracklesham. A leprechaun was helping me select from my ear worm library to take to Kirsty Young. The best he and I could find was 'Molly Malone'. I settled for a Gang Show favourite in the end, 'Riding along on the crest of a wave'. The sun was in the sky, eyes on the distant horizon, heading for Hayling Island. 'We'll do the hailing', but there was little joy as we went, domestic friction in the air. We had decided to avoid the inner parts of Chichester Harbour and stick to our 'outer coast'. That would see us to Portsmouth, onto the Isle of Wight where we had connections, and off to Lymington, by-passing Southampton.

I had secured us a rib ride from East Head beyond the Witterings to Black Point where we walked the south coast of Hayling. Amusements and a little railway with its own 'fat controller', itself amusing, with windsurfers on the ocean and kitesurfers above it. It was a colourful scene resembling hornets and dragonflies skirmishing. A free ferry ride took us from a landing stage at the west end to Southsea.

The 'Yomper' marine statue at Eastney should have been inspiring, our packs were bigger than his, but instead, more acrimony and an atmosphere as deflated as the skirt of the hovercraft, a potential ride to Ryde. The air was blue, I really have no idea or recall why, but things were 'unbearable' and if it was my 'aggressive behaviour' I offer my apology here. We had a complimentary ticket, and I was determined to use it, if Wendy wanted to quit here, she held the button. As the air bags filled to speed off over choppy Solent waves she hopped on, and our three party adventure was on again to see Parkhurst, Tennyson, Queen Victoria and Jack Douglas!

Hosts on the IOW were members of the island hash. P-rick and Bumps and their dog Boykie took us to the Sunday run. Not perhaps a restful day, but all three of us enjoyed running with other packs, meeting new people, exploring new venues, seeing the good and bad habits of other groups. A forest venue near the prison and Havoc couldn't decide whether he liked Boykie or not, he certainly wasn't about to step aside for our mutt.

We met well-wishers at Wetherspoons in Ryde; Tina, Sally and Kim and Havoc scrounged a bacon rind before seeing painted foot high homemade Dad's Army figures at the Battery Hotel. Little gems like this amused the mind and cut through drudgery for a few miles but the walk to Ventnor was one of the most varied we had experienced. A bright day, with a cold wind, a few wintery showers in the afternoon. Havoc had a swagger, a cockiness that said 'I've walked from Scotland' until he put his foot etween two slats on Bembridge Lifeboat jetty and looked pathetic. Old mill ponds, an obelisk at Culver, Zoo at Yaverland, coaches at Sandown, the chine (ravine) at Shanklin, expensive houses, waves breaking over

sea walls, hail, snow, lightening, the sky an artist's box of colours. We were picked up and taxied back to Bembridge for a night with hashers Bilbo and Follyfoot where an onlooker gave us two tins of 'Chum' and chews, Havoc was smiling again.

Bilbo walked with us for the day, and we left Ventnor soon swallowed up by bushes, woods and the undercliff of Binnel Bay. The lighthouse at St Catherine's Point became visible but in a buffeting wind it seemed ages before we looked down upon it from the cliffs at Niton. More chines as we headed for Freshwater, the amusements at Blackgang, giant pirates and a totem pole seemed strange after the openness of the point. By the time we reached Afton along sections on soft sand, we were all shattered. It had been the first time someone had walked with us all day, and Bilbo had bigger feet than normal.

The grass downs at Freshwater are manicured by rabbits and the Tennyson monument stands tall. From the Needles views to Bournemouth and Purbeck and across the Solent to Gosport. Sheer white cliffs and stacks, a flat capped lighthouse and the remains of former rocket testing gear. Coloured sands at Alum and we stumbled on another little gem; a garden devoted to raising funds for the Freshwater Bay private lifeboat. Amongst Bart Simpson and Buzz Lightyear, a myriad of signs, one read:

"If only the good die young, what does that say about senior citizens?".

Yarmouth provided fond memories of sail training trips with the London Sailing Project. Years later we might rent a cottage if it's not too dear, but right now we took the ferry to Lymington.

Chapter 18 – Lymington to Durdle Door

All you wanna do is criticize

"A hero is an ordinary individual who finds strength to persevere and endure in spite of overwhelming obstacles."

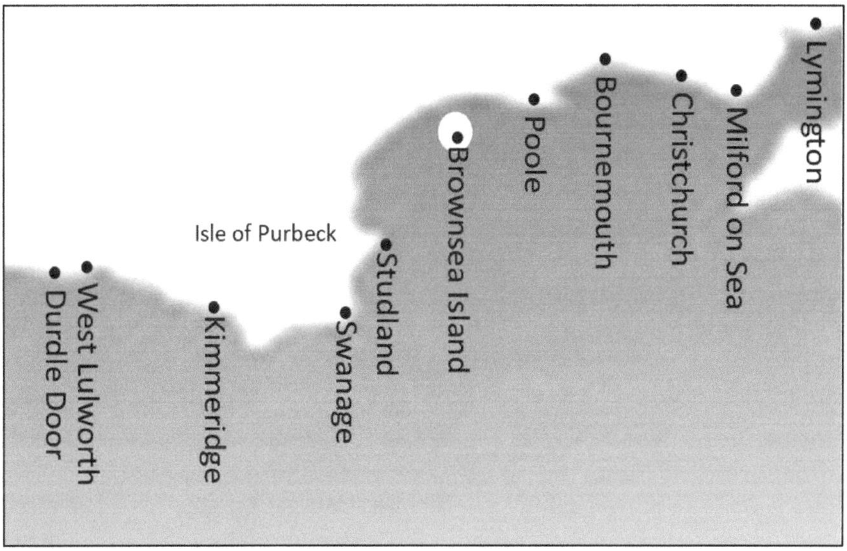

BACK IN BRIXHAM, Broken Man, a hasher, had secured us an open letter from the commodore of the sailing club there, supporting our venture and flashing this at other sailing clubs en route earned us the possibility of overnight accommodation. Hence the changing room floor at Lymington sailing club was our bed for the night but prior to that we sat at the back of a talk entitled the New Forest in the Second World War. We might have been asleep a bit earlier than we expected.

Lymington to Christchurch is about 12 miles, a good bit more if you go via Pennington Marshes, Keyhaven, Milford, Barton and Mudeford. We had tea with the ironing lady at a launderette, after which I just had to call in at a Conservative Party office to view an uncompromising portrait of a former leader, our second 'iron lady' of the day. Chips at Highcliffe and we were offered deck chairs and sit down at one of Mudeford's many beach huts. It was tempting just to stay put, feet up, retire, but I had to find a shop for Havoc's supper and got the best deal of the walk, a reduced tin of meaty chunks for 25p.

From Christchurch we were joined by Barbara and her retired GD, Jeff. That made for polite slow going around Hengistbury Head but were able to pick up speed to Boscombe and Paul, a GD marathon runner and his partner Nicky, injected a bit of pace through Bournemouth. Havoc was teased senseless by squirrels in the park, lead throttled and on back legs, adrenalin made his heart beat out of his chest.

We headed past Branksome and Canford Cliffs turning right into Poole Harbour. A huge man stopped to donate at Lilliput, he could have been Gulliver. Ferries were racing to Brownsea Island, and we found our way to the RNLI College, where the Devon fund raising manager Claire, met us. She had travelled up to see us combining it with a business meeting. The headquarter facilities are special with amongst other things a deep-water pool for capsize drills. I did wonder if the scale of the premises, in one of the most expensive locations in the country was really justified, paid for of course by voluntary donations. It did highlight that the RNLI is a 'wealthy' charity, it wasn't really up to me to question their business management or austerity commitment, but it did signal that our hard-earned efforts might just buy a couple of door handles. I 'might have been on my best behaviour' around Wight, sufficient for Wendy and Havoc not to abort, but apparently, I was about to be in the doghouse.

Claire had arranged for us to stay at the RNLI hotel, but a strict rule was that dogs were not allowed. She had made provision that Havoc could sleep in her car, and although he couldn't really give a howl, it went down like a lead balloon with Wendy, not even the RNLI could rescue. I was caught in the crossfire, not at all bothered about 'shower, meal or bed', the suggestion is quite false, just wanted to appear other than 'ungrateful' and keep the peace. It was true Havoc had endured and helped raise money for both charities over some 2,000 miles and perhaps an exception could have been made, but it was outside my jurisdiction. I was just as keen to see him settled down with blankets, safe, late at night and first thing in the morning early to check he was OK, which indeed he was.

The episode was not dissimilar from a Scarborough front porch it seemed to me, that was perfectly acceptable to Wendy, from this point onwards in her eyes the RNLI could sink, me with them. I wanted to go to Brownsea and join the Girl Guides, keep my head down and learn how to make a washing up bowl stand, but was four months early for the centenary of Scouting. Criticize my lifestyle, the conversation wasn't right, I was with Alexander O'Neal, right fed up, when 'all you wanna do is criticize'.

Instead, we went hashing near Verwood in Ringwood Forest with Wessex H3, picked up by Legover. That raised another £50 - enough for doorbell batteries. Afterwards, he dropped us back to Sandbanks and looking at the real estate realised it might not cover even that. We were in time to catch the chain ferry to Purbeck, Shell Bay. This was the start of Britain's greatest coast path, the Southwest. The sign read Minehead 630 miles - funny that, if you go the other way, according to Mark Wallington and Boogie, it's only 500 miles! On the deserted sandy beach at Studland another sign read 'Naturists area starts 900mts from this point'. I wanted to be a man behaving badly, change the 'm' for an 'i' and prefix it with an extra 't', but Wendy insisted on keeping abreast of such mischief.

The Foreland has its own sewing kit of chalk stumps that used to be connected to The Needles on Wight. The eastern end of the Jurassic Coast, a World Heritage Site (UNESCO) since 2001 was gleaming in the sunshine. Teeth like cliffs that had their own 'ring of confidence', think Rylan Clark-Neal's veneers. Old Harry, so named arguably after a Pirate, a Viking or the Devil, take your pick, was untouchable so we sat on the visitor worn grass waiting for the hygienist. Harry's wife I read had collapsed in 1896, due no doubt to overdoing the housework, keeping the chalk white, but Harry has since remarried. For some strange reason, the tune Jerusalem was in my head, with half the WI for company, and did these feet walk upon England's greens. Swanage was just around the corner and that would be our destination for the night. (The Jurassic coast is some 96 miles long. I have read it can be done in three days. JM took the best part of four. We would need to eat considerably bigger buns to get anywhere near that. Instead, we took considerably longer and I could find no arrows of desire.)

Now deep into Dorset, Thomas Hardy called Swanage, Knollsea, set between 'finger and thumb'. We had spent too long with Old Harry (thumb), and it was getting dark by the time we reached the thenar webspace (Swanage) and the many listed buildings left little space to pitch a tent. Between the pier, Wellington Clocktower and an Amphitheatre complete with Greek style pillars, we found a spot above a small park. It was not the first time we had put the tent up, but it was the first time we slept in it. Why carry even a lightweight backpacking tent halfway around Britain before using it? The only answer I can offer is bedtime security and bad planning. As it happened, we had our own small drama next morning when a council worker, complete with jobs worth cap and digital camera told us,

"You can't sleep here".

Bit late mate. Before he returned with the cavalry, we were off to Peveril Point (finger) and on top of the world at Durlston Head. The 40tonne globe was quite a find after a sour squib at Swanage, but I was resolved to return one day for a sweeter look around. (I would in October 2021 in search of relics marked 'City of London', lamp posts and facades, transported here in the 19th century to make the resort 'fashionable'. Boats took stone to London; these eccentricities provided the ballast for the return journey.)

The quarrying giants Mowlem and Burt had a lot to do with the look of things here. Chiseled cliffs, caverns and ledges where limestone and marble were once extracted and shipped to cathedrals across the land. Tilly Whim and Dancing Ledge conjured up images of derrick jibs, a 'whim' was a crane, with waiting barges below and dark shadowy regular entrance holes in the rock seemed like perfect roosts for any type of bat. The equally square St Aldhelm's Chapel; said to have been built by a desolate father who witnessed his bride daughter and groom drown off the head, and the streamlined, smooth, symmetry of the Dorset Marine memorial table and benches at Emmet's Hill, guided us west.

Steep deep steps are unforgiving for short fat hairy legs, and right in front of us, a walker, not Ernie Wise, slipped and attempted to save himself by grabbing hold of a barbed wire fence. I distinctly remembered that was not in the Boy Scout expeditionary guide and consequently we searched deep in our ruck sacks for plasters. His son was at uni in St Andrew's, and we shared tales of the Fife coast path while viewing uninterrupted coastline in both directions, 'Dorzet', stemming blood flow, and pondering what Bear Grylls would make of it all.

It had been a bright, sunny day, some cooling breezes over a dry, dusty, cracked path shared with climbers looking for crags. Scenery had been on a par with anything we had seen so far but the going had been hard and slow. By Kimmeridge the bangs from an army firing range were getting louder and Havoc was a frantic flavoured jelly. Red warning flags were not to be ignored, look what the tank corps had done to nearby Tyneham village, now a 'ghost' hamlet. We put up the tent next to a stable with a dead horse, there was a water supply, but it was only after we were set up, we found we had rats for company. Nodding donkeys dipped into the underlying shale drinking up whatever oil still existed, the site of the world's oldest continually working oil well.

We were up early and walking before 7am keen to beat firing restrictions on Lulworth ranges, joined by deer, pheasants and rabbits. Paradoxically the army are conservationists. This early you can hear an unusual sound, that of cows tugging at grass and a herd was engrossed in eating, eyes on stalks, totally disinterested in us. By 9am we were in Lulworth Cove and helped put out café table and chairs in return for morning tea. This for me marked the western end of Purbeck and I read the estate, bequeathed to the National Trust in 1982 by Ralph Bankes, included Kingston Lacey House at Wimborne, Corfe Castle and 16,000 acres of land. That takes some dosh to manage and conserve, hence the car parking fees at this World Heritage Site with half a million visitors a year, fortunately we were on foot.

Chapter 19 – Durdle Door to Torquay

Stop pretending, tell me what's in your heart

"Dinos and doors in Dorset and Devon."

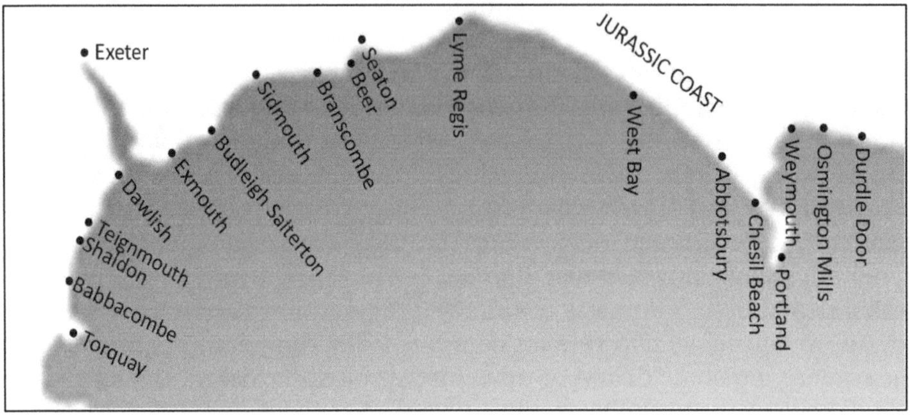

WE CLIMBED HAMBURY TOUT. I half expected a Del Boy-esque salesman to pop out from behind a bush with tickets for England's game versus Andorra (UEFA Football qualifiers – we would win 0-3 but still never got to the 2008 finals.) Instead, sea kayakers had a bit of a kick about emerging from a Duchy College minibus, as a warmup, before hitting the waves.

The arch of Durdle Door is best looking back from the west, and I was busy looking for Gabriel Oak's sheep. The Hardy classic, 'Far from the Madding Crowd' with Alan Bates was partly filmed here in 1967. Indeed, lambs were in the fields. A very young one was chasing a shepherd on a quad bike, the trailer behind carrying a barking sheep dog. Another was stuck in a cattle grid. All I could see was a skinny back with less covering than a worn dish cloth, motionless. Then I noticed a slight rib cage ripple and lifted it from its steely squeeze. It was a bit dirty but soon stood and went to find its mum. One ewe let out her dinner gong bleat and two lambs raced from opposite directions colliding under udder and when hooked on their little tails began rotating like kitchen whisks. Elsewhere, others had put their butting ever hungry charges into nursery to be overseen by a single mum, but a group of ever naughty boys had escaped through a gap at the side of the gate. Sports day included straight forward races, evasive skills any half decent England rugby three-quarter would be proud of and competing for a vertical high jump event where the rules were to take off all four feet simultaneously. How do they do that? I helped

'Alan' get the 'springs' back in and left him to his naked wrestling, 'Women in Love'.

After escaping a milliard of questions from a group of children who themselves had escaped PGL at Osmington Mills we waltzed into Weymouth. I had first been there in the early 1970s, arriving by train which ran through the main street, to catch a boat to the Channel Islands. My AA Book of the Seaside (1972) said you could always see a British Rail ferry. It had changed a lot. There were still some rails in the tarmac along the Georgian esplanade and a statue of King George III, who came for a swim noteworthy, along with sand sculptures. In places it was outdated, rundown, but some regeneration had occurred causing an article to describe it as 'the new Salcombe' - what was evident was that it was almost entirely dependent on tourism. (Visitors seemed to either like it or hate it! Delightful, retro, kitsch, award-winning, the 2012 Olympic sailing happened here, others say the legacy of that is unseen finding it overpriced and tacky. SH described it as 'a beautiful woman wrapped in a tatty coat.')

From the old harbour we were picked up by hashers from the Hardy's pack, Gravel Rash (Pauline) and Welly Wanker! Lamb dinner for ten and a bath after two nights camping, the latter occurring before the mint sauce. A lovely house at Wyke Regis worked hard for from plastering and dry lining, Pauline was also a world record holding nettle eating champion. They weren't an accompaniment. The experience also taught us Hardy's Hash didn't hold back with the nick names; their daughter was Hooker.

The base meant we could have a lightweight walk on the circuit of Portland crossing at Ferry Bridge. Had we arrived 168 years earlier we would have had to walk to Abbotsbury and crunch Chesil Beach. (Or take a ferry.) Havoc had the morning off, resting with a lamb bone. We went clockwise through a foggy Fortuneswell, passing prisons, Church Ope Cove and onto The Bill. We climbed Pulpit Rock - no miserable Man Utd supporters - Ross Bullock (RB) and after another Ope, this one Clay, collected Havoc, still licking his lips and marrow revitalised, turning left to East Fleet. My memories are I was glad we did Dorset's Gibraltar. Not 'great', except for the hospitality, and we would have to see if it put 'Land's End to shame'. It was one big block of dusty rock, somewhat characterised by old quarries and a fear of rabbits, (long associated with bad luck on Portland), tall fences, council houses, rod fishermen, old gun emplacements, former dock yard offices and coaling sheds.

In our tent in the garden of The Elm Tree Inn, Langton Herring (free dinner, a donation and packed lunch next day) I dreamt of preaching, line caught wrasse, omega 3, Watership Down, Dutch Elm, and swollen tonsils from toxic perennials.

Abbotsbury has a famous swannery and about now, late March, pairs select their nesting ground. Established by Benedictine monks in the 1040s, partial to an extra-large drumstick, the feathers hardened in hot sand formed quill pens. I pondered their role in England's cultural and literary development before meeting two coach loads of school children, armed with surveying quadrats, measuring stones at West Bexington. Whoever wrote the National Curriculum? The stones at the Portland end of Chisel were big compared with almost pea shingle here. I managed to convince some of them this proved beyond doubt God at the creation stood in the sea up to his knees, facing the shore, taking a sieve full of stones, and with a swing of the shoulders laid down the beach. Furthermore, it was indisputable from this evidence God was left-handed. Having emptied both coaches we sheltered with a driver chatting, eating our packed lunch sandwich, testing him on the whereabouts of John o' Groats - I was glad he wasn't taking us home!

We passed below Othona (II) thinking of acquaintances back in Dengie, forded Burton Freshwater and arrived at West Bay along the beach, buff, pale mustard, horizontally banded cliffs overhanging our heads. Avoiding rope and nets, the principal historical products, we carried on to Seatown and camped. I had a pint on my own in The Anchor Inn, another sign that all was not well on the domestic front.

Overnight and morning rain meant we were packing up soaking canvas in a laundry room before heading up Golden Cap (191 metres) the south coast's highest point. We made it up relatively easily, indicating good physical shape, and bumped into other coast walkers on a large-scale sponsored event heading east. They were in far worse shape only carrying day sacks, but we shared views in both directions and Wendy reminisced about burying a childhood pet budgie here.

We reached Charmouth via Cain's Folly (2007), the 2016 guide now takes you inland via Stonebarrow. A similar situation was encountered towards Lyme Regis. We found a way over Black Ven and The Spittles, although it involved some 'blind eyes' cast towards signs and vertical climbing. A flag at the golf course was at half-mast and we were told an 82-year-old had dropped dead after making a drive. It perhaps put things in perspective that we shouldn't be so reckless.

Wendy's mum and dad turned up to cheer us on at Lyme Regis, it was nice to see them. The Blue Lias cliffs to the east were not as well visited as they are now, fossil hunting has been made more popular since the

Jurassic Coast became advertised and those following in the footsteps of Mary Anning and Kate Winslet (Ammonite 2020) now count into the thousands. Others flock to the Cobb with their head shawls mimicking Meryl Streep (The French Lieutenant's Woman - 1981). Just up the road I started my teaching career in that very year.

We had the wooded Undercliff to negotiate to Axmouth and Seaton, seven or eight miles of strange overgrown landslip, forgotten by all except dinosaurs and Neanderthals, it takes little to imagine pterodactyls overhead.

All Hallows School used to sit on the cliff tops at Rousdon, where I once played cricket, and the square had a good tilt on it even in the 1980s. The Bindon slip occurred on Christmas Eve 1839 when an estimated eight million tons of rock moved towards the sea. I always believed it was witnessed and recorded by two vicars who must have thought they had incurred the wrath of God. However, on research it seems Buckland and Conybeare were leading geologists of their day and probably understood the science behind 'The Great Catastrophe'.

Crossing the Axe we entered Devon, we had walked there. The valley running group would aid us in the East, they organised The Grizzly long-distance multi-terrain run which had been part of our preparation in 2006. Two cheques were also received, and we had £500 to bank from collecting in Dorset.

Most of my comparative walking commentators barely give East Devon a mention save MW decrying the caravans and RB his pint at Beer. This was my early adult life backyard after leaving university. I bought my first house up the Axe valley in Musbury. Put my foot through a lime and reed ceiling wrecking the only remaining living space and cried for benevolence.

I renovated a small boat which went on to offer fishing trips to grockles around Lyme Bay, taught at the Grammar school described to me in pedagogical sense as a 'pasture between two dung hills!' Got married under the octagonal lantern church tower at Colyton. Its coastal description could not be overlooked.

Seaton had a chalet holiday camp (until it was lost to Tesco in 2009). Its launderette washed my smalls on a Friday night while I ate chips. It had its 2foot 9inch tramway that would whisk you up the valley. Beer had its picture-perfect appearance. White chalk cliffs the most westerly in England. A stream running into an open conduit at the side of the main road to be avoided when parking. Flint faced buildings hid people laughing from behind curtains when you did! The coast path roller coasts to Branscomb's pebbles from which we saw the stricken 'Napoli' that ran aground two months earlier.

Now looted of its nappies, cranes salvaged, and a giant electromagnet dropped scrap into containers. Popping up where violets, cowslips, sticky buds, lots of primroses and some bluebells; Spring's riotous arrival had begun. Also popping up again, like the proprietor of the costume shop in Mr Benn were Havoc's Grandpa and Nanny and my daughter, at regency Sidmouth. By now the cliffs had turned terracotta and we camped at Blackmore in the heart of the town, the rugby club where I had played many times.

We were joined by three hashers through Ladram Bay with its striking red sea stacks and passed by other hashers going the other way as they competed in the Exe to Axe event. Budleigh Salterton is the mouth of the

Otter River. It is a retirement town. When I first walked into an estate agent there 25 years earlier, I was told 'You can't afford anything here!' (I would later buy a house up the valley at Colaton Raleigh.) At the Millennium most towns had their fireworks at midnight, Budleigh had theirs at 8pm, by nine everyone had gone to bed. John Everett Millais painted the 'Boyhood of Raleigh' here, a favourite of mine. Another of his works was Bubbles' who became a Pears soap character. Bubbles is also my hash name, not 'TEB!' The pet shop in town also had a collection tin for us on their counter. There were more well-wishers at Exmouth, including my son, and we were about to enter Teign Valley Hash territory and receive more good wishes.

We stayed in Exeter where Wendy had always fancied living, close to the river near Countess Wear. The joys of the Exe estuary include Turf Lock, the Double Locks, and at Topsham, The Bridge where RB might have been better trying the 'Bass'. (The late Queen went there!) In my ear space that night, for some strange reason, Odyssey, 1980, 'If you looking for a way out'.

Arbie and Doris and a TV crew were amongst those who joined us from Starcross through Cockwood, and on to 'parochial' Dawlish. Wendy and I had both done shifts at the (Black) Swan Inn, experiencing the worst licensed victualled treatment, but if you wanted the country's most unusual pub name, the Ferret and Radiator was a good shout. (Permanently closed 2010, but I reckon Richard Hunt (RH) or his Great Aunt Alice could vouch for it.)

Teignmouth was our nearest lifeboat station (to Bovey Tracey) so there was a bit of a reception there, our fundraising efforts for RNLI would go to this station targeted towards the 'Train One Save Many' initiative. We took the ferry to Shaldon and started to climb. The coast here is indeed 'deceptive', eight miles to Torquay but it had taken JM four hours to negotiate the bays and hills. We reached the lovely old-fashioned model village at Babbacombe, set up by the Dobbins in 1963, and as it was a Monday evening, TVH3 run night, we were whisked to Brixham. The final leg to the Yacht Club was by rib, where a special evening had been planned on our behalf. We were still under halfway, but this sort of reception really ought to have been saved for a finish. It was great to see faces and friends, family in the form of Wendy's children, and a further £400 was raised on the night, the hash had already done miracles digging deep into pockets prior to the walk, and a £500 cheque from Blaster (Glendinning Quarries) was extra icing. Then it was back to Teignmouth for a night with Coldtits. (Another hasher, and we were only in her spare room!)

Chapter 20 – Torquay to Plymouth

Hey there Mr, Blue...I'll remember you this way

"Is there anywhere they do French food?"
"Yes, France, I believe. They seem to like it there. And the swim would certainly sharpen the appetite. You'd better hurry, the tide leaves in six minutes."

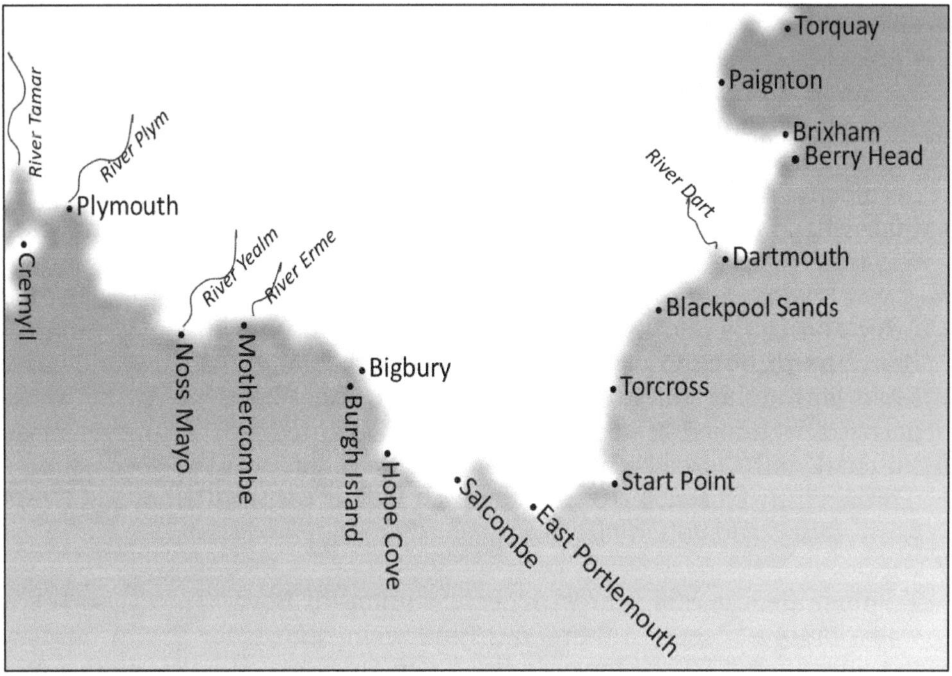

RESUMING WHERE WE had left off, next to a burning house, dragons' castle, and Stonehenge and joined by Wigwam, Migman, and Big Issue we strutted around Torquay's Hopes Nose, Meadfoot, and the Bay to Brixham again. Fallen Woman and Broken Man our hosts, but not before joining Ashburton Hash (Tuesdays) at Idford.

Our companion on a bright sunny morning, day 143, over rugged paths to Kingswear was Flowery Twats, so named, as his family in Torquay owned a small hotel close to Basil Fawlty. I was beginning to feel the hash didn't trust us and were collectively spying on our moves. Flowery was also a coach driver, but we already had a Hatrack. He had helped us set up a 'Just Giving' account and helped with IT publicity and was amazingly supportive. At Berry Head I stopped to admire mauve wild cyclamen and wondered if they were planted by Anglican minister, Henry

Lyte, he was into his flowers. Vicar at All Saints, he was credited for writing 'Abide with Me', (1847) sung at Cup Finals since 1927, 'Praise my soul the King of Heaven' was also one of his.

Later, we passed Coleton Fishacre, purchased by the National Trust in 1982 as part of Project Neptune, focusing on acquiring chunks of the coastline for the nation. A large exotic garden, 24 acres, enjoys a microclimate in a combe leading to the sea from an Arts and Crafts house, with Art Deco interior. The ferry took us to a bustling Dartmouth. The Dart Valley to bohemian Totnes, the lowest bridging point, had formed a lot of our practice, to include it again now would add a 30-mile trek, a detour for JM but not for us, 'short cutting bastards'!

Dartmouth had its fortifications guarding the entrance to the estuary, Royal Naval College and quayside canon. It looked familiar; its cast iron cousin was the one we saw at Berwick-upon-Tweed. In 1896 the town was stripped of its lifeboat, it only made one effective rescue. The many masts in the harbour have since necessitated a new 'D class' to be placed here covering the Dart (2007).

Chaucer visited and Brunel brought the railway to Kingswear. Strange Dartmouth should have a station but no railway - the bridge was never built. Many Elizabethan buildings add to Dartmouth's charm, our late Queen, Elizabeth II came to meet her 'Philip'. Little did I know that three years on I would be delivering sausages to the Royal Castle Hotel.

We would stay with another hasher, this time from South Hams, Pepys at Stoke Fleming. A pet turkey: blue, red, brown, black and white with wattle and long snood having survived Christmas gave us a macho bravado welcome. Havoc responded as only he could. Roughly translated it echoed 'get stuffed!' SHH3 run on a Wednesday, so it was off to East

Portlemouth for an evening run on the coast path and fundraising raffle. I bought my own ticket and won the Easter Egg, but never got to eat any of the chocolate - South Hams hashers, 'greedy bastards!'

Everyone warns of the severity of north Devon, nobody ever speaks of south Devon being hard, according to SH. Those same people might expect to find the Tower Ballroom at Blackpool Sands, they would be wrong. The A379 hugs the coast, one has little choice but tread tarmac, MW hitched in a boiled Hillman unable to read the bus timetable in Strete. Slapton offers field trip opportunities for sixth formers desperate to get away from mum and dad, the Ley a SSSI and Torcross selfie opportunities next to a battered Sherman tank for American tourists tracing their lost loved ones. D-Day landing practice exercises would see some 1,000 U.S. troops killed here, many by 'friendly' fire, 'Tiger' went badly wrong. Today cormorants skim the water surface, just a few feet from getting their wings wet while racing cars, as they in turn head along The Ley Road, bound for naturist bathing opportunities at Pilchard Cove.

Turning left to more remote spots Shally Hunt's coast was about to become 'unrelentingly tough'-er! but jaw dropping in its beauty. Beesands and ruined Hallsands lead to Start Point, 168 miles done from Poole, only 462 to Minehead. Cottages, homes of 128, went to the sea at Hallsands (1917) after the 'beach' had gone to Devonport. Also here, Devon's own "Grace Darling", Ella Trout and her family, saved lives, fished and ran a hotel. (Developed into apartments in 2008.) Lannacombe was lovely, a spectacular rocky, rugged coast with the path etched into it. Just as you think it is about to run out, it curves and pops up again dropping into idyllic coves. The Pigs Nose (East Prawle) offers a perfect pint, take refreshment while you can. Past Prawle Point gargoyles peer down on you, smirking at your efforts to ease your way on. (It's easier in daylight, last night we had our own practice "run", in the dark, with head torches.) Celandine and gorse now provided colour, daffs in peoples' gardens were almost over.

The 5pm ferry from East Portlemouth took us to Salcombe. I knew it well from dinghy sailing (Egremont) with children and a cross channel trip (Provident) to London via Cherbourg. Pi finished teaching maths at Kingsbridge and whisked us back to Blackadon on the southern edge of Dartmoor. There with Pinki we were made extremely welcome with a curry. (I would get to know Blackadon Barns and The Studio much better but didn't know that at the time.)

It was Good Friday and the views from near Sharp Tor back down the Salcombe estuary were heavenly. Bolt Head and Tail, Hope Cove and Thurlston, its rock pierced by an arch led to Bantham and the river Avon. Soft sand underfoot made fording difficult, it was tidal up to my waist, but I did my usual three shuttles, watched by a somewhat mesmerised beach lifeguard. A rendition of 'Bridge over Troubled Waters' came on, a favourite of Wendy's. I'm on your side.' Many criticisms could be levied at me, but dearth of 'loyalty' was not one of them! (A legend exists the Simon and Garfunkel hit was penned after a trip to Bickleigh in Devon - but that's a case of locals doing their own entrepreneurial bit!)

Safely on the Bigbury side we looked across to Burgh Island. The depositional spit, the sea tractor not needed at the moment to visit the tombola island. I looked past the ancient Pilchard Inn to the Art Deco Hotel and imagined Agatha Christie and Noel Coward enjoying aperitives before the dinner gong. Hosting us in Challaborough were Ging Gang and Goolie. Dinner for all of us was at Gara Bridge with Pullit and others. (Pullit was the vet who when Havoc broke his leg just a week or so before we were about to start the walk advised cutting it off as a three-legged dog would gain a more favourable reaction from charity givers!) (Torcross to Bantham was the route of Rambo's coastal marathon (26 miles) which I did a couple of times when it was in its infancy.) RIP Rambo, thanks for everything.

Reference to hashers in this part of the coast is unapologetically extensive, such was the support. It is said you can hash every day of the week in Devon so there was quite a lot of help spread over several packs. The vast majority of members are lovely, generous and warm. Thank you all, you know who you are. I would discover that one or two were charmers, chancers and moles, but more of that later.

We were due a late start and got it. We needed our strength for the ups and downs of Ayrmer Cove. Timing is also important to cross the Erme, as Andy had attempted to tell us back at Worthing. We got it just right crossing to Mothercombe and avoiding the eight-mile detour. From the caravans at Stoke we picked up the old Revelstoke Drive, a former carriage route. Even here hashers had left us a well-wishing note, pinned to a stile. Along the Warren ribs of rocks stretched out to sea and the Great Mew Stone, an island, looked like a giant shark fin. We stayed with old friends Steve and Kathy, these two had more sense than to hash, overlooking Noss Mayo creek. The voss (causeway) had dried out and we could walk to the shop for wine, chocolate and newsprint. Havoc read the paper. A border collie, Ben, had fallen 80ft over the cliffs at Burton Bradstock two days earlier. He survived. However, Havoc made me promise not to tell his mum, he would never be off his lead again.

The extra hashing miles in the evenings had left us shattered. We decided to take the Sunday off, apart from playing rugby with Steve's sons on Bigby beach, some rest! I was godfather, not a very good one, to Alexander the youngest, and Malcolm Collins, an old student mate and keen rugby guy came down too. I actually had far more to do with Tom (RIP), Steve's eldest son who attended the school I had worked at and, despite being in a wheelchair while at the school, completed the Ten Tors Jubilee Challenge, on a tricycle. (Okehampton).

It was Xander and his parents who saw us off, calling for the ferry across the Yealm by dropping the highly technical semi-circular call sign to reveal a white disk. (£1.50 each, single to Warren Point, Havoc went free!) My back ached, who was it who thought they were still up to rugby, and I was glad I wasn't pulling on an oar like gig rowers at sea. I hoped they didn't capsize, that 'shark' guarding the entrance to Wembury Bay looked even bigger today.

Bovisand became Jennycliff and we met a GD puppy walker who had 'walked' 38 dogs, some achievement. I think Wendy had done three before she had her last, Avon, who was the size of a wolf but as scared as a mouse, when it came to loud noises and consequently failed his formal training. Wendy had him back as a family pet. After which came Havoc, just as scared of loud noises and as long as you don't say it too loudly, half as intelligent.

There is a great sign in the form of a door mat which welcomes you to Plymouth, 'Please wipe your feet'. In fact, there are quite a few novel signs around the city for the coast path. Mount Batten and around Cattewater we arrived at The Citadel, with photo opportunities at the Mayflower Steps, fundraising ones around the Barbican and fuel at Cap'n Jaspers.

Local couple Rosemary and Pete provided more fuel, spag bol. We first met them while collecting at Sainsbury's prior to starting off and Rosemary organised all manner of events to aid our charity cause. ELO in the head, 'we were pleased to be with you.'

Chapter 21 – Plymouth to Mullion

And the tears rolled into the ocean

"Haunted shores rearing up against westward oceans, pasties and cream teas and the gulls fly free. Sandy toes and salty lips."

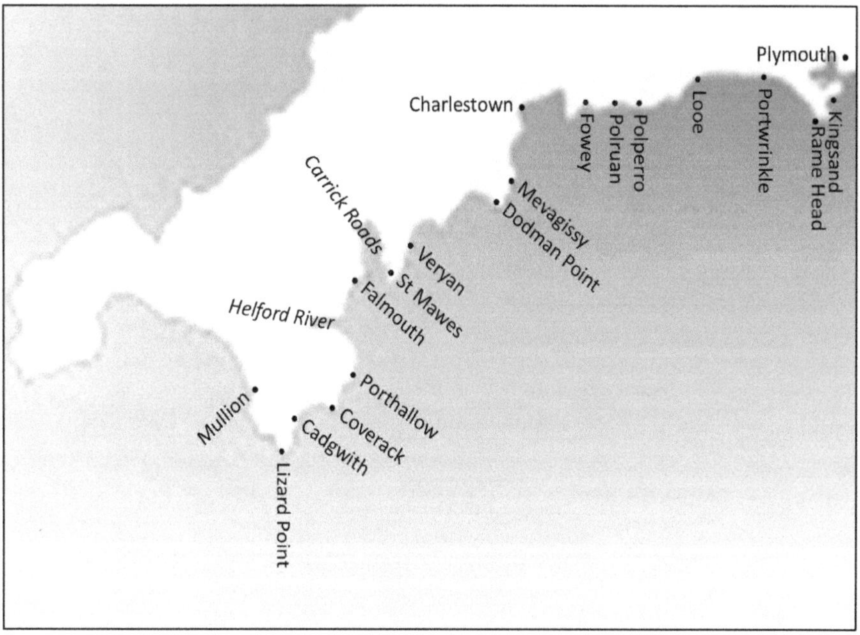

A PAIR OF LOVE-STRUCK swans had set up a home of drift rubbish from the Tamar on the Stonehouse slipway. Bright sunshine and smooth waters led us to Cremyll and Cornwall. My preconception - grey rather depressing cottages, peeling paintwork, spoil heaps, newer build eyesores that should never have passed planning - we had a few miles, 422 to be exact, to corroborate. However, our map case had been left back with Rosemary and frantic phone calls and ferry favours were necessary to retrieve it. It meant hanging around a bit, time to view Brittany Ferries heading past Drakes Island, destination Roscoff. They had donated a female teddy bear which we auctioned off having christened her Jemma Pell (je m'appelle). Back on the Devon side Mutton Cove, Mount Wise, the dockyards and around the corner the Tor Point ferries upon which we had also collected pre-starting.

Like those swans, pigeons were equally amorous, but less quiet, serene and reserved about it. It was that time of year, the riot of spring.

Cleaning feathers soon became obvious flirting. Cooing and chest puffing drove other birds away, they had seen it all before and knew what was coming. Nestle up close and playful, pecking became a game of hard to get 'chase me'. Frantic fluttering and what could only be described as rape concluded the whole drama. The sounds, other than climactic wing flapping, falls into one of two camps. 'Take two towels Taffy' is reserved for Welsh birds, (but not the ones seen in Cardiff nightclubs!) Here near Plymouth it's more of a 'Green Army' chant, echoing Argyle terraces. Having read this you will forever be plagued by that vocab whenever you hear a pigeon cooing. Make sure you know where they come from.

Trees were breaking into leaf at Mount Edgcumbe, violets peeping through the green undergrowth. Tadpoles wriggled in shaded pools and peacock butterflies basked in the sun on dry dusty paths. It was a hot, still, dandelion day. Havoc chased bumble bees and chewed on a bone he had found that looked like a pork scratching. People had their windows open to the sea air in cosy Kingsand cottages, there was a smell of coffee, fresh bread, a rustle of newspapers enough for the cash machine wheels in estate agents eyeballs to spin furiously.

At Cawsand men played on expensive catamarans, boys on jet skis and women sat around slugging from wine goblets in a midday alcoholic stupor. All was well in the world, or at least in this Cornish cupboard.

We dumped our bags to climb up to the small, rustic St Michael's Chapel (1397), that crowns Rame Head without a pair of knickers or an elasticated waistband of slacks in sight. We met a lady cyclist; I hope she had done her shopping at M&S, who turned out to be an Irish doctor from Norwich who was about to go off on an Antarctic expedition and be stationed at South Georgia. Amazing what you can find out from an Irish woman in 30 seconds! Hey, but that was a real adventure challenge, not like our ramble in the backyard. We were not brave enough to go off to some foreign wilderness, exposing ourselves to real hardship, bandits, wild animals and the like, plus Havoc didn't know if they had pork scratchings there.

We hadn't come far in a day. Near Millbrook we could still see the Tamar Bridge, but we were in a laid-back mood. Chalets on the cliffside at

Whitesand have an equally laid-back 1950s air. It reminded me of long days as a child, when a day lasted a week and stinging nettles really hurt. A farmer did his best to plough up colonies of them from a field boundary, shadowed by sea gulls. We decided to camp on a reclaimed site, a former gun battery and while Wendy cooked sausages with instant mash, I opened a tin of Pal for Havoc. (He also got a sausage!) I went to find a temporary loo and was directed by a small boy who said,

"That's the men's".

I wondered if he liked stinging nettles but before I had chance to ask, he fired off.

"Do you want a pee or a poo?". Inquisitive these Cornish pixies.

Red warning flags on the firing ranges at Tregantle meant we had to detour inland via the road before picking up fields to Portwrinkle and a golf links to Downderry. It would have been easy to stay with the sunbathers at Seaton, there are at least seven 'tons' around the coast, without counting the 'owns', but we carried on tilting to the left, that foot somehow always seemed lower than the right one. There were plenty of other walkers about, some seemed like they were about to keel over in the heat, I can't recall we were ever overtaken. Others sharing the path had all the gear, the complete Millets' range, shiny boots, they probably had breathable jock straps, none looked like they had come far, Millendreath at a push.

A carpet of wildflowers led us into East Looe, red and white campions, periwinkles, violets, buttercups and stich wort. The 'Bango Pier' was distinctive, but I wished I had a drone camera to appreciate it more. James Lynes, a former pupil of mine, and his family put us up. In an immaculate bungalow overlooking the two creeks we enjoyed kedgeree, wonderful hosting skills and James told us all about his volunteer role at the RNLI shop and his GD Jacob.

The path from West Looe, with views of St George's Island to Talland Bay did not disappoint. Polperro was hiding in a narrow harbour entrance guarded by more natural cliff gargoyles. A 'fishing village with quaintness cultivated for the benefit of picture postcards and visitors'. Pasties and ice cream, most folk arrive by shuttle bus from the car park at the top of the hill, few by the coast path from Scotland. Pretty streets and alleyways between whitewashed cottages actually provide good hashing territory, if 'hares' are combining it with a pub crawl. (Lay your flour unobtrusively to avoid upsetting locals.) Those same natives told us the path to Polruan was the toughest on the coast, but all locals placed this honour on their bit. A good business would be to sell badges to communities around the country for re sale saying, 'Probably - the most indefatigable coastline in the world!'

Rod anglers tried their luck from rocky outcrops whilst the sea played merry-go-rounds at their feet. Polruan had the most thorough volunteer journalist in the world - probably, who interviewed us in a cluttered front room for the Cornish Guardian. Very methodical, we had to divulge our life histories from conception and all things that had gone wrong; journalists are only interested in the negative, indeed several times, as she was also quite deaf! We were there that long it was getting near time for Ovaltine, and we needed to catch a ferry to Fowey.

Keith Stuart, coxswain, met us at the lifeboat shed. He was father to Shelley who we had met in Amble, and his Harley Davidson had pride of place in the three-storey building. We never got to find out if it went on water. Large ships made their way upriver to the docks, speed boats bobbed on moorings and stylish expensively dressed holidaymakers looked for restaurant tables. When it came to leave Keith escorted us out of town like a sheriff in a Western and Havoc donned a bandana to keep up with the shoot 'um up portrayal.

At Readymoney I knew I should have bought my metal detector with me, and at Gribbin Head a red and white beacon looked like a Caractacus Potts 'toot sweet'. If it were made of candy, I would have expected to see the letters 'k-e-r-n-o-w' running through the centre. Par Sands caravans gave way to Carlyon golf links and a controversial development still a construction site.

At Charlestown, once West Polmear, the square rigged Hespaniola was under repair. In 1791 Charles Rashley had a lot to do with creating this harbour basin, he put up the money for it to be dug by hand. Behind it seven miles of leats, pools and keep docks controlling the flow of water, a straight approach road, and a hotel. Pilchards and some tin had found their way out of here until Rashley changed all that for china clay and copper. The latter very useful in conducting electricity, in development at this time, when Cornwall was the biggest copper supplier to the world; the former was dried in kilns, a chimney of which could still be seen. Today, the site and collection of old ships provide back drops for film projects and TV series like Poldark.

The coast path was closed due to a landslip, and we were told 'you definitely can't get through'. I was in no mood for a mile and a half diversion and went over an old battery point to check it for myself. I returned to tell Wendy, 'Come on, were doing it, tear up that risk assessment' and we climbed over safety barriers. We held on to rusting fence posts and bits of hedge as we tiptoed on four inches of clifftop over sheer drops, below the remains of a once loved garden. JM had similar problems near here, even he went on the road.

Lower Porthpean was covered in beer bottles. Either a beach party or disillusioned coast walkers approaching from the other direction and finding that detour.

Inland the brewery must have been doing a roaring trade. Black Head marked the western end of St Austell Bay and we had to turn inland to find a campsite we had been offered. The owner had seen something in the Western Morning News and had rung with an invitation. It proved quite difficult to find, but we couldn't look a gift horse in the mouth. Fresh paint work at the house, personalised number plates on the drive, flat well drained manicured grass for camping it was nothing like Bates Motel in Hitchcock's Psycho, but somehow, I had got that in my head. Perhaps it was the reference to a sick mother who needed lots of looking after, I still slept a little uneasy waiting for a knife to come through the tent wall, I didn't have a shower. Hotel California (Eagles) stayed with me all night. Would we 'find the passage back to the place we were before?'

It was Saturday 14th April, Grand National Day. I felt a bit like a racehorse as we posed for pictures outside a campsite in the Pentewan Valley. Not that I was a fit thoroughbred and hate saying 'cheese'. With our goodbyes saddled, we headed off for Mevagissey at a canter. The cafes and gift shops were busy with visitors. The inner harbour crammed with boats and the narrow streets congested even by one or two cars. These ancient roads were built for sledges like the one to be seen in the free seafront museum with its artefacts on three storeys. The working harbour was a delight, we munched pasties and a small hardware store gave us meths (to cook with, not to drink with our pasties) and a new pocket-sized dog bowl for Havoc – the last one had been left behind somewhere. We counted out coins in the Post Office to the tune of £104. I had a look at the racing form. Havoc put his paw on an outsider – Silver Birch. Since a lot of the coins were silver, was this an omen? £104 at 33-1, a tidy sum if Silver Birch romped home? But it wasn't my money so we couldn't risk it.

Steps out and over the cliffs to Port Mellon turned the corner at Turbot Point and dropped into Gorran Haven. This was another super spot. A harbour wall protects a tiny bay, notices on a community board proclaim this as an active little place and dogs are welcome on the shingle beach if owners clear up after them. Alongside is a cellar like café, The Mermaid, whose owner provided us with a free cuppa and 'Blue Band' biscuit. She was pleasant with a warming smile and interested to know we were heading for Portloe, where she told us, she had spent her honeymoon night. It would have been easy to stay put, dunking chocolate biscuits into hot tea while fanaticising about a honeymoon night with a mermaid but we had a winner's enclosure to reach.

A large stone cross greeted us at Dodman Point. Mentioned in Spanish Ladies, this tune took root as an earworm. Farewell and adieu with me trying to remember the lyrics from singing this as a primary school pupil. In land from Porthluney Cove is Caerhays Castle – an impressive 19th Century John Nash creation. The local gamekeeper was well worth his bonus, for the fields and gardens alongside were alive with pheasants. I couldn't help wondering if the nearby Forty Acre Wood, marked on the map, was where Winne the Poo had downsized to. On the skyline was a tree that looked for all the world like a giant feather duster, how tickled we were!

The cottages of Portholland were quaint in contrast to the majesty of Caerhays Castle but I couldn't help thinking of renaming this pleasant spot – Portdutch. (Anything to rid the world of the unfortunate name 'Holland'. Try as I might I could extinguish this red light.) We headed over National Trust land, Tregenna with signs saying 1.5 miles to Portloe. With fine drizzle most of the afternoon, we could see the very top of Dodman Point headland looking back and could barely make out Gull Rock ahead. I began to wonder if Portloe was another Brigadoon, for if Polperro was hiding a few days ago, Portloe had now vanished. Eventually, we staggered down and up steps, over a small stream, the rusty railings of a private slipway and into the small car park of a posh hotel – must have been where a mermaid had her wedding night! We were to stay in our tent at the bottom of The Ship public house garden.

The landlord kindly gave us two pints, a shower and dog food and as we supped, we compared the pub's OS 1:25000 map with our one inch, cost 5s 6d. Inland to the west, I could see a village marked Veryan. It reminded me of an old college mate, Veryan Pappin, so named after this Cornish village, from St Luke's in 1977 where I had trained as a teacher. Veryan went on to play hockey for Great Britain as a goalkeeper. It got me thinking as to whether he was conceived in the village and hence named like a certain Brooklyn Beckham? The sports news reported a victory for Silver Birch. That would have been a tidy little earner of

£3,422. He who hesitates – must work harder tomorrow with rattling collecting tins.

The next day was wet and misty, an ideal day out for all manner of slugs, snails and puppy dogs' tails (actually – grass snakes). They shared our path to Narehead and Porthscalho with juggernaut like beetles, the size of Havoc's paws. Their heads and bodies seemed to be articulated, while the head moved forwards, the body was still going at 45 degrees in the previous direction. Havoc had to do a similar manoeuvre to get through some of the kissing gates. Meanwhile, I was showered in blossom like confetti as the flag sticking upright from my rucksack collided with overhead thorn bushes, the path tunnelling its way through such obstructions and causing me to curse as I stooped and occasionally became entangled. The ground became flatter and grassy around Greeb Point, Killigerran Head and Zone Point. We passed the lighthouse at St Anthony's Head and continued on to the landing spot of the Place Ferry.

I dozed quite happily spread out on a bench waiting for a free ride across the Porthcuel River to St Maws enjoying the Roseland sunshine. We had little time to admire the castle built by Henry VIII or the old-world fishing harbour, now a tourist spot and second home haven where vintage coaches do wedding rides, as we needed to catch the last ferry of the day, 4.45pm across Carrick Roads, the entrance of the Fal river to Falmouth. Since 1869 ferry passengers have crossed the third largest natural deep-water harbour in the world, some 2.6 miles (in case you didn't know, this is the same distance as the world underwater cycling record). I was glad I didn't have a bike and admired the large ships of Falmouth's working docks. An attractive barefoot wooden carved model of a girl reading a book was another ferry passenger. Havoc couldn't quite make her out.

We were to find refuge at the Seamen's Mission who allowed us to sleep on a lounge floor while drying out tent, trainers and socks. We could have done a 'particularly savage detour' some 32 miles via Truro but were happy to be in Falmouth. Once the second busiest port in the British Empire in 1817, mail, supplies and wage packets for troops fighting abroad for good old Queen Vic would have left from here. Now it hosts the National Maritime Museum and Trago Mills (although a bit smaller than the one at Newton Abbott – there is nowhere like it!). It is also the place where in 1978 I was one of a football team to lose 6-0 in the Rothman's Western League.

One can soon go off a place, so we headed for Maen Porth beach and Karl's Café where breakfast had been arranged for us. Rounding Rosemullion Head we headed west, along the banks of the Helford river to the ferry point. This was the last major river crossing of the South Coast, but it was low water and we had to wait an hour and a half for a free passage to the picturesque Helford. Our path took us through woodland, around creeks and bulb fields to Porthallow where Wendy and I literally parted company.

This was a big fallout. The reason for this I really cannot remember. It may have been her wish to go via Gweek where there is a seal sanctuary, but somewhere there was a breakdown in communication. Wendy went off with Havoc, I continued on carrying two rucksacks attempting to catch up with her. As I trudged uphill, I remember shouting to her that I would have a heart attack in the heat, only to get a reply,

"Good, and no one would care or come to your funeral!"

Heat, tiredness – whatever, can have its effects but I remember arriving at St Keverne, depositing both our bags at a garage for safekeeping and going off again to look for her. After what seemed like several hours of Kissinger like negotiation, we eventually camped in a field at the back of The Three Tuns pub. Buried in the churchyard are the victims of shipwrecks, more than 400, and I wondered if anyone had gone to their funerals. It had been a relatively short day and we were expected in Mullion the next day, so we had some miles to make up as well as tempers.

Reflection: I could only base this latest row on the assumption that skipping the seal sanctuary was somehow a catalyst – I had no better reason. At risk of boring the pants of you, let's try an almost judicial - like analysis.

Prosecution: We didn't go to Gweek instead wasted time waiting for a ferry. This was just the latest example of my controlling behaviour, getting what I wanted. We had no hard and fast schedule, always saying if we wanted to stop and do something impromptu, we could but I am almost certain Wendy never said that is where she wanted to detour to. If I had used my emotional intelligence, I could have suggested it. Add to this my character; dominant, assertive, liking to be in control and having my own way. It all fitted with a stereotypical view of a PE teacher. Recall the character played by Brian Glover in the film Kez (1969) - you had a blueprint for me, just a little more hair and not so keen on Manchester United. Could be intimidating, unapproachable, often arrogant, condescending, even sexist. I put my hands up, just add stubborn and egotistical for good measure. Macho, perhaps coercive, not by physical force or threats, but good at persuading others to do something they didn't really want to or making choices for them.

Defence: The only further mitigation I can offer is that Wendy knew very well what I was like from before we had become romantically involved. We had worked together for years. Been away on countless field trips together. Colleagues had probably warned her about getting involved. I recall very well telling her in a rented Exeter flat that she really shouldn't get involved with me. I don't think I somehow became more belligerent, if anything, the opposite with a degree of mellowing. Did she see me as something of a challenge? Someone she could model only the clay was more unworkable than she had anticipated. Naughty boy makeover, only this one Gok would have struggled with.

Was such a personality attracted to a career in PE or did training and experience, somehow living up to the stereotype, make me like it? Who knows? I've done some personal psychological scrutiny, on reflection I have to admit to some of the traits displayed to a greater or lesser extent depending on circumstance.

On this occasion to conclude, I have no recall of a discussion about going to Gweek. Perhaps Wendy, by this stage, felt it not even worth bothering to try and even suggest it? Or perhaps she did, and I was too tied up in my own wishes to even hear it. Logistically at least, it was a six mile walk there and six miles back again in order to continue on to the Lizard. The official Southwest Coast path takes the ferry. Would the seal sanctuary even be open on a Monday? Wendy had also done an excellent job networking at getting stays for us around the country. Hosts obviously needed some heads up as to when we would be arriving. Wendy would liaise with them by telephone, fixing the details. All this she controlled. We were due in Mullion, the other side of the Lizard on Tuesday night, 17th April 2007 to meet a couple from Bovey Tracey. What Wendy sometimes misjudged was just how far we had to travel and how long it might take.

One could not fail to realise that things in our relationship were not right – indeed, they could best be described as toxic. What I failed to see was what Wendy, must have been feeling – an ongoing sense that the relationship was wrong. She was often unhappy, perhaps anxious more often than not. Tiredness, aches and pains, cold, wet, haggard – the odd fall out was only to be expected. I had no appreciation of the level of volatility or didn't want to think about it. What was lacking was talking to one another. You would have thought that walking around Britain, just the two of us, plus the odd bark, we would have had plenty of time to communicate, really express our feelings, desires, dislikes but we didn't. This was a joint failing that would take its toll. We were 'making up much more than we were making love' and if that is not a song lyric, it should be. Here ended the Frasier style psychoanalysis. An entire science devoted to the study of just two people, Hitler and Sybil! Perhaps I needed to be added to that list.

We were up early and crept out of St Kevern before they had chance to fire a warning shot from the cannon in the churchyard, a relic from HMS Primrose, wrecked on The Manacles in 1809. We reached the first of several interest spots around The Lizard, Coverack. We were given a free Cornish breakfast at a B&B while chatting to some other walkers. They had highly polished dry boots and telescopic walking poles that still telescoped and all manner of paraphernalia from outdoor shops, none of which hardly looked used. Compared with our gear begged and borrowed, assembled on a meagre budget and by now scraped and worn, we really must have looked like the poor relatives.

Between Coverack and Cadgwith with its thatched cottages, (JM - I counted at least seven which hadn't burned down) we stumbled across a field of all manner of wild animals. Goats, antelopes and bulls! We literally hit upon it by surprise rather like the teenagers who first discovered Lascaux in the Dordogne. It truly was a 'taureaux taureaux taureaux' moment. It was in fact a sculpture park of modern metal works by Terence Coventry and made for some good pictures with Havoc trying to sniff their bits. A large hole with a distinctive arched entrance, formed when a cave roof collapsed called the Devil's Frying Pan, is a landmark before reaching The Lizard lifeboat station. Bacon and eggs were off but coffee and a Mars bar were forthcoming before riding the cable car back up the cliff. This is the only such wired access to a lifeboat station in the country.

Reaching Lizard Point, Britain's most southerly, should have been a high spot especially as the weather was wonderful and wildflowers; thrift, violets and squill carpeted our way. However, Wendy was still smouldering like a spent firework. I don't say this flippantly, but I was conscious of giving her plenty of space.

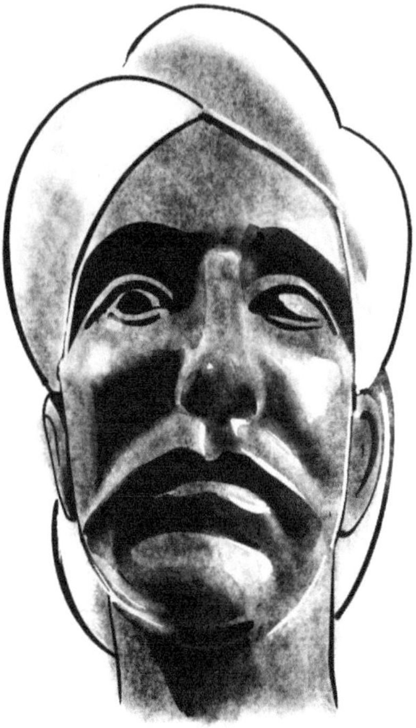

We reached Kynance Cove a particularly attractive National Trust spot, one where visitors normally arrive in their cars, pay for parking and dogs are not allowed on the beach. Arriving via the coast path has its advantages; no parking fee and it's a bit late giving notice of a dog free beach when you have already walked along it. Reaching Mullion Cove, we were greeted by a black moustached scary gentleman wearing a turban. He was in fact a figurehead and owned the sweet shop. On the scary stakes he came a close second to Admiral Lord Howe from HMS Impregnable who resides at The Lee in Buckinghamshire. When you come around a corner on a winter's night and your headlights hit his image, miles from the sea, it certainly is a menacing sight.

Margaret and Tony Wright, a couple from Bovey Tracey with a holiday home in Mullion, were far less terrifying and much more welcoming. They had arranged for us to have a meal at The Old Inn before offering us a bed for the night.

It wasn't just us who found circumnavigating Britain taxing. Between Kynance and Mullion SH/RH reported 'pulse rising, agitation, four letter words and simultaneous cursing of each other' - I wonder just how close they came to 'destroying their marriage'? (Sunday Express).

'Filled to the top with fear, the stars don't even matter'. Post walking, at the time of writing, Sam Sparro's lyrics, Black and Gold, 2008, would provide the haunting.

Chapter 22 – Mullion to Portreath

Crying, Laughing, Loving, Lying

"England's greatest escape - turquoise waters and dramatic serpentine rocks."

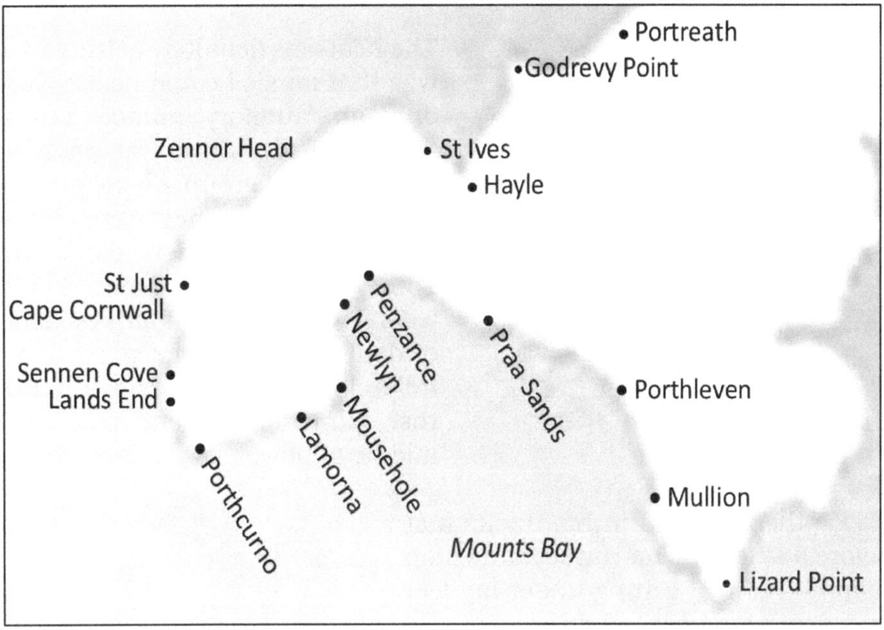

IN THE PROCESS of rounding Vellen Head in the failing light, I had lost our flag, it had somehow fallen from the rucksack. As Wendy was trailblazing (I wasn't always in the vanguard position) she wouldn't have seen it go so the following morning we put out a 'May Day' with BBC Cornwall. Then I retraced our steps and found our colours near Predannack, and leaving Mullion, we headed for Poldhu. A plaque here commemorates Marconi's 1901 wireless message to Uncle Sam. The station here would later tell of the arrest of Dr Crippen and the sinking of the Titanic.

Gunwalloe rivals Cadgwith for prettiness on the western side of The Lizard peninsula and just as the large square clock tower dominates Porthleven so do old mine workings at Trewavas and Rinsey Heads. Here we had done some rock climbing a few years earlier but now choughs, Cornwall's best loved birds were climbing the cliffs and mine chimneys for somewhere to nest. Conservation groups were offering 24 hour 'protection' for these rarities but not in the form of DMM nuts or wires.

I was to lose our colours again after Praa Sands, this time carelessly leaving them outside a public loo block near Pentreath. To my relief they were still there when I went back for them and hence those loos came to my comfort twice.

The heat was definitely getting to me, was that music I could hear? Surely only an 'auditory mirage' but no, near Prussia Cove we met and chatted to a group of people on a music course. They were dressed eclectically like they came from Totnes, clearly their creative juices were flowing and their enthusiasm so evident I had to take a cooling off fully clothed under a single shower rose found on a metal pole in the middle of nowhere.

Havoc then stopped in his tracks just before a stile – 'Go on Havoc, don't stop there dithering', getting under my feet and doing his best to trip me up. He was having none of it and refused to budge, four bony anchors embedded in baked earth. From the undergrowth the diamond pattern of an adder emerged, its vertical split pupils eyeing a prey and its forked tongue tasting the air. It coiled away to the relief of all three of us – a lucky escape.

Narrow undulating paths and tracks lead to Marazion. St Michael's Mount dominates the bay. The church and castle looked as if they could be made from marzipan with icing, and crowned the Island cake but after walking the cobbled causeway as it was low tide, we found the National Trust were not dog friendly and we couldn't go in. Instead, we watched as surveyors with their staffs, tripods and theodolites measured the height of the beach – nice to know someone was taking global warming and rises in sea level seriously. I couldn't help noticing also that even though it was only late April some topless bathing was taking place on the beach – one of the benefits of rising planet temperatures.

Prior to setting off we had an article placed in the Western Morning News. A Penzance hotelier and businessman Peter George had phoned me on my mobile offering accommodation (I was at the top of a ladder at the time). Consequently, we were to stay at The Yacht Inn in Penzance. Peter was a big man, a cricket lover and had a broad Cornish accent. He spoke very quickly so we could hardly understand a word. An England rugby shirt donated by Stack Stevens hung on one of the walls. Chatting to Peter reminded me of another Cornish rugby player I went to college with – Malcolm Collins, best known for his goal kicking, we had met up with him briefly back in Noss Mayo. We also met other locals including Penny and Eddie Wood who in turn, would offer us a bed near to Land's End. This is how it worked, offers of support as we leapfrogged every few miles. We were also given a sweet tin of 1p pieces, about £5 worth, as if my rucksack needed any extra ballast.

It was fine and sunny as we walked to Newlyn. Some 20 years earlier MW commented that the Cornish fishing industry had been centralised at Newlyn, at the commercial expense of villages like Mousehole, and went on to be quite scathing of its position and practices alongside Russian and Spanish 'factory' catches. 'Hundreds of boats, diesel fuel staining the water, convoys of juggernauts waiting with refrigeration units buzzing.' It still had a fishing fleet, kept going, we were told, largely by the efforts of the Stevenson family. We found our way to a tiny Post Office to bank some £250 including all those pennies. I couldn't help noticing a somewhat dishevelled looking couple with children all of whom were huge. They clearly must be employed to eat all the town's unwanted pasties, doughnuts, chips and fish batter, finished off with Cornish cream and fudge. We were to hear more of them that evening.

We looked down on the current lifeboat on her mooring before passing the former station at Penlee Point. Some workers were doing some remedial work to the shed, so we were able to have a look inside. It had a quiet, easy but solemn feel about it. The interior winding gear and all, was just as it was last viewed by eight crewmen on 19 December 1981 before losing their lives on the Solomon Browne rescue attempt.

In Mousehole ladies taking a break from their shops sat in the sun putting the world to rights – either that or they were awaiting to take their star gazey pies out of the oven. Some boats rested on their moorings while others lay on the sand of a half empty harbour floor. It still had indeed the 'soporific air' MW commented upon. As we climbed up and along to Lamorna Cove, old quarry waste looked as if it would slide and

take out the cottage at the bottom. I couldn't help thinking that a gorgeous spot and house near St Loy, which had also served cream teas, would be a great retreat to return to after the walk to pen a book.

Porth Curno and the Minack Theatre lay ahead. In Cornish, Minack means rocky and until 1930 local fishermen had this spot to themselves. From 1931 to 1983 Rowena Cade, a woman originally from Derby, planned, built and funded this remarkable coastal showcase. This stretch of coast with more sandy coves like Pendower and Mill Bay interspersed with rocky outcrops and sea arches is mesmeric. Sunshine on the ocean making it look like glass or wet paint, the eye is led to the Longships lighthouse. Blocks of granite littered the way like giant Lego and in the distance a tented oasis appeared. It could have been a mirage but out of the haze the theme park of Land's End emerged.

Peter de Savery (owner of Bovey Castle on Dartmoor who had made us a generous charity donation) had given this spot a facelift in the 1980s. One of the tourist features was the RNLB the James and Catherine MacFarland, to remind us of our starting point in Scotland. It was only 874 miles back to John o' Groats. We had, however, come by the extreme eastern route and it was probably safe to say our journey was nearer the 3147 miles signposted to New York than the straight-line distance back to our starting point. (JM had done over 1100 to here from London and although we had not trodden in every one of his footsteps, we must have done something like 1000 ourselves from there. SH/RH had done 530 from Eastbourne.)

The extreme western route was even further, and all uphill, as we were so often told but this wasn't a time for thinking of that. It was a great feeling. I wanted to tell the world and all our friends; however, I couldn't reach the door handle on the giant Dr Who police phone box so was reduced to texting just a few. Time travel didn't take us to Hendra a few miles north, but we were picked up by Penny and Eddie who we had met at The Yacht (Penzance). They were to be our hosts for the next two nights.

'Hendra' - it had a name like it had come straight out of The Thorn Birds, Gone with the Wind or Poldark. It was a rather ram shackled old farmhouse and over salmon and salad we were to talk of our respective days. Just yards from the sea, Eddie referred to us and all the 'upright turtles' struggling along the coast path with their back luggage. A few drinks later conversation would lean to less guarded and less complimentary content. The 'fat family' from Newlyn also had nits and would use Eddie's garage for MOTs. They would test the suspension of said vehicle while munching away on sandwiches while he did the smoke test. All they needed now was medicated Hedrin and Slimming World. The slag at Lamorna was from a quarry where Eddie once worked, closing hastily, in his opinion, as 'it never made a loss'. The spot where I thought of writing a book was where Spycatcher was hatched, (not Tasmania) at least according to Eddie and in his opinion the lifeboat in 1981 should never have been launched - The Union Star should have accepted help before the weather worsened.

Knowing we would return that night, the next morning we left Havoc to play with Bosun, Eddie's dog, and look after our bags for a day. It was great not to have the weight of a rucksack. A morning sea mist accompanied us into Sennen Cove where surfers were busy in Whitesand Bay - waiting for that elusive wave. JM was met by three inches of snow and sheets of ice on this stretch in February 1978. The path was very broken. You were either stepping onto or over boulders, zig zagging a way forward. The flowers of the south coast had gone to be replaced by dry bracken, colourless heather and gorse. We negotiated the Cot valley getting ripped up by brambles and the rough stones underfoot were torturous.

Cape Cornwall is the only cape in England and Wales, there are only two in Britain, and is capped by a sentinel, the 1864 chimney of a former mine. Heinz bought the site in 1987. It looked a bit like a salt cellar - did they really need a 58th variety that much?

The ocean views are dramatic here as two great bodies of water meet. Huge seas, relentless wave force on rocks, it made the three of us feel very tiny and insignificant. 'Mordros' we were told is Cornish for sound of the sea, a constant accompaniment. Today, it was middling, but we knew it's potential to abate or escalate.

The Cornwall and West Devon Mining Landscape is a UNESCO World Heritage Site. Old mine remains punctuate this stretch of coastline; some have been partially restored. Tourists can visit a working Beam Engine or Pendeen Watch lighthouse or compare the scenery across the White Downs with that of Dartmoor, with its Tors, as we did. (That's the bit done for the Tourist Board!) We got as far as Treen near Gurnard's Head where Penny picked us up and took us back to see how Havoc was doing.

We dined out with mead at Trewelland, were shown the 'world's smallest house' (although folk in Conwy, Wales might disagree) before hitting The Star at St Just. This was a place that surely hadn't changed much, the sort of place you would think twice before getting out of your car, let alone attempt fundraising. We all felt very conspicuous. I explained to Eddie walking without rucksacks meant you were unable to 'advertise' what you were doing. Nobody carries a day sack the size of our packs and particularly on today's section, since we had hardly seen a soul, we had collected precisely nothing. The Star landlord was to ring the pub bell, announce suspension of service, before going around with a dregs bucket and demanding money or eviction. The generosity was fantastic. We wished everywhere could do the same, a third party asking on your behalf was so much more forthcoming and profitable. Thank you.

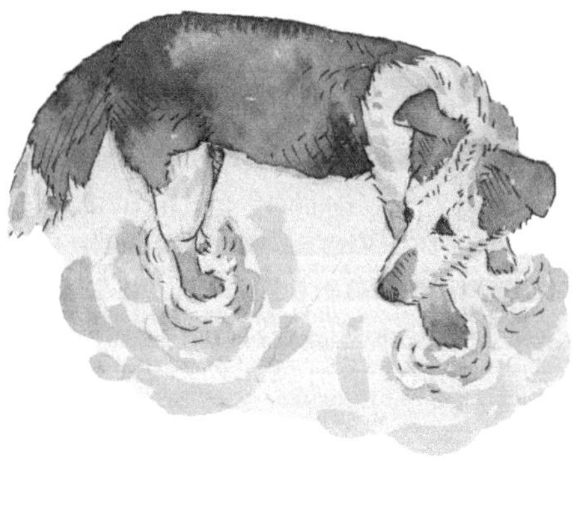

Penny returned us to Treen the next morning so we could continue along the north Cornish coast, 'a dynamic and dramatic interface between land and sea.' SH said the path here is tough, rugged and unforgiving. Certainly our 1958 sheet 189 OS inch map didn't reveal the severity of any inclines. I could hardly see the contours, let alone identify the contour interval. In addition to the ups and consequential downs, the underfoot conditions were haphazard. Where to place your foot, on a stone or in the spaces in between, one thing was sure, you never had a flat foot placement. This brought another drawback. Concentrating on where you put each step meant you couldn't look up to give the view and scenery the attention they warranted. This made it ankle sapping and in 2007 the summer came early.

Two thirds of the way through April and we were seriously thinking of taking afternoon siestas and walking on into the evening when things got cooler. Global warming? We were being grilled and Havoc with a fur coat was the most well done. He would scamper off into any gully in search of a thirst-quenching stream and take the first available spot, to collapse if there was a bit of shade. That from a gorse bush was all he needed, it didn't matter how rocky or dirty it was beneath him. Bluebells would turn a head in admiration and cast blue freckles over his exhausted form. We were back with our full packs and through Zennor Head to St Ives did many an impression of upright turtles, trudging forward, reduced to small steps, with our world on our backs.

A seal checked on our slow progress and a handsome fox, probably hungry as he was out in the day, stopped doing a double take. 'What are you idiots doing?', before silently disappearing. A long-horned bull was not so quick to scarper. With steam emulating from his nostrils like a kettle, he hooved the ground in a very clear gesture of annoyance at being disturbed. We stood there transfixed with a realisation that he could charge at any second. Wendy, not good with livestock of his proportions was in tears, and Havoc never said a word, knowing his place. We beat a rapid retreat over a fence rather than play matadors.

Approaching St Ives and before we had time to rehearse any limericks, we were met for the first of a number of meetings by Will Smith. Not, the American Hollywood actor, producer and rapper but a local chap, a keen coast path walker who had somehow been monitoring our progress. It seemed he was keen to check up on us, making sure we stayed to the path, 'not taking any buses.' He was an old boy, short, bespectacled and balding with a small day sack and two walking poles. With one, if not more front teeth missing, he looked like a cross between Max Wall and Jiminy Cricket. He was to come looking for us several more times before we got off the SW Coast Path catching a bus himself and doing sections of the path. He was clearly a man who loved walking, being outdoors, exploring and re-visiting parts of this National Trail. Either that, or he was escaping 'her indoors' and had never discovered coarse fishing.

Fast forward to 2020 and in one survey I discovered St Ives was voted the happiest place to life in the country, average house prices £413,000. They never stipulated, so it could have been the one in Cambridgeshire! That's a nice river port, Cromwell's old stomping ground. The town mayor in Cornwall, 2023 was advocating a tourist tax, so multitudinous are visitors.

The narrow streets of St Ives led us to Carbis Bay. Here Devon and Cornwall's finest were out in force. The entire constabulary were armed with shovels and metal detectors. Was it buried pirate treasure? Gold doubloons? Pieces of eight? An historic hoard buried by Mary Wolverston (Lady Killigrew) in the 1500s? The reputation of piracy deserves some mention while here in Cornwall and to think it was a pursuit exclusively for men, women were just as shady.

Could the police presence be searching for a crime ring led by Del Boy? A short distance up the road was parked a yellow, three-wheel, Reliant Robin, Trotters Independent Trading Company embellished on the side. I did my dutiful citizen bit, and took down the registration - D366 TFR. In the rear window, an inflated blow-up doll. New York, Paris, Peckham, Carbis Bay - did this car owner know no boundaries in his efforts to make a pony? Lovely jubbly! In truth, I have no idea what the police were doing. We were still rolling along. Not sure if we were being chased by Lee Marvin or Cherokees. The imagination running riot was morale boosting as we swept around Lelant, Hayle, crossing the Red River towards Godrevy Point. Labi Siffre took over, 'laughing sometimes does somebody some good somehow'. 1972. 'Don't cry, can't love, why am I lying now?'

Peering down from the cliff into a small cove we saw the biggest colony of seals we were to find anywhere on the walk. Over a 100, I stopped counting when I got to three figures, mainly motionless on a beach, looking like a disturbed box of cigars. We had the sight to ourselves perhaps due to the combination of burnt gorse and pig dung in the air. It was a welcome flattish walk with steep drops to our left, and a deep valley to negotiate near the Carvannel Downs. The razor-edged rocky cove of Ralph's Cupboard reminded me I needed a shave and we descended to the beach at Portreath.

A group of teenagers were clearing broken glass from the sand. Yes, you did read that correctly. A window at the Surf Life-Saving Club had been vandalised, not by them, and club members were putting it right. Surfing and surf lifesaving to the youth on this coast is a bit like football to youngsters in Liverpool. They are passionate, with competitions and opportunities to travel abroad, to the like of Australia to work, if your skills are good enough. We were allowed to throw our sleeping bags down in the clubhouse for the night thanks to Dave Green. We were even invited to join in the evening circuit training class but frankly were too knackered to partake. Questions on a life-saving worksheet about flags, rips and swell, none of which I had a clue about, served to illustrate how ignorant I was on the topic. I sat there as bewildered as listening to Jeremy Paxman on University Challenge night, where were Monkman and Seagull when you needed them? (Here's a good tip to impress the mother-in-law. Watch it twice, once alone, securing all the answers, then invite her around and play it again on the iPlayer pretending it's live. When Jeremy (or Amol Rajun) asks, 'who painted Nu conche, Reclining Nude, 1917', you can real off Amedeo Modigliani without hesitation and reap scores of points.)

Now, what does a club hall, right on the beach need as a must-have? Correct, a broom - to deal with all the sand traipsed or blown in. The size of this thing, you needed Ralph's Cupboard just to store it. You could get a coven of witches on this beauty. Harry Potter might have had his Nimbus 2000, but this beast was something else. With this baby you needed in-flight entertainment and courtesy drinks, it was a PSLC A380. (Portreath Surf Life-Saving Club - and as big as an Airbus).

Chapter 23 – Portreath to Welcombe Mouth

I've had my share of sand kicked in my face, but I've come through

"Life is a lot like surfing. When you get caught in the impact zone, you've got to get back up. Because you never know what may be over the next wave."

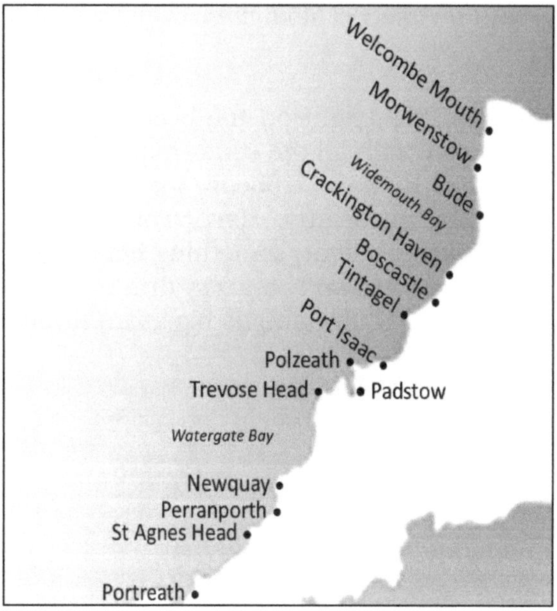

AN OVER-CAST MORNING greeted us, and by 8.30am surfers were in the water, boards waxed. Much of the old harbour at Portreath has been built on, 1970s style housing replacing ships. Not to be outdone by Cape Cornwall's salt cellar, a Day Mark Lighthouse called the Pepper Pot, stands over the town. As if purely to amuse us, Havoc sneezed several times. Signs saying 'Cliff Path Closed - due to landslide' meant a short detour to reach Porthtowan, another surfing village. We were ready for a cup of tea but at 10.30am there was nothing open. A local told me, 'We don't rush in Cornwall'. We did manage a free one at Chapel Porth before rounding St Agnes Head and climbing up to the Atlantic FM Radio Station. Housed in a former tin mine, we were interviewed by Chris Edgecombe on 105-107 FM air waves. Publicity was all about raising charity funds.

We headed on for Perranporth, the cliffs were spectacular and at their base some of the biggest, whitest wash we had seen. Saints of course abound in Cornwall, St Pyran is Cornwall's patron saint. His name creeps into all sorts of place names, this being one of them. The silver cross on the county's black flag represents tin spilling from the rock. Mine shafts lined the path, fenced off and capped with shallow cone shaped covers – a bit like a Chinaman's hat. These allow bats to fly in and out, the shafts are the homes for many rare species.

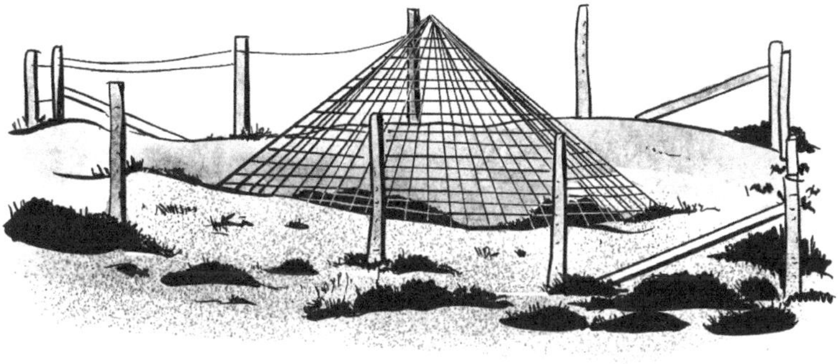

As if to say 'Just checking you hadn't taken the bus' - Will Smith, our spy on the path from St Ives, popped out from behind a bush. I was trying hard to count just how many front teeth were missing but couldn't help thinking of a Cornish Pixie crossed with Ives (The Mole) from The Great Escape - (the little chap so desperate to get out, he made numerous hair-brained attempts and was eventually machine gunned while scaling some barbed wire). Razor wire wouldn't keep this guy from us, and to machine gun him down might have been a bit extreme to stop him stalking. In reality, he was good company, and it was nice to know we had captured his interest. It was only a fleeting 'hello', and he was gone, Pixies can vanish like that.

Perran and Holywell beaches are a holidaymaker's dream, interrupted by rocky points like Ligger and Kelsey Head. The name Porth Joke alone brings a smile to the face.

The tidal inlet of The Gannel lies just south of Newquay. We had been treated during the day to great spreads of bluebells, buttercups and cowslips. Less pleasant was a plague of big hover flies, of biblical proportions, all with black swollen abdomens. Following this we were now to walk on water. A low tide footbridge was covered by a couple of inches of sea, a Red Admiral butterfly showed us the way. With boots in our hands and Havoc on a lead we crossed to Pentre and the promised land for surfers, Fistral Beach and Newquay. Watching each other, and to any onlookers (including the camera) it resembled a holy moment.

'Bill a Bong, Salt Rock, Reef and Wicked' - they were everywhere in Newquay and there were some 'Weird Fish' too. I knew a little bit about aquariums and zoos, Newquay has both, but nothing of surf life-saving, and even less about surfstreet fashion – 'Cool', I was not. We had been to Newquay with hash friends for a cheap weekend away, staying at a backpacker's hostel and had a great time. What I can remember of it! Lots of drinking, being daft, dressing up, drinking, cruising pubs, drinking – Monkey brains I seem to remember, Baileys (other Irish Creams are available), vodka, lemon juice, grenadine, served in a shot glass, or in the case of this trip, flower vases. We did exactly what stags and hens do when they go to Newquay. We could have some good times.

In Newquay now, coaches were loading up with the pink rinse, perm and trilby brigade. We waved. 'Oh, what a lovely dog, how old is he?' 'He's catching you up' I replied. It made me stop and realise that in dog years Havoc would be walking for seven years. We also said to one another that the next time we go away we are not hiking, we are going on a coach tour. There was something appealing about a snooze during an afternoon drive, before high tea, dinner, bingo, and a hotel bed. I also noticed on the map, Newquay airport, at St Mawgan. Another place where Wendy and I had been on a day trip with pupils from school, to sit in a simulator and help man a fire tender. Good memories.

There was no time to linger and reminisce, we had to go and call on Jamie. A certain Mr J Oliver, celebrity chef, had a hotel at Watergate Bay but he wasn't in. Visiting some school kitchen, I expect and winding up the dinner ladies, kettle on, not dino nuggets. (Unfortunately, the Fifteen restaurant/hotel closed in 2019, with the loss of 100 jobs.)

We continued north to Trevose Head to take in the lighthouse and the 'new' RNLI station overlooking Mother Ivey's Bay completed in July 2006. This is a hybrid. A wheelless gypsy caravan crossed with a conch, perched on stilts, with a ski jump for a slipway. The Tamar class 'Spirit of Padstow' must do a 'Telemark' landing when launched. The 'shed' has won several design awards.

Past the caravans of Harlyn Bay, the cameras and celebrity reception at Trevone made us rush for our hairbrush and make up. Alas, the small village of RV vehicles, cars, marquees, screens, lights, camera track and potted plants, to say nothing of a crew of three million, was not for our benefit, but for a Renault Clio TV ad. Several professional surfers had been hired along with two numpties, equity card holding actors, complete in wet suits, for a shoot which must have cost more than the entire budget of a small country. All for a ten second spot between Emmerdale and Corrie. The two cool surf boards strapped to a roof rack were going to blend the cool surfing image with that of a cool French tin box – the trouble was, no one had ordered any surf. When we got to see the edited version on TV later it was less than memorable and wouldn't get me rushing to part with ten grand just to be in the cool club. Memorable however the event was, for we were able to sleep in the marquee, providing night security and got an Oscar winning breakfast from the shoot canteen next morning. Wendy had woken with a spot on her lip but make up couldn't do anything for her.

We met up with Wendy's Auntie Ruth and Uncle Maurice. They treated us to a meal in Padstow. They were down holidaying in the Southwest and had come to see us, not the Renault Clio ad. They went back to their B&B in north Devon and through this networking we were able to stay there in five days' time. I invested in a new pair of approach shoes – 'Merrill's'. I thought they might be after a bit of a hero of mine, JM, and I might get a bit of his stamina. It turned out they were Merrell's and had nothing to do with John. The trainers I had been wearing for a few weeks now were well past their 'wear by' date. They didn't owe me anything. I had done all the training for and completed the London Marathon 2006 in them (h4:36:41, placed 20721- yes!) I had sewn the holes in the canvas toes up with fishing line and the cushion insoles, the gel shock absorber bit, were now as thin as an ice cream wafer. They based the McDonalds Saver Range advertisements, 'Like getting your money's worth' on me. Wendy and I did quite a lot of mileage, when weather allowed in trainers, they somehow were more comfortable than high ankle boots.

We had been to Padstow, now we had to walk there. We were dropped back at Trevone and headed for Pepper Hole and Stepper Point. We followed animal prints in the sand at Harbour Cove. Fortunately, I had done my Cub Scout tracking badge, even had a pair of Wayfinder tracking shoes in the 1960s, with secret hidden compass. These had turned me into Mohican Chiagachgook's lesser known second adopted white son and I could tell they were deer tracks. The roebuck a little further ahead was a bit of a giveaway.

At Padstow a number of coach trippers were unloading. It was a bright sunny day, Padstow looked idyllic and with a carefree and charitable feeling people rushed up to throw money at us. In no time at all we collected over £200. A delivery van opened its back doors for a similar number of footballs to fall out the back and roll all over the street. Havoc was in his element. He loved chasing a ball. Wendy would have it he was an England trialist. If putting your front paws around the ball and sticking your canines through the surface until you hear hissing makes you good, he would have had more caps than Wayne Rooney. I was left wondering how much of the £200 we would have left after paying for damages. Fortunately, a couple came to our rescue and offered us accommodation in the Scilly Isles. I was on the boat, but Wendy politely had to say it wasn't on our itinerary.

Padstein, as it is now known, due to Rick Stein's influence on the town was getting ready for its Obby 'Oss celebrations, 1st May, we were just a bit early. Rick must have been busy with that; we didn't see him. We avoided JM's long detour to cross the river Camel at Wadebridge. Instead, tightened our saddle girths for a free ferry ride to Rock. After all those footballs Havoc went for an extensive swim from the jetty on arrival in a waveless sea. The RNLI Southwest office in conjunction with the Rock Lifeboat Station had arranged a sort of half-way (although it wasn't) reception for us and we were treated to a cream tea on board the lifeboat. The crew turned out in force, in full oil skins, the press was summoned, and Havoc licked Cornish clotted cream from Wendy's fingers.

Our pre-walk networking had also put us in touch with some Slimming World members. We had been members back in Bovey Tracy early in 2006 and an article in their magazine had brought some offers of help from around the country. We were to stay overnight with Karen and Mark Meneer, their daughter Lucy and Fudge the spaniel. It was a Slimming World dinner - roast lamb and all the trimmings. After cream tea, just a few sins.

Rock has some of the most expensive real estate in the country, and certainly in this part of the world. (Average house prices 2019 - £1.6 million.) However, these paled into insignificance as we watched the splendour and spectacle of gannets diving for fish off Daymer Bay. One of the top sights of the entire walk. Seeing them retract their wings before arrowing the water and emerging with something very tasty, 'this one's not for you Mr Stein, all mine'.

Polzeath was where on an earlier holiday the idea of our walk had been hatched. Wendy's idea, she had read Spud's book, *"two feet four paws"* and this was the real inspiration. Walking bits of the coast we always wanted to see what was around the next corner. We would walk to a headland, then the next, but there was never enough time to go around the one after that. I wanted to enable that for her, she had the idea, but it was me that said, 'Ok, let's do it!' I remembered news items from 1978 when John Merrill completed his marathon. I was at college at the time in Exeter, my second year of a degree, living in Rowancroft House with about 30 other guys. I said at the time, 'I'm going to do that one day', they laughed, and I was immediately bundled by half a dozen of them and given a 'wedgie'. If I could help Wendy achieve this dream, then I would have given her something long lasting, more than any material thing.

Polzeath was where she and I took a couple of youngsters for a few days away surfing. We were working at the time, managing teenagers excluded from school, and we were employed to help reintegrate them. It was a very successful few days away in a caravan. We were to go back a little while later, to the same caravan with both her and my own children. Despite very careful shopping beforehand, my impatience with perceived food fussiness, and without saying anything, a raised eyebrow or facial gesture was enough, Wendy and her children upped and left. A less successful few days away. It wasn't the first. A similar thing had happened before in Dorset. I wasn't the greatest at forging a relationship with her children.

I can see the lion's share of responsibility for this in a family split/re-shaping is the adult's responsibility - I failed. Youngsters having 'lost' their own father might be hard to win over, I never did. I am sure I am not the only guy who has experienced this sort of situation. I didn't learn from earlier experience either, given a second chance, I blew it. It placed Wendy in a very difficult position, torn in a way between loyalty to her children and anything felt for me. Managing children in a relationship who are not your own flesh and blood is a minefield but my failing at it is, I think, one very important reason why our relationship was strained, and it has a cumulative effect. Brady Bunch calamitous.

With these memories of earlier visits to Polzeath I watched surfers trying to get upright, few did. I was beginning to wonder metaphorically if I would in my relationship with Wendy. At least manage to stay on the board, if only sitting/prone? Or wipe out completely? With no 'Sub Scorcher' in reach I picked up my air guitar. Brian May the inspiration. Bad mistakes, I've made a few, no bed of roses, no pleasure cruise, a challenge for all the human race. No place for losers, keep fighting to the end.

Rumps Point looks like a whale's tail on the map. We dumped our bags and ran around it. In profile on approaching, it looked more like the rear end of a dinosaur. Perhaps that is how it got its name? A group of bird watchers were visiting, one lady was terrified of falling off the path. She was on all fours, I hung on to Havoc's lead tightly as it looked like he might try and mount her. They said they had seen a puffin and a seal eating cuttlefish. Between them they did have at least half of Cornwall's telescopic lenses aiming at the poor creatures, who were we to argue?

Lundy Bay, Port Quinn and picturesque Port Isaac followed. It was all too easy to become blasé, the beauty we were being subjected to was stunning and spectacular.

We bumped into some people who knew Spud while freeing ourselves from an alley in Port Isaac. These were not made for folk carrying massive rucksacks. Tourism seemed to have taken over from the traditional fishing in this village now used as a set for Doc Martin, which in itself of course draws more visitors. I wondered how the locals wrestled with the fame, but then many of the cottages seemed like second homes or holiday lets. No wonder they don't show too many film clips of the maze of passageways we enjoyed exploring, Doc M (Martin Clunes) would have had to lose his love handles to get through these cuddle crushes. We climbed the hill to the chippy and Havoc got given a saveloy. I stood there doglike with my tongue hanging out, salivating, but was given precisely nothing. Somebody obviously thought my love handles needed no developing.

We camped at Port Gaverne, sharing our site with two guys, possibly gay, who were trying their hand at a spot of rod fishing while knocking back bottles of White Lightening cider from the Co-op (other supermarkets are NOT available). I pondered the difference between a saveloy and a sausage? The best I could conclude was that to those who could afford a posh restaurant in Rock or Port Isaac it was saveloy, to folk like me it was a sausage. I thought about asking the two guys sharing our campsite, but then thought better of it.

The hills and valleys of Cornwall just come at you like tracer missiles. At the Port William Pub, Trebarwith Strand, people stood and applauded as we came down the hill. Then one of the family having lunch took our collection can and went around on our behalf. (Many years later I would meet the lady from the party again, this time in Barnstable, small world!) Hi Jacquie!

Gull Rock (another one) shimmering in the ocean looked more like a lion to me than a gull and the stalker from St Ives, Will Smith, reappeared. We were now used to seeing his bowlegs and knobbly knees, and yes it was definitely two front teeth missing.

Tintagel can easily cast a spell on you. Its dramatic windswept Atlantic location, the myths and legends of King Arthur, the steps and walls of this once 13th century stronghold of the Earls of Cornwall. The site here has 2000 years of history behind it, it's just a bit mixed up. An Arthurian endorsement, while inaccurate is great for business. The ruins of the monastery, the thin bridge joining the Island and castle to the mainland. Rather like Will Smith, Ben Robinson would pop up here to uncover some Cornish secrets. The wonderful, isolated position. Like MW said, it was a great place for kids to have sword fights with pens, we did the same, a moment of fun not exasperation, resentment and anger.

The spell was to take effect for me as we approached Boscastle, how the moment can change. Havoc was off his lead. He caught sight of some sheep, and I didn't respond quickly enough to Wendy's warning cry; I was still at the Round Table. Havoc began his 'out run'. Phil Drabble would have been proud of him, sheep scattered in all directions, not such great marks for 'the lift'. I got an ear wagging, for not controlling her dog. On Havoc's return, a guilty look on his face and shame etched in his body language, Wendy snatched him onto his lead and strode out for Boscastle. I was left to give sedation to the sheep, and follow along half a mile behind, tail between my legs.

They were still doing remedial works to the village after the flash floods of August 2004. A former engineer from Birmingham turned Cornish Mr Whippy gave Havoc an ice cream. How did Havoc do it? He single handedly re-enacts a scene from Far from the Madding Crowd and is rewarded with a '99'. There was nothing offered in my direction, and I was beginning to think the dice were loaded against me, first no saveloy, now no ice cream. A reward for sheep rustling, all I could do was dream of the flake girl, who would have looked great in the waterfall at Pentargon.

A short distance to the northeast of Boscastle, the hamlet of Beeny. Here in 1870 the architect Thomas Hardy would meet his Emma at The Rectory. The poem Beeny Cliff and other novels would follow. The surrounding area would be the backdrop of their courtship.

We continued over High Cliff, imaginatively named, the highest cliff in Cornwall at 223 metres, before bumping into, you guessed it, 'just William' again, for the, I can't remember how many times. Through Crackington Haven and a long climb over Pencannow Point to a clifftop above Dizzard Point to make camp. Nearby, a dwarf oak wood, trees stunted by wind, salt air and shifting slopes. I collected some water from a cattle trough. Hold the ball cock down and collect the water direct from pipe, before it mixes with trough water (one for you Bear Grylls) and the inquisitive cows clustered around me. 'Who's stealing our water, get off my land!' It turned out to be a very windy night with heavy rain. The tent walls flapped nearly as much as Wendy had done earlier, but we stayed dry, and the tent pegs held.

It was still windy the next morning as we followed a wooded path through bluebells and primroses and admired the zig zag rock strata at Millook Haven. Whoever designed the distancing chevrons on motorways must have been here first. We saw many more adders between Wanson Mouth and Widemouth Sand, distinctive diamond marking, red, black - I felt a bit like Indiana Jones. Ahead on the horizon a satellite dish array at Cleave Camp, known as GCHQ Bude, between Coombe and Morwenstow.

On the canal at Bude a mum mallard had 20 ducklings each the size of a ping pong ball, how could they all be hers? There were no other adults around and she looked calm like a school playground attendant - at least above water. Her charges, growing in confidence were like hashers trying to find the trail and I couldn't help thinking they would be better off at 'Duckpool' (seen on the map) about five kilometres north. We grabbed a fry up, Havoc had two, before we headed that way to be met at Morwenstow by Mary M. She was the B&B lady acquainted to us via Wendy's aunt and uncle. We were to stay with her for two nights, at Clovelly.

Without bags again, and Havoc-less, having another rest, we started the next morning by visiting Morwenstow church. In the mid-19th century Parson Robert Hawker is credited with creating the modern harvest festival (1842), it was good harvest. I loved these at school as a child. We would distribute tins of beans to old folk after ploughing the fields and scattering. From Lucky Hole we crossed the Cornwall/Devon border at Marsland Mouth. It had taken us 22 days to cover our Cornish coast path. JM had taken 18, following a longer route, walking estuaries, clear evidence of his achievement.

Chapter 24 – Welcombe Mouth to Highbridge

She only reveals what she wants you to see

"Dimpsy days me 'andsome, alrite my luvver."

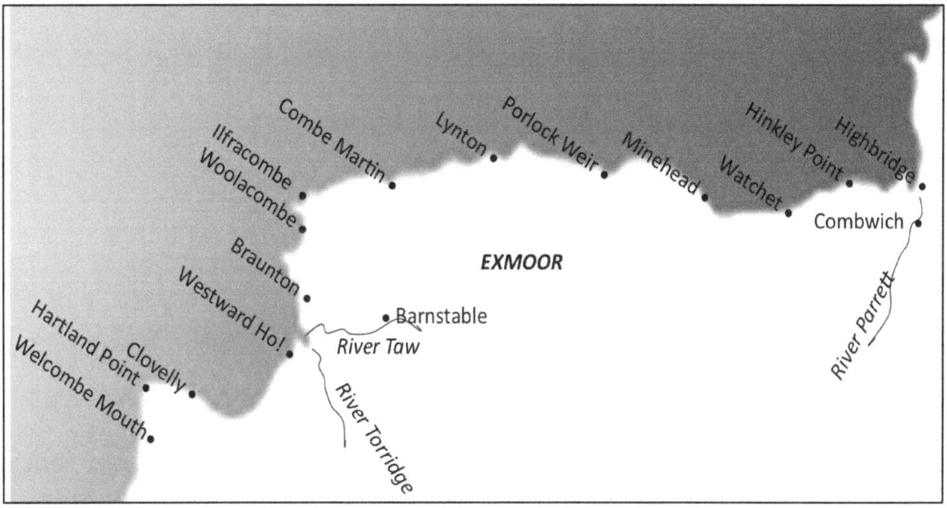

NORTH DEVON BECKONED. We passed and mentally noted a great camping spot at Welcombe Mouth with another waterfall, and immediately bumped into our travel guide nee companion, Will Smith, again. A slightly older Mr Bean crossed with Nobby Stiles? Anyway, you get the picture. He was to recount a story to us that will be a lasting memory of him. A day or so earlier out walking on his own, struggling over some of the high stiles with achy, stiff and aging knees he was finding them a bit unfriendly. So, he decided to go for the great escape and tunnel through the dog flap that some stiles have. Forgetting he had a day sack on his back he became trapped when the sluice like flap dropped, with him halfway through. He couldn't go forward or back.

"I would have been buggered if the wrong person had come along!"

He left us in stitches, hoping to join us again somewhere in Scotland. Goodness knows how he recovered his misfortune. He had become a good mate, we looked forward to him popping out from behind a bush, it was a pleasure to have known him. (This was actually the last time we saw him. Alas, he didn't join us north of the border, suffering a serious stroke, we were to discover on finishing our adventure. My best wishes and thanks, go to him and his wife.)

On this dramatic but tough section, waterfalls often tumble from valley mouths but the one at Speke's Mill Mouth takes some beating. We shared some cheesy chips at Hartland Quay and studied the wall map of SW shipwrecks reminding us we still had more craggy outcrops to stumble over. Children with Skern Lodge Outdoor Activity centre from Appledore summoned the courage to abseil on the rock slaps over the sea. I had done the same, 20 odd years earlier, 'showing off' to the kids I had accompanied there as a teacher from Wantage. Around Hartland Point, a lighthouse has done its best from 1874 to reduce the number of wrecks, (in 2012 it was decommissioned, replaced by an LED beacon and put up for sale.) Lundy came into view. Deep wooded valleys with more bluebells and wild orchids, and fields full of pheasants led us to Blackchurch Rock at Mouth Mill, a large arch stack with shales containing goniatite fossils. (My son with a masters in Geology would be impressed!) To me it was a giant capital letter 'A', but with two holes in it.

Donkeys welcomed us at the top of the hill above Clovelly. They used to carry provisions on the steep narrow cobbled street, 'Up-Along and Down-Along'. It is said Charles Kingsley had a soft spot for Clovelly, and perhaps wrote his 1855 novel Westward Ho! here while living in Bideford. The donkeys are now retired but remain for tourist interest perhaps made redundant by the animal welfare league or a quad bike. Garden courtyards, sledges, bags of coal all made great resting spots for the small army of cats. Clearly Clovelly didn't have a vet that believed in spaying. What with these and the donkeys, Havoc was hepped up and frenzied.

The builder in me noticed the pitched slates on chimneys stopping rain and Santa from dropping in. Youths competed to make the biggest bomb in the sea off the harbour wall. When I was smallish child and on holiday, I found a silver cigarette lighter among the pebbles on the beach. It led to a life-long aversion to smoking. Clovelly remains a magnet for grockles and film makers alike seeking the quaintness of a whitewashed fishing village, the New Inn Hotel ready to empty their pockets. While overlooking the harbour here MW spoke of being lectured by an enthusiastic little man from St Ives, wearing shorts! I would like to think in 1982 it was Will Smith.

Intrigued, I read more of Clovelly's uniqueness. The name seems to come from its location in a cleft or ravine. It has been in private hands since medieval times. A labouring fishing village that once claimed 200 men working 80 herring boats. The Carys may have extended the harbour and raised the height of the cob, but it was the Hamlyns and in particular Christine who had a vision for the village. She gave it its charm, made it beautiful. Restored, added decorative arts and crafts details, made it more refined for tourists. Steam ships and trains brought people from industrialised towns for romantic countryside and clean air. Artists arrived to paint the 'steep stair of houses'. Tens of thousands of cars arrived as early as 1936 and land was acquired from the church at the top of the village to build a car park. Hundreds of thousands now visit annually although it remains a working place. Houses are rented from an estate office and prospective tenants may be interviewed by owner John Rous for suitability.

Hobby Drive, a former coach path, leads out of Clovelly eastwards towards Buck's Mills. The seasons were moving on. It was early May and trees were in full leaf, the smell of newly mown hay in the fields. North Cornwall only really had dwarf stunted trees. I wondered if they had a word for these hardy, thorny survivors bent double by the ever-present onshore wind. I never heard one and the best that seems to be available is 'krummholz' borrowed from the Germans. By contrast the beech and oaks in Devon provided a green, shady canopy for even more bluebells now at their most abundant.

A scurry of squirrels had woken up and were determined to have some fun. Word was out in the trees 'let's tease this dog walker, who cares how far he's come'. An appointed gang member would start it off. 'Cooee, little dog, chase me.' Havoc would duly oblige. Just as he got close another bandit would stick a grey head up. 'Hey, fang face over here.' Havoc would be distracted and begin another chase. This would go on with the rodent army taunting until one led our hero into a dozing cock pheasant. Tail feathers flew and the disturbed bird just escaped to the air. The truncated cry was aimed at Havoc and the squirrels, the translation of which cannot be repeated.

We chatted with two workmen contracted to put up new gates to replace stiles. I couldn't help wondering if the cost was justified to allow an easier passage for a few. At least William wouldn't be 'buggered' in North Devon.

One of the Devonian articulated fellows recounted a tale of doing similar repairs when he met his future wife wearing sweet smelling perfume 'backalong'. I had never heard of it and asked,

"Is it Estee Lauder?"

"No, twas 25 year ago" came the reply. Like Bill Bryson in Oxford (Yvette story), I was probably the most exhausting idiot and work he had done all day.

I had attempted some surfing at Westward Ho! when I was with school children. Wendy had too. She came home one day in the months prior to starting the walk with a black eye, heavily swollen. She told me at the time that while on a staff training day in North Devon, supposedly doing climbing, she had been hit by the carriage on a zip wire. Turns out it was really a surfboard, but she was too wary of telling me. Only reveals what she wants you to see, brings out the best and worst I could be, but always a woman to me.

Westward Ho! town purpose built for bucket and spades providing holidays for all classes now behind us, we dodged golf balls around Northam Burrows to Appledore. Two large estuaries, the Torridge and the Taw, lay ahead. Between the two Instow. I read 'Time and tide are with us'. The local council had picked it as a bit of a strapline, by Thom Flaxman I think (a local from East-the-Water). Wendy and I had enjoyed a great weekend, staying at nearby Bideford RFC, on a hash away weekend in the early 2000s. We were scheduled to hash on Lundy, but nobody remembered to book the ferry tickets - hash mismanagement for you. We ran to Appledore instead. Years before I had 'seal' launched in a kayak off the parapet walk from Bideford old bridge, which won me huge credibility from the watching school kids, lower jaws on their knees. What we needed now was a boat. I had considered buying and carrying an inflatable dingy for times like this. Foolhardy! Fortunately, I hadn't, and Appledore lifeboat crew came to our rescue. They gave us rides across both rivers with an overnight stay in a pub in Instow. Time and tide were certainly with us. Short-cutting 'bastards' hashers would say, we would certainly have got 'down-downs'. I didn't care, JM had called this a 'messy bit of coast', MW caught the bus. There were no rules for us, we were following our own outer coast, we had seen RAF Chivenor before.

We walked shoeless from an inflatable rubber dinghy and began the trudge from the southern end of Braunton Marsh towards Saunton. The Burrows and dunes are made mainly of crushed shells, 'glued' together by marram roots. The soft sand was draining and littered with dead jellyfish. I began to think could they be collected and recycled, turned into some form of biofuel. Watch out for me on Dragons Den.

The surfers of Croyde Bay and the climbers at Baggy Point led us to Woolacombe sands. In the village youngsters with their team managers and parents had gathered for a football tournament. They taunted one another and the language was ripe, and that was just the mums. 'Get him, kick his legs', 'come on referee are you blind?'. What great examples we set our children. We were still at least eight miles from Ilfracombe via Morte Point where we had been offered a room at the Woodland's guest house and a BBQ. Watching kayakers at Lee Bay meant the coals were almost cold when we arrived at 7.15pm.

In 2007 Ilfracombe was one of the most socially deprived places in Devon if not the Southwest region. High levels of unemployment, relatively low qualifications and skills among inhabitants. I was once overlooked for a job here! In the High Street, rough sleepers in doorways, and Wendy and I reminisced about coming up to the Landmark Theatre to see Max Boyce a few years earlier. Now it reminded me of Madonna's conical bra, a fact not lost on many others. Capstone Point, Hillsborough and Hele Bay - it was tempting to follow the A399 and miss out Widmouth Head, but we didn't. At Combe Martin we tried buying meths but were given a swig by another walker, enough for a brew that night. It now seemed as if we were going at breakneck speed but actually, we had switched to a 1:25000 Exmoor OS Explorer map. The climb up over Great Hangman and the stony valley of Sherrycombe didn't deter Havoc who pulled like a husky. On his lead, restrained or lose him due to the gun shots in the distance. We detoured to Hunters Inn in the Heddon Valley for a meal as we hadn't picked up provisions. With little meths to cook on we camped in a nearby field, next to a babbling brook and heard our first cuckoo of the year.

That evening Havoc needed to calm his nerves and promptly climbed on the lap of a drinker demanding to sup his ale. He was a youngish chap, half dreadlocked with a hoody, the look of a typical surfer. His drinking partner was an older guy, balding and hoodless. I couldn't help wondering if the former in 20 years would look like the later. Havoc had begged an ice cream from a stallholder earlier in the day, now in this oak filled, bottomless valley he helped himself to the older guy's pint and half my steak.

While looking at the map that night in readiness for the next day I realised we were close to Parracombe, Martinhoe and the hamlet of Dean. Here we had stayed at a farm on a family holiday 40 years or so earlier. No wonder the feeling of deja vue. I remembered the journey down from Hertfordshire on 1960s roads in an Austin Somerset. What now takes four hours or so then took about what seemed like four weeks. (Dad, are we nearly there yet?) I wanted to ask the question again now, in respect of the walk, but the answer was straight forward - NO!

We climbed up to Highveer Point turning right to Woody Bay. Lee Abbey, a conference and Christian centre looked immaculate. The goats on the crags and pinnacles at the Valley of the Rocks had somehow avoided the cull and curry pot and ushered us to Lynton. The tarmac path, improving access for more and allowing the mobility impaired to explore, somehow spoiled 'Rugged Jack' for me.

Lynton's cliff railway was exactly as I remembered it, green paint and all. Powered by water and gravity it has carried the curious traveller and tourist since 1890. Lynmouth still seem haunted by the 1952 flood disaster which cost 34 lives. From here in 1899 locals hauled the lifeboat Louisa over Countisbury Hill in an attempt to assist the brigantine, Forest Hall. We hauled ourselves over the same hill, around Foreland Point and crossed into Somerset.

The leper colony long gone, the small church at Culbone remains a delight. Porlock Weir offered up little by way of camping spots, and we were forced to pitch tent on a patch of grass next to public loos. This turned out to be a canine toilet and not one of our best campsite choices. The lights of Wales beckoned us on across the Bristol Channel. Little did we know that even despite going via Gloucester we would be delayed before entering the land of the dragon.

Back in 1993/4 Spud had done a lot of her fundraising at holiday camps and was lucky to stay at many too. Not wanting to feel left out I had completed protracted negotiations to stay at Butlin's Minehead with a chance of shaking a bucket as well. Porlock, the pretty Bossington and Huntstone Point remained between us before we descended the zig zag path to the harbour and the giant hands and map, that mark the Somerset end of the Southwest Coast path. The Sarah Ward Minehead marker meant we could leave the acorn signs for other travellers.

The Butlin's bonanza turned out to be a disaster. I was always the driving force on the charity fundraising side. I would often leave Wendy and Havoc in a village hall or lifeboat station to go around a town at night trying to rattle a tin. I was always conscious of our pledge to raise £50,000. Roughly, £1000 a week, over a £100 a day - every day, for nearly a year, when sometimes we would see nobody. We had got off to a great start raising about £12,000 before starting, collecting at supermarkets, Trago Mills dressed in a Guide Dog suit, Sandy Park Exeter, the Torpoint Ferry to name but a few. We had entered Bovey Tracey carnival dressed as Dorothy, the Tin Man and Toto. I had collected all sorts of things new and second hand to auction. We had written to businesses and grant giving organisations. I knew we needed to work at it and on reflection I think that this was one major cause of fallouts between Wendy and me as we walked. I would not leave it alone, being very focused, perhaps over enthusiastic.

I remain just as compulsive on all sorts of topics, a fault I recognise but find hard to alter. I wanted the charities to do more to promote the thing. Like in Scarborough where we had walkers and publicity ahead. I felt the RNLI stations particularly could do more, blind to the fact they of course had their own ongoing yearly schedule and events to raise funds. Wendy was more realistic, often too tired in the evenings to go back out. She was also very self-conscious about the process, as I was, but to a lesser extent. We argued in the Butlin's chalet, voices raised, paper thin walls. I was hopeful she would join me in the bar and ballroom, with Havoc too, with all three of us the reception was more fruitful. That didn't happen, as well as the anxiety, I managed a meagre £91 for my efforts. Billy Joel had monopolised my eighth cranial nerve – leave Butlins out of it, he had built hotels. Carelessly cut you and laugh while you're bleeding, blame it all on yourself, Stranger. Havoc might recall the fall out in his autobiography, but the reasons for it are less well explained.

It some ways it was nice to be off the Southwest Coast Path. To have that behind us, not to see acorns every day. The white concrete blocks which now marked the West Somerset path however were hideous. (Described as 'secret and elusive' in 2014, at least the ammonite signs now seen in places are more stylish.) We crossed a golf course in wind driven drizzle to Dunster beach and caught a whiff of the steam trains on the West Somerset Railway. We hauled ourselves to Blue Anchor (we didn't meet

Vic) a SH acquaintance, and on to Watchet. The attractive harbour is said to be 1000 years old, watched over by a bronze of the Ancient Mariner and I would agree with JT 'it alone is reason to visit'. PH thought it 'run down, slightly sad, needing a bit of love and pride reinstated' (2014).

The path was fast becoming a joke. We side stepped ammonites on a beach where JM had collected them nearly 30 years before and trespassed our way nervously through holiday parks and caravans to St Audries. Here, in the distance we caught sight of two ladies, dressed in their fineries, one, a rather portly lass, in a green and cream bridesmaid's dress the other in an equally fetching off the shoulder blush pink ball gown. As we neared them, with a thought of gate crashing a reception, we were flabbergasted to realise they were actually fellas in frocks. Wendy and I both liked fancy dress/ dressing up, but here we just looked at one another. It was a strange time of year for panto and there was no sign of Cinderella. Having been tense in the caravans we were even more uneasy as we retreated up a side path sniggering to ourselves around the edge of the Quantocks.

Steep Holm and Flat Holm bobbed like two hippos in the Channel, and we carried on to Hinkley Point, with its platonic solid power station. All it needed was a coating of tin foil and Somerset would have the world's largest Oxo cube. A herd of deer and a badger in broad daylight, none of which had a fluorescent glow, shared the view. We stayed nearby at Holford in the Richardson household. An army of dogs were partly controlled by water sprayed from emptied 'Jif' lemons. A particularly alpha male Airedale took an instant dislike to Havoc's intrusion. Far from him having a particular dislike for bulldogs, Airedales seemed to be his great nemesis.

The 9th May, day 178, of our odyssey proved to be an eventful one. It started well enough in fine weather as we walked to the Anchor at Combwich. Ahead lay the river Parrett and a long detour via Bridgwater. We were due in Clevedon that night to do a talk at a Rotary dinner. It was obvious we weren't going to get that far. We would try to get as close as we could and a boat ride over the Parrett would also avoid any lingering pungency of the cellophane factory in Bridgy closed a couple of years earlier. (My son would later be involved in the site's decommissioning.)
I went off to find a boat owner and was pointed by the WI in the direction of the harbour master.

"He lives at the house with the silly barometer outside" I was told.

Arriving at his doorstep I knew I'd come to the door of a right character. Bill Johnson was upstairs dismantling a wardrobe. Balding, bespectacled, possibly in his sixties with a gammy leg and a heart bypass. The wind was blowing downriver to the sea, a more than moderate current running out leaving boats already marooned on the steep muddy riverbanks. He was hesitant about helping out, his brain telling him 'Let

them walk to Bridgy'. His heart 'let's give them a hand'. His old, dilapidated rowboat looked like the one Steve Mc Queen bought on his escape from prison in Papillion. As I stepped into it the seat gave way. We pushed and pulled to get the little hull off the mud. As we left the relative shelter of the tiny river harbour the current and wind hit us. I rowed for all my worth upstream against both elements in an attempt to make a diagonal crossing so Bill, returning alone, would have the elements to assist him to get back to the harbour. Wendy helped from the stern. Bill gave a novice oarsman advice from the bow as the rowlock-less gunwales came out in sympathy of the broken seat which Havoc trembled under, not daring to look out. Fighting a losing battle and exhausted we did not reach as far upstream as we had wanted and were forced to anchor up on an oar thrust at an angle into knee deep mud. We disembarked up the steep muddy bank at Pawlett Hams carrying rucksacks and Havoc in shuttles.

Bill now had to make his return and we watched in horror as the aging invalid struggled alone to avoid overshooting the harbour entrance and being swept towards the Bristol Channel. Blue flashing lights of a Police car and ambulance could be seen opposite us. We never found out if they were summoned to assist him, but we breathed a sigh of real relief to see him just make the safety of the harbour. I felt guilty about being too pushy at getting Bill's help. I can boast I have put myself out to help others, Wendy too, but this act of assistance was beyond comparison. Thank you, a true champion, saint and saviour.

We washed our legs and feet in a farm shed and headed off for Huntspill and Highbridge. Within a few miles I was feeling very ill. Was it the dog poo of a couple of days earlier, the river water or mud, some sheep dip I had come into contact with, nervous exhaustion or just fate - revenge on me for overbearing with Bill? Whatever, I was going down with a severe dose of Bridgwater belly.

Steve Maloy, a Rotarian and ex-copper collected Wendy from Highbridge, and me from the toilets, for a quick shower at his immaculate house, riot helmet in the porch, before taking us to a hotel in Cleveland for a Rotary dinner. Wendy did a great job of a talk, a grateful audience presented us with £350, and two bottles of wine. I sat in the corner, making frequent visits to examine the sanitary ware.

Andrew, Wendy's brother-in-law, was to Mondeo us back to Bath that night. Her sister's house was to be our place of rest for the next four days, in return for two bottles of wine. With a bum like a tap, I watched raindrops race down windowpanes and took time to see how quickly cloud filled skies changed. The Premiership season came to an end, Bolton's 2-2 draw secured them a place in Europe for 2007/8. Tony Blair announced his standing down as PM. While Gordon opened the bubbly, I dipped into Andrew's bookshelves, the most energetic thing I could manage. Wendy had her hair done. This was surely an opportunity, with the back-up of family to call a halt if she felt so unhappy. I am not suggesting for one moment she is a quitter, but as far as I'm aware she raised no concerns. It wasn't until a dose of antibiotics turned off the tap that we were able to resume from Highbridge on 14th May.

Havoc's Walkies Album

("all my pictures seem to fade to black and white")

Send off from loyal Guide Dog supporters. 11 November 2006 — Newton Abbot Station.

Solitary scenic submission. Stacks of Duncansby. 13 November 2006. It was often as special as this.

Sausages! Along with frozen crabs and live rats. Fisherman's cellar Keiss Harbour. 13 November 2006.

Meeting Granny Vera, long distance walker. Helmsdale —18 November 2006. Pair of size 5 sling backs please!

After recuperation with my friend Chris Bonney. Forres.
28 November 2006. Posh, plastic, Crufts candidates in tow!

Pet Cemetery, Cullen - 1 December 2006
RIP Benji

My Baloo impression -"oh that itch! Thank goodness for all this sand"

Tentsmuir, Fife — 17 December 2006
Is this the way to Amarillo?

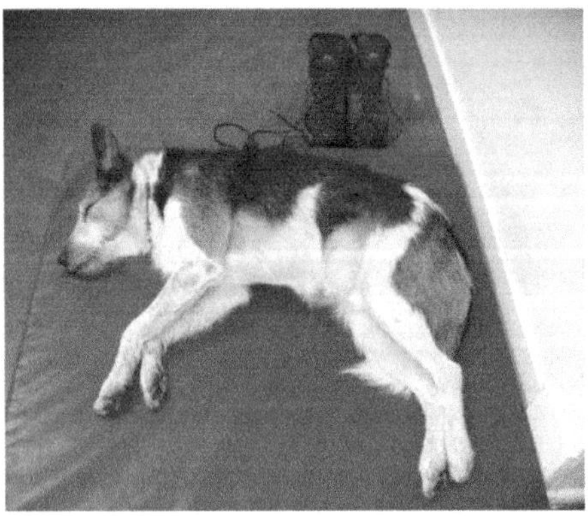

Early night! These boots stink!

My lovely friend Roz, in Edinburgh with all her dogs. Xmas 2006.

Spud and her husband Rob enlist "TEB" to wrestle a ram to the straw for foot spray. Kelso. 6 January 2007.

Heading for Redcar. Gas pipes, chimneys and eyesores.
16 January 2007.

Spume. Dissolved fat and dead algae. Turkish barber, Fat Larry singes my ear hair! Flamborough.

"I'm not wearing a life jacket or doing any pole dancing!" The Humber.

Call RSPCA Dog Line!

The fall and rise of Reginald (Havoc) Perrin. "I didn't get to where I am today!" East coast.

"Ok Mr Drabble, where are the 'bloody' sheep?"

Girlfriend — Norfolk.
6 February 2007

"Please sir — can I have some more?"

Martello tower - Clacton-on-Sea.
18 February 2007

Sold into piracy! Greenwich.

Holy Lifeboats Batman! "I never thought I could love again but you've shown me it is possible." River Thames.
26 February 2007

Happy Birthday to me! Bexhill.
"There ought to be a law against, anyone who takes offence".

To corrupt an old sailor's adage — "a bitch in every port"!

"Has anyone seen my sun glasses?" March 2007.

Barking mad! Pagham Harbour.
15 March 2007.

Primroses and blossom on the South West Coast Path, but wait, what lingers in the Devon undergrowth?

"500 mile walkies! Huh!"
24 March 2007. South Haven Point.

Global warming in South Devon.
19 April 2007.

Bluebell freckles. "They play "Havoc" with my hayfever." North Cornwall.

"Keep your ice cream, give me another pint!" Hunters Inn, North Devon.
4 May 2007.

"I've seen one of these somewhere else?" Newport, Wales.
20 May 2007.

"When you've finished with the press, can we go for a wriggle in the sand?" Llansteffan, Wales.

Cairn building. "This one needs to be on the top!" With my friend Ellie on the Pembrokeshire coast path.

"Here's one I made earlier."

"It wasn't me who made this mess!" Pistyll, Lleyn.

"Can you eat seaweed?" The Isle of Walney.

"Are you sure we're supposed to be up here?" Foxfield Viaduct, Cumbria.

"I can't get the lid off my coffee!" Resting with my friend Leakie Willie. Cumbria.

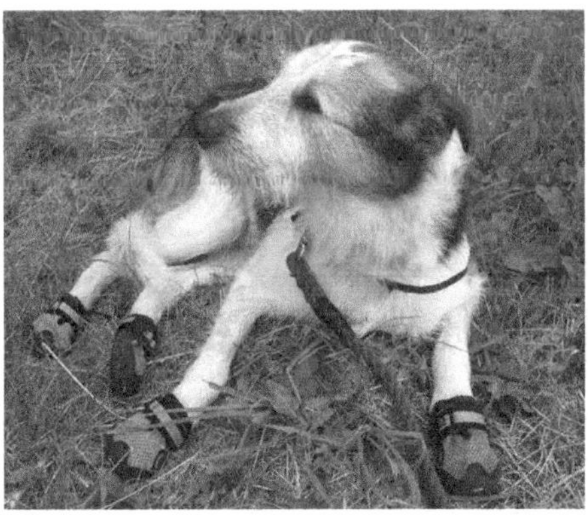

"A hate them so much, I'm not taking another step!"

'I can follow you no more. Why should the world take notice of one more love that failed' (David Essex)

"Dad being stupid again." Dumfries — The home of thick chips!

"I'm bored - pay up or I'm not moving off this step". Kirkandrews Kirk.

Pork scratchings! Islay.

"Mirror, Mirror in the lake, who's the fairest dog of all?" Islay.

"Excellent camouflage comrade" Hamster watching in Port Askaig.

Flower of Scotland! Dunvegan, Skye.

Lying in rocks looking for an otter.

10 September 2007. Fine weather in search of Gavin Maxwell's croft and Edal. "I must check out Ring of Bright Water".

The North West Highlands. Heading from Scourie to Kinlockbervie.

"If I get drunk, well I know I'm gonna be
I'm gonna be the *dog* who gets drunk next to you
And if I haver, hey I know I'm gonna be
I'm gonna be the *dog* who's havering to you" (The Proclaimers!)

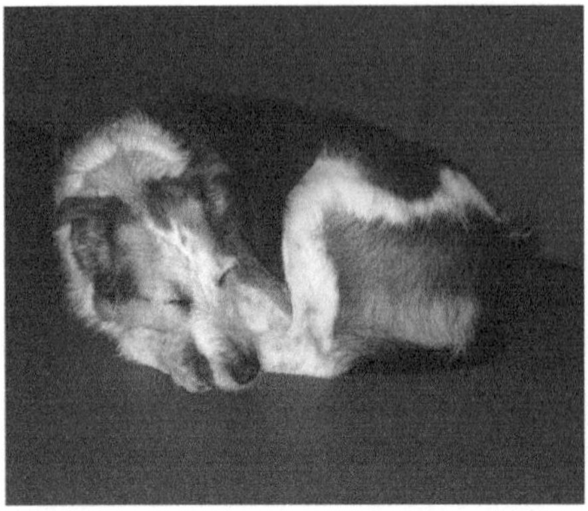

"I'm going to curl up so small you won't be able to see me". Isle of Lewis.

"I prefer mine with a squeeze of lemon!" Fish Farm, Highlands.

"Don't let the sun go down on me!" 5 miles south of Cape Wrath.
29 September 2007.

"Is it ready yet?" BBQ near Dounreay.

"The Old Man of Hoy did this to me". Heading for The Orkneys.

All over at Whaligoe Steps.
14 October 2007.

Chapter 25 – Highbridge to Cardiff

Sad, so sad…it's getting' more and more absurd

"Every day you wake up, you have one job - to be better than yesterday."

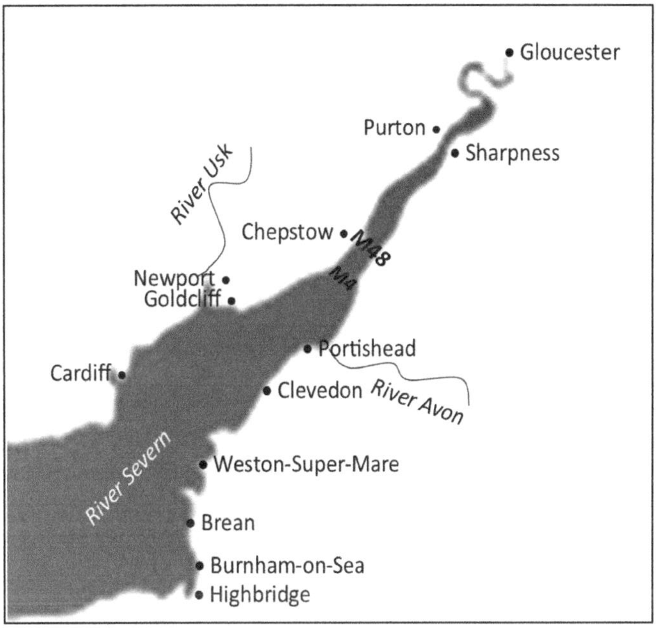

WE HAD PLANNED just a bag free short walk to get back into our stride. The legs felt heavy and achy as we headed off for Burham-on-Sea with its unusual low beach lighthouse. We then followed the beach to Berrow and Brean. The amusements offered Somerset's answer to Blackpool. Row upon row of static caravans, visitors often too overweight to climb Brean Down and get 360-degree views, shared with grazing cattle. A lucky find, the Brean Cross sluice near Diamond Farm, allowed passage across the Axe to the harbour at Uphill with climbers top roping on the cliff below the church. Then it was back along the sands again to Weston-Super-Mare. The Grand Pier allowed dogs - up yours Southend! A sign which should have read 'Tropicana Bar' now read 'ropi ana Bar' and made for a laugh.

(Fast forward to August 2022 'See Monster' was meant to champion innovation, creativity and renewables, the ultimate re-use. A converted North Sea offshore oil platform with trees and waterfalls was meant to attract visitors and boost tourism over the summer, right on the sea front.

By the bank holiday it was still in wraps, running late, something of an anti-climax, but would hopefully roar come the autumn.)

2007 - we stayed with another of Wendy's family, Auntie Anne at Sandford a few miles inland, allowing more recuperation, where we regained our bags. A large bungalow, with electric opening curtains on a timer - 'Um Betty!' They would have been perfect for an episode of 'Some Mother's Do 'Ave 'Em'. It did cause a bit of a surprise the next morning.

The challenge for the day leaving Weston was to cross several 'insignificant' rivers before arriving at Clevedon. Guide Dog puppy walker Tracey and the very handsome Bumble reminded us of our task as they joined us for a stroll along Weston seafront.

A church warden cobwebbing the bell tower at Wick St Lawrence, using the longest bamboo cane brush you can imagine, was pretty unhelpful with directions to find sluice gates despite having lived there all his life. I couldn't help thinking an old woman tossed up in a basket (17 or 19 times, depending on your nursery) could at least give us a birds-eye view. A drone would have been handy, or another Brean Down. Inquisitive cows would now do their best to block our way. Somehow, we crossed river after river, Banwell, Oldridge, Yeo and Kenn plus numerous other ditches all of which we had sped over effortlessly many times before a few miles inland on the M5 motorway. Like PH we must have committed act(s) of 'semi-deliberate' trespass. We avoided angry tractor drivers. Sea walls and isolated farms led us to Salthouse Bay where we met up with five more puppy walkers and their dogs. The Clevedon area Guide Dog volunteers were great uniting behind us and giving support.

Low arched bushes caused us to play 'Oranges and Lemons' to Portishead and there were plenty of brambles to decapitate yourself on. Being a responsible dog owner Wendy always cleaned up after Havoc. With the absence of bins, she had to carry this deposit for six miles. I teased Havoc saying it was a stool sample to take to the vet. He should prepare himself for a surgeon's thermometer or doggy colonic irrigation. His eyes widened and he swallowed as if he knew exactly what I was on about. We passed the impressive former National Nautical School building near Battery Point, and I wound him up even more by saying,

'If you don't stop pulling on your lead you can go and join the destitute and neglected boys housed there'.

A rarity in Portishead, we ordered a fish and chip lunch. I was in the wind-up zone. Local school teenagers were finishing for study leave prior to exams. They were all in mufti. I said to one dressed as a builder,

"Is that your white van, can you move it please!" He was very taken aback. "PPE - where are your steel toe cap boots?"

Wendy had to step in and say I was only pulling his leg, had he the boots he would have knee-capped me.

Our path took us through car pounds brimming with every conceivable model of Toyota and Fiat cars. Motors as far as you see in any direction, millions of pounds worth of metal, various colours, all covered in their protective wax. A foot/cycle path at the side of the M5 took us over the Avon. Looking down at the houses of Shirehampton it was clear there was a good business to be made in garden toys, especially trampolines. However, even the rubberiest 'Tigger' would have their work cut out reaching us on our elevated causeway.

The fuel depot, fertiliser works, and smouldering boilers meant there were plenty of 'for sale' boards at Avonmouth and serve to illustrate that not all the coast is cliffs and beaches. Denny Island was like a plug someone had pulled out, allowing all the water of the Avon to escape, exposing the muddy basin. The Severn Valley Way was interesting. Its signs were riddled with air gun pellet holes, fly tipping was epidemic and it was clear local magistrates weren't walkers, or they would have been issuing community work orders to sort it out. An attempt had been made to strim the metre-high grass, nettles and bramble but Havoc would stop in his tracks, confused and get frustratingly under my feet.

A walking pole or boot in his ribs encouraged him to get moving only for him to stop again, sniff and contemplate cocking his leg. His urge to pee was like that of an old man, lots of regularity, not much volume. (I now know exactly how he felt). He couldn't be marking his territory, who would want to inhabit these bad lands? We resorted to tarmac and lead walking before returning to wilderness again. Now Havoc would catch a glimpse of a rabbit and restrained would walk on his back legs doing a dancing bear impression. I swore him in as an honouree member of the animal 'where the fukawi' tribe.

A campsite at Salthouse Farm, Severn Beach near the 'new' bridge was home for the night and our Trangia smouldered like the boilers seen earlier in the day, with hot pot and extra vegetables for tea.

Next morning, we found our way barred by a locked gate. The wall seemed climbable, but little did I know it had been daubed in thick black anti-theft grease. We were trying to get out, not break in! We managed to avoid getting any on Havoc, we had needed to put him through a car wash before after a rotten egg incident some years earlier. With care the bags and Wendy escaped unscathed. I was covered in the stuff. All that was missing were the feathers. A family laughed at me from behind closed curtains in a park home. The dad looked like Captain Mannering and grinned at my predicament. Stupid boy Pike!

We headed for Aust and the 'old' Severn Bridge. Even that wasn't shown on our map which only showed a ferry. Oldbury power station came into view, Hinkley Point's long-lost twin. Fields of yellow saucer size buttercups, a green carpet of four-leaf clovers and a posse of stud rams escorted us to a tidal reservoir - really a paddling pool for power station workers! Two fellas in a van, flashing lights and siren approached. They weren't selling ice cream. I thought they might be bounty hunters armed with a dead or alive wanted poster. After months on the road, we resembled Al Qaeda activists, but they only produced a Geiger counter and proceeded playing in the mud. Instead of arrest they gave us a fiver for our collection.

CCTV must have caught an amorous courting couple who we came across. It reminded me it had been a long time since I had received a kiss. What have I got to do to be heard? Sorry seemed to be the hardest word. Havoc decided to be 'busy' mooning for the camera. I couldn't help thinking 'why are we doing this?' It was four miles to Chepstow, but we were headed for Gloucester. More inquisitive prime beef on the hoof met us at Berkeley. What looked like little bits of loin cloth, possibly tampons, hung on poles monitoring pollution, this time from the nuclear station there. We met up with Cupcake, to reminisce about a very great fun event we had been to at Berkeley in 2002. Organised by the brilliant hasher Mad Dog, a guy who reminded me of the Razorlight lead singer Johnny

Borrell or a young Jagger, the unofficial Hash Olympics, I still have my medal. I kept telling myself in the morning, you know it's gonna be alright.

We followed JM's lead and joined the canal at Sharpness to walk the towpath to Gloucester. It would have been just too easy to cross the Severn estuary at the M4 Bridge. We hoped we might spot something of the river's famous bore and the Forest of Dean on the north bank. I was very nostalgic about canals having been brought up living in a toll house on the Grand Union. It was one of the locations for a British comedy film, The Bargee staring Harry H Corbet and Julia Foster in 1964. In our efforts to get more publicity and hence more money for charity we had contacted all sorts of people. Ben Fogle, presenter and a bit of an adventurer himself is the son of Julia Foster so a letter had winged its way to him. Havoc had written to Paul O'Grady (RIP 2023) knowing his love of dogs. At Shepherds Patch Station near Slimbridge we had a phone call from one of his programme's researchers. It seemed they might be keen to have Havoc on the show. We waited hopefully, but it was in vain.

I couldn't help wondering that our next walk should be along the canals of Britain, no hills. The barges had fantastic names: 'Cherry and Whites' (Gloucester RFC) had just lost heavily to Leicester the previous week, 'Bristol Rover', Rovers had just won a play-off place at the new Wembley and best of all 'Foxy lady', most intriguing. For about £55k you could buy a barge, moor up at a pub like Pilot Inn at Saul Junction, perhaps do odd jobs, work for the Waterways (After 2012 the Canal and River Trust). It was just a thought for the future, Wendy and I both had to find jobs when we finished the walk. Lots of people thought this was a big risk, but it was one we were prepared to take. The itch had to be scratched. Neil, a cousin of Wendy had offered us digs in Gloucester and met us at the historic docks.

We took the opportunity to pop into the cathedral began in 1089 and the burial place of Edward II. Who might have admired the impressive cloisters previously to us in the centuries before? What pilgrims had visited here? I saw a definition of 'pilgrimage'.

"A journey on which we offer ourselves in God's service and ask for his healing power to guide us". We were making progress.

I wasn't sure how much we were offering but we needed a helping hand or two in Wales. We had received fantastic support so far, particularly in the homelands of the south, but our contacts were more dispersed as we travelled further west and north. I certainly felt as if someone was watching over us and gave thanks for that.

We said goodbye to Beatrix Potter's tailor and headed over the Telford Bridge towards Lydney. Then it was Westbury on Severn's water gardens at Newnham. The churchyard here offered great views. It was Saturday 19th May, our last day for a while in England and Cup Final day. Pubs en route had to be visited to try and find out the latest score. Come the final whistle Chelsea beat Man Utd 1-0. It was the first cup final at the new Wembley, a certain Didier Drogba got an extra time winner and none other than Frank Lampard was named 'man of the match'.

We never got to see the bore. I would have to return to Minsterworth a few years later for that. Aylburton, Alvington and Stroat (sounded like a posh firm of solicitors), led us to Chepstow. The castle, I read thought by some to have great defence and beauty, overlooked the Wye. I was taken by the main streets paving inserts. The names of shop owners over the years were something I had not seen elsewhere. A building now a chemist was once a butchers, bakers or candlestick makers - interesting, at least to me.

The very grand St Pierre golf course had to be crossed as we headed for a camp site at Wallstone Farm only to find it was closed behind Heras fencing. We continued to Portskewett. It was time for a drink. In the pub we met Tim a financial adviser, drowning his sorrows ahead of the 2008 crash. We stayed in his garden, didn't even have to put up our own tent, his daughter's play tent was already pitched, so we squatted for the night.

Caldicot gave us a surprising and generous friend welcome, scores of invalid scooter riders came up to offer us cash. It was either a Welsh welcome (croeso) or 'go away now or we run you down!' It was like running to get the fastest dodgem at the fair after the siren had sounded but before the last riders had stopped. This was the invalid scooter capital of Wales, as Bognor had been in England, when was the international robot wars?

The Rogiet seawall led to Goldcliffe. We followed the cycleway to the transporter bridge across the Usk at Newport. Not only do roads and railways get squeezed into a bottleneck along south Wales's bottom but powerlines feel the same compression as they sing over-head and dominate the skyline. A gang of painters were busy doing their thing on the pylons. Not red or green or aqua marine but something else. A sort of mucky grey colour. Heavy overalls hooded and masked, a bucket clipped to a harness and cow's tails attaching them to the steel work. Swaying in the wind, self-spattered and 60 feet up over our heads. What a job, nearly as precarious as the barefoot scaffolders I had seen on bamboo poles in Thailand just before starting the walk in October 2006.

It was a good job we had used the transporter bridge in Middlesbrough back on January 16th (2007) because the Newport sibling, opened in 1906, was now closed (for lunch!). We crossed the Usk upstream on a new bridge and got our lunch free from Ranaldo's in the form of chips and a can of coke (not quite Egon Ronay recommended but Eager Ronnie had endorsed it!)

The Usk revealed itself in its full muddy glory with green weed in places which Havoc mistook for terra firma and promptly sunk straight through.

"You might think you can walk on water" I said, "but you're not JC!"

He shook himself in embarrassment and headed for the nearest bush to relieve himself.

Tredegar House Country Park campsite proved to be very pleasant - lake and woods, a surrounding wall, just difficult finding an entrance. The area seemed even harder to get out of the next morning as we attempted to return to the sea wall. Past Asda and Marshfield School then it was drainage ditches, what seemed like a Native North American Indian reservation with skewbald and piebald horses as we neared Cardiff. One last country scene before we reached metropolis - Shetland ponies with foals. They were the size of Beswick pottery models which adorn mantle pieces and good playmates for Havoc. It is interesting that SH here described,

"The mud, as like potter's clay before it is baked."

These realities had all their legs and ears, you could put away the super glue.

Chapter 26 – Cardiff to Three Cliffs Bay

Asso Asso Yogoshi

"Land of my fathers. Ar hyd y nos."

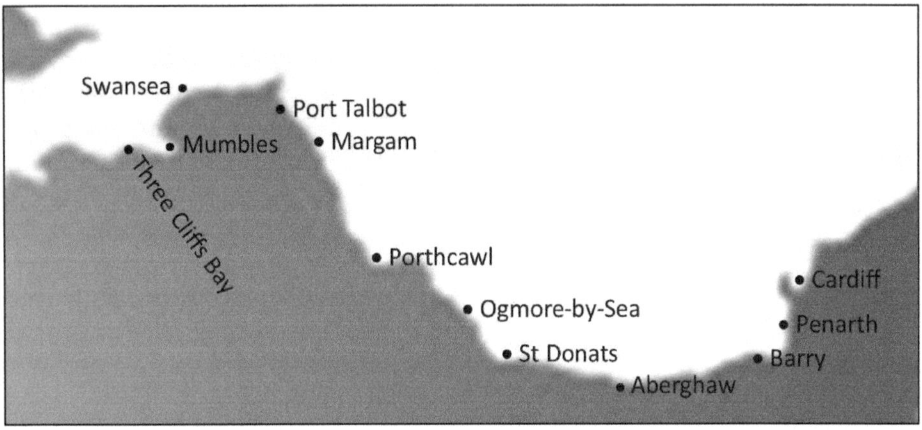

IN CARDIFF, UNLIKE JM, we weren't met by the Lord Lieutenant of Glamorganshire or any other dignitaries. We did meet up with one of 'the Taffia', Ponce Charming, a Cardiff hasher, after he'd finished work. His daughter, Daisy, immediately fell in love with Havoc, which was a good thing, because his wife, who didn't really get the whole hash thing (she's not the only one) was very unsure about allowing us across the threshold.

"You can walk over the Cardiff barrage" he said.

No access at the Cardiff end at the time meant we detoured some three miles over ground we had already covered to cross a bridge over the River Ely. On the Penarth side, in very sizeable letters a sign reading "NO PEDESTRIANS". Another indiscretion, but there were no signs on the Cardiff side, so tough, too late, and we headed for Penarth prom. A beach at Lavernock Point, Sully Island and we bumped into a BBC film crew. At last, celebrity, bring it on! Turns out they were doing a bit on a future barrage across the Severn. Somerset, some ten miles away was clearly visible. Will you be able to walk that in years to come I thought? (2024 - no!)

Coal yards and docks at Barry proved another headache. Again, we found ourselves lost. Negotiating the Welsh coast was proving to be hard; they need a Coast Path I thought. (It wasn't until 2012 that they managed it.) We briefly stepped onto Barry Island, just to check Butlin's had gone, closed 1996 (I had been there with a group of primary age children from Tavistock in 1978 - hoping to impress a young female teacher employed there.) 'Truth be told' it was 'tidy', 'I'm not going to lie to you' visiting old haunts. 'Fair play' Nessa, 'Crackin!'

New houses and caravans in old quarries at Porthkerry and Rhoose, then East Aberthaw before St Athan. Our host there, another through Slimming World, was Melonie, who I would discover was a South Wales Policewoman. Now I'm a bit hesitant in the company of any police but her bubbly personality soon made us feel welcome and we were whisked off to a Slimming World meeting at Cowbridge. This surely was a first. Two round Britain walkers, one dog still slightly smelly, a police woman and a posse of well-rounded Welsh maids in the land of Charlotte Church. What is more we were given a juicer, that would come in handy! (We auctioned it for the charities.) Talking of hands, fortunately Constable Melonie didn't have all my details, so I avoided the handcuffs!

The coast here was actually a 'Heritage' one. Cliffs looked like courses of brickwork, some done by a master craftsman, others by his apprentice. Path 'byur' (excuse my Welsh) 'is a bit hard to find' we were told. Fields of wheat, very green considering the dry baked earth it was growing from, barley, peas and newly mown grass for silage. My legs became very inflamed with the grass seed, scratches and nettle stings, 'man-up' I was told. My allergen credentials, 'v, m, gf, hp, w, pn, sf, cn,' disregarded.

Atlantic College, St Donats is somewhere I had stayed before with Devon students in the late 1990s. It is also the site for an RNLI inshore lifeboat (withdrawn 2013) and a sandwich and hot chocolate were on offer, more sins, before we went on to Nash Point Lighthouse.

The brilliant white paint work of lighthouses sparked my mind, I had done quite a bit of decorating both private and commercial, leading up to October 2006. Who paints them? I was told Welsh winger JJ Williams (deceased 2020). I had played against him at Strady Park, Llanelli (now developed) in the late 1970s. A quick and elusive star for Wales then nearing retirement. With only a Rizla of space to work in, tight to the whitewash, in front of the grandstand I lined him up, I would sink him into the mud in touch, I couldn't fail. The crowd would applaud, we would get the line out and those silky white shorts of his would be caked in hallowed Strady mud. I ended up with an armful of nothing, tackling his shadow, the white shorts still straight from the washer and the crowd roared - with laughter! JJ, who graced the golden era of Welsh rugby, unscathed, went on to run an industrial painting business, become a self-made millionaire and was awarded an MBE, all because I missed that tackle.

A waterfall at Nant Cum Mawr and a 'secret' walled garden at Dunraven Bay then Ogmore-by-Sea, skylarks and what I thought was a peregrine falcon made up our afternoon. Havoc thought this was a kite, (the sort on a string not the ones that proliferate in The Chilterns) and went quite berserk. He tended to do just that if anything appeared, particularly in the sky. Sea gull, helicopter, 'Quidditch' centre forward. Kites were a favourite. Blood pressure off the scale, doggy adrenalin, flight and fight, true excitement. He would chase his tail as a pup, attack lawn mowers, children on scooters, wind-blown leaves - an intelligent little chap. A wade through a river and scramble over a rough beach meant we reached the huge caravan park at the eastern end of Porthcawl. The jungle drums had warned them, and we were politely ushered away to a rival at Nottage, who let us camp, but charged us a fiver.

I banked £101 at a Post Office the next morning for our charities. In 1978 JM had been weighed down by cheques and publicity, particularly in this part of Wales. He recorded on March 8th,

"Everything was getting out of hand. I knew that I wouldn't be able to cope if the pressure didn't ease."

This was in sharp contrast to our experience nearly 30 years later, we had to work for every penny and every bit of publicity. I would pick up coins, coppers and the odd 5p from the street when we saw them in a gutter. We used our own money to invest in two printed T shirts. With 'Charity Walk - Please Donate Now' embellished across our chests we reached Sker Point, Kenfig Burrows wading a river with the same name and onto Margam Moors and the steel works.

The sandy beach right in front of it was completely empty. I couldn't help wondering but for the factory, a beach this perfect would be covered in sun burnt bodies, bathers eager to top up their skin cancer. Instead, any brave enough would have to wrestle chronic lung disease from the atmospheric pollution. We turned inland, rounded the can workshop and stayed, thanks to Father M (Margam - as I never caught his name), camping in the grounds of a Catholic Church.

The adjacent social club filled our water bottles, and we were invited to join a private birthday party. 'Help yourselves to the buffet, stay for the cabaret.' The ensuing acts with a young Down Syndrome girl as Dorothy from the Wizard of Oz, to rival Wendy's impression from Bovey carnival, brought tears to her eyes. (The Tin Man remained as 'heartless' as ever!)

To cap it all, they handed us a cheque for £100 for our effort. Sometimes a cheque did come our way, when it was from 'ordinary folk' like these Saints in Margam it was all the more appreciated.

We walked past Taibach RFC and into Port Talbot. Being a Saturday, the shops were busy, and we browsed the tabletop market stalls before burrowing our way along a tunnel under the M4. Baglan, then a bridge crossing over the River Neath before taking a subway which allows golfers from one green to the next tee. What would Peter Alliss make of it?

Swansea beckoned, collecting from cars stopped at traffic lights, past new marina developments and posh flats. The cycleway to Mumbles was busier than the M5 at the start of the school holidays. The road train nearly ran us down and we dodged skateboarders, roller skaters, scooters and all manner of bikers past Black Pill to Lilliput. There to meet us was a giant, not Gulliver, but Leaky Willie a hasher from Swansea Jack H3. Now Leaky stands 5'1" in stilettoes, a centre parting like a golf fairway and a moustache out of a spaghetti western. What he lacked in stature, he made up for in personality and along with several other Swansea Jacks (and Jills), plus half the Mumbles lifeboat crew we were 'pissed yn dda' having seen Wales loose to Australia (29-23). (England had already been thrashed by the Springboks, so I didn't make a big thing of it!) Havoc had a set to with the Commodore's dog in the sailing club, we jumped from pub to pub along the Mumbles mile, gate-crashed a private BBQ and eventually settled down for the night complimentary at the Carlton Hotel.

Mumbles Lifeboat has some history over 180 years. Three lifeboats have been lost over the years in 1883, 1903 and 1947 - some might say a bit careless. However, 33 gallantry awards have been won and 18 volunteers over its history have lost their own lives in rescue attempts. The 60th anniversary of the 1947 disaster (23rd April) had recently been remembered, when 47 people lost their lives. The pier still houses the old boat house but with slipway problems the current boat sat on a mooring. (A new boathouse opened in 2014.)

We followed low craggy cliffs, green with bracken and trees, past small beaches like the gem, Bracelet Bay. Mumbles is also the start of Penrhyn Gwyer, the Gower, 97 miles of coast, give or take. The rain followed us all day and the wind picked up too. We tucked in behind a hedge to put up the tent at the campsite at Three Cliffs Bay. This was Welsh soprano singer, Katherine Jenkins' choice for best view in Britain.

I had stayed here before when my son was only a baby and washed sand from his scrotum in an outside sink, while others washed pots and pans. It had also been a destination of a hash run as part of the 2004 Cardiff Inter Hash, another fond memory of good times with Wendy. Today, it was where large tents hung over the cliff, some abandoned, their twisted poles and torn flapping nylon just left where holiday makers had not bothered packing up, just gone home to the TV. They would never trust Katherine Jenkins again.

'All through the night' I dreamt. Leaky lost in five-foot grass now, me on a *lugby* tour, a nine-foot outside half named Tommy David. Max Boyce karate chopping a giant leek and Katherine as a gosha girl giving me a *lub down* while feeding me bamboo shoots and wearing platform boots. It was The Vapors (1980) who provided the soundtrack. 'I'm turning Japanese, I really think so.'

Chapter 27 - Three Cliffs Bay to Angle

Take a black cat and sit it on your shoulder...in the morning you'll know all you know

"Happiness is a warm Welsh cake."

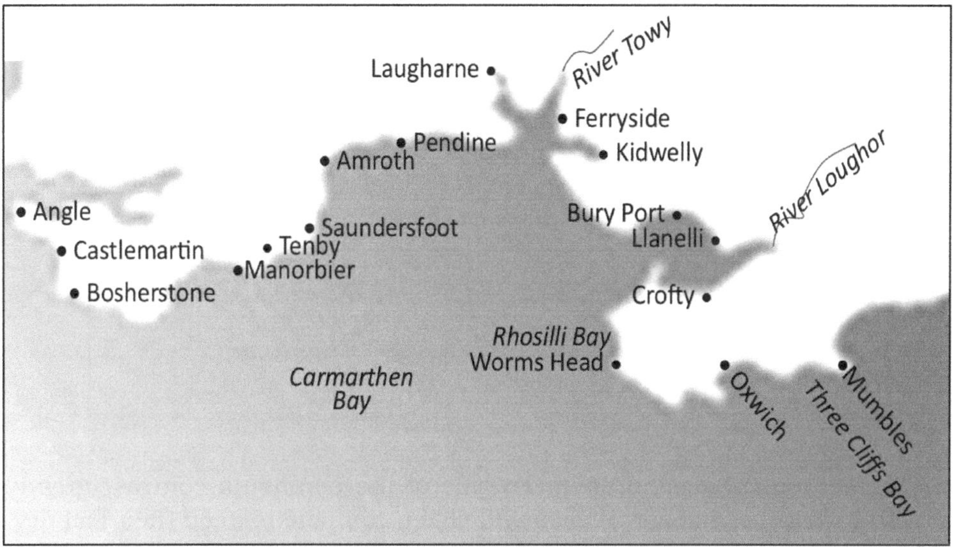

WE WALKED THE BEACH to Oxwich and briefly admired the Castell which is a grand Tudor manor house built by Sir Rice Mansel to aid social climbing from about 1520. Here, on the Gower in Wales it gave solid meaning to the phrase 'Keeping up with the Jones".

Being a Bank Holiday, Horton and Port Eynon Lifeboat Station had an Open Day with a cake stall. We were treated to hot Welsh Cakes which were simply fab-u-lous. It wasn't the best weather, hail stones meant the coat was on, off, on, off, and with ten more Welsh cakes in our pockets we headed off for Mewslade Bay. The griddled 'pic ear y maen' delights lasted all of two minutes once we were out of sight, we simply devoured them. Mochyns barus, I can still taste them now.

We were told the sheep, just to change the farm animal, which graze the turf on Worms Head produce superb lamb meat, but one in our path, dead with eyes pecked out by magpies, caused Havoc to cringe. The tidal island Pen Pyrod, it sounds better in Welsh, gets its name from Norse or old English, meaning serpent or, I prefer, dragon. Although remaining windy, the afternoon and evening continued bright and we enjoyed foxgloves, sweet peas and honeysuckle to Rhossilli, and the aptly named Hillend. Amid the dunes the campsite didn't take dogs and wanted £15 to camp. After a bit of gentle coercion, a complementary exception was made. With the dramatic sand and limestone cliffs and sandy beaches of the south Gower behind us we enjoyed a sunset that was worth 15 quid just to see it.

The marshes along the northern side of the peninsula contrast greatly with its southern coast. Ponies and sheep compete to keep their feet dry. On high tides the farmers take the sheep off, but the ponies remain using their necks like periscopes to keep their heads clear of the water. They could well be victims of rises in sea level if the heaters stay on. The early 14th century fortified manor house of Weobley Castle overlooks the bleak expanses of marsh and saltings.

From Crofty and Penclawdd we crossed the Loughor River and joined the Millennium Cycle Path that goes some 12 miles to Burry Port. This seemed pure overkill. The Welsh speakers might say, 'Dros ben Llestri' (over the top). Dressed with tarmac, scalpings and in places Redgra, it was some six to eight feet wide and surely the result of some 'over-generous' grant. It proved less than pleasant walking, better suited to bikes, but you could land a Eurofighter Typhoon on this surface, and I guess some Brussels' money helped pay for it. The National Wetlands Centre provided a welcome break, named in honour of Peter Scott, we were reminded of walking at Slimbridge and Sutton Bridge.

One could see few signs of Llanelli's industrial past. It didn't 'swallow us up' and we didn't meet its 'Ukranian Mayor' as Spud did. It certainly wasn't SH's favourite picnic spot,

"Litter, dog shit, peeling posters, weeds and the smell of industrial decay."

The power station at Burry Port had gone, decommissioned in 1984, and we hurried onto the 202 hectares of parkland, known as Pembrey. Cefn Sidan, (which always sounds to me like Kevin Sheedy, a professional footballer with Everton 1982-92) is actually eight miles of sand, fringed with dunes and forest. The park was once the site of a Royal Ordnance Factory and 3000 people once built Second World War munitions here. Nudity, the sign read is not permitted, but getting lost was. We were supposed to be heading north, but at times our compass read south, west and east. Eventually, we reached Kidwelly, where you can get two pub meals for £6.

The castle here, every hill in Wales has one, is built on a bluff over the River Gwendraeth. It was used as a location in Monty Python and the Holy Grail. We had no intention of coming back and didn't want our legs bitten off. The spire of St Mary's church has twice been destroyed by lightening. Not wishing to risk a 'third strike and you're out' I looked to pitch our tent in the grounds of the large Welsh Congregational Chapel, Chapel Sul. In the end we camped just outside of town. We didn't want to upset either the ghost (ysbryd) of Princess Gwenllian, wife of an ancient Welsh prince and Boadicea-like figure, or the town's black cat who struts the streets, both of which are celebrities here. We needed our legs in full working order. Ride a White Swan (T. Rex) filled by ear tubes. Da-da-di-di-da!

It was the back end of May and off we trekked to Ferryside in driving rain. The River Tywi is the longest flowing entirely within Wales. The coast path takes you to Camarthen and back down the other side of the Tywi to Llansteffen, about 17 miles. From its name Ferryside, clearly there used to be a crossing here. Now, if Gerald of Wales on his travels could use a boat, so could we. A friendly boat owner and a bit of a wade and we were in Llansteffen, a place where golden memories of Sunday School trips from Chapel would be had by many. (Sul's congregation told us so, see!)

A BBC Wales reporter, a young Hywel Griffith, met us but was only really interested in what had gone wrong. Unless there was adversity, there wasn't a story. We needed to master the art of Welsh yarn spinning, embellish things a bit, give it more 'Jackanory'. Think, The Boyhood of Sir Walter Raleigh painting (John Everett Millais) and there, you've got the picture. The odd broken leg, loss of consciousness, attack by roving 'Gwylliad Cochion Mawddwy' (bandits), but we were mere novices at interviews. The art would develop as we heard more 'hwyl' and got further west.

Wharley Point, an expanse of Carmarthen Bay rippling and swirling, despite more rain and we arrived at an old bell shed at Black Scar opposite Dylan Thomas country. The estuary of the Taf, an arranged boat ride through twisting marshes, two more wades, and we stepped foot into Laugharne, right by the Castle, 'As black as owls'. (Nice one Denzel – boat owner.) Thomas, when not exercising his turbulent personal life, is said to have written Under Milk Wood at his writing room a few yards away in 1953. He apparently wasn't the only man to 'behave badly' here. Neil Morrissey had pub business interests, lost a lot of money, made few friends and described himself (2009) as 'a rat leaving a sinking ship'. Certainly, in 2007, sat in Brown's Hotel, there were few who would buy him a pint.

A local bard told us, best hywl rolling off his tongue, the old ferry used to transport pilgrims on route to St David's, three visits to which were equivalent to one to Rome. 'The ferry did a roaring trade but strangely passengers were mysteriously going missing only to be found dead,' ychafi/erchyll (horrible). The ferryman, the obvious protagonist. The local constable was heard to say,

"If this continues, we will have to have an enquiry".

Hence, the ferry was closed. I pledged to come back one day and see more of this hardd (beautiful) place.

We bought a few bits at the Spar shop, still raining, carried on to Broadway and bumped into an old boy called Cecil Davies. He offered us a small caravan for the night and a chance to dry out. How generous, little did we know he was once a ferryman.

Having survived the night we now had to avoid the firing ranges which bordered us over Pendine Sands. In the 1920s 'boy racers' would attempt land speed records here. Malcolm Campbell and JG Parry-Jones duelled for honours. The latter was killed here in 1927. Six years later Amy Johnson with her husband took off from here only to crash at Bridgeport, Connecticut, short of their intended New York. In 2000 Don Wales, grandson of Malcolm Campbell set the UK electric land speed record on these sands in Bluebird Electric 2, achieving 137mph.

We followed the beach all the way to Amroth and the start of the 186-mile Pembrokeshire Coast Path. Passers-by were generous through Wiseman's Bridge and a tunnel leading to Saudersfoot. Havoc was attempting his own land speed record clearing sea gulls – 'Get off my beach!' Wendy recounted to me a story from holidaying here when her children were young. She was peacefully sunbathing lying face down, rays pleasantly warming her back. Her young son emerged from the waves, wet, cold and sandy and leapt onto a prone sun kissed figure; trouble was, it wasn't his mum! I told her of staying nearby in the aptly named Pleasant Valley in a caravan. I went off one morning for a run, nose leading, through woods, only to find the skinned carcass of a dog/fox hung by its back legs by a rope from a branch. I duly reported it to the Police, but when asked where it was had to hesitate as I wasn't sure if I was trespassing. What are the punishments for such in Wales? I don't know any outcomes, but we were talking at least. 'Rhyw' was still a bit far off! Past wooded hills at Monkstone Point and into Tenby.

I banked over £200, and we met Bob Fish, former singer with Darts (successful back in the 1970s with hits like 'Daddy Cool' and 'The Girl Can't Help It'). Other less 'cool' dads were queuing to get tickets to visit Caldey Island. The Monastery Island off nearby Giltar Point is home for Cistercian Monks. Twenty or so, we were told, have seven services a day, one at 3.15am, make perfume from gorse and other flowers and only have their peace disturbed by boat loads of tourists. I remembered going there as a teenager on a tour. Someone asked,

"Do you have many coming to join your ranks?"

The wise sage, on his own 'spiritual journey', with polite but masterful linguistic frugality replied,

"They come, they go, but mostly they go!"

The new lifeboat station, 2005, costing over £5 million and Tamar Boat, £2.6million, were very grand. (My £200 might buy a fender). We had been promised somewhere to throw down our sleeping bags, disappointingly it never materialised, or any other offers of assistance. The Salvation Army wouldn't help either, too busy selling War Cries or vanquishing foes. It seemed like we would need to walk out of town, find a green space and camp, but the tiny Christadelphian Church, wishing to get as close as possible to the early Christian practice, were lovely and welcoming. We were made comfortable; the heating was put on and we were left to settle down. Later, members brought cake and chocolate for Wendy and Havoc, while checking up on me. Good Samaritans.

We had a bit more of a look around Tenby the next morning. Majestic harbour, beaches, 13th century walls, arched gatehouse, viaduct, and many narrow streets and alleyways. Dinbch-y-pysgod in Welsh, literally, 'Fortlet of the Fish'. Again, noted as a place to revisit, we headed off, passing Old Castle Head and King's Quoit Neolithic burial chamber. We camped near Manorbier's Castle, thinking we would be safe, but more importantly, it was a few hundred metres from the Castle Inn. Close to a hedge providing a great scent of elderflower, we would surely be fine and out of sight. We saw Wales lose again in the second test to Australia, this time 31-0. Tears in beers here, and all over the principality.

Wedding guests at a reception hosted by the pub were friendly. We weren't offered to 'help yourself from the buffet', so bought a mixed grill. No one was interested in seeing my 'dad dancing' either, so we retired to bed. In the early hours the disturbance of cars leaving and guests in high spirits was annoying. Pranksters decided to take out our tent pegs, probably because they couldn't find the honeymoon car to decorate or the matrimonial bed to desecrate with rice. Havoc, never vocal when you needed him could hardly rise from his slumber. In my deepest, most vociferate voice, practised many times over the years, I howled, 'bugger off!' (I should of course have used 'bugger I ffwrdd.') Still, we did have some misery to tell the next reporter.

Past Swan Lake Bay (did we both need to leap in for a happy ending?) and on past Freshwater East to Barafundle Beach. An earworm came into my head, Stranglers, 'Walking on the beaches looking at the peaches', I was in 'punk' mood. It would have been easy to 'stay stuck here the whole summer'. Stackpole Head, and a little later we found ponies with foals who were feeding from their mothers' teats. I couldn't remember ever having seen that before in real life.

We used paths by Bosherston Lily Pools to go to St Govan's Cawl (Country Inn). In the hamlet there was a rabbit hutch, with a dog in it. It seemed dog mistreatment was rife in these parts based on this and my years earlier experience near Saundersfoot. I had to usher Wendy away and we warned Havoc to be on his best behaviour. In the pub, photos on the walls showing that this coast has great challenges for climbers and their scaling efforts were recorded. Once around the Head, St Govan's Chapel, a former hermit's cell is built into the cliff. The sea was a bubbling cauldron, fit for a witch, rather than a saint. Huntsman's Leap, a deep chasm lies a bit further west. It is within the Castlemartin military training area but access was open, even if you didn't have a steed, perhaps as it was a weekend. Folklore says a hunter on horseback jumped it, on looking back to the gap, he died of shock. Some horse, must have been to NCT and been breast fed!

The MoD control over 6,000 acres here. Depending on weapons being tested the exclusion zone can expand or contract. We heard gunfire, aircraft overhead and saw Centurian tanks at Merrion Camp. Havoc was trembling so much he had to be carried. Fortunately, we were able to get to Freshwater West and with sunshine and tea we could all regain our calm, while surfers waited for the opposite from an Atlantic wash. Watching boats enter Milford Haven was a further distraction as we turned the corner and arrived at Angle. Innogen, disguised as a boy, Fidele, (Shakespeare's Cymbeline) sought to make her fortune in Milford Haven. Euclid, the Greek mathematician may have visited, he measured angles, but if he did, he surely would have stayed permanently in such a beautiful spot. Since he died in Egypt, he probably never set foot in Angle or Wales!

Chapter 28 – Angle to Fishguard

But these two...Gumshoes. Picking up the slack

"Foxgloves shall adorn thy dells. They are loved by fairies as well as bumblebees who wear them as hats. They nod on windless days as good folk pass by."

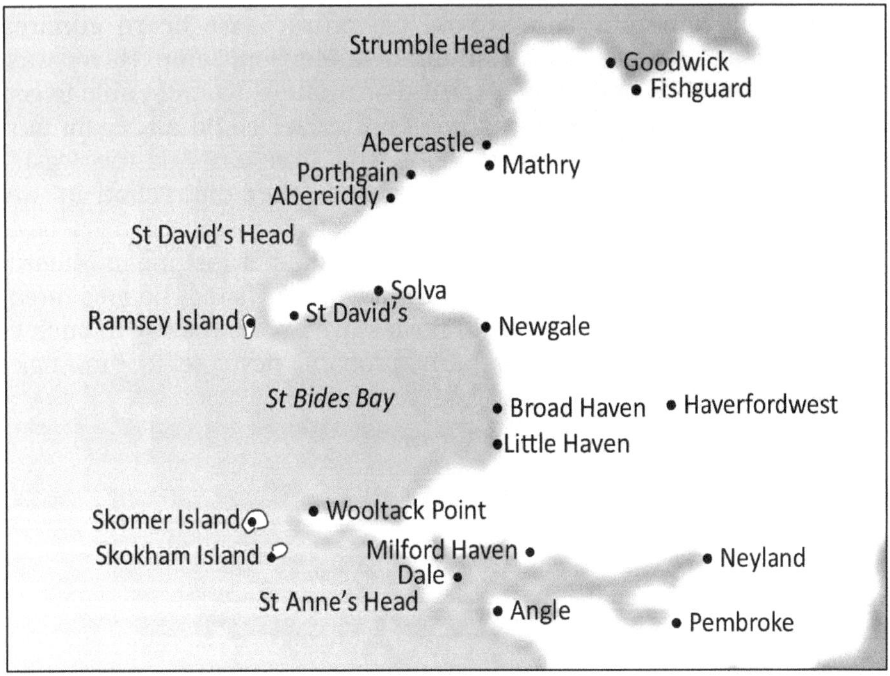

MILFORD HAVEN WATERWAY is a ria and natural harbour. Freight and passenger ferries, tankers, crane ships and drilling structures shared the waters with Stack Rock Fort. Wendy had set a new high for us finding a couple, Alan a lifeboat crew member, and Elisha his 'Slimming World' wife, who were to be our hosts for the night. Next morning, we had a tour of the lifeboat station, were briefed about the Watkins' family history of service to the RNLI and together with Bessi their dog, A and E walked with us.

Pembroke Refinery borders Angle Bay, its neighbour Pembroke Power Station was in the process of being converted from oil to gas. Jetties to jump, storage tanks, gas flares and flues and a good whiff of oil. Juxtaposed to these, tree lined paths, flights of foxgloves, oxeye daisies and very busy bumblebees. PH heard his first cuckoo of the year, 2014, here on 22nd April. We had to wait until 5th May in 2007 and we were back in North Devon. I knew Milford Haven was industrialised but had no idea how green and beautiful it was. One could imagine how it must have been before the late 20th century brought terminals and shore processing facilities of the oil and power industries. Liquefied natural gas (LNG) terminals were now under construction in light of dwindling North Sea supplies. I wondered if the Haven would be returned to its natural self when all the industry is no longer required, and fossil fuels have been eclipsed.

We passed a lovely old Welsh lady, quite resembling Hilda Ogden, sitting on her doorstep at Monkton who insisted we stay for early afternoon tea. It was a hot, beautiful early June afternoon and that was really welcome. We paid for it however, as it turned out she was the 'All Comers Talking Champion' of champions, and left Hilda and for that matter Vera Duckworth, in her wake. After hearing her life story and that of her mother, grandmother, chiropodist's neighbour, Uncle Thomas Llywellyn who used to live next door to Barry John, what an awful place Haverfordwest was and why St David was an ascetic, we finally managed to escape to Pembroke, just before sunset, as she paused for her first breath.

This time guide dog owner Eifon and his 'Slimming World' wife Jane were our hosts. They had two teenage children, an older Down's son, Lucy a retired guide dog, Bart, a working white Labrador, another visitor, and now additionally two itincrant foot sloggers with their dog. We had enough for a football team. What's more, they lived in shoe box. They could not have been more welcoming. We did have broth, but ours came with bread, we were never whipped and when it came to bed, we had a blow-up mattress on the dining room floor. It was all sublime, the queue for the bathroom extensive.

I must come back some day to look at the castle, I thought. We crossed the Cleddau on the A477 road bridge. It partly collapsed during construction, became operational in 1975, but was not even marked on our map from the same year. Between Neyland and Llanstadwell my phone rang.

"Hello, is that Paul Barber?"

"Yes, it is."

"Roy Noble here, you're live on BBC Radio Wales."

The Welsh broadcaster OBE, had somehow picked up on us. We had a chat, signal not great, me very tongue tied through surprise. What transpired is that Roy would ring us weekly to see how we were getting on through the rest of Wales. I may not have been Terry Walton scrunching up a compost bag on his allotment in the Rhondda on Jeremy Vine's programme, but I felt like a bit of a celebrity, and it helped with publicity. We were frequently told over the next weeks, 'I heard you on Roy's programme'.

Past more terminals and at one point I counted 25 pipelines running under a footbridge we crossed. Steppingstones at Sandy Haven and more at Musselwick and we reached Dale to camp after a meal at The Griffin Inn. Henry Tudor, born at Pembroke Castle, landed at Mill Bay near Dale before moving east through Wales gathering men before his fight with Richard III at Bosworth Field 1485. Result? One nil to the Tudors, Richard went to car park in Leicester.

The 200 or so villagers at Dale enjoy a pleasant spot. Children were sailing in dinghies, but the bay was as still as a millpond. I have taken children to do similarly on many breezeless days. Moving the tiller from side to side in an attempt to get some progress through rudder flapping. This half of the two villages guarding Milford Haven's entrance had set itself up as a bit of a water sports venue. The other half, Angle, across the water should have renamed itself 'Chip' and the Disney tourist attraction would be complete. Time for a Rescue Rangers' rendition. We were detectives, finding out what was around the next corner.

We left our bags at a campsite and quickly rounded St Ann's Head. The dramatic folding of Old Red Sandstone at Cobbler's Hole was nature's attempt to make a roulade. Having reached Westdale Bay we nipped back to collect our kit before paying another £91 into the Post Office account and breakfast. Marloes Sands on the peninsula of the same name, led to Wooltack Point. Stockholm (260acres), and Skomer (720acres), neither of which are tiny compared with Gateholm (10 acres) were like a giant's steppingstones around Wooltack to St Bride's Bay. Boat trips run from Martin's Haven to puffin watch on Skomer and we had a paddle at St Brides.

Little (and Broad) Haven lifeboat station allowed us sleeping bag space and The Castle Pub gave us evening meal. (Mum's sausage cooking wasn't needed here.) It is only right that the generosity of the landlord should be acknowledged. A glorious sunset, with St David's in the distance, and no washing up to do. The kindness of The Castle keeper extended to breakfast the next morning too, more reason to accurately record our stay. We didn't have anything for Havoc, so we fed him a little later at Broad Haven, 'PAL', from Londis.

Right on the coast path we came across The Druidstone. This venue hosts artists and had a very Bohemian feel. A wedding party was taking place, the collection tins were made obvious, and a cream tea enjoyed. Alas, not all was well. Two donkeys were resident, and we were told 'Jenny' had just died, leaving 'Jack' widowed and lonely. Wendy was all for taking him with us. Could be handy with the bags I thought, but how would I get him over stiles. It stayed with me to Newgale, on a dusty road, don't give up now!

Solva lying in a deep valley at the mouth of the River Solva, once an important lime burning anchorage, still hosts many boats. We met some Americans who were very taken by the nearby named St Elvis. I could not help wondering if local entrepreneurs were not missing a trick. A bit of marketing akin to Tintagel or John o' Groats. Get Scouting for Girls over for a festival ('Elvis Ain't Dead' was released in 2007), and this bit of west Wales would be on the map. The King lives. On the other hand, it could have been me who needed 'A lot of lobotomy'.

We were headed for St David's. This is the UK's smallest city; its status was bestowed by Queen Elizabeth II in 1994. David was the son of St Non, who's bay we rounded, born about AD 500 and later became Wales's patron saint. We circled the headland, with Ramsey Island across the Sound, to St Justinian's where we camped. The turbulence seen in the water here was crying out for some form of turbine harness. We still had a bit of energy to go back to the city and look around the Cathedral and the ruined medieval Bishop's Palace. The slope on the floor in the Cathedral was really marked. If you had dropped your collection money as the plate was passed round it would have rolled to the west door. A lady in a café took £120 from us all in coins, we could really do with less weight, this happened quite a lot around the walk, and we had the notes to bank at the first available Post Office. The only issue back at the campsite was spending a penny, the toilets had crispy loo roll, and this 'Bronco' is rather sensitive.

Whitesands was busy and we quickly strode out for St David's Head. The volcanic rock path around this plateau-like headland, with jagged outcrops, which reminded me of Dartmoor's Tors, was 'scorchio' and at Abereiddy we took our first swim of the walk.

Later, we saw dolphins, a peregrine and heard her chicks. An old, flooded slate quarry is known as the Blue Lagoon and teenagers were tombstoning. I don't think Leonardo DiCaprio was one of them, and we didn't smell any wacky baccy. All manner of water sports, kayaking, coasteering, diving and climbing were popular here. (The lagoon was later used for the Red Bull Cliff Diving World Series in 2012 - now they really should be on drugs.)

Once a prosperous industrial village, Porthgain is now something of an historical relic. Slate from nearby quarries was dressed here before export. Bricks were made, up to 50,000 a week, until about 1912. Other stone was crushed for road making. Some local houses, like The Pilot's Cottage, showed that poor quality slate must have been used for roofing. Some have been given a coat of mortar to aid protection. I had noticed similarly back in St David's. Now, Greater Horseshoe bats inhabit the old quarries.

Havoc met and seemed to have a conversation with an aging Pyrenean Mountain dog.

"Yes, I'm the dog walking around Britain, why don't you come with us?"

"I'm a bit too old I'm afraid, I would love to, but the hips aren't what they used to be."

"I could help you if you like."

"What would I eat, my teeth are nearly all gone, I don't have to floss anymore. You go on and have fun."

I had to tear Havoc away, on towards Abercastle, stopping for a look in at Carreg Samson, a 5,000-year-old burial dolmen. He wasn't the slightest bit interested. More so in a cow who had just given birth, its calf and sniffing at the afterbirth. The wildflowers, dog daisies, pink orchids and dandelions growing from stone walls were more pleasant to my sense of smell, but each to their own. I saw from the map the A487 runs almost parallel with this stretch of Heritage Coast through Mathry. Back in the late 1970s, on a touring holiday with an aunt and uncle, we had played football here, Wales versus England, with locals, using gravestones as goal posts.

We met up with Ellie, a Guide Dog contact of Wendy's at Pwll Deri Youth Hostel. I think they may have met when Wendy was preparing for or doing her across Russia tandem cycle ride, with a blind partner. We added our own small stones to a cairn before going to Treathro where she was putting us up.

Ellie would prove to be a great support in this far western corner. She was keen on nature and pointed out all sorts of flora and fauna the next day. Lesser Sand-Spurrey, Common Vetch like a sweet pea and 'Veronica Spicata' Spiked Sweedwell. This we were told was quite a rarity, protected in the UK since 1975 and a favourite with bumblebees. While accompanying us we also saw choughs, seals, more dolphins and more ponies suckling. It was great to have an informed guide and made me realise how little I knew; every day is a school day.

Around Strumble Head and into Goodwick lifeboat station to eat lunch. To the west the Isle of Man and Ireland. I was tempted to add them to our itinerary. Keen to see if *Jezza* had managed to obliterate his eight-foot singed seal (13th August 2006) or where Tony Hawkes (1998) had left his fridge. However, those crusades would have to wait at least until I had grown a third leg and could handle my Guinness.

Chapter 29 - Fishguard to Aberystwyth

An invisible force pulling me close to you... don't stand a snowball's chance in hell

"Lay not up to yourself treasures upon earth, where moth and rust destroy and where thieves break through and steal. But lay up for yourself treasures in heaven, where neither moth nor rust corrupt - where rust has been seen off by WD40 and thieves are caught on CCTV."

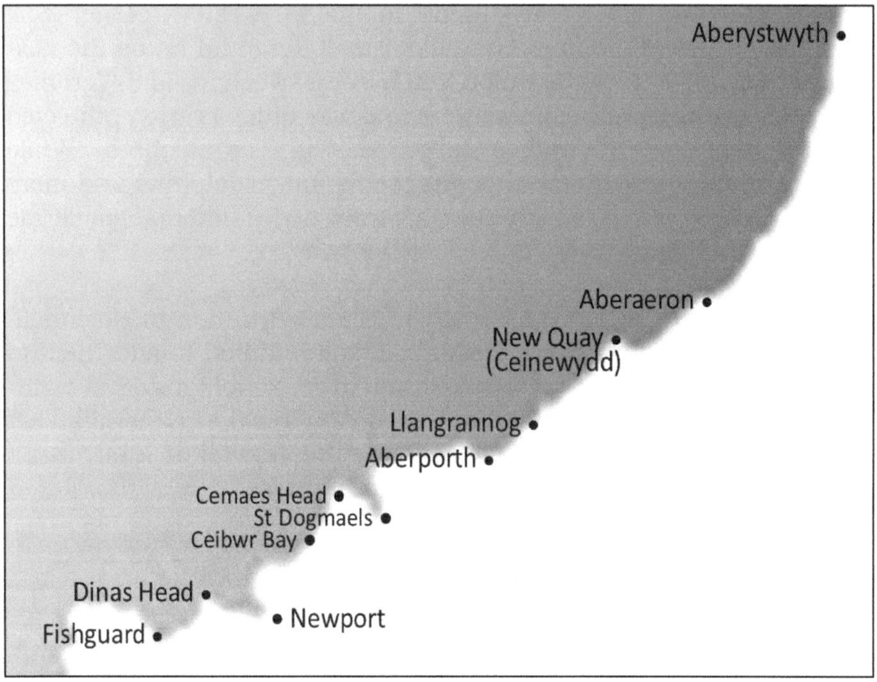

WHEN THE RAILWAY arrived with its head at Goodwick and the new harbour was completed in the early 1900s, Fishguard was once an important trading centre. It remains an Irish sea-ferry port. We carried on to Castle Point and found the remains of the 18th century fort. I learned from an information board, which I loved to read, that an American ship in 1779 had tried ransoming the townsfolk for £1000. Some canons were fired from both sides and the 'Black Prince' sailed away. To stop similar things happening again, the fort was built, completed in 1781 and some 16 years later was under attack, this time from a French invasion attempt. Folklore would have it a local woman, Jemima Nicholas, captured a dozen Frenchies single-handedly. The lesson for all is clear, don't upset Welsh girls wearing tall black hats and long red cloaks! Our day finished at Pwllgwaelod, the Sailors Safety pub near Dinas Cross, but not before Ellie had introduced us to Peter Byles and his wife Ruth.

They were to be our next hosts. We rounded Dinas Head with views to Fishguard and Newport Bays. The 12th century church of St Brynach, hit by storms in the 1850s and finally abandoned in 1859 was a landmark at Cwn-yr-Eglwys. We waded a stream (goodness knows how many that had been in the last seven months) at Newport Sands and continued on to the Witches' Cauldron at Pwll Y Wrach near Moylegrove. This is a striking geological feature, greeny-blue water and the tourist leaflets tell you to look out for 'daredevil canoeists and bathing seals'. In truth, nearly all of the Pembrokeshire coast which we were coming to an end of, had been striking, dramatic, sensational with friendly people, warm hosts and left great memories.

Peter and Ruth lived in a house right on the coast path near Ceibwr Bay. From their conservatory windows the views over the Irish Sea were breath-taking. Welcomes we received were always appreciated. When they were in a house where you could walk in off the path and walk out the next day directly on to our coastal course it was somehow special.

Peter was an ex-doctor, GP and anaesthetist, a former Cambridge student and a gentleman. An old sweater, white moustache, very honest, decent values, with a twinkle in his eye. He talked rugby, fair play, wood turning and moths.

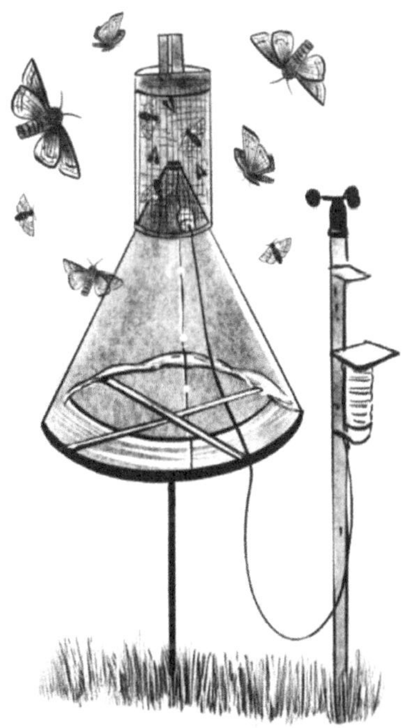

He could also spin a good yarn, but one packed with a wealth of knowledge. The house was full of a lifetime's clutter. Books on shelves, in piles. There was hardly a surface or square centimetre of floor space uncovered. Memorabilia, unusual objects, accumulated paraphernalia, hoarded stuff. Three bean curry, rhubarb and a carafe of red and it was time to go and set some traps. A selection of boxes, bulbs, funnels, gauzes and tents, we were after big game. Peter was a keen lepidopterist and our catch Gatekeepers, Speckled Woods, Commas and 'Lycophotia porphyria', True Lover's

Knot. How could that not be an omen. Three varieties of butterfly and one moth. It was a unique experience; how many other coast walkers could boast an encounter like this. Jethro Tull might have been past (1978) in order to write their anthem. Olivia Newton John, Moth to a Flame (1985) was certainly in my ear space.

Havoc was quite taken by Peter's dog, Jess too. They did one further good turn for us by dropping our bags at the Webley Hotel (now Teifi Waterside) but once known, according to Peter, as the Poppit Inn at Poppit Sands. The latter did not go down to well with certain chapel going ladies and hence the change of name.

We needed to navigate Cemaes Head before turning right along the Teifi. A dead sheep was being dismembered by a vixen to carry off for cubs and a murder of crows, more like vultures, fed or waited their turn at the table of scavengery. It was a feeding frenzy. Other sheep seem to have been genetically modified with two legs longer than the other two across the centre line for standing on the cliffs. The strata of these were fascinating, corrugated like a sheet of box section roofing material and then mangled by forces one could only imagine. This surely must have been home for a Harry Potter monster.

Although we had some mist and drizzle, we watched a great gathering of dolphins holding their annual swimming gala. Inquisitive cows seemed more interested in Havoc than they were in the 25-metre side-stoke or breaching puissance and did their own impression of Babs and Bunty from Chicken Run. Later, sheep wanted a piece of the action too. Some stood chewing like teenagers, others were cockier and more arrogant. They stood in the path like a western gunfighter, ready to draw, then they would lose their nerve and flee like startled school children playing 'what's the time Mr Wolf.'

We popped in to the former 'Poppit Inn', collected bags and carried on to St Dogmaels seeing off Pembrokeshire's western border. It had taken us just under two weeks and had largely been couple trouble free, I had managed not to be 'horrible'. It wasn't 'Endless Romance', and a verdict was still awaited to see if we had 'Fallen in Love Again'. We had at least 'Ysgafnhewch Y Baich' (packed up our troubles) for a while.

Crossing the Teifi we entered Ceredigion, turning north to Gwbert-Verwig and onto Aberporth. The 65-mile coast path to Ynyslas was not opened until 2008, but our maps indicated existing paths and rights of way. At Aberporth we stopped to shop at Londis. Bumping into a rather portly vicar we dropped lots of hints about where to stay. The advice we had been offered back in Erith at the end of February fell on deaf ears. We were directed to a campsite; on the way we saw a huge house which Wendy joked was a manse. When we got to the drive the sign read 'Rectory'.

The campsite officially didn't take tents, but they let us pitch next to a summerhouse full of children's toys, they all enjoyed a bigger space than our little tent. A clown puppet looking out was a Dick Van Dyke look-a-like (Chitty Chitty Bang Bang) and completely cosy. Through house windows one could see many empty bedrooms. Wendy was feeling sick, didn't want to eat, but had to manage overnight under canvas. Aberporth needed a 'friendship' bench and one or all of us needed to go sit on it. From generosity and Freddie many mates, we had quickly flipped to Billy no mates.

This little bit of coast had its own armada, in the form of pubs named 'The Ship'. Firstly, Aberporth, then Tresaith and lovely Llangrannog too, all within a yardarm of one another. Either, a sign writer was offering preferential terms for a job lot, they were all trading off each other's advertising or imagination in these parts was sparse. It did get me thinking however, centuries old pubs, from a time when customers were probably illiterate, could probably only recognise a pictorial sign. So, either the locals saw a ship and immediately the brain said 'ale/ rum!' or the local old master paint wizard could only do 'ships'. Looking it up, I found King Richard II in 1393 actually passed an Act making it compulsory for pubs and inns to have a sign. Who knows, there might be an Act to say every pub in these parts had to be named 'Ship'.

Showery rain and a couple of hills that took us a bit by surprise, we were ready for a cup of tea by the time we got to Cwmtydu. Over this, rather milky, so not so hot a beverage, (there was no charge, so I shouldn't really complain) we were asked,

"Where have you come from?"

A reasonable question, I just wish I had a £1 for every time it had been uttered. The problem was, how to reply. If you said, John o' Groats they would either come back,

"Where?" or "Oh, you're going to Land's End are you?"

If we said no, we are going to John o' Groats, they would say,

"I thought you said that's where you'd come from?"

A lengthy stop and conversation were sure to develop, which was fine if the tea was hot but in this case it was clear we weren't going to get a donation and we really needed to be on the move again.

If you replied, the last place you had been through or where you had started from that day, in this case Aberporth, the reply was sure to be, oh you're going to the next town, in this case New Quay, which we were, but the reply came back,

"Oh, you're going to Ceinewydd."

That brought me to another dilemma. Our maps had been almost exclusively borrowed from Wendy's dad, a great traveller in his own right, so he had lost some over the years. What remained were old and out of date and he never possessed the entire A to Z, or the equivalent in OS terms for the whole coast in the first place.

I therefore had no idea where 'Ceinewydd' was. It could have been next to the Sea of Tranquillity or somewhere you sit in a bucket seat and eat popcorn for a couple of hours for all I knew. We eventually discovered after quite a lot of arm waving, lots of 'dd,ll and wys' that Ceinewydd was indeed New Quay, one and the same. I knew we should have stuck to England. That wasn't the end of it however, because once the direction of travel had been established the next retort was,

"Did you go to Mwnt?"

At which point I should have offered round the Imperials and made a quick run for it. Dilemmas come in packs. To reply yes, might have been a lie, I wasn't really sure. One cove or beach tends to run into another, I could barely remember my right from my left leg, let alone one inlet from another, when they usually weren't labelled, and I had no map. I would be putting myself on a vulnerable footing, so I replied "no!" (However, on checking later, we had been there!)

"Should have gone to Mwnt, lovely there see!"

Mwnt was lost down the side of the sofa, and with the afternoon now gone, we weren't going to get beyond New Quay, by now it was antique Quay anyway. It was raining heavily when we arrived and our hoped for stay at the lifeboat station disappeared in the downpour, bit like the mints. We had no option but to camp. It continued to rain all night and by the early hours, we could tell because we were awake, we were witness to new meaning of the term 'water beds'.

Dylan Thomas lived in New Quay for a short time at a house called Majoda, 1944-45. He rented it for a £1 a week and called it his 'wood and asbestos pagoda' where his children 'hopped like fleas in a box'.

He drank at the Black Lion, still there, and after a scuffle one night had his house shot at. The perpetrator, a Commando Captain William Killick, said to have not been pleased with his wife's close friendship with the bohemian Thomas and his wife Caitlin. Jealousy, exclusion, suspicion of a cosy ménage a trois plus lots of liquor all may have contributed to this colourful New Quay narrative. We had had three in our waterbed, but it was time to head up the coast a bit further.

In this neck of the pren, (woods) 'Aber' basically means river outlet or estuary. There were more here than tribute bands in Sweden. Nearly as many as there were 'Ships'. Aberaeron was the next. It was a day which would force philosophical reflection on the term 'Circle of Life'. At one point a bird was hit by a car, it flapped, spiralled hopelessly out of control and died right at my feet. Small and colourless, my ornithological skills were insufficiently developed to know what kind it was. Later on, we came across another one squashed flat on the road. This time too wafer-like to identify. By contrast Havoc was full of life, literally having the time of his chasing rabbits, until he got scolded for not coming back. Wendy asked,

"What do rabbits do?"

I just looked at her dumfounded. Other than silflay, it was pretty obvious what they did, judging by the number of them! If they took too long about it, Havoc might have sent them off to meet Frith, faster than myxomatosis.

Caravan sites and little used paths led us to Aberaeron. After drinking half a bottle of kaolin, JM slept for 16 hours here. It was very pleasant with unusual architecture for rural Wales. Elegant, regency style houses, many brightly painted, quite a few with at least three storeys. Boats were regimented on moorings in a harbour only built in 1805. Before then apparently, there was little here at all. Now it has a population of just under 1500 and is the seat of the County Council.

By the afternoon my thoughts were returning to the Lion King. If Ceredigion's capital has one and a half thousand folks, its fields have many thousand sheep, as well as rabbits. The remains of a rabbit kitten were distributed in front of us. We also came across a ewe in a very bad state. Buzzards had started to have a go at her, magpies were gathering not wishing to miss out. It brought back memories to me and I could see from her reaction, Wendy too.

At this point there is a need to rewind a little. Before starting the walk, we had worked very successfully with children excluded from school, attempting to re-integrate them. A re-structuring brought a third party into our group. On one occasion trekking across Dartmoor with a couple of children, we had come across a similarly dying ewe. Miles from anywhere, no mobile signal, we wouldn't have known who to contact anyway, this poor creature had prolapsed, her back end was hanging out, eyes had been pecked out, and was hardly moving, but was still alive and clearly suffering. I suggested the others move on so they would not witness me putting the animal out of its misery. I took no pleasure in any of it, and certainly sought no heroism.

Months later, wrapped up with other 'misdemeanours and accusations', just as the organisation was undergoing another re-shuffle where we all had to reapply for our jobs, this third-party colleague brought up this (and other) events. My suspension followed and full investigation. At the authority hearing, in front of a panel of senior executives, I was told to return to work. When summoned to a briefing before this, the newly appointed head of the programme ignored the verdict and said I wasn't wanted. There were probably good grounds to dispute this, but I decided to walk away. When you know you are not wanted there was no point in contesting it.

I went on to work elsewhere, Wendy stayed with the organisation, continuing to work alongside the colleague who originally made noises of concern. It led to many rifts between Wendy and me. I felt unsupported, betrayed. If I asked about her days or made comments, probably often loaded with resentment, arguments ensued.

This latest dying sheep brought it all back to us both. The circle of life is not just biological, creatures surviving often on the remains of dying others. 'Musafa' was of course betrayed. 'Scar' or Swahili 'Taka' (the translation is worth looking up) did what he did. My resentment clearly remained at the time and although less so, still does. Life, however, moves on. Hukana matata.

We didn't discuss this much on the day, it would have been dynamite, but we both knew what was on each other's minds, albeit from different perspectives. I didn't have the temerity for another argument. We gave the ewe some water and moved on, hoping a farmer would find her soon. Through Penparcau to Aberystwyth where we had been invited to stay at a B&B right on the seafront. We didn't arrive until 9.30pm totally shattered, physically, mentally and emotionally.

Chapter 30 - Aberystwyth to Criccieth (Lleyn)

Open up your beach umbrella

"Nostalgic yearning in itself more pleasant than the thing being yearned for...my favourite place in the world, the south beach with its sewage outfall. Where's Dot Cotton when you need her?"

MARISE WAS OUR landlady. She had done some fundraising on our behalf which was a welcome surprise.

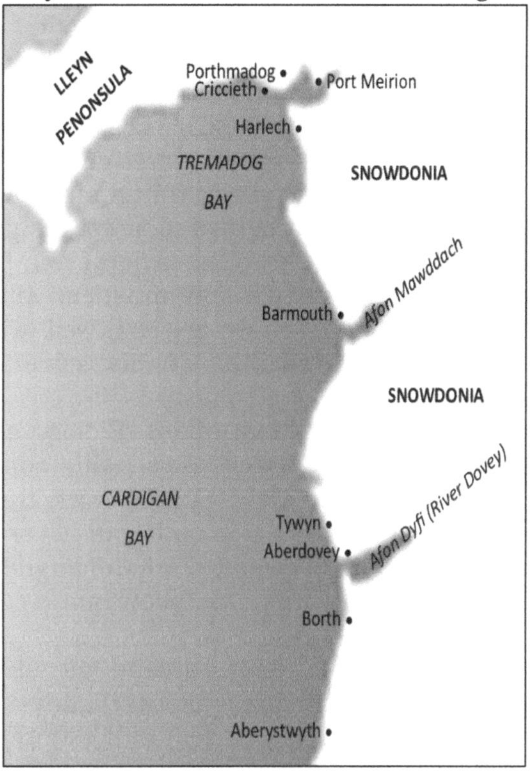

It was Father's Day and we decided to have a rest. We did some fundraising ourselves, went to Constitution Hill, known as 'Consti' locally, and to Pen Dinas where there is a monument to Wellington. Put up around 1858, it is an upended cannon, 18 metres high. Rumour has it a statue was to be placed on top, but it was never installed. We were told they ran out of money. The day also allowed us time to speak to our kids, dry things out and go to a launderette.

Havoc had emulated MW's travelling companion Boogie, and really let the side down. In fact, he had gone one better than even the roguish Boogie and had wet the bed. We were therefore desperate to get bed clothes clean, dry and back on the bed without anyone knowing. Hanging them from the back of a rucksack as we walked around town was a bit of a giveaway. Marise had two dogs of her own and would probably have been quite understanding, but how to tell her? I explained to Havoc if he got caught short again, go by the radiator. At least that way, one could blame it on leaky plumbing.

Gemma, a lifeboat member gave us soup for lunch, and we watched more dolphins in the bay. We had a very pleasant, relaxing day. Quite coincidentally, we bumped into an old colleague, Colin Harrison. Colin was an Habilitation Officer, who provided one to one mobility instruction for those with, or working alongside, blind and visually impaired people. He had trained both Wendy and me before moving with his family from Exeter to mid Wales. He was as surprised to see us as we were him.

From the seafront looking north, the Lleyn Peninusla looked a very long way off. That's the direction we would be heading the next day, Monday 18th June, after a second night courtesy of Marise and hopefully no more accidents.

We climbed 'Consti'. Apparently, I 'puffed' up it. I don't mind the term, it is 97 metres, clearly the powers that be thought most folk would find it tough, or they wouldn't have built a funicular railway. I had been nicknamed 'puffa' by some of the building site work mates back in Devon. With many faults, one of my strengths was my willingness to do hard physical work. I enjoyed it. If humping and dumping was required, I was your man. In fact, a hero of mine was Boxer, the workhorse, from Animal Farm. I would go as far as saying I was frustrated by others who didn't have the appetite for it and impatient with those without the aptitude. I probably wouldn't have got on well with Harold Wilson or Jeremy Clarkson. I still retain this quality, sometimes referred to as a whirlwind.

MM (Greenlights) talks about 'Biology and giddy up, DNA and work, genetics and will power.' He's right, 'some do get the genes but never develop the work ethic. Others work their ass off, but never had the innate ability. Some have both, but never rely on the first.' I like to think of myself in this category. McConaughey, should know, he's 'alright, alright, alright' words that follow him everywhere. Time to giddy up.

Over rugged cliffs to Borth and the lifeboat station, or should I say container - they do come in handy. The new station was under construction and not opened until later that year. The Ynyslas dunes now mark the end of the Ceredigion Coast Path and we had made good time along the route, heavy breathing, 'puffing' or not. At low tide near here, ancient, submerged forest stumps become visible.

Without maps, we were just keeping 'the sea on our left' (SH) and had not really noticed the detour that was necessary via Machynlleth, to cross the Dovey. Fortunately, Robin Goodlad, (appropriate surname) gave us an unexpected call. He was an Aberdovey lifeboat volunteer and offered a lift in his own boat across the Dovey, picking us up from the northern end of Ynyslas nature reserve. (I think Havoc may have been watching too much 'Only Fools and Horses', it was Robin, not 'Dave', or Rodney or Trigger.) This was a most welcome saving in time and energy. Boat rides take a lot less 'puffing', using the DNA.

A beach walk and across golf links to Tywyn. Here we became one third of a trio of divers. Diving for cover to avoid stray golf balls, while gannets dived for lunch much more spectacularly. Hazel, Fiver and company dived for their warrens to frustrate Havoc. We were moving into mountain country. Inland was Cadair Idris and Snowdonia National Park in the distance.

The saltwater lagoon of Broad Water and the Afon Dysynni were the next obstacle, still map less we needed local advice. JM had used steel girders of a partly dismantled railway bridge years earlier, even then taking a risk. We followed the A493 via Brycrug and onto Llangelynin. There is a narrow coastal strip here, the road and railway hemmed in by dry stone walls and Cardigan Bay. Footpaths veered inland. These were however very overgrown, other walkers or maintenance teams were making little impact on nettles and giant thistles, so probably just like any foot soldiers before us, we followed the road.

It was meaningfully coincidental that BBC Radio Four contacted us here and asked how we were finding the coast path. At this time (2007) there was a drive to establish an all Wales and indeed all Britain coast path, linking up existing sections, with better maintenance and encouragement for people to use them, establishing new routes where necessary and the media were keen to know what it was like on the ground. Then, we could only report there was a good lot still to do. The Dysynni Bridge shows, opened 2013, things have now improved.

At Llwyngwril it was our turn to do a Samaritan bit. A lady had turned her ankle and was in some distress. Unfortunately for her we were the only available first aiders! We sat her down as she was feeling faint, applied borrowed frozen peas, compression and elevation and with Havoc providing the distraction she improved. Just what she needed, leg stuck up in the air, toes blue and a tea towel strapping crushing her tarsals. Still, we left feeling good about ourselves. Our reward was tea and a sandwich, Havoc got extra ham, it was never fair. She was probably glad to see the back of us and get her peas back in the deep freeze.

On to the Mawddach estuary and the toll foot bridge, next to the railway, took us to Barmouth. SH/RH had to pay 30p each, but the wizened little man waived the charge for us. We looked for RH's father's pork pie hat, but it had washed up on an island somewhere miles away and years earlier.

We half expected a little karma for our earlier ambulance actions but there was none on offer at Tal-y-bont. By now it was raining, and we found ourselves dodging the heaviest in bus shelters to Llanfair and Harlech. Wendy was suffering again with her own planters, and there was no chocolate to be had as comfort. Shops had not replenished from JM's visit.

For some reason Jeff Beck's Hi Ho Silver Lining came into my head. The sun wasn't shining. Wendy wasn't making a fuss. Frozen peas may have brought back flies in the pea soup baby or thoughts of karma may have sparked lies are gonna get you some day, just wait and see. Whatever it was, there was little need to open up a beach umbrella. The only thing that was in anyway meaningful, was to carry on down a bumpy hillside.

It is interesting JM describes Harlech Castle as 'imposing but 'ruined'. SH calls it 'well-preserved yet bleak and inhospitable' on a grey day. It was grey and wet, I teased Havoc he wasn't the only mad dog as there were as least three more somewhere, the sweep of the coast here is called Tremadog Bay.

The very square castle, with rounded corner flanking towers may be an 'all-seeing sentinel' but I was not blind to the multi-story Harlech College. How on earth did planners allow this monstrosity? The castle seemed to be guarding an ugly swimming pool and a town full only of antique shops. (Hark at me, one half of an architecturally critical, carbuncled pair of old gits - I should invite myself to Highgrove.)

One man's coastal erosions are another's deposit and the Castle in 1283, once a 'sandcastle' with the sea at its feet, now over half a mile from enjoying a paddle, across a golf course and nature reserve.

The tune of The March of the Men of Harlech came into my head. The lyrics however where a bit of a struggle. 'Hark I hear the foe advancing' pom, pom, pom, 'Helmets in the sunbeams glancing', pom, pom, 'Men of Harlech on to glory, see the banner famed the story' de dar de dar de de de de, 'Cymru fo am byth.' Inspiring for another few miles, if Harlech's men could endure a seven-year siege in the mid-1400s, we could manage a stroll to the river Dwyryd.

At Talsarnau we met purely by chance, two visually impaired adults, Bryn, a carefree loveable rogue, and his partner Wendy. We needed somewhere to stay and were warmly welcomed to sleep on their sofa bed. We pulled out the bed, we could have just as easily pulled out a gun. They were completely trusting, but then again, they had nothing to steal. There was no kitchen, water from an outside tap, but they shared what they had. It was all very humbling, all we could do was to leave them a bit of cash the next morning, by way of a thank you. They probably put it in a charity tin somewhere. Travel restores faith in mankind. It was very true here, and replicated so often in our adventure.

Across the old toll bridge at Penrhyndendraeth (it closed in 2014 and had to be replaced) and onto Portmerion. The village is 'a tribute to the Mediterranean' and to its creator Sir Clough Williams-Ellis. It took about 50 years to complete and although very different reminded me of Cornwall's Minack at Porthcurno. Pottery, ponds, pools, it needed a lick of paint, but we could hardly complain as we were given complimentary entrance, Havoc was allowed in too! About when I was born, the iconic series 'The Prisoner' was filmed here. It must have been re shown many times and looking out over the sands I visualised the giant bubble rolling down to sweep us up, along with No. 6.

The Cob to Porthmadog (Portmadoc until 1974) was busy, the Ffestiniog railway, the oldest narrow gauge in the world, was beautifully nostalgic. Its paintwork, somehow in old fashioned colours, brown and beige, the smell of steam and the 'Cha, cha, cha' of rolling stock, slightly drowned out by the squeak from my shoes. We were after all in the land of Ivor the Engine. My shoes somehow sounded like 'Idris' when he just hatched from the fire box and the old lady on her knees washing her front doorstep was surely the wife of 'Jones the steam' waiting for his return after Ivor and his latest adventure.

Borth-y-Gest and Black Rock Sands led us to Criccieth. We were about to embark on a circumnavigation of Wales's little pinky, the Lleyn Peninsula. Lambs were keen to suckle from their mums, but this was a place steeped in modesty. Even the ewes would shun their attempts 'not in front of visitors Larry.'

Wendy particularly loved the smell of steam and coke. I think it reminded her of family times with her dad who was a bit of a steam anorak and loved to collect tickets from journeys. She was still troubled with sore feet, horrible as it was, there was little to be done. We tried various chemist products. She complained very little, was certainly not a shrinking violet but they were making her miserable. I just got the feeling sometimes that because I wasn't suffering too, and clearly by the rules of karma I deserved to, she felt fate was letting me off the hook at her expense.

Chapter 31 - Criccieth (Lleyn) to Carmel Head (Anglesey)

I see the crystal raindrops fall

"Soch's, wellies, umbrellas - what we really needed was a strimmer!"

I READ UP A BIT about Lleyn (Llyn). It was some 30 miles long, covered 150 square miles, had a population of around 20,000. Beaches on the south coast, cliffs on the north, mainly dispersed settlement of farms and small cottages, some compact villages, tourism took more of a hold after the railway reached Pwllheli in 1867. Thank goodness for 'Jones the steam'.

It looked quite remote on the map I bought, just to be on the safe side. I thought Llyn meant lake but couldn't see many of them shown, a dry spring or someone had left the plug out. I later found out its name is probably of Irish origin. I could barely see enough towns or villages for a six a side team, if I tried to find eleven, I certainly wouldn't have had any subs. It proudly boosted a coast path, so we wouldn't need the map!

We reached Criccieth and found out from the lifeboat station their last shout was for a beached Minke whale. I joked with Havoc if he wasn't good, he might end up with Pinocchio, in the jaws of Monstro.

This was Lloyd George country and the obvious ear worm kept wriggling in my head, 'he knew my father'. A huge campsite, JM noted it as Butlin's, it now seemed to be Haven, (2020 - Caravan and Camping Christian Fellowship), passed before reaching Pen-ychain point and onto Pwellheli. Nevermind 'P-Fweli or F-Whelli' (SH) a new worm took over. This time an even more persistent one, Billy Connolly's 'If it wissne fur yer feet in yer Pwllheli's.' Bastardisation inspired by Wendy's feet, and the need for wellies as it was now raining.

We even had a small boat owner give us a lift from the marina, it must have had at least 400 berths, across the harbour. Still with Billy's boots in my head we carried on to Abersoch. I was still missing one from Talsarnau, I knew that Bryn was dodgy! This is one of Wales' top sailing venues, with St Tudwal's Islands out to sea. Inland, more sheep. The Llyn breed are raised for meat and wool and did look like they were good mothers.

The perceived remoteness of the peninsula was not so born out as caravan parks seemed nearly as populous as the sheep. We were of course getting closer relatively to the urban conurbations of the Northwest who no doubt had discovered this unspoilt pinki and were doing their best to alter that. We heard that holiday homes were a bone of contention in what was a Welsh speaking stronghold. Meibion Glyndwr, were a group responsible for arson attacks on properties in the 1970-90s. Opposition to loss of culture and language dies hard, we didn't see any burned-out houses, but there was a sense of antagonism in some that we met towards 'outsiders'. SH mentions this too, a Welsh disapproval of the incomer, 'the thumbs down bit starting at Abersoch'.

The 91 miles of long-distance footpath around Llyn was opened in 2006. We discovered to our cost that paths like this take time to mature. It needed more use, from outsiders or whoever, better signage and less vegetation. It was very overgrown in places, they needed to issue visitors with a strimmer. We found it cut inland too much away from the sea, not what you want from a coast path. Reading up, I understand it has now been improved. We found it hard to get onto the eastern end of Hell's Mouth, the five miles of beach leading to Aberdaron but struggled on.

We camped near to St Hywyn's Church. It was a great location and resting place for all the souls in the graveyard. While shopping for supper at the Spar, sausages, beans and mash, we bumped into a guy who had seen us in Hastings months earlier. He gave us a £20 donation, but more importantly it was a whole lot of encouragement. It brought it home to us what a venture we had undertaken, and his words allowed us to reflect on our achievement to date (23/6/2007). Umbrella by Rihanna was No 1, but fortunately the weather had picked up and we didn't need one.

We woke to the sound of rain lashing the tent, Rihanna where are you now? We dropped down into a cove with boats at Traeth Porth Meudwy before rounding the fingernail of Uwchmynydd. Bardsey Island with lighthouse and remains of St Mary's Abbey, once a highly ranked pilgrimage site, lay across a racing Sound but was beyond our distal phalange. JM had difficulty finding his way here in driving rain and gale force winds, - snap! The Whistling Sands of Porthor were something which Havoc enjoyed. Perhaps his hearing was more acute than his smell had been back near Southend. A squeak or whistle is emitted from peculiar shaped sand grains when rubbed together. I could hardly hear a thing except the wind or perhaps age was catching up on me, pardon!

We needed somewhere to shop and went to Tudweiliog where we met Andrew, landlord of the Lion Hotel. He provided us with food and drink, two tins of dog food for Havoc, made an online donation and pointed us in the direction of a campsite at Towyn farm. Andrew at the Lion, far better than any supermarket express.

More rain and strong winds, the walls of the tent bellowing like we were going to take off. Even the on-site peacocks were crying for help. Amazingly golfers were out on the course at Porthdinllaen and we visited the lifeboat station stuck out on another wee neck of land, a protuberance only about a kilometre long. We continued to Nefyn and having picked some wild mushrooms had them with dried paella and a side helping of Super Noodles.

It had been a miserable day weather wise, and we needed to try and dry out. The evening entertainment was provided by two black and white tufted ducks and their six ducklings. After much debate they were named Homer and Marg with offspring, Bart, Lisa, Maggie, Huey, Dewey and Louie. We knew a long trek lay ahead tomorrow over Yr Eifl, a volcanic peak the highest on the peninsula and on to Caernarfon. An early night and I dreamt of Mr Burns, was I really getting more like him?

The first stop of the day was at the chapel dedicated to St Beuno, patron saint of sick children, at Pistyll. The sense of it being untouched by time may have been because of the reeds spread on the floor. There was a basket at one side, I thought it must have been John The Baptist's. It is the final resting place of actor Rupert Davies who played TV detective Maigret.

Yr Eifl, turned out to have three peaks the highest being 564 metres. In English it means The Rivals. The mention of this had me humming Green Grow the Rushes O, but I don't think there is actually any connection. Old quarry works near Trefor and onto Clynnogg-Fawr. This time a much larger church dedicated to St Beuno. The story goes that an old 'treasure' chest is where pilgrims on their way to Bardsey would place their donations. We were told farmers would put money in it too if they had a calf or lamb born with a split ear. It was said the creatures had been touched by the holy one and this was the Beuno mark.

We came upon Aberdosach first and then Dinas before picking up a cycle path leading to Caenarfon which ran alongside rail tracks. We were to glimpse a steam train once more which Havoc tried to chase. That got him into all sorts of trouble. Hashers Mo and JJ met at Norwich, had not long moved into Caernarfon and put us up, metres from the Castle and on the estuary of the Seiont. From here we could plot our conquest of Anglesey.

Caernarfon is dominated by the 13th century castle used for the investiture of Charles, HRH Prince of Wales, in 1969 (Now King Charles III). At the suggestion of the Labour government of the day, his acceptance speech was delivered partly in Welsh by way of quelling Nationalist sentiments. Two defence movement terrorists were killed by their own device in events leading up to this. Portrayed in an episode of The Crown, (Netflix) the actions of HRH helped to establish better relations between Wales and England. We certainly had received warm welcomes thus far apart from a bit of 'outsider' syndrome.

On reaching this part of Wales many coastal walking 'coadjutors' either skip along the Menai Strait coast and /or take in some mountain air climbing Snowdon (now Yr Wyddfa) - JM, and SH/RH. The motivation, a bit of fun, self-indulgence, whatever, Wendy and I had ticked that off together previously, but we had seen very little of Anglesey together. At the Straits narrowest a couple of hundred metres, widest a couple of miles, Anglesey just sat there invitingly. 260 square miles, (Isle of Wight is only 150sq miles), only a bit smaller than Singapore, half of Wight's population, about 70,000, 124-140 miles of coast and 20 coastal towns and villages plus many highly recommended beaches. It was also part of our 'outer coast' and would add about a week to our walking time. It just had to be included, if only to be different and we were 'expected' at Penmon.

I figured if we could get across onto Anglesey's bottom left hand corner we could continue around clockwise. Apparently, I did 'one of my disappearing acts'. Shazam! I walked into Menai Marine at the harbour. 'Hi, Tim.' I knew his name was Tim, it had to be, unless he was wearing someone else's label badge. I leapt forward doing my Wizard pose from 'Goblins, Giants and Wizards' (similar to Scissors, Paper, Stone).

"I need a boat."

"Well, we do sell boats." He said,

"Can I get a one-way test drive over to the island?"

To shorten the story, phone calls were made and Alan Price, not the one with a dancing bear, collected us in a rib and we crossed to the old Mermaid Inn. Ferries once ran from here back and forth to Caernarfon. We were just re living a former custom. We had great views of the castellated city, waters of Menai in the foreground, mountains of Snowdonia behind. It began to rain. There was just time for a rendition of 'I may go out tomorrow if I can borrow a coat to wear'. I skipped along keeping a special lookout for dancing bears.

We made our way to Newborough Warren, heavy showers, and sheltered for some lunch in a farm building, surrounded by orange vintage tractors. What was the collective noun for these? We decided it might be a 'cultivation!' Havoc and I had broken biscuits, Wendy had flame hot Doritos. While munching on these, directly above her, sitting on a phone wire, a crow decided to poop, directly into her savoury snack bag. Take That. This certainly extinguished any flames; she would need to 'Relight the Fire.' Anyone for dipping sauce?

We moved onto Malltraeth and Aberffraw where a keyholder allowed us to stay in the village hall, now surrounded by a cluster of six computers. En route today I had been given a walking stick by a guy from Liverpool, they are known for their sense of humour, and Havoc had spent most of the afternoon chasing hares, dodging piles of seashells in fields, presumably left there in readiness to spread as soil fertiliser. Wendy was deciding if she liked guacamole. In the end we had fishcakes, peas, rice and mash for tea.

We were still in St Beuno's backyard as we couldn't help noticing another church dedicated to him. We were headed for the small tidal island of Cribinau and St Cwyfan's, the 'Little church in the sea'. It had its own history of employment controversy, based around the Welsh and English language disputation. At the centre in the 1760s Dr Thomas Bowles, an English only speaking priest was appointed, which upset the Welsh speaking parishioners. Bowles actually stayed in post until 1773 when he died. The new signing was a Welsh speaker. It was also closed for our visit. I never had the opportunity to 'confess' my employment wrangles.

We passed Trac Mon motor racing circuit and Barclodiad y Gawres, a chambered Neolithic mound. Rhosneigr is a surfing town. Clearly, we didn't look like surfing customers as the staff in all merchandise outlets never looked up from their computer screens as we passed. We paddled over Afon Crigyll and along the beach. In the air, jets and helicopters from RAF Valley. Havoc just had to give chase. A narrow neck of water at Plas Cymyran looked as if we might be able to wade over to Holy Island but there was no way of knowing just how deep it was. Instead, we carried on up the channel to Four Mile Bridge, underfoot soft sandy mud, worm casts, a couple of rocky, cockle covered breakwaters, lining our route with sea holly and sea lavender.

In heavy rain and strong winds, this was late June for goodness' sake, we decided to follow the B4545 to Holyhead. Bill Withers was in my head 'we can make it if we try, just the *three* of us.' We would back track a bit tomorrow if the weather improved. Being a ferry port and one which offers Irish Sea shelter, this west coast bad weather refuge was welcome, the lifeboat station was ours. It has a long history with over 70 awards for gallantry. The latest award, an MBE to coxswain Bryan Thompson for services to sea safety.

Next day we turned left and headed for North Stack. From Holyhead Mountain, on a clear day, the Wicklow Mountains in Ireland, the coast of Cumbria and the Isle of Man can apparently all be seen. We were able to just make out Bardsey to the south and The Skerries to the northeast. We took in the lighthouse at South Stack and Abraham's Bosom before heading back to Holyhead and collecting our bags. (Proposed tidal energy schemes in this area, 2020), were said to cause concern due to environmental influence both in terms of visual and wildlife impact.)

The coastal scenery was stunning and in the harbour a replica of The Matthew, the ship that put North America on the map. The breakwater tentacle stretching a mile and a half into the bay is the longest in Europe. Inland too, all manner of interest, beauty and engineering genius over the ages. The Breakwater Country Park opened in 1990, once an old quarry, seven million tons of rock were dug here to construct the spidery arm. An old brickwork with stalagmite like chimney, the Wild family made heat resistant bricks alongside until 1973. Its half-brother was the stack of Anglesey Aluminium, a familiar landmark for many, (AA closed in 2009). It was just like the inner tube of a giant roll of tin foil.

The stainless-steel Celtic Gateway Bridge, opened in 2006, crossed the Old Harbour and Telford's Stanley Embankment (1822/23) known locally as The Cob, crosses the Cymyran Strait carrying the North Wales Coastline for trains, the A5 and us to destinations West and East.

We were headed back to the heart of Anglesey and turned left up the coast to Church Bay. I scavenged some potatoes from fields as we walked north wading the Afon Alaw. They would form the basis of our tea, with soup as we camped at Porth Swtan. I enjoyed the sense off living of the land, even if our endeavours could more accurately be described as 'scrumping' or less than lawful foraging. Our dining experience wasn't quite like those who were eating at the Lobster Pot restaurant we saw but in its own way was just as enjoyable.

We chatted about the number of horses we had seen on Anglesey. They seemed to be everywhere. Wild ones grazing back near Llanddwyn Island, but there also seemed to be loads elsewhere with a plethora of opportunities for trekking, beach riding and the like. Was this in some way linked to our proximity to Ireland, we could only wonder?

I read somewhere, it wasn't Mrs Clarkson, that there are over three million 'horsists' in Britain. All costing the NHS a fortune in rider injuries, missing out on skiing holidays because of falls, blocking roads and generally projecting a sense the whole world revolves around their pets. I tend to agree with *Jezza,* just to be controversial, that when it comes to horses on roads they should be allowed 'in the same way that the (monarch) is allowed into parliament - briefly and by invitation only'. (Have a great coronation, Charles!)

At least here in Anglesey there was plenty of room for them, and few chairs. Fast forward to April 2023 more horse controversy, this time at the races. Three horse fatalities at Aintree, animal rights protesters and trainers blaming them for horse deaths due to delays. Still, the number of deaths was one less than 2022!

Chapter 32 - Carmel Head (Anglesey) to Neston (Wirral)

I get up when I want, put on my trousers and have a cup of tea

"A dead mouse a day."

ROUNDING CARMEL HEAD, we could now see The Skerries close up and a little later West Mouse Islet. Nursery rhymes and poetry were filling my head space, a change from other songs. Hickory, Dickory, Dock, even something Welsh about building a small house. I knew there was one of them ahead at Conway, and a small mouse sleeping, waking up and 'off she goes' reverberated between my ears, mixed up with 'see how they run.'

There are other 'Mice' along this coast, Middle and East. As if by fate we came across another dead mouse on the path. We saw them with some regularity during our walk, so much so we began to think they were some kind of sign. Research suggests this can mean almost anything. They are said to be symbolic of good and bad luck, along with giving too much proportion to minor issues and an indicator of needing to be more detail orientated, take your pick.

I was sure I didn't need to focus more; I was very nearly OCD. I thought of a mate back in Devon, who knows he is, and has to refer to the condition as CDO!

I was equally certain I was taking all opportunities offered and regularly released anxiety, albeit it would seem, in ways unpleasant to others. Lennie from 'Of Mice and Men' (Steinbeck) kept a dead one in his pocket, I read it at school, it was about the only bit I understood. I concluded that coast path walkers all carry warfarin and have holes in their pockets, and that the three out at sea were very wise mice not blind and didn't need to run. What happens to all these dead mice? They must be burbled up by a Jabberwock!

Quietly and stealthily we made our way to Cemlyn Bay and on to Wylfa power station, resting briefly by a Tumtum tree. (Wylfa Magnox nuclear generator was decommissioned in 2015). Next, we whiffled through the Welsh wabe to Cemaes Bay and into Amlwch. This was an 18th century copper town, nearby Parys Mountain providing the ore. It once had a population of some 10,000, now it's shrunk to between three and four thousand. After copper the town dabbled in shipbuilding, brewing and even tobacco. It's claim to fame as far as heavy metal lovers are concerned, Lemmy of Motorhead went to school here. This was one of the places where my efforts to rattle the collection tin was challenged.

I had left Wendy and Havoc resting while I went out around pubs. A group of girls were happy to splash some loose change but one of their boyfriends was more than suspicious. I had ID with me, saying what we were doing, from both charities, but it wasn't washing. I sensed things were getting quite tense. While I was happy to just walk away, the boyfriends were having none of it. It required a bit of quick thinking. I left them with the collecting tin, while I went back to a hotel to collect my vorpal sword. Instead, I found a local paper with photos and an article about us in it. I took this back to the group, who could hardly argue with something in their own local rag. I retrieved the collecting tin, and everything ended amicably, Twas brillig. One of the few occasions when I played my 'ace of spades' just right, Callooh, Callay!

We reached the lighthouse at Point Lynas. Some of the buildings there were available as accommodation, but it was early in the day and too soon for us to stop. Instead, we were given coffee and a £50 donation. Havoc certainly wasn't sure about some of the residents. A raven which was hand reared and two huge Irish wolfhounds. All looked as if they belonged in a Harry Potter film. Havoc was very quickly out of the door before Hagrid and Dobby showed up.

I read that due to intensive mining activity in the area many of the streams and rivers were polluted. The Afon Goch (Red River) got its name because of this, once said to be the most acidic river in Britain. That led me to think about some of the livestock we were coming across. At least two cows with badly infected hooves, several sheep carcasses. One ewe was drooling and going around in circles. I knew this was sometimes seen with Listeriosis, causing abscesses in the brain. I don't know if the ecotoxic situation on the ground was to blame but there was work here for Erin Brockovich and a few vets. Perhaps we should have stayed a bit longer at Lynas lighthouse Havoc?

Dulas and Ligwy Bays lead to Moelfre. The village wraps around a small harbour with a headland to the north. This is the place to holiday if you are into Scheduled Ancient Monuments, there are some 14 in the area, Neolithic, Bronze and Iron Age. Much more recent on the harbour side (2004) an alloy statue of Dick Evans, highly decorated lifeboat man. In a service of over 50 years, he is credited with saving 281 lives, and was awarded the RNLI Gold Medal twice. In 1959, as coxswain, for his efforts to save crew from the coaster Hindlea and again in 1966 while attending the Nafisporos. Born in Moelfre, I remembered seeing him on This is Your Life in 1970, he died in 2001 aged 96.

As we neared the end of our Anglesey adventure we were swept up by Turtles, not TMNT Leonardo and Raphael or leatherbacks, but Pam and Ron. They were long friends with Wendy's parents, and I think the jungle drums had messaged to spoil their daughter. They lived at Penmon and we ended up staying with them for three nights receiving Ynys Mon (Mother of Wales) treatment. This meant Havoc could have some time off and we could walk without bags after a bit of a lie in except it was a Wednesday, and we were rudely awakened by the dustmen. (Blur,1994, actually got it wrong, it was a Tuesday!) Slumbering and confidence are no preference for the habitual voyager.

A muddy path to Benllech and around Red Wharf Bay. It was a good thing Havoc wasn't with us because a very handsome red fox was advertising this as his territory. We had begun to notice Havoc was getting a bit snappy at other dogs and sometimes people too and we put this down to the fact he had nowhere to call his own. We had stopped briefly in a bus shelter for a sit down and a perfectly behaved Labrador and its owner happened to pass by minding their own business. Havoc had shot out from under the seat, snarling, top lip curled back, canines poised. This was unusual, just protecting our bags or space, but the change in behaviour was evident.

Puffin Island came into view as we approached Penmon Point. At the ruined Priory a massive, domed dovecot, it would have held over 1000 nests when the meat and eggs from birds were part of a staple diet. After visiting the World Heritage castle at Beaumaris, 'perfect symmetrical concentric planning', we banked over £400 at the post office.

We had arrived by boat, but we would leave Anglesey via Telford's Menai Bridge. We looked across to Stevenson's Britannia Bridge, not quite its box section original, I remembered it being burnt down in 1970, but soon rebuilt to maintain the link between London, Holyhead and on to Dublin. The university town of Bangor our next stop. The obvious ear worm, at least to all 'folkies', loosed into my auditory cortex. Fiddler's Dram, 'A beautiful day, we had lunch on the way' but it was a bit more than a pound.

JM had spoken of a pair of dog tongs at the cathedral, they might be just what we needed for a bad-tempered Havoc. We popped in, were given tea and biscuits, the tongs were no longer on display but a kindly member of clergy led us to the vestry and there in a cupboard were the oak carnivore pincers used for removing unruly dogs from the bishop's seat. We took some photos just to remind Havoc he better be on his best behaviour. It seemed a bit odd being driven back to Penmon for our third night thanks to Pam and Ron, but they insisted. Wonderful generosity and much appreciated support. We had eaten all their Welsh lamb shanks, so now it was time for roast beef and the following morning we said our thanks and goodbyes after they dropped us back to Bangor.

Bangor Garth pier looked absolutely splendid. Built in 1896 it was almost demolished in the early 1970s. Bangor City Council bought it in 1975 for a penny, did it up and it was reopened again in 1988. The silver turrets on octagonal kiosks gave it a look of eastern promise and a black and white cat sat next to the entry honesty box and below a sign reading 'No Dogs on Pier.' Mel's Ices advertised would have to stay frozen for us, but the cat seemed to come and go as she liked. Much later I read a further £1 million was thrown at it in 2017 and the historical no dog rule was abolished. Havoc's lobbying surely had something to do with it.

Some of us saw sheep on the beach as we approached Llanfairfechan. Everything, including those sheep is rammed into a narrow coastal strip here shared with the A55 Expressway, viaduct arches, railway tracks, tunnels and raging traffic. Snowdonia and Penmaenmawr shadowed us to our right. Spud spoke of fence lines made of hundreds of pieces of slate here, which we saw and shared her anxiety of finding a path, crossing roads, 'with or without horse and carriage', even contemplated swimming.

Llanfairfechan was a nice seaside town, even in the rain, developed in the late 19th century as a Victorian holiday resort. A nostalgic looking wooden beach pavilion did a great cup of tea, and while "sunbathing" in the rain on a deckchair Wendy asked if the footprints in the sand were sheep or deer? She clearly hadn't seen the earlier flock, which I could empathise with. Sometimes, you just switched to auto pilot, almost oblivious to your surroundings, alone with your thoughts, eating up the miles bit by bit. A chance to stop, relieve the drudgery of carrying your world in a rucksack for a while, stretch out, it was just hard to get going again.

"Come on" I said, "Only a few more Welsh towns and we will be back in England."

Again, like Spud we struggled with Dwygyfylchi, before Conwy and the first pub we came across the Liverpool Arms. Some scousers led us into a bingo hall and between two fat ladies and Kelly's eye we rattled our collection tins. It was as if we were detached from reality, news and events affecting everyone else. I picked up a paper the headlines read Terrorism welcomes in Gordon Brown, I quickly turned to the sports pages, where Wimbledon was washed out, with the wettest June on record in GB. We could vouch for the last bit, but frankly we were well divorced from all the other stuff.

The walled medieval market town, with its own Edward I creation, cobbled streets, and numerous attractions was very majestic. If you were born within the walls you were nicknamed 'Jackdaws'. Stonework splattered with clumps of vegetation, alleys all jumbled and the river snaking inland 27 miles to Migneint Moor. At the quay we found out Conwy is famous for mussels and while my prime movers were aching my eye was drawn to a small boat named 'Wendy the Witch'. Wendy the Walker, to disambiguate, was more taken by the brilliantly red painted Smallest House in Great Britain, Y TY LLEIAF YM MHRYDAIN FAWR, as verified by Guinness Book of Records (Sorry! Trewellard, Cornwall).

In St Mary's churchyard the grave that inspired another wanderer, Wordsworth's, to write his 1798 poem 'We are Seven'. Telford's suspension bridge, spanning the river Conwy since 1826 is constantly in need of ongoing maintenance and 181 years later it was needing of a coat of paint. It had been a practice run for his bridge at Menai, now it looked sad and was closed waiting for the decorators to arrive.

The Great Orme is a 300 million year old limestone headland over 200 metres high to the north west of Llandudno. Dominated by bronze age smelting sites, copper mines, riddled by caverns and passageways which archaeologists still excavate, and tourists descend upon by cable car, tramway and vintage coaches. We navigated the marine drive, overlooked by former gun artillery emplacements, the occasional Kashmiri goat not selected as a Royal Welsh mascot with wild thyme providing the aroma beneath our aching feet. The Victorian pier, curved promenade and covered shopping walkways all came into view. We stayed at the in-town lifeboat station, still unique in 2007 as its location allowed launching on both the West and North shores. Ten years later would see all that change. We treated ourselves to a takeaway curry.

We said our goodbyes early and headed off east. White horses were skimming over paddling pools and boating lakes and hanging baskets were trapezing outside hotels. Residents may have been entertained last night by a Dad's Army sing-along thing at the theatre but they were still up early. It was only 7.30am but coaches from Aylesbury and Ashby-de-la-Zouch were loading the OAPs wrestling for window seats. Some had even forsaken breakfast to bagsie the front seats with uninterrupted views. They weren't going to be moved, handbags armed with yogurts and bananas.

In fields outside of town we came across Shire heavy horses. One could only admire their rippling muscles; how could this physique be achieved on grass alone without any visits to the gym? One grinned as I struggled with my bag over a style and the very square rear end of another reminded me that last night's vindaloo was coming back to haunt me. Fortunately, the relative remoteness of Little Orme Head came to my rescue. With the remainder of a worn gusset from my shorts surgically removed I was more comfortable as we continued to Rhos-on-Sea.

St Trillo's is a tiny chapel here, the alter directly over an ancient spring, which Havoc had to have a good sniff around. Sixth century, with whitewashed walls and just six seats, the founder's brother and sister were also great chapel founders, a very holy lot. We made our way to the post office to try and deposit some collection money. Unlike many others this one sold nothing else, just PO transactions. We were to discover the postmaster was the slowest in these parts, if not all of Wales, if not the world! We were invited into the back room for coffee, which I had to wonder may not have been allowed from a security angle, but his rather fungal infected fingernails resembling something from a Dickens novel caused us to urge on the side of caution and beat a hasty withdrawal.

I had never been to Colwyn Bay. All I could remember of it was a mid-1970s edition of Seaside Special with Diddy Hamilton and Tony Blackburn. It was as if they were still there. The pier was straight out of the land that time forgot, rigor mortice had long set in. It was actually dismantled in 2018 although I understand much of its metal work still remains. In an attempt to re manufacture itself some attractive willow sculptures. The comedy was provided by Havoc, who must have been practicing his Gromit impersonations. He had the ears and eyebrows off to a tee and would easily have won a Saturday night competition with Diddy and Tony.

SH describes this stretch as dreary and was glad of company. Caravan parks proliferate, and we were mainly on cycle track, like JT who describes this coast as flat as the fens. Raynes Jetty near Llanddulas was where the local giant had left his jackstones. Huge concrete tetrapods or dolosse, serve to protect the shoreline, their geometric shapes designed to disperse the force of the sea. Spud described Rhyl as 'waiting patiently for the first hint of summer' (springtime) we were there in July, and it was forgotten fairground rides none of which seemed very amusing. We saw very few holidaymakers. Prestatyn marks the start of the 177 mile Offa's Dyke path.

"You off to Chepstow, are you?" we were asked.

It took us a while to explain otherwise. JM had been given a large bagful of chocolate not far from here, his first pair of boots were still in good nick, after 2,400 miles and felt like slippers. We struggled to get free camping at Nant Mill, (they wanted £12 a night) and wild camped at the Point of Ayr instead. My boots worn, I needed re shoeing. Chocolate, not on offer but a passerby did flash the wine gums.

Between leaving Wales and getting back into England we got ourselves into all sorts of pickles. Some ten miles along the west shore of the Dee should have been straightforward. Near Mostyn the beached former passenger ship the Duke of Lancaster. It arrived here in 1979, has had a chequered history, was rusting white for our visit, saw graffiti added over the years and was apparently painted black in 2017. It brought new meaning to the call 'Abandon Ship'.

Before Flint, we found ourselves scaling an eight-foot fence, which ended in Wendy grazing her wrists. We had thought we could cross the Dee on the Flintshire Bridge but found this was non-pedestrian so kept going to Queensferry. We then turned left to stay as near as possible to the east shore of the Dee but encountered industrial estates, steelworks and flooded fields. We literally had to take off our socks and boots at one stage to wade through knee deep mud. Wales did not want to let go of us, the border swings north away from the bridge at Queensferry for another couple of miles. We eventually got to Burton, we were in England and headed for Little Neston where an aunt of mine let us shower and recover. Hwyel fawr Wales, Yaki Da (for now) Roy.

Chapter 33 – Neston to Fleetwood

You'll Never Walk Alone

"She loves you yeah, yeah, yeah."

IT WAS A LANDMARK day to have Wales behind us. Neston, Parkgate and West Kirby with views across the silted-up Dee back to Wales. Wendy was in good spirits and as we walked, we played 'who am I?' Off the coast Hilbre Island, through Hoylake stopping for photos at the lifeboat station and onto New Brighton. It was here in 1931 The Guide Dogs for the Blind Association was founded at The Cliff, thanks to Muriel Crooke and Rosamund Bond. Havoc humbly doffed his cap at the bronze Labrador statue but then the moment got the better of him. He had to run away and hide behind a bush. In the afternoon, as if to emphasise the other of our charities the RNLI rescue hovercraft was launched to assist at Crosby. We were staying with hashers at Greasby and in the evening joined a small pack of the Wirral and Chester Hash for a run near Two Mills.

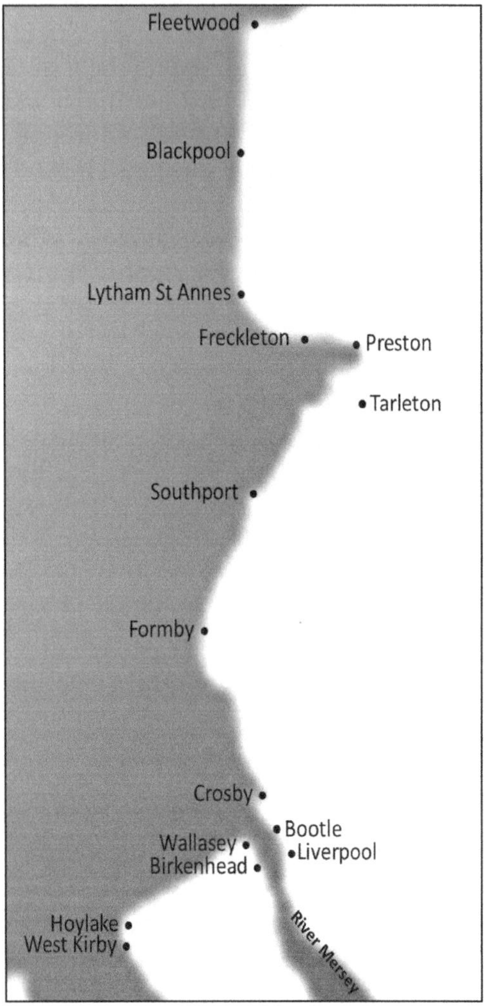

Seacombe is where Michael Portillo lived briefly in 2003 doing a bit for the BBC and working at Asda in Wallasey before he discovered trains. Bradshaw's Guide wasn't going to be a lot of help to us, and we climbed aboard the 'Ferry 'cross the Mersey' with Gerry and The Pacemakers the latest ear worm to wriggle. High rise buildings and aerial cranes to arrive at the Albert Dock. The clock on the Royal Liver Building said five to nine (am) and we peered up at the Liver Birds giving very different meaning to the term 'up skirting'.

Liverpool was basically a building site. Hundreds of builders, hard hats, high vis jackets, the occasional bum crack. The morning coffee shops were doing a bomb, there didn't seem to be a lot of manual work going on, but there was a lively fun atmosphere, lots of banter aimed mainly at two aliens resembling Himalayan sherpas with a black and white pooch wearing his own high vis.

We walked around the Old Cavern quarter, Freddie and The Dreamers, The Hollies, The Drifters all bricks on the Wall of Fame. Wendy had her photo taken with John (Lennon) casually leaning outside and Havoc grabbed a free drink offered in a Tupperware container. We were challenged trying to save 20p by only paying once for two usages at an auto loo which left me squatting with the door still open. Fortunately, no one came too close to find out what Chester Zoo had to offer from the advertising hording outside. They might have found a silver back gorilla's ass!

The automation failing raised my level of belligerence and street comments about my footwear gave me Liverpudlian confidence and downright cheek. I had only bought my Merrell shoes in Padstow and now they were worn more than any rough sleeper's. I had worn them every day and every mile since Cornwall, 340 miles driving distance without going around Wales, but what the heck. Passing Blacks, they had been good mates with JM, but hadn't helped us yet, I walked into the store,

"Do you think you could possibly exchange this pair of shoes; I've only had them a couple of months?"

If you don't ask you don't get and after a bit of haggling, I was given a new replacement pair. I bought some new shorts to replace the ones I had cut the gusset out of back in Llandudno and threw the old shoes in a bin, no one rushed to salvage them.

We had taken the ferry across The Mersey, to a land many people love. We had received don't care what your name is boy treatment, been welcomed warmly but we couldn't stay. We needed to walk on. I would never let Wendy walk alone, but would that be replicated? Dreams tossed and blown, but with a love of some sort, I knew I should be glad.

Concrete pavement as we headed down the Waterloo Road out of town. I imagined meeting Spud going in the opposite direction on her trek from Carlisle. She describes the dock terraced scene so well in 1994. Things had improved but there was still rejuvenation work to do. It would be very interesting to see this stretch again now.

Crosby revealed Antony Gormley's 100 life-size cast iron figures forming Another Place. A plaque read the installation 'will move to another site in November 2006'. Clearly no one had booked the removal company, and we were very glad of that. We practiced the standing anatomical position at low tide when most are exposed. Visitors are reminded not to attempt to walk out to the furthest figures risking changing tides and soft mud. The idea is to 'harness the ebb and flow of the tide to explore man's relationship with nature'. Havoc chose to have a good bark at the creations, cock his leg and forage the tideline of flotsam and jetsam. Some risk the tide and others think the most extreme figures are people in distress and summon the emergency services, hence the RNLI craft from New Brighton are sometimes launched. We crossed The Alt at Hightown and moved onto Formby practicing our west Lancashire pronunciation on the likes of Ormskirk and Scarisbrick.

I read that towns like Ainsdale now provide large lavish homes for Premier League footballers, but they must have all been training or advertising razors. Equally, rare red squirrels occupy the woods protected by the sea to the west and an absence of trees to the east preventing their more common grey cousins infecting them with the equivalent of squirrel HIV. We saw none, just miles of sand and a single dead porpoise. Eyeless, it was being recycled by birds. I didn't remember this aspect of food webs being mentioned when I studied it at school.

This stretch is known as England's Golf Coast, with clubs too numerous to mention, please excuse the pun. However, the sight of Army cadets exercising, running, log carrying, pressing and sitting up in the surf may have caused some of the Formby Ladies Club members to go slightly out of bounds. We found a coconut washed up and momentarily wondered if it had come from a sun kissed remote tropical island. Then seeing first, the Tower at Blackpool in the distance, followed by the ski jump shaped end of Southport pier, realised it probably came from a much nearer shy.

Southport warranted much more time than we could give it. Exploring its Victorian architecture, pier, Lawn Mower Museum, monument to the lifeboat Eliza Fernley lost on 1896. Other boats went to aid the German barque 'Mexico' from Lytham St Anne's and were also lost, the event was the worst disaster in the history of the RNLI with 27 crew losing their lives. The RNLI withdrew from Southport in 1925 and years later an 'independent' was founded. We did see something of what remained of a sand extraction plant on the north foreshore. Sand winning as it was known ceased in February 2007, and restoration of the site was supposed to take place but by early July nothing had occurred. I read later that sand removal had recommenced in 2015.

Turning inland we had been offered a stay at Tarleton with Ross and Elaine Bullock. This came through Southwest Coast Path links, Ross was about five years into covering England's longest National Trail, covering about 40-50 miles a year during vacations with a friend, completing in 2016, admirable longevity. (He got his book, 'Good Days and Great Days' out well before me.) This 'traditional bank manager, with quirky eye and wicked sense of humour', mm, mm, mm, took our collected change (I thought I could trust a bank manager) pledged to try and get a few extra donations and paid in the money on our behalf for our charities. Havoc made friends with two bearded collies, Charlie and Abbey.

Tarleton Holy Trinity Church boosts a tall spire and the surrounding area crossing the river Douglas and through Much Hoole, picking up the Ribble Way were black soiled, all manner of veg and salad produce, glass houses and the voices of Polish and Portuguese workers. The skyline as we approached Preston was full of pylons, power lines and more church spires and towers. I glanced at the map and counted 18. St Walburge's spire is the third tallest in the UK after Salisbury and Norwich cathedrals. They liked their church spires round here; this was the last one to be worked upon by Fred Dibnah.

At Freckleton we came across a memorial to 61 people, including 38 children killed when an American bomber crashed into a school in 1944. Although fewer casualties, I wondered if during wartime this drew comparative attention to that of 1966 and the Aberfan disaster I remembered as a child. We were stopped a little further along at Lytham by a lady and both events were among prayers said. On leaving she made a generous donation to our charity effort.

I had just turned eight when a colliery spoil heap collapsed at Aberfan in South Wales killing 144 people, 116 of them children. The prayers stayed with me as we made our way north. Aberfan remains one of my most saddening memories, 21st October 1966. The Crown, third season, aired in 2019, portrayed the event poignantly and mournfully. I have a hashing friend in Devon, just a bit older than me, who as a child, was taken regularly to church. The wretched event impacted on him too, overnight he became a lifelong atheist.

Landmarks as we approached Blackpool: BAE Systems (aerospace), the black capped white windmill, two separate boathouses, unusual with the inshore ILB at Lytham opposite the Queens Hotel and the main all-weather ALB at St Anne's. Havoc found himself a cosy cubbyhole next to the teddies in the shop sheltering from the rain. A three-metre-high figure of a lifeboat man looking out to sea marks the losses from the 'Mexico' disaster 1896. Also, another 'Royal' link golf course and until 2009 Pontins.

Havoc recalls an argument over a wee stop. My diary records only a face being pulled and the missed opportunity to ambush a crowd at Pontins' gates. I have no issues with calls of nature, we all need them, but fundraising opportunities, crowds, England and the summer were all running out.

Hashers, Simon and Rhona, who owned the New Guilderoy Hotel in Blackpool had kindly given us a room for two nights. While Havoc might have been enjoying a cosy little room, I was getting an ear bashing at the dinner table.

"I would have thought someone who went to St Luke's would have learned how to eat and use a knife."

I had never been criticised for my table manners before and someone's perception of college life was slightly confused. However, I noted the existential disapproval and pondered if it would be seminal? With a bit more work I thought, I might be ready to show off to friends, and if not, another fault to go on my eulogy that no one would be around to listen to.

The rain on arrival at Blackpool had put paid to most fundraising. We caught a tram back to the Pleasure Beach the next morning and re-walked Blackpool, collecting and sightseeing. Hens and Stags, men in drag, pony and traps, one with a super long mane it must have had hair extensions. Donkeys by the lifeboat station, some very obese contestants in a burger eating competition, The Tower, every conceivable sort of rock. Even pigeons were joining in playing football with a discarded doughnut. Wendy had her palm read and while waiting leaning on a lamppost a George Formby ear worm burrowed into my head, this was his window cleaning round. I have no idea what the fortune teller told Wendy.

A street market at Cleveleys, past Rossall School (I would be offered an interview there six years later), and onto Fleetwood, home of the Fisherman's Friend. Slightly more tasteful, certainly than some of the exploits seen at Blackpool, the Welcome Home statue as a landmark here. A sculpture honouring families, the anxious face of a mother with children waiting for the safe return of a fisherman husband. With a generous cheque from Simon and what we had collected in 48 hours we had swelled the collection total by £660.

Tram Sunday, with all manner of vintage vehicles, steam buses, a white police dog patrol Morris van, which Havoc was very suspicious of, town criers and marching bands provided more tin rattling opportunities outside The Legion in Fleetwood. Then we boarded the Wyre Rose, the red and white ferry bobbing like a fishing float across the estuary and arrivaed at Pilling. The Methodist church was generous, gave us a donation and a lady vicar prayed for us. Two formal expressions of gratitude and hope for God's grace of safety in as many days, what were we about to enter? The answer was Morecambe Bay, its mud flats, quick sands and any number of river mouths from here to St Bees Head. I already had a feeling we were under a guiding, protective gaze, how else could we have made it this far? I felt we were three quarters of the way there, a bit more of England, only the Scottish west and north coasts to negotiate, that was surely a highlight.

Chapter 34 – Fleetwood to Ravenglass

Past rack and samphire...walking through the tide as rain cuts through the spray

"I was playing all the right notes, just not necessarily in the right order."

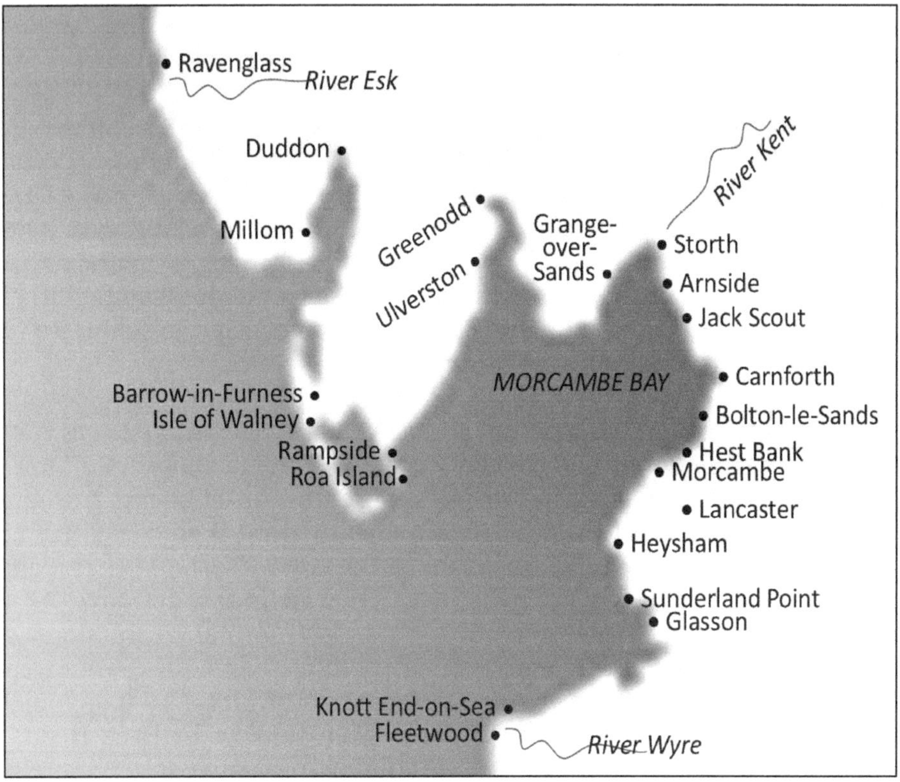

WE HEADED FOR COCKERHAM and onto Glasson Dock. Then it was into Lancaster, and we visited St Peter's Catholic Cathedral, the Blessed Sacrament Chapel and stain glass memorable. From Williamson Park the Ashton Memorial, the 'Taj Mahal of the North', since 1909 dominated the skyline of Lancaster.

We met up briefly with Lune Valley hashers, turning south to Overton and Sunderland Point. Cut off at high tide, this community is only accessible via a narrow road, once a favourite haunt of artists. Also, the site of 'Sambo's Grave'. A wooden cross, painted pebbles and flowers with

a plaque, eccentric old English, telling the story of a young slave boy who died in 1796. This point was once the port of Lancaster before docks further up the Lune were opened and West Indian slave ships would unload their cargoes. A name which struck political correctness shock in 2007, and even more so now, I could not help thinking this simple moving and sorrowful grave served well to inform, remind and educate of the horrors of the slave trade. An enclosing low wall was added in 2019.

Claustrophobic iron railings prevent all bar pole-vaulters entering Heysham power station, itself looking like an early Kenwood blender with Lego-like brick mobile homes just metres away. Tracking north again we came across stone hewn graves in the ancient St Patrick's Chapel ruins. Local legend has it, St Patrick himself landed here from Ireland on his missionary travels, but these hollows now filled with rainwater and chapel remnants post-date him by several hundred years. Heavy metal lovers of Black Sabbath might have seen them on CD covers.

Hashers Ron and Ruth 'White Noise' were to help and host us in the area, with a sleepover inland at Caton. Ruth was very aptly named having clearly inherited a talking gene and Ron, all I put in my diary was 'Off his Trolley'. If it wasn't his hash name, it should have been. They guided us to places to try nettle tea and beer, into Galloway's at Morcambe, a local sight loss charity, and gifted local buttered shrimps. They clearly wanted to give us a welcome, their house offering phenomenal views of the Lune Valley, tree fringed pastures with grazing cattle.

Morcambe itself was a place of contrasts. Some sad shops and houses boarded up, contrasting with a promenade which clearly had received funding. One slab read 'On which side does a Lapwing have most feathers? ON THE OUTSIDE.' Perhaps straight out of an Eric Morcambe joke book, whose statue, piano less, we grabbed a selfie beside. Thora Hurd once lived here but as far as I know has not been cast in bronze and was no pianist. In the first couple of years after our visit the art-deco Midland Hotel saw great refurbishments, but the proposed sea front Eden Project North and Tidal Bay Bridge remain ambitious dreams. It would be four years, 2011, before Christy Moore penned On Morcambe Bay paying respect to 23 migrant workers. Tyson Fury is reported to have lived in a £1.5 million house but was forced to leave his corner and sell it. In 2019 ITV launched their series The Bay with a sex scene in a pub car park set here.

From Hest Bank we picked up the Lancaster Canal with boats moored on both sides. One called 'No Chance' surely was not prophetic of our intended plans over the next few hours to cross Grange-over-Sands. The birdlife on the waters seemed to be out of kilter with the seasons. Ducklings still the size of table tennis balls, while geese played a courting tag game and moorhens their own version of kick boxing. Perhaps it was still spring in these northerly lands, but the mother duck needed to keep her wits about her as we saw a large pike eyeing the ducklings with fervour.

We were met by Marion Inchmore, another Southwest coast path tie-up, and went on to Storth. We had phone calls to make and arrangements to put in place to meet up with Cedric Robinson, Queen's Guide to the Sands, a title from the Middle Ages allowing a highway from Furness to Lancaster. As well as receiving £15 a year and an MBE Cedric served for 56 years until 2019, guided thousands over the sand plain and was hopefully to be our saviour. We just had to finalise arrangements. Weather often puts paid to plans and clearly this was something not done every day of the week. He was due to lead a large-scale charity crossing on Saturday 21st July, which meant we could follow him laying a trail on Friday 20th. That allowed us Thursday 19th to walk south from Storth to where Marion had collected us near Bolton-le-sands.

Heading for Arnside everything seemed to be saying 'you're going the wrong way', the waters, the trees, all wildlife. Skirting nature reserves to Silverdale, Warton Sands and back to Carnforth taking in great sounding places, Jack Scout, Jenny Brown's Point and the drainage channel Quaker's Stang. Views across the Bay and a backdrop of the Lake District make this quite a unique spot. Designated an Area of Outstanding Natural Beauty the walk was well worth it with tea at The Shovel chatting to a window cleaner.

I had had my own round back in Bovey Tracey, weekends and evenings really to bring in a little extra cash, and now realised what I was doing wrong, his rates were double mine. (Early 2006, detached house, 10/12 windows, cleaned by hand using ladder where appropriate, my rate £7.50 would take best part of an hour. 2023 standard semi-detached, 10/12 windows, done with reach lance in between 5-10 minutes, £25, as quoted to me. Guess I will be doing my own.) On the same day on the radio, 1970's children's pocket money quoted as 1/6 - 4 shillings a week. For Vernon Kay's benefit, 4 shillings is 20p. Actual figures seem to speak louder than percentage inflation rate.

2007- We carried on to where we had first met Marion who collected us once again to return to Arnside. The Albion pub gave us a generous donation and we collected in the bar as well. A sunset over Morecambe Bay, not to be missed, concluded a great day. Marion would join us tomorrow across the Kent and in time hand stitched a customised bed cover/quilt commemorating our walk as a personal gift. Thank you, fond memories, you were a star.

The next day was a hugely memorable experience for all three of us and Havoc. We met Cedric, his two 'trainee' friends and tractor at White Creek near Arnside. With full packs, what started on soggy sands became shoes off and then knee deep wading through eddying waters following a rusty tractor which came to look like a dot on the horizon. Tyre tracks to begin with, we needed the laurel 'brobs' stuck in at intervals as markers of the route to follow. Cold waters reached way up to Havoc's belly and only when we reached a shallow bit could he cock his leg on one of the green branches. We walked for what seemed miles south straight out to sea heading for Blackpool Tower, surely this could not be right? We just needed to trust Cedric; many Chinese cockle pickers had perished here in 2004. Keep your eyes firmly fixed on that black dot. At one stage I thought I would have to put Wendy on my shoulders to get a sighting. Then we turned right sweeping in a big arc to reach Kents Bank with no little relief. We thanked Cedric and his pals, congratulated Marion and said our goodbyes.

The Hunt's experience here in 1995, straining sheep waiting to receive their last rights, but with slurry seeping through her knickers SH was unable to administer them. SH/RH caught a train and PH pounded tarmac. JT provides her own vivid account of a similar experience to ours but gives no mention of being accompanied by a dog(s). This really was some 'life threatening adventure' especially for an 18inch Havoc.

We were now in Cumbria, our last English coastal county. It got me thinking, how many counties had we visited? By way of a time filler, I started to tally them up in my mind. I made it 19 coastal counties not counting Tyne and Wear, Greater London, Isle of Wight and Merseyside, but feel free to check. I also realised I knew extraordinarily little about Cumbria except it had lots of lakes and relatively few people. I had heard of William Wordsworth, Beatrix Potter, Alfred Wainwright and Stan Laurel, Cumbria's finest, but that was about it. The Leven viaduct heading directly west to Ulverston looked very dodgy walking, so we followed the river north towards Greenodd. Wendy was a bit spooked by walking on sands fearing we might go the same way as those 23 Chinese shell fishers three years earlier and was right to exhibit caution.

Away from Cartmel Sands we were approached by someone on a BMX bike. Wearing a full-face crash helmet, they seemed quite petite, but their message was very clear, we were on private land. When the helmet was removed it turned out our castigator was about ten, barely out of believing in the tooth fairy. I was a bit taken a back, considered deploying my carpet tack stinger but resisted. What confidence, what courage, this was a future Evel Knieval or bailiff in the making. A bit later the message was reinforced by a farmer on a quad bike, probably dad, who escorted us onto a right of way. These two would have given Statler and Waldorf from The Muppets a run for their money. Little laughter in the wallet here. If we all made sense of humour our default emotion, we would all get along better. That was something I needed to keep repeating to myself. So much for Cumbria being sparsely populated, they chase you down here.

We crossed the Leven near to the busy A590, were given permission to put the tent up at the back of the Post Office in Greenodd, (it closed in 2008) and, also were gifted an open bottle of red wine, three quarters full. Something of a strange set of welcomes to Cumbria, it rained all night, cheers.

We picked up an old railway line heading south, and the John Barrow Monument came into view to our right on Hoad Hill. He was a great explorer and founded the Royal Geographical Society. Designed to look like Smeaton's Tower at Plymouth it looked for all the world like a giant greasy spoon café salt cellar. Ulverston Canal Foot is the end of what I read is the world's shortest, widest and deepest canal, the width accreditation certainly surprised me. Glaxo Smith Kline, Chapel Island, and onto The Concle Inn at Rampside.

We left our bags and followed the causeway to Roa Island. From here we could look across to Piel Castle and South Walney the bottom end of a hammerhead of land which we needed to reach. An industrial landscape led us into Barrow, where work making submarines has ceased for the day and Barrovians were out for a drink or three before hitting the clubs. We headed for the Jubilee Bridge and crossed to Walney.

The island is a mile wide with nature reserves at both ends. Shingle, sand dunes and salt marsh provide habitat for the likes of natterjack toads and a host of bird life. Wind farms proliferate with turbine masts seeming to germinate everywhere from the ocean in all directions. A concrete and kelp covered causeway visible at low tide enables foot crossing of the channel near North Scale and we carried on to Ormsgill.

We had heard there were guides who led people over Duddon Sands but were unable to contact anyone. Instead, as it was a Sunday and there were no trains running, we crossed on the viaduct at Foxfield after summoning up courage at The Prince of Wales. Millom lies on the north shore of the Duddon only about six miles from Barrow as the crow flies but some 20 around the estuary. Not for the first time I wished I had wings.

Turning north again and off his lead Havoc was being bold having his own mini capers exploring the beach. At that moment he reminded me of Snowy, Tintin's companion in Herge's adventures, but then the weather changed. First lightening and then thunder, although distant, his knees went, and he became a quivering wreck. With added gunfire at Eskmeals ranges he was more jittery than Scooby Doo locked in a warehouse with a janitor donning a sheet.

He now had to be carried, the viaduct over the river Esk being our way to Ravenglass. This was surely a secret gem on the coast of the Lake District. Here we met up with hasher Leakie Willie again, last seen in Mumbles, who had journeyed up to see how we were doing. He had organised our complimentary stay at The Holy House Hotel, bought us dinner at The Ratty Arms and was going to join us the next day for a real taste of what walking the coast was like. He was on his way to Turkey via Glasgow, his soft sided suitcase full of holiday brochures, wearing compulsory Swansea Jack H3 rain top, check shorts, pristine trainers and brandishing a large umbrella, perfectly equipped for what we were about to come across.

Chapter 35 – Ravenglass to Gretna

A troubled bridge over swirling waters...I'm on your side

Ravenglass to Gretna

"Born too late, and with a Leakie Willy, but Freeeedommm will be reached."

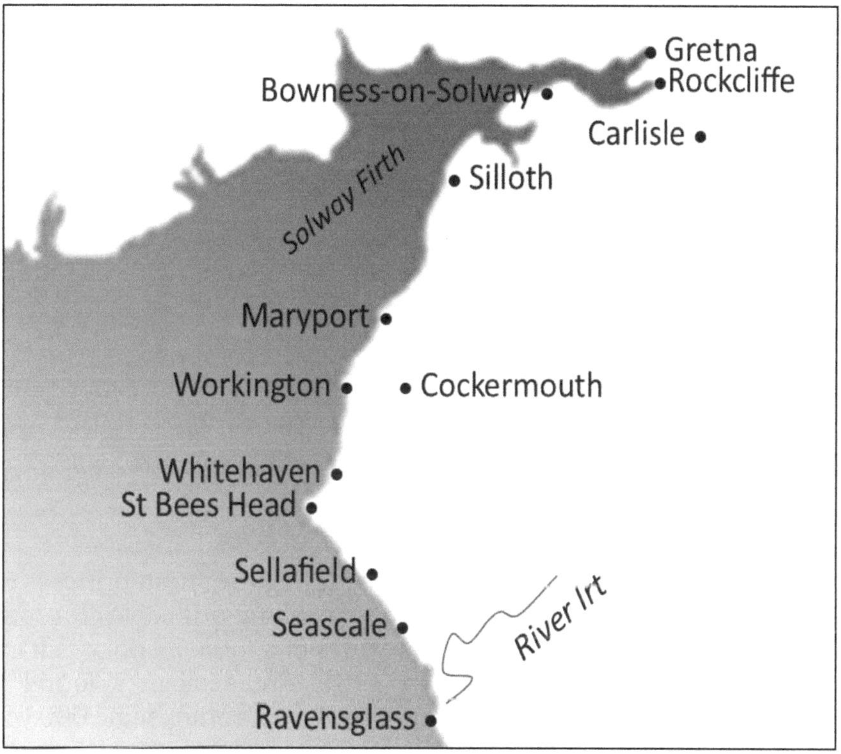

A FOOTBRIDGE ALONGSIDE a viaduct over the river Mite leading to Saltcoats should have been an easy option but workmen had closed it off, saying it was more than their job was worth to allow us passage. I began to wade the river, with my rucksack held at arms stretch over my head the water came up to my chest, but I made it. Leakie, seized his chance while the workmen were distracted by me nearly drowning, and snuck over the viaduct. Super sneaky the Welsh. Which left Wendy and Havoc still negotiating with the workmen to let them pass and after realising they were fighting a losing battle, allowed them across under their closure tapes. Some eyelash fluttering may have been exhibited and maybe a rendition of Paul Simon's 1974 anthem with the correct words. One of Wendy's favourites.

Next all four of us had to wade the Irt. Socks, shoes and trainers removed, the water wasn't too bad, but the steep muddy banks were more of a challenge, even with an umbrella walking pole. Mud caked shank and plantar photos evidence Welsh foot fetish fosse foolery. Cooling towers, chimneys, pipelines and fencing as we reached Sellafield and then wooden beachside chalet bungalows at Braystones where Leakie said his goodbyes. We sent him off more informed about coastal walking, sludge spattered and thankful for his ticket to Turkey. We had been entertained and enthused.

We headed for St Bees. Associated with Saint Bega, an Irish princess who fled here to avoid an enforced marriage to a Viking prince. Coffin routes also lead here from surrounding areas. Parts of a former priory still exist which was subject to excavation in 1981. Archaeologists found the remains of Anthony de Lucy, now known as St Bee's Man, some 600 years old, stomach contents, skin and nails were perfectly preserved in a lead coffin, somewhat questioning the notion of poisoning by Pb!

"Are you off to Robin Hood's Bay?" we were asked, "It's 192 miles."

Wainwright's Coast to Coast starts here, tradition has it, walkers should paddle in the Irish Sea and pick up a pebble to take with them. We politely replied we had been to Robin Hood's Bay, got the T-shirt, arrived here via a slightly less direct route and were too sensible to dip our toes in the ocean if we didn't have to. Rain and a strong on shore wind meant puffins, sometimes seen here, were being equally sensible and were all underground. Wainwright's Wall, an interpretation board marking this end of the trek was erected in 2013.

The candlestick creation at the site of Wellington Pit dominated the skyline at Whitehaven. This was a major mining centre for coal and metals. In the 1790s 'King Pit' once housed the deepest shaft in the world. Chemicals and later silk production played a part in the town's history. The harbour and much of the planned gridiron layout were down to the Lowther family. Three years after our visit, Whitehaven would attract media attention for its focus on gun law reform, following several shootings. Parton, Lowca and Harrington sounded like they should have been a firm of bankers financing former industrialisation stretching to Workington but were actually villages leading there.

Workington sits at the mouth of the Derwent, if nothing else walking around Britain made you well equipped for pub quizzes on the 'know your rivers' round. I had read they played Uppies and Downies here, a sort of mob football/handball but we would have to hang around until next Easter to witness that spectacle. Apparently at least £50 million had been spent on regeneration, the likes of Washington Square uplifted with the addition of several public art pieces, awards won, coal long gone, steel hanging in there, heavy industries always a part of the fabric t'up north. Despite accolades I noted in my diary 'all very depressing, metaphorically, a bit like a nettle patch at the bottom of the garden, underscored by charred wood and mattress springs.' Even a local called Workington the 'Chav armpit of Cumbria.'

The outlook was more pleasing to the eye as we approached Maryport, the marina with some steamships including a Clyde Puffer. A stream ran parallel to the shore with several small bridges crossing it, the concrete promenade was part of a long-distance walk called the Allerdale Ramble, Seathwaite to Grune Point, some 54 miles. Elizabethan saltpans can be found in places, where salt was extracted from sea water.

We met up with more hashers this time from Cockermouth, where we were billeted. The town is just a few miles inland at the confluence of the rivers Cocker and Derwent. Gifted with souvenir T-shirts, wined and dined our dinner host was Victoria, aka Plum Tart. Famed for her homemade jam and other culinary delights. We sampled marrow cookies, beetroot cake, nasturtiums in our salad, all with a 'hint of liver'. The Dibley organist, Letitia Cropley (Liz Smith), 'Queen of Cordon Bleu' had a soulmate in The Lakes.

Havoc got a new collar and a soft toy to play with which lasted all of 20 seconds. Starting with the eyes, he was adept at opening up the face before spreading kapok stuffing from skirting board to door post. Pubs were generous for our collection, the RNLI tin doing particularly well, which as future events would show was quite presaging. The town suffered badly in November 2009 with flooding and RNLI boats and crews helped with rescue efforts. In December 2015 the Derwent burst its banks and brought more disruption.

The wide cobbled streets and The Green of Sillouth were extremely attractive. They were preparing for a Kite Festival the next day and in hindsight we perhaps should have made a stopover. However, the populous here were saved from an ear bashing from Havoc, we decided to move on. Quite a trek lay ahead around Moricambe and the estuaries of the Waver and Wampool to Bowness-on-Solway. This was the start of the Hadrian's Wall Path stretching 84 miles to Wallsend. Some of those setting off commented on Havoc's little boots. Blue with black Vibram soles, held on by Velcro fastenings. Keeping all four on was often beyond him, but Wendy wanted to try and protect his pads on hard ground. He hated being a member of the canine ministry of silly walks, had a highly embarrassed look on his face whenever they appeared and would stand on three legs trying his utmost to shake a paw free.

We camped at Port Carlisle and I got talking to a fisherman. Scotland was easily visible across the Solway and this guy said he could show us where to cross if we were up early the next morning. Crossing would avoid going to Carlisle and the difficult roads leading to Gretna, Liddel Water and the Cumberland Gap. We arranged to meet him at 7.30am the next day. Overnight however I listened for once. Wendy was not happy at all about the risk, probably quite rightly, if we ended up having to call the RNLI having spent so much effort trying to boost their funds, would mean publicity we could do without. The following morning, I went to tell him thanks, but no thanks. Instead, we headed for Glasson and Burgh by Sands.

I was still sulking having been denied a paddle to Scotland, one to tell the grandchildren, but my mood was soon to be lifted. I had always loved everything medieval. At primary school if you finished your work and got cleared up at the end of the day the class teacher, Mr Hill, would read a class story. My favourite was The Battle of Crecy, it probably was the foundation stone. My favourite assembly hymns were 'He who would valiant be', and 'When a knight won his spurs'. Longbows, jousting, claymores, castles, chivalry and fighting, the stuff 'real' men were made off. So, what more could one want to discover than a bronze of a Plantagenet king, Edward I. It had been unveiled on the village green just three weeks earlier marking the 700th anniversary of the King's death on the marshes nearby.

Edward, known as Longshanks and the Hammer of the Scots, was on his way to sort out troublemakers like Robert the Bruce, and was going to cross the Solway at low tide but succumbed to dysentery on the marshes on 7th July 1307. He was 68 and had ruled for 35 years. We had eyed many of his castles en route to this point. A tall sandstone pillar close by is said to mark the exact spot where he died. He was later taken to Westminster Abbey for burial. Great medieval king or conquering tyrant?

He was of course played by Patrick McGooham, (Prisoner and No 6 from Portmerion) alongside Mel Gibson in 'Braveheart' (1995). Cry 'freedom'. Famed for its historical inaccuracies, it still won five Oscars, Longshanks would hang, draw and quarter William Wallace (Gibson) two years before his own death. A short list of names came readily to mind who I might like to do the same to, but I was born too late and had not made it to be king, no divine right. 'Know what it means to hate, now you're ready to be king.'

It was about here on their walk SH/RH had a big fallout. Shally even mentions for a brief moment she wanted to go home. Verbal expletives were directed and returned, two small children had their vocabulary expanded, teamwork was stretched to its limits. She even had a whistle to signal to Richard she could not keep up, that was often ignored, and communication was lapsing into brick bat throwing. She comments,

"No wonder people do this type of marathon on their own."

We had been warned. I vaguely recalled her asking about the strength of our relationship when we met them on the south coast before we even started, she was passing on the warning. Reading back over her comments was in some way comforting for the fallouts we sometimes exchanged. They had been 'married' for years, but still experienced relationship vulnerability.

Next stop Carlisle, across the river Eden and out through Kingmoor nature reserve. We camped on the cricket field at Rockcliffe planning a short day tomorrow. Sunday, day 259 was a landmark day as we said goodbye to England. At Metal Bridge across the Esk we found only concrete. Had the Scots on their way back from Wembley in 1977 taking the goal posts with them, also pinched the bridge metal for scrap? Road improvements on the A74 and new M6 meant a lot of our way was construction site. My thoughts went back to the 2-1 defeat, McQueen and Dalglish, hordes of kilt-wearing Scots. I needed an ear worm to take my mind off it. The Cumberland Gap song refers to a pass in the Appalachians, but this was our Cumberland Gap and skiffle king Lonnie Donegan filled my mental chasm.

Chapter 36 – Gretna to Garlieston

Fox on the Run

"Bitter though it may be to many, there is no substitute for truth. Which is in the right, the young man who sees the best in all and trusts all, or the old man who suspects all until he has probed them through and through...now eat up your lettuce."

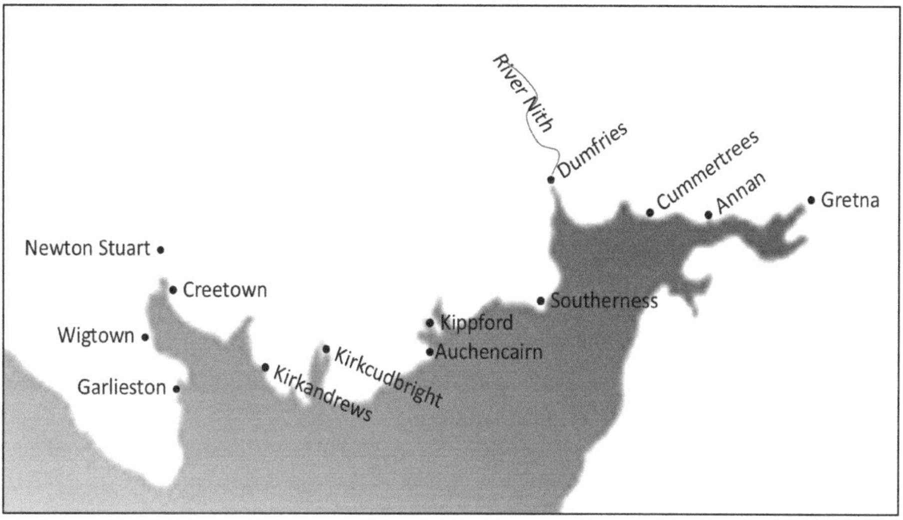

COLOURFUL BEGONIAS, St Andrew's flags and a large green and white sign saying, 'Scotland welcomes you' told us we were north of the border at Gretna, and the First House in Scotland Marriage Room was as good a place as any to camp. We popped over the river Shark to explore Gretna Green. The 1754 Marriage Act meant young couples had to be 21 in England to marry without parental consent. At the time laws in Scotland allowed boys of 14 and girls only 12 to marry. Hence was set a custom of eloping to Gretna in order to fulfil true love. By the 1770s a toll road enabled Gretna to be more easily reachable and the rest is down to the entrepreneurial genius of locals.

Blacksmiths it would seem were the first to diversify. Giving their horseshoes away for luck and using their anvils to conduct services, they forged marriages in the white heat of the hearth. Hugh Mackie had set up a visitor attraction by 1885, thousands flocked there, hotels and all manner of merchandise followed. What 'Nessie' did for Loch Ness, anvils

did for Gretna. They were everywhere, holding open doors, peeping from behind curtains, breeding by the bick and hardie hole (anvil parts). Anvil pencil sharpeners, tin openers, key rings, I just waited to see an anvil loo brush. Now I realised where the 'metal bridge' and Wembley goalposts had ended up, melted down to make anvils.

The local football club, nicknamed, you guessed it, were riding high, living the dream. In 2006 they had been promoted to the top-flight, The Scottish Premier League and reached the Scottish Cup Final. The success however was short lived, by 2008 the money had dried up and the club was dissolved. The whole experience would not have been complete without the appearance of a piper and haggis for tea. On the subject of getting hitched, Havoc records,

"I just thanked God that we hadn't walked all this way for Mum and TEB to do that!"

The topic never came up and why would I raise it and invite rejection.

Much of the local economy is still driven by the marriage industry. It is estimated one in six Scottish weddings take place in Gretna. While the area still awaits its Star of Caledonia, an approved spiral sculpture planned to be twice as high as the Angel of the North, times have seen the emergence of a new Greta star in the form of Miss Thunberg, some might say the angel of activism and the environment.

Heading west we came to Rigg and then Eastriggs, although why the later came to be so named when it clearly lies to the west of the former was something to ponder. This was once the site of a massive First World War munitions factory, codenamed 'Moorside'. Conan Doyle called what was made The Devil's Porridge. Often hand mixed nitroglycerine and the like were combined to make cordite and stuffed into shells, workers often women, from all over the Commonwealth occupying a nine mile long factory. The legacy, still to be seen, streets named Calcutta Avenue and Melbourne Terrace.

The weather was much more in our favour, blue skies, Simpsons clouds and sunshine reflecting off ripples on the water. Dornock, Annan and Powfoot to Cummertrees, my diary entry read 'like Batman and Rowan'. By pure chance and good fortune, we bumped into a couple in their front garden. Mike and Sheila Stubbs were to offer us an overnight stay in their home on Queensberry Terrace, an impressive symmetrical row of some 15 houses. To invite two strangers from the street, with no prior warning into your home speaks volumes for some people's generosity and kinship of humanity. We would 'sing for our supper' but it was far more interesting to listen and treat the experience as a school day. Listening, very under rated, it means putting others before self.

The main landowner in the area we were told was the Douglas family with a mausoleum in the village. The 9th Marquess of Queensbury, John Sholto Douglas, was the man giving the name to the boxing code which governs the sport, Queensbury Rules. His third son, Lord Alfred 'Bosie' Douglas had a much-publicised homosexual relationship with Irish author Oscar Wilde. 'Dad' disapproved of the relationship fervently, arriving at a Wilde play with a bouquet of vegetables, intent on trouble. A cabbage was not thrown, but the incident made its way into folklore. Kinmount House, a family mansion was sold to Edward Brook, a wealthy industrialist, in 1896, athlete Steve Ovett owned it for ten years in his retirement and now a leisure group let out holiday accommodation.

Without meeting such hosts, we would have never been able to hear local tales. Knowing I was a keen sportsman they linked my interest with the locality, if I were a painter or a lover of origami, they would have probably been equally able to captivate. Introduced to Arran Blond beer I could not help but think the slogan on the bottle summed up our evening combining 'substance with zest'. Often asked, 'what was the best bit of the walk?' It was these meetings that surpassed any place or view.

The lower road led us to Ruthwell. As if to confirm the fact that Scots are known for their thrift, the world's first Savings Bank was set up here in 1810. A small, whitewashed cottage and museum mark the foresight of Dr Henry Duncan. A little further and we reached Brow Well. We were in Rabbie Burns country and read the bard took the waters here in 1796 before he died. It was easy to think the reddish iron stained water seen may have contributed to his demise but apparently, he had a dodgy heart before his visit. Grassy banks and wildflowers on the river Nith, sounded like it was straight out of Monty Python, and we stopped to watch Haaf fishermen. Standing chest deep in water holding a giant butterfly net about four to five metres by two metres with the intention of catching salmon and sea trout. The name has Norse origins, and the practice is quite unique to Solway. (The normally colourfully clothed Michael Portillo toned down his wardrobe for his go at it, May 2023.)

An unusual, indescribable noise and around a corner we were greeted by a fox trapped in a snare. The wire loop had been set between the bottom two strands of a barbed wire fence on a known animal passing place in vegetation. The poor creature was frantically trying to free itself by jumping but making the noose tighten around its neck, the wire disappearing into its fur. As you might expect Havoc recalls this but is also victim to mistaken identity as it was me not Wendy who attempted to release him.

The wire was attached to the fence and without pliers untwisting it took all my finger strength. You do not come across such a distressed animal every day of the week; I remember thinking I had never been as close to a live fox, beautiful coat, huge eyes but he was scared and angry. With only about a metre of wire 'lead' to play with I did not want to risk getting bitten with whatever consequent infection a fox might pass on and as I unwound the last turn, he pulled the wire from my grip and was off across the field. I had not really thought the rescue attempt through, how were we ever going to get the looped end from his neck without appropriate gloves and pinning him down?

We could only hope he would somehow gain sufficient slack to be able to get his paw in and free himself completely. I did get criticism for not keeping hold of him, virtually impossible, but took solace in knowing if we had left him as found he would just have been shot or bludgeoned. We had given him at least a chance, left alone he would have had none. The farmer or hunter would not be so happy, but the truth, it would be me not Wendy, they needed to remonstrate with.

Dumfries, the Queen of the South, famed for its Burns connections, was our next stop. Its toponymy is debated I just like to think it was the home of very 'thick chips', so we treated ourselves. Although buried at Dumfries, Burns was born nearer to Ayr. A pioneer of the Romantic movement, many see him as Scotland's National Poet, and he has been voted 'The Greatest Scot' ahead of Wallace and Kenny Dalglish. He died aged 37 but some 900 living descendants dip into 'Ancestry' regularly. Sasanach's might know him best for 'Auld Lang Syne', poorly rhyming epithets and the chance to have a party at the end of January.

Eight miles south down the Nith is New Abbey, home of Sweetheart Abbey. The remains of a Cistercian monastery dating from 1275. The wife of a nobleman had it built in honor of her late husband also keeping his embalmed heart in a casket. The course of true love knows no bounds. A bell tower, pillars, nave and carved stonework remain in 30 acres of precinct with manicured grass like a billiard table. American Revolutionary naval commander John Paul Jones, who we had heard of back at Flamborough in Yorkshire, grew up in these parts, his parents were married at New Abbey in 1733.

We camped at the caravan/campsite at Southerness. In the evening we were made very welcome at the Mermaid Bar, bingo, quiz, children's games, collection and writing letters hoping for sponsorship. Nearby, an ancient and unusual lighthouse, 1748 with a square base, which Jones might have taken advantage of, but for our visit needed a coat of paint.

Walking west along Preston Merse, Havoc, having now refined his hunting skills, caught a rabbit only to be severely reprimanded. We came across several long vertical fishing nets each three to four metres high supported on posts with guys. It was low tide, we were walking in puddled and ridged soft sand, shoes off, the nets draped in bits of seaweed like lametta on a Christmas tree. A small monument to schooner Elbe and her captain Samuel Wilson marks an incident here in 1866. Freshly whitened cottages in Rockcliffe line the eastern side of Urr Water and we continued to the little lifeboat station at Kippford.

There, doing their shopping by watercraft, were a couple, Pete and Sue, with their family. We got chatting and were given a boat ride along the coast past Rough Island to their house near Auchencairn, Havoc already making himself at home on the lap of a teenage daughter. They had dogs of their own including a puppy, Impey, kept sheep grazing on Hestan Island, and we disembarked up a sloping lawn for drinks and nibbles on the terrace. A large multi chimneyed house, part ivy clad, part tower scaffold covered, the exterior of which somewhat underwhelmed what the interior would reveal.

A magnificent entrance hall, internal arches and pillars, silver candelabra, six-piece cutlery place setting, boar's head on the wall with just a few eccentricities, a Union Jack draped over the banister and a marble curling stone as a door stop. We were invited to stay and given the yellow bathroom, County Illustrated and National Geographic reading material, figs in the vegetable garden, and a llama called Brian. 'Who lives in a house like this?'

I do not quite recall if it was Pete or one of the magazines which got us onto the topic of Cadfael style recipes and treatments for walkers but somehow, we discovered a few.

Onion mixed with salt and honey for dog bites, onion and chicken fat rubbed onto blisters and lettuce preserved in brine to allegedly hold men's amorous instinct in check. I wondered why I was being given a lot of salad and it was bitter!

The Auchencairn experience was just another delightful unique one, a further reminder if we needed it, travel restores one's faith in mankind. We left with Pete on the scaffold fixing his slates. With fond, grateful memories we continued to Balcary Point and Rascarrel. Gorse, nettles, thick pine tree wind breaks, barley fields, wire and walls forced us inland to Dundrennan. Mary, Queen of Scots spent her last night in Scotland here at the Abbey in 1568, shortly afterwards being imprisoned in England. The roofless ruins might have been shelter for two hikers but would no longer be up to royal B&B. As it happens, we were on our way to Kirkcudbright, known as the 'Artists Town'. Spud recounts having fun pronouncing it and used it to enhance a 13-stride rhythm. They liked giving towns a second name here, inland Castle Douglas was the 'Food Town'.

For now, at the top end of the Bay on the river Dee, making big of the wonderful light, comradery and inspiration from fellow handicraft types, painters, textile embroiderers, ceramicists and, for all I knew, pubic hair platters plied their skills. Edward Atkinson Hornell and other Glasgow Boys were frequent visitors. On the harbourside a wooden sculpture of two figures hugging, (couldn't do that in 2021) in memory of loved ones lost at sea. The war memorial is a dramatic bronze of a warrior protecting a child unveiled in 1921. The Selkirk Arms Hotel agreed to put us up, we dined well after saying Burns Selkirk Grace, written here during his six-day tour in 1794, we were following in his footsteps.

The Borgue/Knockbrex peninsula lies to the east of Fleet Bay. Between them can be found Kirkandrews. An unusual Kirk is in Arts and Crafts style and dates from 1906. It would be a must for anyone interested in traditional craft particularly if they have a fondness for miniature castles. A couple were checking it out for a wedding in October and Havoc lay across the steps in the sunshine preventing entry until they gave us a donation.

Nearby, cup and ring marked rocks can be found at Tongue Croft. Megalithic art consisting of concave depressions and etched concentric circles, around 5,000 years old, the tradition of artists in the area was firmly rooted. We camped on a grassy/rocky ledge beside Fleet Bay, given dog food and milk by a local and intended to cross the sands next morning at low tide.

We woke to rain and were in no hurry to get going. Hoping things would dry out, it also allowed for the tide to recede. In low cloud and mist we headed off carrying our boots once more. We could see the outline of land we were heading for, I estimated some three kilometers away, tide catching us out wasn't really a problem, the unknown being how deep was the water in the centre of the bay. We reached Mossyard with no real problem, cleaned up and headed for Creetown. On the way we were given brunch at Carsluith smokery and Havoc had chicken skin.

A clock tower and unusual stone globe sit in the centre of Creetown but glistening wet streets and puddles meant we never saw a soul. Close by, Kirkmabreck quarries once supplied granite for Liverpool docks and sites in London. The Adamson Square makeover was the work of Japanese sculptor, Hideo Furuta. Born in Hiroshima he worked waste granite found locally but died in November 2007 just three months after we visited. Six miles later, still raining, we sheltered in the cinema at Newton Stewart and shopped at the Co-op before finding a campsite and trying to get dried out. It was a Sunday and I noted in my diary a possibility for a future book title, 'Should be dry by Thursday'.

Hugging the Cree and Wigtown Sands we headed south and discovered the Martyrs stake. 1685 saw two women executed by drowning for their religious beliefs. Wigtown itself is known as the 'Book Town' with second-hand bookshops everywhere and a bowling green in the centre next to the County Buildings. I looked to the skies to see if I could spot Wigtown Wanderers training ground but could only see a few clouds studding a pale blue merging with the salt marshes. One of JK Rowling's quidditch teams' heralds from the town. After yesterday's chicken skin Havoc was striding out to Garlieston carrying his own Lucozade Sport bottle in his mouth.

He stopped briefly to say 'Hi' to a donkey called Oatie before discovering friendly black pigs at our evening campsite.

All was well in the animal kingdom. My mind went back to 1974, Sweet - was that fox still running?

Chapter 37 – Garlieston to Irvine

You better start swimmin', or you'll sink like a stone

"The sticky out bit, that looks like a propellor." (Galloway)

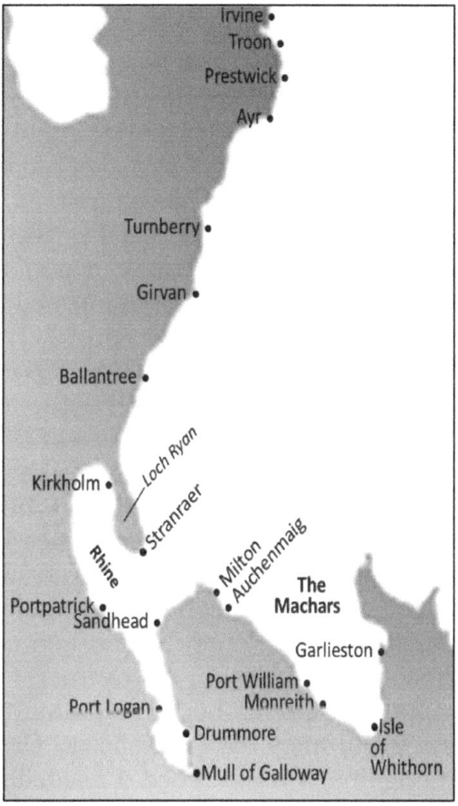

GARLIESTON IS A planned Georgian coastal village. Mulberry harbours were developed here during the Second World War providing temporary, portable landing stages for troops. The eastern side of The Machars, this stubby peninsula in Dumfries and Galloway with a 40mile coastline of its own, provided similar beaches to Normandy and was remote enough to prevent German discovery.

Inland were rolling green hills, good dairy country. Lush pasture, some fine dry-stone walls and we came across more beef cattle. Not the Banded Galloways shown on an Isle of Whithorn sign, but two magnificent South Devon bulls a long way from home. St Ninian, Scotland's first saint brought Christianity here ahead of St Columba on Iona. The remains of a chapel and a cave bearing Ninian's name lay either side of Burrow Head. Pilgrims would travel here from all over with a peak in the 1500s. Today, a 14 mile long distance walk stretches from Glasgow south to Whithorn Priory.

We found ourselves walking on a raised beach on the western side of the peninsula, scrubby field boundaries dotted with yellow ragwort but some grain to run my hand through and pretend I was Maximus Decimus Meridius from Gladiator. A hare left it right to the last second before bolting off and Havoc gave chase, but he was boxing well above his weight. We crossed St Medan golf course and picked up the A747 at Monreith.

A memorial in the form of an otter overlooks Luce Bay remembering Gavin Maxwell, author and naturalist who wrote Ring of Bright Water. Sir William Maxwell, an ancestor, founded Port William in 1775. We met a lady, Joyce Kinnear, on her bike who insisted she gave us a meal. Over pasta, strawberries and a coffee her husband Robin would tell us all about St Medan golf club, which we had crossed. He had been Gents Captain in 2005, their centenary year and did we know it was the most southerly golf club in Scotland! In 1915 the AGM was attended by two members, in 1916 the Secretary was on his own. Earlier in 1910 it was agreed ladies' powers were to be limited to arranging the teas. Just after the First World War sheep were brought in as gang mowers. I was presented with a Club Handbook. I was waiting for us to be retrospectively fined for trespass but managed to sidetrack him - only as far as his pre-retirement occupation as a soft furnishing retailer selling carpets and drapes. Worried I might end up leaving with a role of flock and an Axminster we made our apologies but not before Joyce gifted us double yoked eggs and Robin insisted, he take our bags onto Auchenmalg and leave them at the Cock Inn.

We were fattened up further with tea and fruit cake by teachers on holiday from Barrow-in-Furness at Chapel Finian. Allowed to pitch tent on a lawn next to the pub, as good as any putting green, we had to save the eggs for breakfast as the Cock Inn gave us an evening meal and we joined in the bingo. Between games I took the opportunity to wash my feet in a sink in the loos. A chap came in and for a moment I thought I was going to get a telling off. I apologised for taking the only sink, he uttered 'na bother' and instead told me to find a lady called Margaret in Simpson's bakers in Stranraer. Then, like Rumpelstiltskin he disappeared, no further explanation. Very odd I thought. Was Margaret going to gift me a bar of Lifebouy? Or had he suddenly realised he had a winning line? Dumfounded, I needed to release my big toe from the tap.

I checked out the map, I was not even sure where Stranraer was. Inland, I could see the northwest corner of Machars was more 'fell-like', peat bogs and small lochs. We had also been on the main road for most of the day and I could see tomorrow we could leave it and get back to proper coast. I pondered the Scottish remark made to me in the gents, compared it with memories of Wales 'fair play to you' and dreamt of Margaret's doughnuts.

Crossing fields near Milton, barley had just been harvested. The stalks left in the ground had filled with dew and as I walked on them water shot up the legs of my shorts. It was quite a thrill; I was going to need a lot more of that brined lettuce. An overgrown cliff path took us to the Waters of Luce, we crossed to Glenluce golf club. Another collection opportunity and we walked the Sands of Luce. A further bit of one upmanship over

JM, he was not able to do this as firing was taking place at nearby Torrs Warren. Just miles of sand, the occasional dog whelk and razor clam shell, mollusks of Luce, which crunched underfoot. Time had been taken up earlier with photographs for the Galloway Gazette and we needed to try and do some washing, so we decided to camp at Sandhead.

On a proper campsite I went to the laundry. First soap powder, we had a tiny bit, but the vending machine was empty. I went through the bin, shaking what I could out of old thrown away packets and hand sweep salvaging any to be found on the top of washers. Then the spin function decided to end early leaving our large and smalls still dripping so I did my best to wring out what I could. Oh! for a mangle. Without appropriate coins I tried to stick our things in with other peoples' in unattended dryers only to get everything all mixed up, socks I couldn't match and by now I had forgotten what Wendy had given me. Were these her knickers or Bridget Jones'? I was stripped down to my pants and a lady walked in to recover her things, I gave my best possible Mr Bean impression which required minimal acting, quickly threw everything in a bin liner and shot out of the door. I'm still missing a sock.

We were now on The Rhins of Galloway, a proper hammerhead like Wallney but larger, on the map, a propeller driving the Southern Uplands to the North Sea. Through Ardwell and near Terally we desperately needed the camera out quickly. Two seals, two deer and three herons all in one shot, they must have been having a convention, but unfortunately a companion of ours caused them all to scarper before I could expose my zoom lens (Inuendo intended!) We did some shopping at Drummore, meths top of the list, and camped just short of The Mull, the southern tip of Scotland.

We woke to heavy rain, so we left the tent up to dry, some chance, and skipped down to the rough shard at the bottom of the propeller, through pink heather to the lighthouse. There was no chance of seeing the Isle of Man to the south, we could hardly make out the cliffs just metres under our feet in thick fog. At the Gallie Craig coffee house with a grass roof, I had my first ever Ecclefechan tart (more inuendo!) An absolutely scrummy pastry with cinnamon, raisins, lemon peel and nut filling. I rang Sainsbury's, they put it on as an alternative to mince pies later that year and sold 50,000 packs. That is all true, except the bit about the phone call. Ecclefechan village lies midway between Lockerbie and Annon close to the A74(M), surely worth a visit just to pick up a local tart.

On the way back to pick up our bags and tent, which would be dry by Thursday, I ushered a very inquisitive cow, keen to meet Havoc, back over the fence. August 2007 saw an outbreak of foot and mouth disease. At the time three farms had been hit, way down in Surrey but landowners were jumpy after the disasters of 2001. A widescale outbreak would put paid to our walk. Later in September I read a sheep in Lanarkshire needed testing, fortunately it was negative. The scare lasted a couple of months and outbreaks never materialised on a broader scale in the UK.

With kit now saturated with three kilograms of water we headed up the west side of the Rhins to Port Logan.

The exposed west coast is all together more rugged than the softer east coast with sandy beaches. Steep cliffs on the Atlantic side are interrupted by one or two inlets, the whole peninsula is some 25 miles long with around 50 miles of coast. A small quay, a bell tower, a restored former Victorian fish larder now the oldest natural marine aquarium in the UK and an inn boasting Port Logan was the setting for the BBC TV drama series 'Two Thousand Acres of Sky' (2001-03) were the first sights I recorded. We found a key holder who let us stay in the village hall. Already airing inside was a small marquee so we made ourselves at home in a tent, in a hall; that was a first. Our flysheet and worldly belongings all spread out on chairs and tables drying, even the contents of my wallet, cards, a few notes all wet though spaced out, nothing like making yourself at home when you have the chance. With all this space and knowing things had not always been harmonious between us, one might have expected the sleeping arrangements to have been distanced, but the cocoon sleeping bags were laid out next to one another, if only for heat, but the zips stayed firmly done up.

The hall was once a lifeboat station and old honors boards were interesting. 1867-1926 saw three different boats. Activity ceased in 1913, The Great War would have seen to that, but the next entry was 1926. No incidents for six years or so after the war ended? Or did the war take a longer toll, meaning volunteers were hard to come by and voluntary services slow to resume after such a far-reaching event. Also, the association and physical distance to Ireland was revealed, eight stricken vessels were from Belfast and others too from various Irish ports. Northern Ireland was just over 20 nautical miles away.

We ascended and descended on, making use of chain handrails to the ruins of Dunskey Castle. Portpatrick itself has a crescent shaped harbour, guesthouses and hotels and the feel of a pleasant holiday destination. The Southern Upland Way, a coast-to-coast long-distance route runs some 200 miles to Cockburnspath on the east coast, we had been there on 4th January. JM was here on 1st May, it took him four months from London, we had been going for nine months to the day from John o Groats.

Past Blackhead lighthouse stinging hail brought a mole to the ground surface, Havoc panting with excitement and something I had never seen in real life before. A little later there were hundreds, all hanging dead from a barbed wire fence, barbaric pest extermination or was someone selling on their velvety skins?

From Corsewell Point lighthouse we could just make out the southern tip of Kintyre and at Barnhills another first and unique experience. Owners Horace and Caroline gave us an overnight in one of their horse-drawn caravans. The little round topped, green and red, 'gypsy' style wagons were a tourist rental idea which had not gone exactly to plan but made for a cosy stopover. A Cher earworm wriggled into my head, 'preach a little gospel, sell a couple of bottles of Doctor Good'. Supper and breakfast the next day with a packed lunch to take away all gifted, meant our daily budget rolled over, no need to 'lay any money down'.

We headed off to Stranraer at the droopy end of Loch Ryan, into Hanover Street and found W. Simpson & Son, bakers since 1905. I was stalking Margaret whose meringues were celebrated from Auchenmaig and I entered with a degree of apprehension. I left with a cream puff and a cheque for £50 for our collection grinning all the way up the A77 to Cairnryan. Thanks Margaret, thanks Rumpelstiltskin.

Dozens of swans upended their bottoms in the air feeding on submerged vegetation and ferries departed to Larne and Belfast. It wasn't long before we wished we had caught one of them. The people we met were charming and generous. It was the ones that might be lurking around a corner who we wanted to avoid. Another fence with moles hung evenly spaced out on the wire. They had not been on a kamikaze steeplechase and left themselves draped and rotting, their skeletons becoming exposed. Was this some sort of trophy exhibit, traditional mole trespass warning or allowing natural decomposition to flay the potentially valuable skin. Who knows?

Then, more alarmingly, between Ballantrae and Lendalfoot the Sawny Bean Cave. Legend exists of a 16th century clansman who hunted down night travelers killing, dismembering, pickling and eating their bodies. Folklore has it that cannibalism was rife in his family, 1000 victims, it went undetected for 25 years, and the site now warrants tourist circuit stop-ins. We scampered on to Girvan before it got dark and sought sanctuary in the lifeboat station.

Ten miles due west of here and a similar distance south of the bottom of Arran lies Paddy's milestone or nose, also known as Alisa Craig. 'Blue hone' a microgranite is sourced here to make curling stones, the only other place it comes from is Trefor in Wales which we had walked through.

Two thousand tons were harvested in 2013 and if my estimates are correct, they were due for another rape about 2020/21. Save for sea birds, a few rats and a lighthouse the island is uninhabited, a rocky protrusion, 340metres high, looking like it was a giant mammary implant, 'D' cup, floating on the Firth of Clyde. It was to be our companion on the horizon for many days to come.

I tried my arm collecting at Turnberry golf club but was given short and swift rebuttal, so we moved on to Maidens and the clifftop Culzean Castle. I knew I had seen it before but couldn't think where. Then it came to me, it featured on Royal Bank of Scotland £5 notes. A little further and we stumbled upon Croy or 'electric' brae. Due to the configuration of surrounding land a slope gives an optical illusion that things roll slowly uphill. Termed 'electric', it was originally thought to be a phenomenon caused by magnetism or electricity.

Approaching Ayr, Havoc is correct, a storm brewed between Wendy and me, and like him I cannot remember why. With no defence or excuse I accept full responsibility and put it down to my belligerence and volitivity. Sociopath? Possibly, complex untamed character, like a mustang, never quite broken. It was possibly the worst of the walk, resulting in Wendy crying, which I felt bad about, my guilt probably illustrating I was in the wrong. The tears would subside, we would make up, but underlying animosity was incremental and permanently damaging. Bob Dylan's prophetic creation may have been in my head, but was I taking any notice wherever I roamed?

We visited some of the sites of Alloway, birthplace of Burns; cottage, monument, Brig O Doon mentioned in some of his poems, shopped in Ayr and walked the dunes and links of Prestwick, Troon and Barassie. We were probably in need of some different adult company and at the Water Sports Club on the harbour side in Irvine met lots of jolly folk. After a few drinks ourselves we were equally jolly and one of the ladies, Dawn, arranged for us to stay at the fire station near Dreghorn. It was not quite such a peaceful night as one might imagine, two shouts for blue watch meant alarms sounded and lights came on automatically to remain on controlled by a timer. Their efforts were to help search for a teenager who had fallen into one of the nearby rivers in flood. We saw a search and rescue helicopter the next morning in the sky, a body was later found in Annick Water. Despite this the watch had a whip-round raising £30 and another guy handed us his darts competition winnings, another £25 for our collections.

Chapter 38 - Irvine to Kennacraig (via Arran and Kintyre)

Smiles in the sunshine and tears in the rain

"Sail on a ferry across the Clyde. The finest of Scottish scenery, no word of a lie. Rugged, magical beauty it may feel as if you have left this world and gone to another."

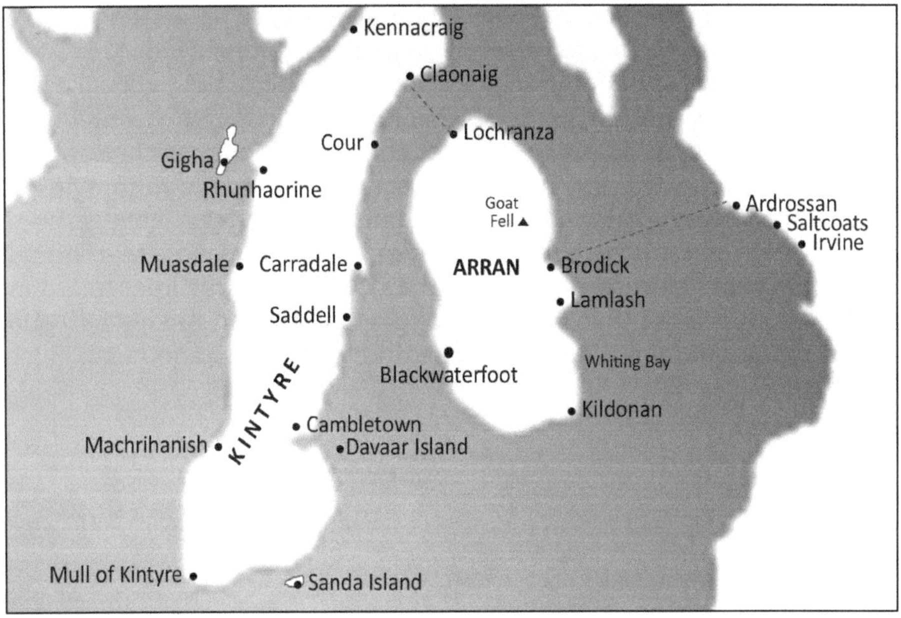

VERY SADDENED AND humbled, we headed for Ardrossan via Saltcoats to catch a Caledonian MacBrayne ferry. We were very naive about many aspects of the walk. When it came to navigating Scotland's west coast, we were downright ignorant. The many lochs and finger like peninsulas, I hardly knew what was mainland or island. I had heard the names of some of the bigger isles, Mull and Skye for instance, but could not have told you which was which. Back in Edinburgh one of our hosts Anne Robinson twigged this, let us look at some of her maps and told us about CalMac, who we had never heard of before.

So, in the intervening months I had written to them and secured a free pass on any ferry we wished to use. The upside was we would get to see some of the west coast archipelago, the downside some of the mainland coast would be bypassed. We were sacrificing good chunks of Argyll and Bute, places like Applecross and Plockton which we had been told of, not to mention other parts of the west highlands and the remote Knoydart peninsula. Looking at the maps however, we could see roads hugging the shores of many of the lochs so we would have been walking on tarmac. An additional downside, we would need to keep to a tight schedule to tie up with ferry frequencies, certainly not daily, and the timing of sailings. The ferry offer was too good to turn down, the absentee locations could wait for another time, we just needed to sort out an island hopping, outer coast route.

CalMac had been serving the Clyde and Hebrides since 1851. We had a hotline for one of their staff, Lesley who would arrange tickets and a large black and white ferry was waiting to take us to Arran. I read,

"The earth belongs to the Lord,
And all that it contains,
Except the Kyles and the Western Isles,
And they are all MacBrayne's."

They sailed to 22 islands, there were little dashed blue lines all over the Sounds. Which ones to choose?

Arran was an obvious, 'Scotland in Miniature', and if you were a geologist, my son had just passed his 'A' levels and was off to study it at Cardiff, Arran 'Rocks'. The ride took an hour, we were accompanied by jet skis and dolphins surfing our wake. Arriving at Brodick the sea seemed bluer, the skies clearer, the trees greener, the air fresher. It invigorated every sense. We had networked a guide dog supporter who ran a B&B and Kendal her golden retriever, put up with our heartbeat. That was Havoc, always under your feet, sometime pillow, a tent farting companion, soldier and friend. He got all the best titbits, here was no different. RB said walking is like life, it has its ups and downs, Ayr paradoxically, had been a down, Arran for me at least was definitely an up. Light after significant shadows.

So much so that the next day we decided to do our own bit of mountaineering and climbed Goat Fell. Open and rugged with jagged ridges it is a beautiful mountain. At 874m (2866 ft) it is one of four Corbetts on Arran, heights between 2500 and 3000ft. Shimmering purple heather, U shaped valleys and back to Brodick via Glen Rosa. The strange thing is Havoc recalls the climb being hard going, but my diary says he stayed back with Kendal at the house. Photos at the summit with him AWOL.

I helped with a bit of gardening the next day moving four lavender bushes and we were loaned a Nissan Micra to explore wider. We did a circumnavigation via Lamlash to Whiting Bay, Kildonan, a paddle at Blackwaterfoot beside steep cliffs, before going to Lochranza, Corrie and back to Brodick. We had to take in the brewery and distillery en route. No drinking and driving however, it was my first time in a car for ten months and an odd experience, my left foot more conditioned to pushing in tent pegs than engaging a clutch.

We had been invited to meet Lady Jean Fforde in the evening at her house, 6.00pm sharp. A keen dog breeder, she had shown at Crufts, but didn't seem to mind our mongrel, and a long-term President of the RNLI having served for 55 years. At the time she was living in a large house and had problems with her double glazing which I was able to fix for her. Posing for a photo outside with us we saw red squirrels on the lawn. At the time she was already in her eighties and had led an interesting life. Born into aristocracy she knew royalty of Monaco well, was a debutante in 1939 and was presented to King George VI. She also worked at Bletchley Park codebreaking and met Alan Turing. I read she died in 2017, but led an active life until then, and had to auction off lands to pay for her central heating. Kind spirited and hardworking, much admired by the people of Brodick who gathered at her funeral in numbers, a collection raising nearly £2000 for a youth group. It was an honour to have been given just a bit of her time.

We walked to Lamlash to get a better view of the lifeboat station and Holy Island. A long-time sacred site, the island is now home to a Buddhist Community and several rare breeds of ponies, sheep and goats. We were to stay with Robin, who provided valuable food for thought on future book writing as we stayed at Hamilton Terrace. This dated from the late 19th century, built and named after Alexander, tenth Duke of Hamilton. It consisted of front and back properties. Alexander was behind land clearances which saw peoples displaced, some went off to Canada, others occupied the terrace, the row behind for estate- workers, the posher front part let out to summer visitors. We were in the back half, which was fine, perfectly comfortable, somewhat smaller than Lady Jean's place, but still larger than my cottage back in Devon.

Robin dropped us back to Brodick with an early start at 7am. We needed to reach Lochranza by midday to catch our next ferry. Even at this time the morning was bright, with my arm outstretched, little finger on the sea, the horizontal rising sun was on the end of my thumb. We saw more red squirrels, quite a beautiful walk despite being on the road and quaint cottages at Corrie. Seals on the rocks, do not be fooled by the Marvin Elliot sculpture, we saw real ones too, and lots of jellyfish on the shore. I wondered again if a use could be found for them if collected, they did not seem to be part of the food chain for squirrels or seals or anything else for that matter. It repeated a thought from north Devon. Fertiliser, biofuel, filling for Paddy's nose, I was in that sort of a mood.

We crossed a small river at Sannox on stepping-stones and climbed up before dropping into Lochranza. Some castle ruins and inquisitive deer grazing but we had no time to dawdle with a 1.15pm sailing to Claonaig on Kintyre. There was no pipe reception but the obvious ear worm? You guessed it, Wings, McCartney, and took me back to Christmas 1977. Sir Paul held real estate on the peninsula, High Park Farm, and we looked out for it and him, but saw neither. If this is still the case, he might now need to up his security.

We passed a large sign with stylised motif telling anyone who did not know they were on Kintyre. The K distorted to form a sweeping wave, the Y a stooping eagle. Havoc stopped to give it a second look. He cocked his head amusingly to one side, analogous to Scrappy Doo, thought about barking, but I put a finger to my lips and sssshed him, akin to Hanna-Barbera's Fred Jones. 'You will be carried away for an eaglet's supper!' Velma Dinkley stepped in, 'You'll scare him into stop wagging his tail.'

We were now virtually out of networked contacts for stops, flying more by the seat of our pants than ever, getting full value from a tent we had been given, the terrain more remote, fewer interactions with people, less opportunity to fundraise. At Cour a lady did let us pitch tent in her garden, her dog Legend, showed Wendy where she could grab a wash,she returned saying she felt nearly as dirty as when she went in. We got some drinking water from a standpipe a little way up the road and had our first real encounter with 'Culicoides impunctatus', midges.

We got up early to try and give them the slip, but they were with us all the way through forest and scrub to Saddell. Here were the remains of a Cistercian abbey dating from 1160. Stone carving was a specialty and carved medieval grave slabs depicting knights in armour are displayed. We reached Cambeltown in time to join the lifeboat crew on an evening exercise aboard a Severn class boat, the largest in the fleet, The Earnest and May Shaw. I got to have a go on the wheel as we headed out around Davaar Island although we could not open the throttle to top speed as they were on an instruction to be economical with fuel. The previous weekend a boat had sunk locally, two survivors were picked up, a third body was still being looked for.

Cambeltown itself sits at the end of a loch. Several large imposing, listed buildings overlook a harbour. We were told fishing had almost gone, some wood was exported, and wind turbine production provided quite a few jobs. It is one of five categorised distinct malt whisky producing areas, although far fewer distilleries exist than in the past. We continued to Southend with views through mist to Sanda Island. At Keil we found an old church and more stone carved tomb stones, figures like warriors. Skull and cross bones, Memento Mori.

Fording a river at Caskey Bay we made our way to the Mull. The mist was rolling in from the sea, the sun had given up trying to burn it off, heather, bracken, moisture on our eye lashes formed droplets which ran down our faces. It settled on cobwebs on a hedge making them look like fairy hammocks. A high point of 428metres and a lighthouse, on the map this really does look like the swollen end of a large but flaccid phallus. The lyrics of '*Macca's*' song kept coming back to mind but there was no beach and pipe band like in his video, the bomb fire would have gone out in this mist and crowds celebrating must have been rented in, we never saw a soul, perhaps because the video was filmed back at Carradale on the east side of Kintrye.

From Machrihanish we headed over dunes and a golf course with surfers bobbing on their boards to Bellochantuy Bay. From Rhunahaorine, with Scotland's lowest trig point at just two metres, we had great views of Gigha, 'God's Island' and further away in the distance the outline of Jura. At times we were following the Kintrye Way set up in 2006 which traverses the peninsula for some 100 miles. Waymarked by short blue posts, etched with what looked like a dangly earring motif, I suppose illustrating that the path jumps from east to west as it passes from Tarbert down the peninsula.
At one point a flock of black faced rams clambered up a rocky outcrop to show off their spiraling sets of full curl horns. Any one of them would

have made a majestic regimental mascot. Havoc was humbled to a silent, submissive, subjugate. Time to exit this west coast knob.

Chapter 39 - Kennacraig to Tobermory (via Islay, Colonsay and Oban to Mull)

Billow and breeze, islands and seas

"Yesterday is history, tomorrow is mystery, today is a gift."

WE TOOK THE evening ferry from Kennacraig, two and a quarter-hours to Port Ellen, and camped right by the ferry terminal. Islay is shaped a bit like a lobster claw, the houses of Port Ellen in the south wrap around a small bay. I had read agriculture and tourism were the principal occupations not to mention whisky galore. We got varied answers to the question, 'How many distilleries are there?' single malt clearly has its effect on memory. Around about ten, the most common reply, mostly characteristically peaty. We headed off for Kintra, an area to our left known as The Oa, (An Obha).

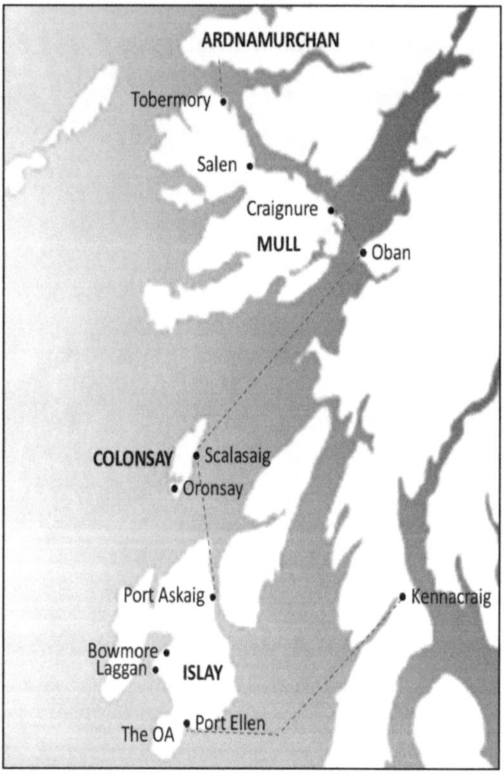

A long beach at Laggan Bay and we were spotted for a second time by Becky. She had been on last night's ferry too and came over to chat. She was remarkably interesting, good company, a bit of a Queen of Hebrides herself, something of a gift. She enjoyed wildlife, photography, artistic stuff and we ended up scavenging beach rubbish to build a dinosaur from rusty corrugated tin sheets, oddments of wood, with golf balls for eyes. She told us the beach was known as the long strand and was herself walking Islay's coast in sections but was not sure how far it was. I estimated it was around 120 miles and she joked saying at her current rate it would take her ten years. A chance meeting and we had a floor to sleep on at her house in Bowmore. We walked there crossing the river Laggon, while she grabbed photos of our joint beach sculpture for her college portfolio and went ahead, with time to tidy up, if that was needed.

Outside Bowmore's Kilarrow Parish Church we met another couple who had seen us at Turnberry. The white church was round, so the devil would have no corners to hide, it seemed like we could not escape the attentions of others either. Over a cup of tea with them the lights flickered, and they commented LIMPET's playing up again. They went on to tell us about Islay's pioneering part in wave power energy, the world's first wave power station was opened on the Rinns on the west of the island in 2000. (LIMPET 500 - Land Installed Marine Powered Energy Transformer.) Who dreams up these acronyms? I read much later it had been decommissioned by 2018. Is this what is meant by renewable energy? Just renew the scheme, less than 20 years old, some light bulbs last longer than that. Other schemes have apparently been approved for the Sound of Islay, let's hope they have more sustainability.

At Becky's in the evening the conversation was easy, helped by more than one bottle of red wine and single malt tasting. On the topic of wild camping and back to nature, Kathleen Meyer's book 'How to Shit in The Woods' entered the exchange. Amazing how relative strangers find a 'spot to squat', and uses of sphagnum moss so amusing with the benefit of alcohol. The floor was fine, although I swear it was a bit on the squint, and Wendy had her new 'therm-a-rest' bought in Ayr, fed up having to re-inflate the old one, to ease her off to dreamland.

Next morning, slightly worse for wear, we headed for Bridgend and then followed the river Sorn through woods to Ballygrant. The path through the Dunlossit Estate gave Havoc possibly his best afternoon ever. Red 'Tamworth' and black 'Iron Age' pigs roaming in the forest, dragonflies which he tried to catch in his mouth and several swims in the Loch.

The surface was perfectly smooth, mirror-like in its reflection of edging trees, white-grey clouds and vibrant sunbeams, the camera could do it no justice. Dave the mechanic of the Port Askaig lifeboat, the Helmet Schroder of Dunlossit II, another 'Severn', provided the digs. Crab on toast for tea, we borrowed his clippers for Wendy to give me a haircut and Havoc stared motionless for hours, his nose glued to the bars of a rodent cage, utterly frustrated, 'we have ways of making you talk.' The enclosed Russian hamster had been KGB trained, stayed tucked up in his shavings, never blowing his cover, a true comrade.

The seasonal ferry to Colonsay only ran on Wednesdays. Day 290 for us just happened to be the last one in August. We hopped on, the Paps of Jura a memorable and magnificent backdrop. Surely it cannot be long before Nicola Sturgeon has something in Holyrood by way of a deed poll to make these more politically correct. We were only really using Colonsay as a springboard to Mull via Oban.

The ancestral home of the Clan Macfie, with a population of a 100-135, had more than its fair share of 'learner' L drivers. We were told learners did not need to be accompanied by a driver with a license, but then there are only three B roads. When you jumped out of your car you left the keys on the dashboard so anyone could move it if needed. 2007 saw the opening of a brewery, the world's smallest island with its own. (By 2020 it had two gin distilleries, showing just how much gin has taken off.) The previous year saw the last crime committed, burglary by a visiting Glaswegian, prior to that little offending had happened since 1623.

On the map it was Islay's apostrophe. From Scalasaig we walked south, the weather worsened, turning misty, followed by cripplingly cold rain even in August. We crossed The Strand to the tidal island of Oransay, the semi next door, just to say we had been there, not exploring too far as we were unsure of tide times and needed to be back at the ferry terminal the next day to board for Oban. No time to go MacPhie bagging, these were the high points over 300feet, 22 in total, it would have taken six/seven hours to cover the 20 or so miles capturing them all. We camped at a farm near Garvard, becoming a staple, sausages and Super Noodles for tea with the addition of a single foraged mushroom. The natural beauty and tranquility were obvious, even in poor weather. There was a sense of calm, a peaceful wildness, quiet yet possibly full of life if we had longer to explore.

After a wet and windy night, we made our way back to Scalasaig where there were quite a few travelers waiting to catch the late morning ferry. There we met Leslie, our CalMac guardian angel, and I was gifted a fleece top bearing a breast badge, the standing boxing red lion on a ship's pennant. I still wear it regularly. We boarded for a long two-hour sailing. I tried to imagine what it would be like to live on Colonsay. Where would you work if not retired? Tourism, the fish farm, crofting possibly. Learn Gaelic to fit in, though we had heard little spoken. Get on with everyone, remember to return the borrowed lawn mower. Essential qualities; multi skilled, versatile, independent, a make do and mender. Materialism low on one's personal barometer. A freezer essential and preserving skills useful. Online dating opportunities limited, must be prepared to travel. For the young, it must be hard, although we heard there was a primary school. The brain was still buzzing but fortunately we reached the Sound of Kerrera and docked at Oban.

It sat in a horseshoe bay, an obelisk on Kerrera Island which shelters the town is in memory of David Hutcheson who was really a founding father of CalMac, although it was his son-in-law who grew the business into today's operation. Over the town, McCaig's Tower, a banker's attempt to build a colosseum to rival Rome.

Oban is known as the Gateway to the Isles, whisky distillation predated the town from the 1790s, so I was assuming there would be a few more folk around than on Colonsay but the numbers were a shock. 8,500 inhabitants, which could grow to 25,000 in summer, quite a step up for secondary school kids from Colonsay who would board at a hostel and fly home for weekends. I was still wondering about life on a tiny island, trying to put myself in the mind of a teenager, this was quite a contrast. I was finding the gulf strange even having been on Colonsay for just one night and Oban was only really a modestly sized tourist town. It is always said kids are very adaptable, but I wondered how those who had to, coped with the transition. Much later, 2019, as a teacher I saw a Headship advertised at the primary school on Colonsay. £51k salary, with a house thrown in, six pupils and a preschooler. Even if they wanted me, how would I manage small island life?

We had been given space to throw down our sleeping bags at the lifeboat station. With somewhere to leave him and a babysitter to boot we left Havoc and went to take in a show. Hardly Broadway, but McTavish's Scottish Show Night was a bit of a hoot. A piper, fiddle player, sword dancing and lots of tartan. All very traditional and some might say cheesy, but we had fun and when asked if we wanted a tune requested, the Skye Boat Song. We were actually heading for Mull the next day but had never heard of a boat song to there. We had survived Culloden, evaded capture the long way around to here, and now needed someone to speed a bonnie boat, like a bird on a wing, to Craignure.

Mull is the fourth largest Scottish island with a coastline over 300 miles long. We were not going to be able to see it all. To the west Iona and Staffa which were draws but the big pull was from Tobermory to the north. We headed for Fishnish Bay, past an old chapel and carved tomb stones at Pennygown, allegedly depicted were former chiefs of the Duart MacLean clan who were into witchcraft. This was MacLean country. Old rotting fishing boats pulled up on the beach at Salen were a sad sight, their seaworthy days long past. From Aros Castle we headed away from the coast, following the Aros River to Ledmore. A forest trail took us to a bird hide, carved eagles adorning a seat, TV web cams but no real-life eagles.

White headed ones were re-introduced in 2005, 'Spring Watch' broadcasts and the growth of ecotourism have put Mull on the map as far as visitors are concerned. We walked the shore of Loch Frisa and then past other smaller Lochs, picking up the Tobermory river which led us to the town.

A colourful sheltered harbour with Calve Island sitting a short way off in the bay. More legend, Spanish gold lay somewhere at the bottom of the Sound from the Florencia, but none has ever been found. We treated ourselves to fish and chips and joined a group of lady cyclists for a few drinks at the pub.

Outside on the harbour steps we spotted two otters in the dark feeding on restaurant fish scraps thrown into the water. Silvery scales and the reflection from their eyes were really all the camera captured in the dark, but the viewing made Wendy's night, possibly her favourite animal. Back in the pub it was time for the best impression of an otter competition - what, what, what! Round two was impressions of Peter Bonetti, goalkeeper for Chelsea and England, retired to Mull and did a stint as a postman, nick named, 'The Cat'.

We were staying at the lifeboat station and next day, being a Sunday, we did have a day of rest, mainly because there was no ferry until Monday anyway. A lazy day, time to look around and all of a sudden, the lifeboat launched needing to offer a tow to a ketch, Asgard II, flying an Italian flag, which had caught on fire. That's wood fired pizza ovens for you. The houses stirred an ear worm, the 1960s social activist anthem, Little Boxes. I pondered who covered it, Val Doonican or Pete Seeger? Not that the houses were made of 'ticky tacky', they weren't even on a hillside or all the same, but there was pink one and a green one and a yellow one.

I filled some time doing some research. Fingal's Cave on Staffa, hexagonally jointed basalt with great acoustics, legend had it one end of an ancient bridge, linking it to the Giant's Causeway in County Antrim. Two giants falling out, baby disguises, cakes filled with iron and broken teeth filled half an hour. Then there was World War II Commodore Sir Gilbert Stephenson, known as the 'Terror of Tobermory' due to his temper. I thought that was a role reserved for me. Tomorrow was a mystery. Our brief encounter with these Western Isles, oh so much a gift.

Chapter 40 - Tobermory to Sandaig (via Ardnamurchan, Mallaig, Skye and Kylerhea)

You and I must make a pact, we must bring salvation back

"All for Edal."

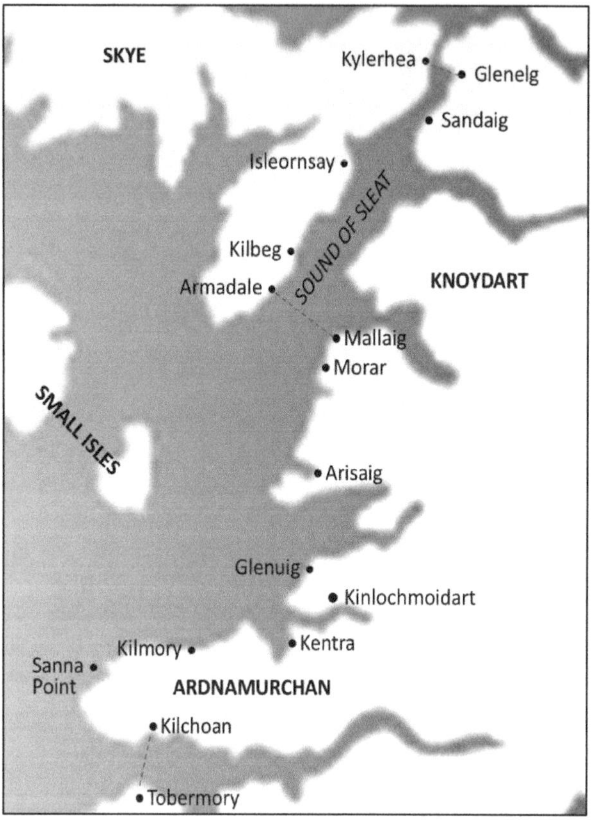

ON MONDAY morning I wanted to get a map at the Post Office and deposit some money. Wendy went ahead with Havoc to board the ferry while I waited in the PO queue. Checking my watch, this was going to be tight, the sailing was at 9.30am. I was next in turn, the dear old lady in front of me couldn't remember her pin number, the next ferry was goodness knows when. I reached the head of the queue, the postmaster was keen to chat, sorry got to go! I sprinted to the boat where the gangplank was being raised, made it by the skin on a giant's tooth. Half an hour later we were in Kilchoan, a little later a sign read 'Welcome to West Ardnamurchan - the most westerly point on the UK mainland.'

A headland of the great seas needs something. On the point a lighthouse, made from pink granite, a single birthday cake candle for Fingal. Built in 1849, 36m tall and standing 55m above sea level. Nelson stands 51m above his lions in Trafalgar Square, but John Noakes never climbed this one, as far as my Blue Peter memory serves. The Stevenson family of engineers, synonymous with lighthouse construction, had a hand, this one the work of Alan. There was a fresh breeze, but it was sunny and everywhere just seemed beautiful. Blue, blue skies and sea with views to Tiree and Coll. Inland mountains, red deer, and birds of prey soaring, they could have been eagles, but we were no Hamza Yassin (wildlife cameraman/Strictly winner 2022) and this was his back yard. Among the rocks at Sanna Bay mink, black against the white sands, easy viewing for us, let alone predators in the air. As the day wore on views of Muck, Eigg and Rum. I thought of celebrities offering their best views in Britain, this had to be a contender, probably Hamza's.

Fascadale and an unusual circular walled cemetery at Kilmory, judging by the church in Bowmore, no corners for the devil to hide here either. Ockle and then Kentra Bay before finding the floor of a transport office, Shiel Buses as a place to stay. Our list of strange and 'exotic' accommodation growing ever more comprehensive. With the keys to all the vehicles hanging above our heads I regressed to times when I sang nursery rhymes to my kids, wheels, driver, conductor, and prayed the horns didn't work.

As we followed the Shiel river towards Cliff a car pulled up. In the passenger seat, with her husband driving and young family in the back, was a face I remembered. A friend from my days at college in Exeter, I had not seen her for about 27 years, neither of us knew or were expecting it, pure chance, but there was Liz Heppel. I had fancied her, even taken her to a summer ball one year. She was a long way from her home in Plymouth, we recognised each other immediately, with equal degrees of surprise, exchanged pleasantries and waved each other off. Strange how such meetings occur, with sixty million other people one could bump into, but plenty for my mind to play with as we carried on to Castle Tioram perched on a tidal island.

We turned eastwards along the southern shore of Loch Moidart picking up a path called the Silver Walk. Rough terrain, climbing over fallen trees and boulders, boggy in places, some vertical drops. It went on for nearly eight miles and took four hours. Twisted oaks, with feathery lichens, birch and rhododendrons, rocky islets and a misty, mysterious background, scenes through branches reminded me of Chinese artwork on porcelain plates.

We met a digger driver making the path more accessible. Alone, miles from civilisation, highly skilled, with his machine looking as if it could topple over at any moment. What was even more surprising was he only had one arm, a cup shaped prosthesis, as if it could have been fashioned from an ice cream scoop, resting on the controls. We chatted as he rolled a cigarette, his caterpillar tracks at 45 degrees to the hillside. The dumpy bags of path aggregate are lowered in by helicopter he told us. I asked how The Walk got its name? A few theories existed. The castle owner Clan chief Alan Macdonald torched Tioram to keep it from the Hanoverians but hid the family silver in the woods beforehand. Option two, a cook from a fancy house would hide items of cutlery stolen on her way home, a knife one day, a spoon the next. A third theory, silver was landed here to fund Bonnie Prince Charlie's 1745 Jacobite rising. I wished I had packed my metal detector, little treasure had ever been found, but then was that a hallmark on that ice cream scoop!

Spud came up trumps for us, arranging for us to stay at Kinlochmoidart House through someone she had met, Nina Stewart. Having completed her walk, she returned to nearby Glenuig to write the bulk of "*two feet four paws*". The turreted Scottish mansion, chateau like, the interior equally architecturally intricate was quite a coming up in the world after some of our experiences. Nina and Duncan our hosts, were welcoming, Willow the labradoodle got on with Havoc, the drying facilities were exceptional, and the roll top bath fit for a lanky bigfoot. A comfortable night was just what the doctor ordered, Wendy was suffering with a heavy cold and worn boots had contributed to my sore Achilles.

Refreshed, but with bags still feeling like lead, we passed the meadow and seven beech trees, seen by some as the seven men of Moidart, loyal to the 'Young Pretender' on landing from France. We saw two otters in the Loch, they seemed to follow us while feeding. These were gold medal synchronised swimmers, agile and playful, backstroking with brunch on their chests. Surely some of the most charismatic creatures, perhaps a close second meerkats selling insurance. We grabbed a snack from the shop at Glenuig, little more than a green shed and carried on to Lochailort. A lone otter, stag and fish farm, hardly a car in sight on the A861. By the time we reached Loch nan Uamh the midges were biting. I lit a fire to deter them, and we camped near The Prince's Cairn, marking the spot the 'Chevalier' fled from in 1746.

The A830 and the railway, home of the 'The Jacobite' steam train, were our companions as we made our way to Arisaig. A few miles east the Glenfinnan viaduct at the head of Loch Shiel, used in Harry Potter films. A powerful waterfall at Morar allowed me some hydrotherapy for continuing sore Achillies and as a sign the seasons were changing, we saw our first conkers on the ground. Mallaig would be our transit point to Skye. On the map this was The Islands fresh ginger rhizome.

One of the few stores was aptly named 'Way Out West', (unfortunately it later closed in 2021) we bought a few bits, said goodbye to the fishing boats and white statue of a seafarer pointing the way to Armadale. On arrival we turned right to Kilbeg and onto Isleornsay and its small natural harbour. Leaving Ornsay behind we camped at the head of Loch na Dal beside a small stream. The round top of our little tent resembled a wheelless pioneer covered wagon somewhere in the American interior, a wisp of fire smoke drifting off into the distance.

This was MacLeod country. I read the Third Chief, Malcolm (1296-1370) while returning from a clandestine visit to the wife of Fraser of Glenelg was supposed to have slain a mad bull with just a dirk. We were heading for Glenelg, back on the mainland tomorrow. As Havoc sat in the coarse long grass, I couldn't help thinking he looked like Havoc MacLoad of MacLoad, Clan Chief, brave, strong and fearless and should have pride of place on the heraldic crest. Then a midge must have bitten him, and he disappeared to the deepest back corner of the tent.

Next morning the path to Leitir Fura, a settlement abandoned in the early 19th century due to forced clearances, was demanding but became almost impassable as we headed for Kylerhea. It is estimated about 60,000 people left the Western Highlands and Islands as emigrants to Australia, Canada and the US between 1846-61, many forcibly evicted. In Isleornsay MacDonald and Elder were emigration agents, One sailing alone in 1837 saw 322 passengers. To put the figures into some perspective the current approximate populations of Mallaig, Broadford, Skye's second largest town and the Glenelg scattered community combined, is less than 3000. There are no roads beyond Kinloch Lodge Hotel, and we never saw a soul.

We slid, slopped, sloshed, stumbled and fell over countless streams, fallen trees and bogs to the ferry point. The Glenachulish car ferry had a rotating top, could hold maybe half a dozen cars, but we were the only passengers going east. This was the site of a cattle crossing, used until 1906, cows forced to swim to mainland markets. Some way to meet your maker. Glenelg was a quiet village, one shop, one pub, white cottages, a few newer houses and an elaborate war memorial which would not have been out of place in Edinburgh or London. The ruined Bernera Barracks, built here by the British 1717-23, guarded this strategic spot, ancient ferry crossing when rebellion was rife. We went to a church service, met some local families and were given permission to stay in the village hall. It would be our base to travel south to Sandaig where Wendy was keen

to visit. Glenelg was twinned with another Glenelg in 2012, the latter on Mars! NASA choose a palindromic name for a site their rover vehicle 'Curiosity' would visit twice.

All community buildings we stayed at were awarded a 'star rating'. The obvious criteria with a few additions. Mugs rather than cups were a plus, the latter in village halls were usually one mouthful affairs. A toaster, microwave, and biscuit tin we could raid were further kitchen points to be considered. Soft toilet paper, shower, hot water urn, use of heating, no early check-out time the following morning and TV would almost certainly achieve a four star or higher. This one was a three star, downgraded slightly for lack of a washing up bowl. To soak one's feet, one had to balance on a chair to use the sink, with heightened health and safety risks.

Sandaig lay in the direction of Loch Hourn, if we were ultimately heading for John o' Groats this was 180 degrees in the wrong direction, and it felt like it. Without bags and in fine weather we headed for Camusfearna, an old croft where Gavin Maxwell created Ring of Bright Water. It was beautiful and fresh. We crossed a stream using a rope 'postman's walk' bridge and found the slab marking the burial point of his ashes and one in memory of the otter Edal and were reminded of his words, 'Whatever joy she gave to you, give back to Nature'. Across the white sands, the broken rocky hummocks of the Sandaig Islands and beyond the coast we had struggled along yesterday. Grey seals on the rocks but no elusive otters. Fast forward 12 months and images captured here of Havoc would be blazed over the side of a van advertising Wendy's newly founded dog walking business. We had to back track to Glenelg and never liked following the same route twice, but it had been a touching and memorable experience and well worth it.

Otters gave Wendy great joy. My mind went back to a time just after Edal. 1970 - The Jackson 5. 'I'll be there'. A pact, salvation, calm in all things, bright waters. I noted in my diary we enjoyed just being quiet together here. The silence wasn't awkward, we didn't need to fill gaps, things were golden.

Chapter 41 - Sandaig to Uig (Skye)

Taken my heart, torn it apart

"Keep memories propped up on the walls of your heart. When it gets lonely take one down and think of me... remember."

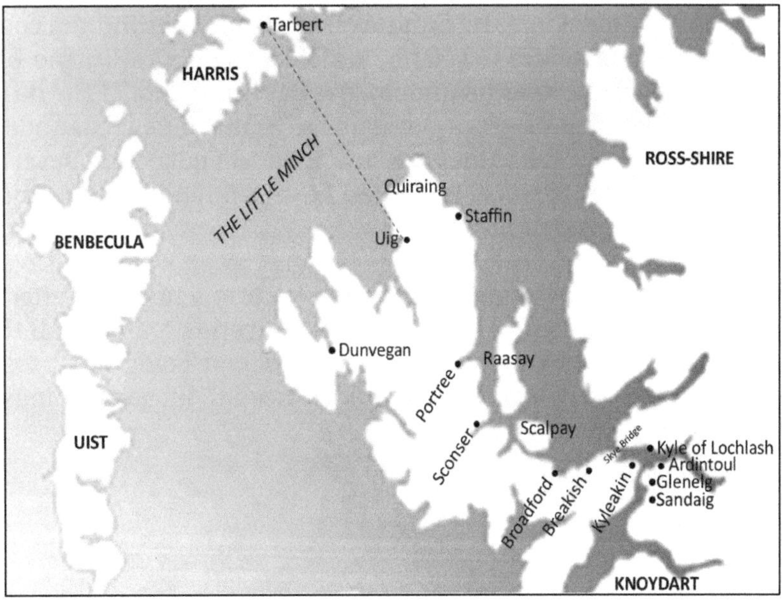

HEADING AROUND Kyle Rhea we reached the fish farm at Ardintoul. With a prior arrangement to cross Loch Alsh to Balmacara, I fancied doing similarly as we had done to Sandaig. Nip back to Eilean Donan Castle, famed in films and calendars, along the A87, but it wasn't to be. Tides and weather were wrong, and we had to take a larger boat to Kyle of Lochalsh. Going back from here was adding another seven miles or so and Wendy was far from keen, otters okay but castles no way.

The Skye Bridge had been completed 12 years earlier and after a quick risk assessment of its concrete arch we followed the A87 over the 500metre span to Kyleakin. A controversy had existed about expensive tolls, but all had been abolished at the end of 2004. Said to be precisely 500 miles due north of Land's End I did some quick math and worked out we were there 144 days ago. At that rate we had walked a measly average of 3.47 miles per day, which completely depressed Wendy.

Totally demoralised we only got as far as Breakish and again found a key holder of the village hall and somewhere to stay for the night. This one only managed 'two star' status partly because we had to put a £1 in the electric meter and partly due to our depressed, miserly mood. It was still far better than putting up the tent. Nearby we had passed a whitewashed rough stone cottage with a thatched roof weighed down at the eaves by boulders hanging on wires. This place could be windy.

At Broadford our luck changed, and our spirits were lifted. The hotel was emptying out a coach party, and we collected £150 in as long as it took to say two Drambuies please. Rumour has it, good old Bonnie Prince Charlie, him again, fleeing Culloden gave the recipe to Clan MacKinnon. (It gets more like The Waltons with every sip.) They passed it to a certain John Ross, and his son James ran the Broadford Hotel. In 1879 he started cooking, tweaking the recipe a bit, and the golden liqueur was born, 40 % ABV, cheers, or should we say, 'Slainte Mhath'. If only it was 30th November. Concocted story or were we really at the original home of 'the drink that satisfies?' You had to admire the sales pitch involving the fair Prince Charlie. In 2014 Drambuie was sold to Grants who make Glenfiddich, price, £100 million. Too many of them and it would be 'Goodnight Jim Bob' and we needed to move on.

The main road took us around the south shore of Loch Ainort, the high points of The Cuillins directly in front of us in the distance, and we branched off on a minor road hugging the north shore with views to Scalpay. It was here we passed a green camper van and Sarah the occupant invited us in for tea to avoid the midges. She was living the dream, wood carving as she toured and her work was impressive, enough to subsidise her travels. The conversation focused on the flying vermin, midges. We were informed how garden predators mimic a perspiring human and use cues to attract them, particularly the females. (Could do with one of one of these!) We were told it was female midges who needed blood to ensure the next generation. The great hunks of machinery were not very practical while walking the coast, on that we could agree. Suits with a hood, Citronella candles, vinegar mixed with Fairy liquid, and Avon 'Skin so Soft' better options. The marines at Fastlane swore by the latter, and had lovely soft skin in the process. The moment we stepped out we were covered in hovering insects and had to cover up quick and get moving fast. I was no longer so keen on all the female attention.

Raasay now came into view, and at Sconser we sat in a small waiting room. Ferries go to the Island, but we wanted to go across the finger Loch Siligachan. It was a long wait for the ferry to Raasay and with no obvious way off at the northern end, it was not on our wish list. It looked like we would end up sleeping in the tiny vestibule when a man came past walking his dog. With that in common, rather like parents meet friends at the school gate, we had our conversation starter. He turned out to be the owner of the Sconsor Lodge Hotel and we were offered a comfy room. Our luck was running over. What is more, in the bar we met a boat owner who would take us over Silgachan the next day to Peinchorran, saving us about six miles of walking, three of which would have been on the A87.

We walked The Braes with Tianavaig Bay to our right. Portree boasted Skye's only lifeboat, a Trent, and when they heard Friday would be my 49th birthday they immediately sorted us out with two nights accommodation at The Rosedale Hotel. It was perfect. Situated between the harbour and The Lump, (a rocky outcrop not an unwanted find when self-examining,) and the Georgian Marmalade Hotel (where Paddington was checked in) we were made very comfortable. A luxurious refuge to rest, and later from which to explore, with a tour to the west by public transport.

A bus took us to Dunvegan to look around the castle and gardens. The home of Clan MacLeod, the current owner Hugh Magnus was not in, but we enjoyed waterfalls, giant thistles, clan heirlooms and long-haired Skye Terriers. A full 12 months on and a big birthday would be memorable for less pleasant reasons. (Tomorrow is a mystery.) For now, a special dinner back at Rosedale courtesy of Paul and Alison with dolphins in the harbour that evening as there had been at breakfast. England were thrashed 36-0 by South Africa in the Rugby World Cup and it was amazing how locals suddenly found affinity with Springboks at the expense of any visiting sassenachs.

Back on Trotternish we headed north past lochs and the pinnacles of The Storr. Rain and wind all day, the cuts from peat extraction disturbing the carbon sink but the stacked sods would not be drying much today. The 'Old Man' played peep-bo with us through windows in the cloud. Kilt Rock, basalt pleats resembling those of a kilt and Mealt Falls hardly visible, and we arrived thoroughly wet and cold at Staffin. With God's blessing we bumped into Rev. Wilfred Weale and his wife Alice who put us up in the manse.

An insight into the customs of the Free Presbyterian Church of Scotland our latest theological cognisance. A bible reading and grace before eating perhaps expected but in the evening when family members left their seats, turned and knelt with their heads in the sofa to pray, came as something of a surprise. A home free from vanity, an experience characterised by humility and puritanism. Comfortable, yet awkward at the same time, as we didn't know what would happen next and were keen not to offend. Having said that we probably did as we headed off over the Quiraing on a Sunday, ignoring any observance of the Sabbath.

The northern end of this peninsula was a mass of ancient landslips with modern movement still occurring causing roads to require regular maintenance. The topography straight out of Tolkein's Lord of the Rings. Rocky features named The Needle, The Prison and The Table were like walking through a mouth full of teeth, jagged incisors, the odd flat-topped molar and underfoot saturated ground. The moors dripped and dribbled, the sound of running riverlets, ribbon streams and waterfalls resembling the water features at a garden centre. In this amphitheatre one felt insignificant, like tiny specks in a giant's world. Looking back Staffin Island and Bay through low cloud, ahead hairpin bends on a road to Uig. We camped at Idrigil at the top end of a campsite field, a picnic table almost floating, some bikers and motorhomes waiting with us to take tomorrow's ferry to the Outer Hebrides the next bit of our outer coast.

Quite regularly we seemed to come across a dead mouse. The one here clearly drowned. We further pondered the significance of these findings. Sacrificial in our honour? A pointer to a future career as a needed pest controller? We were occasionally living close to the edge but surely even on the Western Isles rations were not going to be that limited? I dreamed of being Spencer Tracy, Rogers', in Northwest Passage when his Rangers were forced to eat squirrel, raccoon and the like in Quebec and hoped there would not be too many hostile natives on Harris. Unsure why, but the Reggae tune 'Where did I go wrong' (UB40-1988) was the backing. Perhaps it was the thought that I would be unemployed on our return, touching 50 at my next birthday, and all that would hold.

Two weeks earlier I had been given a new pair of walking boots at the Discount Footware Centre in Oban. Wanting to get maximum value out of the ones I was using I had continued with my old pair, posting the new ones to the Post Office at Uig. The old were now worn to destruction, so I walked back a mile or so to collect my parcel before we caught the Tarbert ferry at 2.00pm.

Chapter 42 - Uig to Stornoway (Elope to the Outer Hebrides)

Leaves that are green turn to brown, wither with the wind, crumble in your hand

"There are two seasons on Scotland, June and Winter - it was winter!"

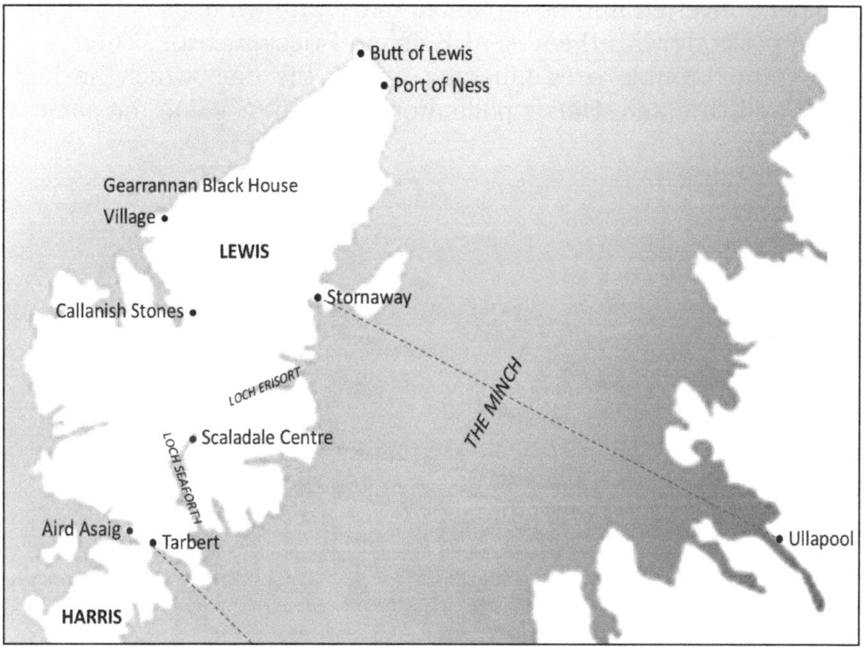

THE TWO-HOUR CROSSING from Uig to Tarbet, across Little Minch was an easy one. Time passed chatting to a local guy who offered us accommodation on Harris just outside the port village. We were only too pleased to accept as we passed Scalpay into East Loch and the tiny harbour. Surrounding the houses, a lunar landscape, treeless hillsides, mainly of exposed grey rock, dark shadows cast by clouds and not a sheep to be seen. Where did they get the raw material for their famous tweed? There were handy craft shops selling the stuff, almost outnumbering the couple of grocers, hardware shop and chippy but the shepherds were all elsewhere, on a hilltop waiting for a proclamation.

Tweed was originally called 'tweel' but somehow the name was corrupted in the 1830s, it has little to do with the river Tweed in the Scottish Borders. The name of your suit is enshrined by law, the Harris Tweed Act of 1993, you wouldn't want to argue with a spinner, dyer or weaver here.

In fact, you might get a handbag, pair of Nike sneakers or Dr Martens to go with your suit, such was the 'on trend' merchandising. The wee 'orb' trademark had to be found, easier than finding a sheep. I read, lichen Parmelia Saxatlis 'crottle', used to give the deep red colour and distinctive scent to the fabric, there was plenty of those algae/fungi mutually getting along on boulders everywhere.

Our stopover was in an old 'Swift' caravan, weighed down by rocks on a hillside surrounded by cotton grass. Havoc had his very own semi, an even older converted minibus, painted black and white as camouflage to blend in perfectly with the absent Holstein Friesian cattle. There were a few flies and bumble bees finishing up for the day, which he had to torment and threaten. Harris pollinators soon to be going the same way as the sheep.

The following morning was wet and windy to Aird Asaig, looking down over Loch Bun the remains of an old whaling station. With tall, square, brick boiling chimney the remnants of any shore-based stations are few and far between.

Harris and Lewis, really a single Hebridean island and it seemed on this morning we were doing all 840 square miles of it. Harris is hillier, the highest point, Clisham, a Corbett, at nearly 800metres. There are over 30 peaks more than 300metres.

By lunchtime we had struggled as far as Aird a Mhulaidh and came across an army green caterpillar tracked 'people carrier' and trailer. Uig Off Road Hire Vehicle company had this one available for rent. The door was open but there were no keys behind the sun visor, it made for a welcome sheltering spot to eat a soggy sandwich. The wind was relentless, water that should have been falling vertically from falls was being blown horizontally forming a mist as if the hillsides were smoking. Whatever Billy Connolly said about Scotland, it was true here, and it wasn't June (20th September.) We decided to seek sanctuary in the Scaladale Centre, offering outdoor activities for youths, the £15 a head tariff was waived.

We woke to a dryer day and views, although cloudy down Loch Seaforth. While one sign in Gaelic read Welcome to Lewis, the reverse side of one we passed read Welcome to Harris. Loch Erisort and a milliard of smaller ones, more peat cuttings and eventually into Stornoway, known only from the shipping forecast. Lewis was flatter, Stornoway, far and away, the largest town having around a third of the total island population. With Viking origins, we found an important port and administrative centre.

For such a remote and wilderness-like part of Britain, with a reputation for conservation and care of the environment I was staggered by the amount of roadside litter as we approached the town. Surely this wasn't part of the gaelic culture? I even contemplated a sponsored litter pick on their behalf, but time was against us.

We were staying at the lifeboat station, Murray the mechanic arranged for us to have a mini tour with his father Ian the next day. I was just amazed by the realisation we had reached this far-off corner. I read up about William Lever of Lever Brothers (First Viscount Leverhulme) who had bought Lewis in 1918 with grand economic plans only to have his finances overstretched and eventually gave Stornoway to the people. How different would things be here if he had not run out of cash? Also on my reading list, HMY Lolaire lost on the 1st January 1919 along with 205 lives, men returning from World War I. Having survived that horror, to be taken within sight of home and loved ones was quite unimaginable.

Our tour took us to see the lighthouse at the Butt of Ness. This one was built by David (Stevenson) following in his father's footsteps. Welsh wizard JJ Williams never visited with the whitewash, this one's unpainted red brick. It was one of the last to be automated, 1998. Nearby, the inlet of Port Stoth and the evidence of 'lazy bed' arable cultivation. Spade dug ridges and furrows, channeling drainage with the addition of seaweed fertilizer, up to about the 19th century here. Often used to grow potatoes, the Irish weren't the only ones to suffer from blight and famine in the 1840s, the same misery would affect the Hebrides.

Dun Carloway Broch, another relic from perhaps the 1st century AD. What is left is described as 'well preserved' masonry on the east side some nine metres high. (If that was a true description, I could add it to my name tag in my pants.) In the 1600s it was used as a stronghold, according to one tale, as a hide up for stolen cattle and the Morrisons. Their embittered nemesis should have been the MacAldi's but were in fact the MacAulay's. Smoked out by burning heather, they were keeping it local, the broch was destroyed and the Morrisons went off to sell eggs and butter from 1899!

The Callanish Stones consist of an arrangement of standing stones in a cruciform pattern with a central stone circle of 13 stones. Thought to be 5000 years old, the largest stone weighing in at seven tons. Theories abound about construction and relevance. Likely to have been an 'active focus of prehistoric religious activity', how they got there, 'Weetabix' only knows? Folklore would have it they are petrified giants who refused to convert to Christianity. Ultravox used them on the cover of their 1984 album Lament. Outlander 2014 on the box, as a fictional circle near Culloden, depicting them as having time travelling abilities when touched. (Who needed a Police box?)

Also of interest at Garenin the 'Gearrannan' Blackhouse Village. This gave an insight into crofting, a lost way of life, from the 17th century. The restored township has several stone long houses with thatched roofs, the reeds/straw weighed down by boulders. Inside, box beds with curtains, dressers of crockery, flag floors and washing drying over open fires. The smoke with little way of escaping and the soot gave the houses their name.

Unspoilt beaches, the sea at places whipped up to a white foam frenzy crashing at cliffs and stacks. We had experienced something of the wind, a treeless horizon and this additional evidence showed Lewis could be a wild place.

Off the west coast the Flannan Isles. In 1900 three lighthouse keepers mysteriously disappeared. Speculation and conjecture followed, sea serpents, giant sea birds and abduction by spies postulated, one could see that even on our limited exposure to this corner of the Atlantic, swept away in a storm was a more likely explanation. The Vanishing (2018) is a good way to see off a Scottish winter afternoon. We kept our eyes peeled for Sea Eagles, apparently they can be seen on Lewis - just not while we were there, they had all 'gone fishing'.

Stornoway is often described as 'bustling'. For our time there it seemed very quiet. I began to think everyone had followed their Viking forefathers and gone off raiding. From this anchorage ships would sail for the Isle of Man, Ireland, Wales and northwest England in search of booty once upon a time. I knew the Sabbath (Sunday) was likely to be hushed, services, shops and businesses closed. Presbyterianism and religious types had made this place 'the last bastion of Sabbath observance in the UK'. But it wasn't a Sunday, where was everyone? A large funeral procession, the coffin being carried through the streets, provided the answer.

A fine send off. The town and everyone looked down upon by Lews Castle and Lewis War Memorial. Also, notable the turreted and majestic Townhall from 1929. Rather grey houses and a contemporary article in the 'Gazette' caught my eye. Land Rover had introduced 'Stornoway Grey.' Councilor Angus Nicolson, feared the term would hurt the local image, associating it with being boring and dull. He even called it 'offensive' and wanted a 'Silver Stornoway' relabeling. Land Rover stuck by their quarter panels, 'defender' (ing) their 'discovery' of a bestselling colour and saying the name would keep Stornoway 'on the map.' (Sod off! In car manufactured speak.) I see their colour range now includes 'Carpathian' and 'Tweed', so perhaps they took offense.

Colours change. Ours were too. Leaves that were green were turning brown. I threw a pebble in a brook, like Paul Simon, and watched ripples run away. Was my girl fading in the night? No time to write a poem. As we prepared to return to the mainland, I was taken by a couple of works of public art. A bronze of a herring girl, her basket resting on her hip, and the birds, boats and fish of a mural (Iain Brady) on a gable end in South Beach. Many fond and timeless memories of touching this outer extremity.

Stornoway now has I understand a more relaxed view of the Sabbath. You might find a shop open but not many Land Rovers. Calmac started Sunday sailings in 2009. The economy a mix of the traditional – Tweed, crofting and fishing, inshore for prawns and crabs, plus ‘aquaculture’ (fish farming.) Tourism, the remnants of an oil industry, the growth of wind turbines, they now sell them to Turkey. A distillery opened in 2019 and ‘black pudding’ popular. The proposed tunnel link to the mainland - still a ‘pipe dream’.

Chapter 43 - Stornoway to Bay of Keisgaig (via Ullapool)

Feet start to pound...what you see is what you get

"You've got to know when to hold on, know when to fold, know when to walk away, know when to run."

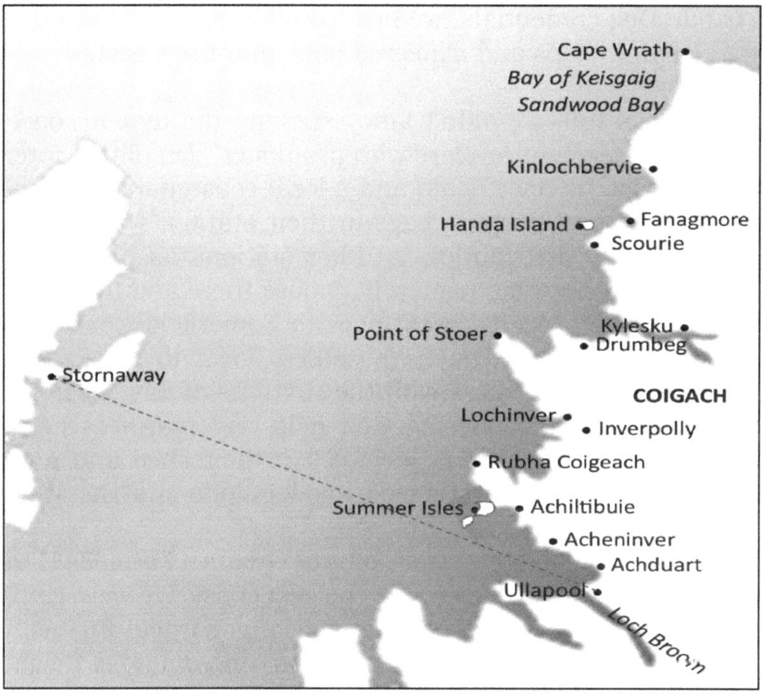

A LUMPY LAST LIFT across The Minch took us to Loopallu. Sitting near the mouth of Loch Broom, Scotland's largest sea loch, the painted houses of Ullapool looked inviting. It had moved on a bit I guessed from its days as a grid iron late 18th century herring station. It was a Saturday in September, the Rugby World Cup was in full flow and the town was hosting its music festival, Loopallu, now in its third year. It was quite a music hot spot, and what better way to prepare for the long cold Scottish winter, it would be quite a while before the next knees up, Hogmanay.

Franz Ferdinand were headlining; the place was jammed, and I thought 'I'm gonna make somebody love me' and pushed our way into The Ferry Boat Inn through swing doors like a wild west saloon. It was late afternoon, by now few of the locals were even standing, let alone coherent.

Understanding 'jock' is an acquired art at the best of times, heavily inebriated and in a noisy bar, rugby recitals including Kenny Rogers, The Gambler, all we could do was nod politely when spoken to. England had won, but Scotland were not even due to play until tomorrow. The Lochinver lifeboat crew were present in force, one female crew volunteer promptly downed the contents of her glass, rung from a 'J-cloth' by a young bartender trying to clear glasses, wipe tables and serve Magners over ice, all at once and on a measly minimum wage. With evening food orders beginning to be served and the bar owner beginning to question Havoc's Guide Dog credentials, we headed off in search of somewhere to stay dodging flying chips and squeezed back into the street.

The campsite was full, we didn't fancy sticking the tent up on a grass verge for fear of late-night revelers with prankster, demolition intentions. Lady Luck followed us once again and a local coastguard officer allowed us to throw down our sleeping bags in their station, with coils of new abseil rope awaiting distribution to other stations as pillows. Had I a crystal ball, I might have made myself a noose there and then. As it was, we were conveniently located, next door to Somerfield's and two doors away from a Chinese takeaway. We settled down to black bean beef, complimentary prawn crackers with the rhythms of Saw Doctors in our ears. I could not help wondering God help any mariners lost at sea tonight, the coastguard couldn't have got in their shed and a crewless lifeboat wouldn't make it from its mooring, let alone into The Minch.

Leaving Ullapool, a road sign read John o' Groats 170 miles. I guessed that was via Lairg and Golspie and up the east coast. We were going west, north and then across the top of Scotland, a good deal further, but at least we were getting close. After Ardmair we turned across Coigach and a safety notice from the Keanchulish Estate saying,

"Bridge crossing unsafe and temporarily out of use."

Surely this wasn't one of those Scottish diversions you hear about on radio traffic news requiring a 50 mile detour. In fact, no alternative was offered, and the timber sleepers were perfectly sound. A while further and another sign,

'You are entering remote, potentially dangerous mountain country.' Eleven miles to Achiltibuie.

The occasional newish looking slate post marked a path which was seldom used. Steep cliffs, waterfalls, gorges punctuated our way, under foot thick mud, wet and slippery, craggy boulders tripping you up. I stumbled several times, each one harder than the last to get up from with our packs, windblown showers adding to the task. At least there was no one around to hear the cursing. It took nearly five hours to cover eight miles and we arrived at Acheniver Hostel shattered, only to find it closed for the winter.

“I thought you said JM slept on the floor here.”

“He did,” I replied, “18th August 1978, and with the warden’s blessing.”

What to do? Camp, I was almost too tired to pitch a tent. I hardly more than collapsed on a poorly secured door and it opened. Chairs and mattresses were piled up and the contents of an open fridge had been left on a work surface. Someone tidying up at the end of the season would be back, perhaps not tonight, and since we would be gone first thing in the morning, we convinced ourselves no one would mind our intrusion. We cooked a meal, Havoc found another stiff mouse, and settled down for the night. We were woken by a returning warden, or so we supposed, himself shocked and somewhat angry at our presence.

Embarrassed, ashamed and guilty it was left to me to placate the guy and take a slap on the wrist. I would no doubt get all the blame, but my breaking and entering was not solely for selfish intention, it was for all three of us. It was my shoulder that opened the door, and I was now taking one for the team. I saw no retreating over the threshold once we had entered, so any future accusatory comments need to be tempered with a degree of balance.

I may have been economical with the truth when groveling to the warden, but to be criticised for lying in this context, without any mention of mitigating factors, is rather lacking in solidarity. It’s well documented how one lie can lead to another, and those liars do succumb to believing their own stories, I might even admit to a tendency and possession of a ‘billy’ gene but slander me not.

I did put some money in the Scottish Hostel Association collecting tin by way of appeasement. At the time of writing, 2021, I looked online at the hostel’s web page to find four camping pods had been erected at the back of the building, so perhaps the donation went to good use.

We all probably slept very lightly, with uncomfortable feelings of shame. I dreamt of Goldilocks, being caught in The Three Bears’ house. However, we had not eaten any porridge, broken any chairs or anything else for that matter. Perhaps it was a wake-up call for the warden, get the dodgy lock sorted on that door and furthermore what a bloody stupid time of year to shut for the winter!

For me lots of nights on the walk were dream accompanied. Often about my children, how I had let them down or what job I would go home to. In this shallow sleep it was as if my eyes were open with a bird's eye view looking down on my life, misdemeanors too frequent to list. Steve McQueen walked in, as Papillon, the scene where he is being tried for a 'wasted life'. I was 'going underground!' (The Jam, 1980.) A judge in a wig appeared to sentence me, it was the hostel warden, in place of a gavel was a dead mouse, I shook awake before he gave his verdict.

By way of recompense allow me to apologise here to the warden, The Hostel Association, and for bringing the good names of The GDBA and The RNLI into disrepute.

Needless to say, we were on the move good and early next morning and by 9am were sitting outside the shop at Achilibuie eating cream crackers for breakfast. The Summer Isles, there seemed like about 20 of them, bobbing in morning sun. I opened a large tub, thinking it was a litter bin, and jumped back grimacing. In it were fish bits. Later I discovered it was the bait bin, local fishermen would use the contents to set their crab pots.

We rounded the headland called Rubha Coigeach and with boots off paddled the beach at Achnahaird and moved on to Loch Garvie. Like Spud we seemed to see the same postman for several days and found the friendliness of people just as warm as she experienced, offers of lifts, blocking roads for a chat.

Stuart and Julie, who managed Inverpolly fish farm were completely in keeping. They fed us (roast beef) and we chatted about raising salmon, oxygen levels, toxins and antibiotics. We discovered farmed fish were lighter and pinker, with greater fatty marbling, good for smoking, which many of the couple of million raised each year go for. We did learn that rather than being offered a last supper before slaughter, they are starved before harvesting, to empty the gut. No last breakfast orders here then.

I heard more recently that storms damaging enclosing pens leading to farmed fish escaping is a real problem. Not just because of the loss of stock but those creatures can breed with wild salmon, whose numbers are significantly lower and who may then be genetically weakened. Termed genetic pollution, it's just one of cons of intensive farming in the oceans.

We were also told it was the start of the rut. We had seen any number of red deer does. Preening themselves, pretending not to be interested, putting on their make-up and dancing around their handbags. Now it was time for the boys to puff themselves up, act macho, stick back their heads and bellow. All over the Inverpolly Forest, on the slopes of Stac Pollaidh and Suilven beasts were competing for the best totty on the block.

We were offered the floor of the mess room to kip, making another unique entry for our varied list of stop overs. Fate, or a generous cat had left us a gift on the doorstep as we left next morning. You guessed it - a dead mouse. We began to start looking for them and secretly I kept an eye open for a witch stalking us too.

A familiar accompaniment, the sound of rain and by the time we reached the lifeboat station at Lochinver we were ready to strip naked and put everything in the tumble dryer. The wee stone primary school on a peninsula in Loch Culag, stuck out on its own, must be the only location like it in Britain.

Just back at Achiltibuie, Spud described the crofts. In a bad state of repair, rusting barbed wire, scrap metal, flaking paint, their inhabitants eking out a living reliant on subsidies. Lying between smart holiday cottages, 'juxtaposed, the obscene, empty neatness, and the subsidised shambles!' Here, we saw a sign for The North Assant Estate, 21,000 acres purchased in 1993 for £300,000. Crofters own the land in a trust, controlling mineral, fishing and shooting rights, the first cooperative of its kind. To be truthful it was hard to know what-was-what, without spending more time investigating. We were just passing through and could only make cursory observations.

There were lots of old baths stuck in the corners of fields. It reminded me of Wendy (Soapy) in hash terms and the charity calendar done by the harriets of Teign Valley before we started the walk. In Calendar Girls fashion they had stripped for photos, and we had gone up to Dartmoor on a winter's day to capture a tastefully nude 'piccie', taking a bath with us.

There were also some very passable dry-stone walls and wire fences.

The livestock also looked good. Heathy sheep and hairy, horny, Highland, herds of cattle, perfectly at home, bred here since 1885. The herd book makes them the oldest breed in the world, but the term 'fold' should really be used as a collective. The late Queen must have seen something in

them, feasibly characterful and cute, as she introduced them to Balmoral in the 1950s. Perhaps Charles feeds them now when on holiday?

Some small sandy beaches peppered the way out to Stoer Lighthouse and the rock stack known as The Old Man of Stoer. The weathered chap brought on a feeling of déjà vu, I was sure we had passed him not that long ago on Skye. One had to admire the 60metre monolith, was there more than one or was he on the move? Thoughts drifted to the film Spartacus, 'I'm the Old Man', 'No I am'. The Monty Python team might have had material for a great sketch, with old women throwing themselves off the cliff into the white surf breaking at his feet. With ideas becoming more ridiculous by the stride we carried on to Eddrachillis Bay and found the keyholder of Drumbeg village hall very amenable.

Inside on display were old black and white photos. Tinkers from the 1930s and a travelling man known as 'Forty Pockets'. Would we be on the wall in another 80 years and what would our names be? The hall had doubled as a primary school and in the 1880s the numbers on roll were 80+. Dropped to 50 by 1909, 20 by 1930 and two by 1995. It closed the following year. Here was evidence of Spud's comments regarding depopulation in parts of Sutherland like this. At the time of writing any number of articles could be found describing shrinking communities apart from holiday cottages and tourists, aging permanent populations but no real influx of younger blood and conditions of a 'perfect storm' for rural parts of The Highlands.

A super kind Post Mistress offered to take our bags on to Kylesku Hotel. Unlike SH/RH we were willing to risk our stuff with someone else. We had little of value, everything was more worn by the day, and if you can't trust one of Pat's mates, who can you trust? Free from being weighed down we enjoyed the finest, sunniest day in September so far. Cyclists shared their lunch with us, instant mash, bolognaise sauce from a bag, and ready-made custard dotted with 'Refreshers'. All washed down with 'Irn-Bru', Heston Blumenthal eat your heart out.

Inshore freshwater Lochs shone like precious jewels and Quinag loomed over us at 808metres to a curved box girder bridge over an unpronounceable sea Loch at Kylesku. It was quite a sight, especially as the AA Book of the Seaside (1972) led us to expect a ferry. Opened in 1984 and costing £4 million, a 276metre long serpent, except this one had eight legs. In 2019 it became 'A' listed as 'visually striking and technically innovative'. Nearby a memorial listing 39 names of the 12th Submarine Flotilla, in the Second World War submarines would hide further east, local folk knew so much but talked so little.

Reclaiming our rucksacks, we bumped into a chap named Bass, from York but now living in Scourie, a trek up the coast. A former public schoolboy, keen on fishing but today was a hunting day dressed in tweed plus fours and with two Labradors in tow. In return for his address at The Beacon, we entrusted him with our gear and made our way shadowing the A894 north. In 2015 this would become part of the NC500. A scenic evening with wine, cheese, BBQ and oatcakes. More amorous stag grunting from the hills and a sunset that only the west coast can do. A molten glow ball and halo of flame descending into the horizonal ocean one could imagine the steam rising as it finally disappeared.

Next morning, I hoped Bass did not think I was impersonating a stag during the night. I had stumbled along a corridor, pitch black in an unfamiliar house to use the bathroom, falling over a step and into his bedroom by mistake.

'Hello' he said, in restrained schoolboy tone, as I apologised for the interruption and sculked away to my own bed.

We returned a football back to the playground as we passed the school and tried to find a non-existent path that led to Tarbet. It was supposed to be marked with small stone cairns but either naughty schoolboys had pinched them, or roadbuilders had run out of aggregate. Handa Island came close, and I read in days gone by burials used to take place here when wolves still roamed the mainland. You could imagine it would have been hard to bury anyone too deep with all the slabs of glacier smoothed rock, boulders and scant soil.

In a treeless landscape adjacent to Loch Laxford, surrounded by mountain peaks and ameba shaped lochs, we blundered upon some remains of an enclosure. All that was left on a moor, miles from anywhere, a rusting metal gate between two angle iron posts. Any wire fencing on either side long gone but Havoc waited amusingly for the gate to be swung open rather than pass either side of it. Next, the hamlets of Fanagmore and Foindle, with me misbehaving in my head with the names, before wading the river at Laxford, Rhiconich and the north shore of Loch Inchard to Kinlochbervie.

KLB as it is sometimes referred to is a scattered harbour village with a large fish handling depot. Landed here from all over, refrigerated lorries are just as likely to be heading for Europe as Edinburgh. A family put us up in an attic store above a domestic garage. It was our first Anne Frank style secret annex, another to add to our hospitality peculiarities. The children, four of them, to whom we were something of celebrities escorted us to the Spar shop next morning, arguing over who would hold Havoc's lead. Hidden in an industrial estate, portable provisions were a necessity where we were heading for our last night on the West Coast.

From Balchrick the road runs out and we needed rubber ankles and shock absorber knees to reach Sandwood Bay.

This was a contender for Britain's Best Beach. Remote, empty, untamed, dunes backed by lochs guarded by another rock stack at Am Buachaille. Before it could be awarded our 'blue flag' I had to test the water with a skinny dip and naked crab impression of sideways skipping.

By 5.30pm we had pitched tent for wild camping at the Bay of Keisgaig. The stream was our water source, kettle on, Havoc had had his tea and curled up into a ball asleep. Wendy went down stream to wash and I watched another wonderful sunset with a slight breeze keeping the midges to single figures. The ear worm Martha and the Muffins, Echo Beach, watching the sun go down, far away in time. Although I say it myself, I think my air saxophone solo was pretty good.

Chapter 44 - Cape Wrath to Strathy Point

Footprints in the sand... washed away when the water hit the land

"Iconic cornerstone, moorland wilderness and a last boat until May 2008."

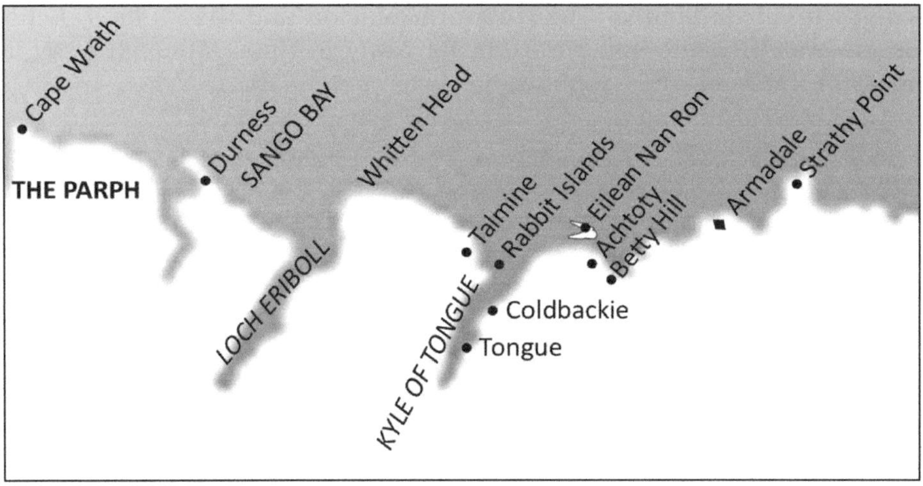

CAPE WRATH WAS ominous sounding, but if that was down to inclement weather it did not live up to its name. The MoD blow the hell out of the place each year, but the war game exercises had just been white flagged. Although we had to keep an eye out for live ammunition, nobody seemed to be dropping 1000lb air born bombs at least. On reaching the lighthouse, perched on one of only two British capes, I thought the Armada had landed. Spanish tourists followed by two minibuses of people for a poetry reading. They had come from the opposite direction, Durness, and the last weekend in September, the Northern Lights Festival. Tourism adds about £500,000 to the local economy each year and when John Lennon puts his name to the gig, local Scot businesses are on to a winner.

The cape is a dramatic headland and the most northerly point of the Western Highlands. We could consider ourselves 'serious travelers.' (BB - there is no caravan park or tearoom.) We turned right along Clo Mor the highest sheer cliffs on the British mainland, over 280metres to the sea, not the place to fall off Havoc. We caught the last ferry across the Kyle of Durness at 4pm, the next one, May 2008. I asked the ferryman how John Lennon came to be involved in these parts and he explained his family used to holiday this way and the 'future Beatle once had a pee', so anointing all local entrepreneurs for eternity.

Stepping off the boat Wendy fell, hurting her back. She was never one for laying across the gunnels, howling like a Banshi and waiting for her Bafta. She got on with it, I was uncertain what happened, or how seriously she had hurt herself. At the time she managed to limp on to a lovely campsite overlooking Sango Bay. It wasn't until I read the account in "*Wherever I hang my lead*" that the full consequences of the fall were realised.

It is said I 'never show sympathy to anyone'. My diary records an excellent Spar shop where I bought Ibuprofen gel and paracetamol. We had a meal out, and the next day rested up with a gentle explore of Faraid Head and Smoo Cave only and a second night at the campsite. The weather, a lovely sunny day, making for some great photos of Wendy smiling and Havoc bursting with life on the beach.

Wendy's position on the anthropomorphic sensibility spectrum, slightly further left than Saint Francis of Assissi, differed from mine. I sat nearer the pragmatic marker. Regarding this incident, there was little more we could do in the circumstances, but I think it is right the true events should be recorded. Matthew McConaughey warns us all to 'learn the consequence of negligence - it's not just what we do, it's what we don't do that's important as well'. I guess I was guilty by omission and hereby own that mistake.

We found the Lennon Memorial Garden, 'There are places I remember all my life.' John returned with Yoko Ono in 1969 but crashed his car. Ceannabeinne Beach would make it to the January entry of the 2021 Coastlines of Britain calendar.

The lid of Britain is quite wild and on a grand scale. Mountains provide a dramatic backdrop to the coast. Here, hidden among cliffs can be found resplendent sandy beaches.

It is secluded, few people, few roads save the A838 and A836 as you get further east. Balnakil near Durness was once the site of a 1955 rocket warning system. By the sixties it was a cradle of creativity for crafty types. Eriboll, a safe anchorage for the home fleet during two world wars. Bettyhill, named after Elizabeth Leveson Gower, Countess of Sutherland, 1765-1839, we were to find offered some river game fishing opportunities.

It was now October, and we walked around two sides of Loch Eriboll. Somewhat monotonous on road, past scattered crofts, but at least the underfoot conditions were reliable for Wendy's sore back. Pine trees near a river at Hope provided a great place to camp. It was tougher going out to Whiten Head passing a bothy at Freisgill, we stopped for a break. The exterior looked more hotel like compared with a hovel like interior. New slates and pointing on the outside contrasted with humble, rustic furniture and stained, grubby plasterwork on the inside. A selection of pots and pans, a sooty fireplace and three candles (but no fork handles) would have been handy for a stopover.

Stacks and geos, narrow deep clefts in the shoreline, and cliffs where we were often higher than gulls below. We even looked down on some military jets, and loud bangs were sure evidence of some remaining ammunition. Old chrome hub caps and tin saucepan lids were a novel way of waterproofing the ends of gate posts, handy I thought if you ever wanted to form a marching band. Achininiver, provided a great spot to go in for a paddle, Talmine shopping and ground at the back of Craggon House Hotel somewhere to put up the tent. The Rabbit Islands got me jabbering to Chase and Dave.

Hammish, a big guy and former railway man, now in charge at The Craggon served us breakfast. As so often, when it came to paying, the tariff was waived. Havoc and I now felt less self-assured about our earlier private referral to him as 'The Fat Controller'. The causeway and bridge over Kyle of Tongue provided great views inland, locals said the best one in Britain, with Ben Hope and Ben Loyal each side reflected in the water and seals playing beneath us.

Sometimes to occupy the mind, counting strides helped, especially going uphill. After a couple of hundred that was getting mundane, so I switched to etymology and toponymy of Sutherland place names.

Tongue must have come from the shape of the inlet or was everyone here a rival for Sybil Fawlty and that little old lady back in Pembroke. Next Coldbackie - surely rating Frosty Mackay was the country's equivalent of Walmington's Private Walker. He only possessed a short overcoat, but punters knew where to get their illicit tobacco. This was very much Mackay Clan territory. When they evacuated Eilean nan Ron off Caol Raineach in 1938, there were nine of them on a list of no more than 30 names. Mackays that is. I pondered whether Ron's nan was named Eilean for a mile or so. At Achtoty I was dreaming of meeting a hot attractive thespian but there was no such drama.

Rounding Torrisdale Bay we crossed the Naver to Elizabeth's Mound, I renamed it, elevating it somewhat from Bettyhill. During the day we passed two superbly located cemeteries. One at the end of the bridge at Tongue and another overlooking Torrisdale Bay approaching Bettyhill. Souls had some fine final resting spots in these parts. My christening of places would drive anyone to their grave.

Monsoon Drain, a hasher from Musselburgh had given us the contact details of family of his who ran the village Post Office come General Store for a stopover. Susie and Pete assisted by two cats welcomed us with some apprehension. In true hash fashion Monsoon had forgotten to tell them he had volunteered their services for more than just cashing a Giro.

We were probably a security risk for the strongroom making use of mailbags for pillows and they could not accommodate us, but we were fed and packed off to stay with Susie's mother Joan in Armadale with a menagerie of more cats. We did not get time to find out the first cats' names, and as we were still in naming mood, Havoc and I decided they should be either Arkwright and Granville or Ike and Godsey. The Armadale entourage were too numerous to baptise.

We were zoomed back to Bettyhill next morning, logistics the Pony Express would be proud of. There was just time to post the OS maps of The Islands back to Anne Robinson before the pension queue formed and we walked bagless back to Armadale via Swordly, Kirtomy and moors. Collecting our packs, we headed for Strathy Point. The lighthouse was the same age as me but had weathered less, despite its remote, exposed position. The A836 would have been the easy route to complete our circumnavigation barely a mile or so from the coast but we were keen to stay honest to the cliffs as far as possible. It meant finding lots more baths in corners of fields, this must be the world's reuse and recycle centre for tin and plastic tubs turned drinking troughs. It also meant crossing fences and I began to curse grants for crofters to spend on wire.

This could be a bleak and lonely place. Seemingly endless moors, purple heather, dark pools, black peaty soils. Ferocious sea, battered cliffs, deep ravines. I thought of those forced off the land in the great 'clearances.' We at least could enjoy the remoteness, appreciate the forces of nature, bathe in the solitude, mellow at the relationship interface. We were true 'edge landers' and could 'revel in being part of the elements' (Raynor Winn).

Like John Lennon, we would remember this northwestern corner. We had crossed moorland wilderness, rounded the iconic cornerstone, left footprints in the sand. Our time walking was slipping away. We needed to live every moment, love every day and not throw our love away. (Paraphrasing REO Speedwagon, 1984).

Chapter 45 - Strathy Point to John o' Groats (via Orkney)

Never Forget... We've looked each day and night in the eye

"Feet don't fail me now. The perfect end to any project - finish strong."

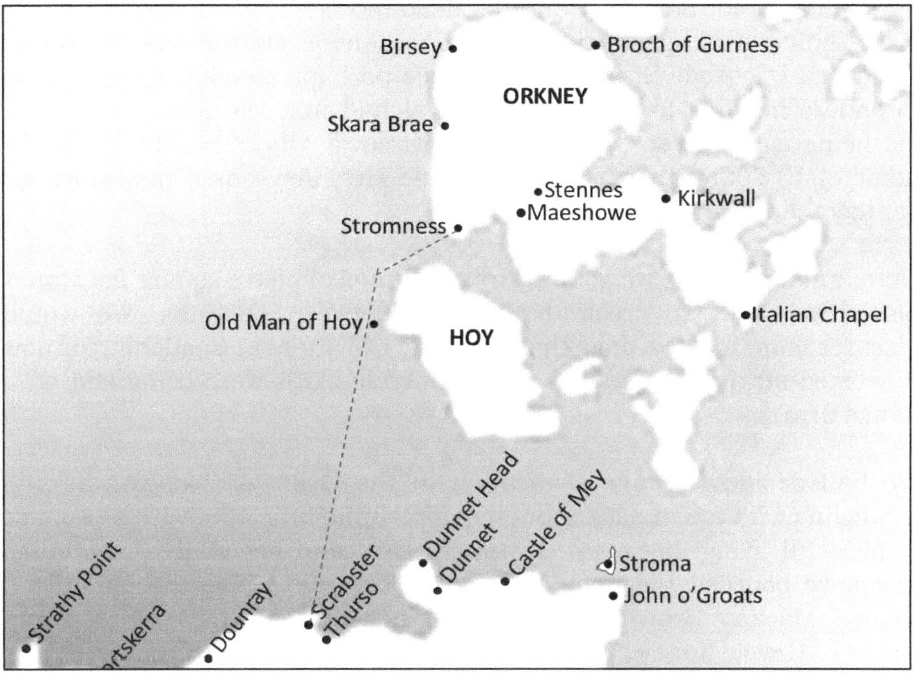

STRATHY AND PORTSKERRA to cross the Halladale river near Melvich on a footbridge and onto Reay. Dounreay came into sight even the name sounded forbidding. Dominated by a golf ball like sphere, the nuclear power station's short operational lifespan was long over. Decommissioning started in 1977. A submarine reactor testing facility was also there behind fencing, guards and grazing cattle. I read a 1988 report highly critical of operations here with 143 recommendations for improvement.

By 1994 all nuclear power generation ceased. It would cost billions to continue making the site safe, brownfield status would not be achieved until 2336. Long after we had passed, over 500 jobs would still be retained, one of the costs, a two-kilometre ban on harvesting any seafood.

Nearby at Forss Business Park six wind turbines, surely safer, and we camped by the river in woods. Andrew and Alex were our neighbours, both keen wood carvers, and we shared a cookout with saucepans on a grate. A smokey open fire, tree trunk seating, licorice tea, judo and jujitsu instruction, more the former than the latter as rolling around in wood ash was less than pleasant. Havoc was content with Whisky the cat and secured a £20 donation which most people in our shoes would have willingly paid for the experience.

As we headed for Scrabster another dead mouse. It was not glowing, but it certainly wasn't going to 'fast breed' anymore. On the road countless discarded Lucozade Sport plastic bottles perhaps chucked away by end to enders heading for John o' Groats. I had just learned of a Serbian mathematics professor, Tomislav Radovanovic, who had built himself a home of 13,500 of them. Someone could rival Jewsons if they got their act together here in Caithness.

On a building theme we got our first sightings of metre square flagstones placed vertically to create boundaries between pastures. We would discover more in a few days the other side of Thurso at Castlehill, for now it seemed strange to see this when concrete slabs were being laid on a house drive.

We had decided to take a vacation in the Orkneys. Wendy was still struggling with a bad back though complaining little, and with a promise of peaceful living, big skies, historical sites and negotiated free return ticket we boarded the noon Hamnavoe ferry. It is also the name of a George Mackay Brown poem learned off by heart by children from Orkney. Havoc however, was something of a problem. Dogs were not allowed inside unless kenneled for which they wanted £7.60, and you can imagine what Wendy thought of that idea. Since we didn't have a car to leave him in, which would have been allowed, the option was remain on open deck and freeze for an hour and a half. With an officious steward with his beady eye on us, perhaps this wasn't going to be so 'peaceful', but I told Wendy to pretend she was blind and say Havoc was a guide dog.

The iconic Old Man of Hoy welcomed us, 137metres of vertical red sandstone. I remembered Chris Bonington climbing it in 1966. The cliff scenery was nearly as dramatic with the wrecks and dive waters of Scapa Flow to our right. Havoc peeked his head through the white railings for a better view and resembled a cow in cattle crush.

Stromness appeared, a grey collection of stone houses, many gable-ended to the sea, all about to throw themselves in, backed by shallow green and brown hillsides. One or two whitewashed but most thought the prospect of freshening décor too much to bear. Private jetties, a smoothed flagstone high street, one car and washing lines empty, it was a Sunday and that could wait till wash day.

We needed somewhere to stay and found Mrs Humphrey's House, marked by a heritage blue circular sign. It was a temporary hospital in 1835 for a year serving 'scurvy ridden whale men who had been trapped in the ice for months.' Per Mare, unimaginable. Why were we moaning about 90 minutes on an open deck? We left Mrs Humphrey to Jonah and Captain Ahab and instead found lodgings which were donated 'sine crimen' or 'frjals'- free! We were in the money, so I hired a car (£40) for some sightseeing, and two lemons.

Skara Brae was a must, clustered flagstone houses and reckoned to be the best preserved prehistoric site in Western Europe. At some 5000 years old, Indiana Jones when lecturing students in 'Kingdom of the Crystal Skull' was not too far out when he dated it at 3100BC.

Also, at the 'Heart of Neolithic Orkney' we marveled at the mound, monument of Maes

Howe. The chambered cairn bears runic inscriptions recording how Vikings plundered the tomb.

The 27 standing stones of the Ring of Brodgar and those at Stennes which feature on the cover of Van Morrison's album 'The Philosophers Stone', are up there to rival Avebury and Stonehenge. Every season reveals new finds, 2023 the Ness of Brodgar is now said to 'blow everywhere else out of the water' in terms of Neolithic importance.

At Marwick Head a memorial commemorating the sinking of HMS Hampshire in 1916 with the loss of 737. Among them Lord Kitchener, Secretary of State for War, who had pointed at future 'tommies' in posters Britons 'wants you'.

The ornate Italian Chapel at Lamb Holm created from Nissen huts by prisoners of war was a bit of more recent history along with the Churchill Barriers they built in the early 1940s to block access to Scapa Flow. The red stone St Magnus cathedral dominated the skyline at Kirkwall with partly ruined palaces nearby.

Two bits in shop windows caught the eye. First, a T-shirt with the words 'feet don't fail me now'. A young Joy Crooks may have seen it and got the first line for her anthem, 'stand my ground...no blames worth buying.' The second a request card reading 'milking cow wanted for family.' How many administrative centres with a population of over 9000 have such irresistible intrigues?

It had been an enjoyable, restful few days. Some island icing at the top of a mainland cake. Even Havoc would say 'all too soon it was time to catch the ferry back to Scrabster'.

In Thurso we met a girl in the paper shop who had seen us nearly a year ago at the start. Simultaneously we said to each other,

"What have you been up to?"

She said she had not been further than Wick. I could not bring myself to recall where we had been and were now in touching distance of the finish.

Low cliffs around Clardon Head and Murkle Bay led to Castletown harbour. It was not hard to see why flagstones were important here. With hundreds stacked vertically forming sea protection, apart from a decaying wooden boat, odd rope and lobster pot everything was stone. We half expected Fred and Barney to come around the corner.

A very extensive Orcadian Basin stretching from Shetland in the north to the Moray Firth in the south some 370 million years ago laid down sediments which formed this stone. The money and pioneering brain behind an industry which thrived in the second half of the 18th and first half of the 19th centuries were James Traill's. While his picture hangs in the National Portrait Gallery, his flags paved Edinburgh's Royal Mile, built fireplaces and provided kitchen surfaces. Thinking about it our rock fences at Reay and all the stone antiquities of Orkney were good indicators of something hard and useful lurking below. Now there were quarries and a place from which the sedimentary slabs could be shipped.

We met Geordie Douglas, a church warden at Dunnet who was to be our good samaritan on this final corner. He let us stay in the church hall, it would be our shelter for the next two nights and received two-star billing. Dry with facilities, nothing wrong there, but it turned out to be the migratory centre for all of Scotland's woodlice. If the floorboards suddenly vanished beneath us, we knew who had eaten the trusses. Havoc nudged them with his nose and when they rolled into balls played solitaire using the cheesy pill bugs as marbles.

Overcast, our last full day took us out around Dunnet Head. We saw a few wind surfers and the sea seemed to be speaking,

"It's our last chance to get you."

There was something of a swell, but we danced along the cliffs like confectionary,

"You can't catch us, we're gingerbread men."

Deep heather and arm pit high bracken with many impressive geos to a sturdy white lighthouse at mainland Britain's most northerly point. At Ham we saw our last two seals disappear and at Scarlskerry a couple we had met at Ullapool gave us coffee. As we sat chatting Roy Noble from BBC Wales phoned to check where we were. I was blown away by his memory and kindness and reciprocated gratitudes to all in the Principality.

Built in the late 16th century, The Castle of Mey had received little recent attention until the late Queen Elizabeth the Queen Mother bought it in 1952. Recently widowed, she needed a bit of a project. Some say she paid £1 for it, others a £100, it may have even been gifted by previous owners. In 1996 now restored in was placed in Trust. Her former holiday home is now open to the public, in 2021 a family ticket cost you £35. Geordie collected us and returned us to Dunnet. I remember thinking how the seasons had changed as fields were being ploughed and gulls fell into the furrows behind, by the drove.

Geordie was keen to show us his kirk. Unusual pivoting pew backs, tower with spiral staircase and summoning bell. Freshly painted, the graveyard was full, and we were told everything about Timothy Pont, cartographer, and vicar here for nine years from 1601. He was among the first to map Scotland, so we actually owed him quite a bit. Our last supper was sausages and pasta. Chocolate 'Chunky' for dessert, while Havoc had the canned variety.

We were dropped back to Mey to do the last six miles with mixed emotions. From St John's Point we could see the Island of Stroma. Very isolated, the hardy, self-sufficient residents, not shy of illicit and illegal brewing and smuggling, dwindled in numbers from a high of 375 in 1901. Sixty years later there were 12 and the last permanent residents left in 1962. Shipwrecks apparently provided additional income in the day, the remains from the last one in 1993 and old crofts provided subject matter for Prince Charles, now King Charles on a painting trip. Pity he wasn't around to capture me taking a heavy fall at Gills Bay, narrowly missing the tumbling water of the Pentland Firth whipped up like a washing machine. Feet don't fail me now. An old hotel at Huna was a final find before John o' Groats.

There to meet us on 13th October were just four people. Geordie, a random Welsh guy (possibly sent by Roy Noble!) and Wendy's mum and dad. They had kindly come up to see us arrive and after a few photos it was all over. No big welcoming party. After signing in, we shared a bottle of bubbly and were treated to a night in a local hotel. Wendy's dad said a thank you to me for looking after her, and

"Not pushing her off a cliff".

An earworm wriggled. Take That, 1995, Never Forget.

'We've come a long way, never forget where you've come here from, we've come so far and we've reached so high, and we've looked each day and night in the eye'. Thanks Gary.

Immediate Tailpiece

A Saturday afternoon, we could hop down the A99 to Wick and send pictures via the RNLI internet back to charity workers. We had somehow missed Whaligoe Steps that lie between Ulbster and Bruan so also visited there, 365 steps down to a natural herring harbour. With feet up we saw something of England beating France 14-9 to win a place in the World Cup final.

We went back to Dunnet church on the Sunday, to say goodbye to Geordie and give thanks to everyone for everything on our journey of self-discovery. I read,

"Above Dunnet Bay stands the Old White Kirk where once a
light was lit to guide the boats
home on dark nights, and now as He has in the past, so
The Light of the World still shines today to guide us to our
Eternal Home."

We had received guidance from so many quarters, but it was soon time to head south and home.

Before that however, a bit of unfinished business and repayment of a favour. We had a few days rest and recuperation in Edinburgh before heading north again to Aberdeen for a shift or two in 'Olympricks' fancy dress shop, 'Party Mania' in George Street.

With Halloween approaching business was busy and he had asked if we fancied helping out for a few days. It turned out to be great paid fun. Either, trying to remember how to drive and delivering helium balloons to throwing hire gorilla suits into the washing machine and fetching them out of the tumble dryer. As well as telling well rounded girls their bums didn't look big in skimpy Wonder Woman suits or trying on everything from Beetlejuice to tartan crotchless knickers and from wet look topless leotards to the full bondage, fetish and S/M range! Our wages were put into our charity tin.

With a bit more time for sightseeing we found the statue of William Wallace, ironically, he probably never visited the city. Friends came up from Arbroath to congratulate us and privately we toyed with the idea of starting our own fancy dress shop back in the Teign Valley.

Very memorable for me was soaking in the bath one night the soles of my feet fell off! Almost like two shoe insoles and about 5mm thick, layer upon layer of skin, a leathery foot lining released, it was no longer needed and headed for the plug hole.

It was 5th November, Bonfire night, before we finally headed for Devon. It was a Monday, hash night (TVH3) and we were collected in Newton Abbot and taken to Torquay for the run. Havoc hated 'Bluebirds' pyrotechnics, he asked to have some words added to the Boomtown Rat's anthem, 'I Don't Like Mondays - when there are rockets!' It was quite a welcome home in contrast to the rather quiet finish we had experienced back in John o' Groats.

Chapter 46 - Aftermath, fall out and reflection

Oh, what about us

"We all have to decide what we let go of, and what we keep."
"Above the parapet, there is bird song."

WE ALL FIND REASONS not to start something. That was evident from John o' Groats in November 2006. Equally, we might find reasons not to finish something - or at least begin the ending. That was my experience here. This was the final chapter (written long after the revisits). I had left it, put it off, it would be the hardest. In November 2007 I didn't want the walk to end. I didn't want to write its ending now, 16 years later, it would inevitably stir emotions, raise misdemeanors, some criticisms.

Have another coffee, make some toast, put the bins out, any excuses. My handwriting had deteriorated in the diary entries as the walk went on, it was even worse now. I didn't have volumes of notes from early 2008, much would need to be from memory, there were many, countless loaded. Song lyrics and titles would guide me, I could remember lots from the time. I have always said the most important part of any outdoor activity or adventure is reflection. It might be the most important thing in all pursuits. I needed to stare into Stevie Wonder's 'Lately' mirror and 'very slowly pick (things) apart'.

We had been warned it would be difficult to return to normal life. Aberdeen Party Mania had provided a steppingstone. By Wednesday 7th November 2007 the phone had rung, and I was back on the building site. (More dressing up or curing jellyfish would have to wait.) Little time to reflect. We needed money. My cottage tenants had moved out, bills were still arriving, we needed to buy a car, the former runabout had been sold prior to our starting, you can't walk forever. I got hold of an old Ford estate, it gave us something to go hashing in. I could just about remember how to drive, going to a garage and putting petrol in it, an unusual conundrum.

Wendy got a job with a local greengrocer - enough to buy Christmas presents - and we moved back in together to my cottage. I had a Black-Eyed Pea feeling 'Tonight was gonna be a good night'. We sent cards and 'thank yous' to everyone who had put us up or helped in any way on the walk. I made a full duplicate copy of all the contacts made, so we could stay in touch, at least every Christmas.

Wendy immediately took control of all charity money matters paying just over £25,000 to each of our two charities by the end of the first week back. We reached our target. Slightly strange, as she was less enthusiastic raising it on the walk, but then, could I be trusted? I offered to buy her the gold charm bracelet, at full valuation, as we had not received acceptable pledges. The drive to get something from the Bovey Tracey bespoke jeweller was all mine, his idea concept to raise us some money and give him some publicity, it unfortunately didn't come off. (Both in terms of pledges, and Wendy's wrist for 5000 miles.) It would have been a nice keepsake, unique good luck gift - but it was returned without discussion with me. The writing was on the wall. Never mind.

"The course of true love never did run smooth". (Shakespeare)

I was hearing Bon Jovi, 'You give love a bad name...loaded gun' interspersed with 'My Way' (Anka or Sinatra) 'And now the end is near'.

The New Year saw Wendy apply for one role in education, I helped her with her application, she got an interview but not the job. I recall saying to her persevere, don't give up, I had no problem with her returning to a role in schools as "*Wherever I Hang my Lead*" states. Indeed, the chapter 'Home for a while' reads more like the one-sided Lionesses' score line against Norway in the Euros 2022!

Truth is there were no 'yellow cards' from solicitors. I recall no crowd control by Police, burly or otherwise, and any fear of a water bearer being left alone with me, while others sold cabbages is pure fiction for tabloids. What's conveniently omitted is that there were some extra players on the pitch. I like Cyndi Lauper, but I am not so smitten with 'Girls just wanna have fun!'

Some have suggested to me what has been out there since 2018 verges on libel, and I should do something about it. Paul Simon's (1970) lyrics come to mind. 'Slandered, libeled, words never heard in the bible'. My reply is how do you sue a former much-loved pet who has now moved on to the big kennel in the sky? I am confident if I ever see him again, he will recognise me immediately and warmly, with a frantically wagging tail and lots of licks. Better to forget bitter, resentful insults. Hang onto compliments, if there are any to be found. I was never much good at micro-navigation and don't own a magnifier. I prefer to offer some balanced defence, which everyone is entitled to, and remember that old bible saying, 'let those without sin, cast the first stone'.

Friction - I recall little, I wouldn't say none at this time. You cannot fully appreciate the light without some shadows. Life is not always perfect, it has bends, ups and downs, that might be its beating. I was no easy mustang, one failing trait not admitted to date, an over sense of importance in what I am involved with, that often precludes the importance of others. Wild or feral, calmness did not exude, that comes from sweet, gentle natured, humble ponies. In a school sense I was rough book, not a jotter.

Wendy's son, and girlfriend did move out of her Bovey flat to a rented house next door to my terrace. The washing machine would not go through the front door so came through my lounge. Wendy's daughter had loads of elbow room now which meant Wendy had an ideal base to a) leave Havoc if she had any fears and b) retire to if ever sabres crossed. Wendy had plenty of space to not be herself, regain her sparkle, take pills without sobbing on the moor. Perhaps, more detail, 'not less' needs to be gone into if you are going to pen a character assassination with no balancing mitigation. Should I feel aggrieved, or take a line from Oasis 'Don't look back in anger'?

If life really was so bad for Wendy at this time I can only apologise. I do remember her listening a lot to Katie Melua, 'Closest thing to crazy'. Perhaps I should have taken more heed of those lines. I am including here a quote from Richard Coles, that young vicar back at Boston.

"I can't turn the clock back, but I can seek the forgiveness of those I've wronged." I do that here.

I can display sympathy, perhaps more here's a hot beverage, than Joaquin Phoenix on the topic of fish, but I am not uncompassionate. Empathy for me comes when I stop and think about it, it doesn't sit on my lap. Realisations arrive quickly, learning takes time.

Fed up with fruit and veg Wendy started her dog walking business, 'two feet, four paws' name borrowed from Spud. She used the Ford estate until it blew up. A smart new replacement white van saw Havoc embellished across the sides in panoramic scenes alongside Scottish lochs. I helped with carpeting it out. Not meant as a cliché, she was woven into the fabric of my life, selfishly I knew if that unraveled, I would be a tangled mess. All those truisms italicised as chapter toppers, delineating fortitude and strength would serve me no disentanglement.

We went to Painswick, Stroud to pick up a dog travelling cage for the back of the van. I stuck flyers on gateposts to help advertise. Things went from strength to strength, to include house/pet sitting. I went along to help; every support was given. It was at one of these, when I wasn't present, in Chudleigh so I am told, when delivery of a second offered cage took place, that would signal the beginning of the end. I don't know how much spewing of discontentment was aired, but it seems Wendy stopped looking for happiness in a place where she had lost it. I hadn't heeded the words of Dr. Hook, 'When you're in love with a beautiful woman, watch your friends'.

I was hugely proud of Wendy, and for that matter Havoc's achievements and made no secret of it. That is both the Walk and the walkies business start. We gave a talk to a group in Bovey entitled 'A dead mouse a day'. Slides from our 'holiday', enough to bore a mouse to top themselves. Perhaps I should have heeded the symbolism of them littering our trek a little more deeply.

It occurs to me now that all through all 11 months, 5000 miles, Wendy was perhaps unhappy. Secretly humming Queen, 'Got to break free'. If that was the case, she deserves more credit than I ever offered. Putting up with a supercilious, capricious bulldog; big, squashed nose to go with it. In the months afterwards was she just looking for a way out, the charms of another eventually providing the way out of a romantic conundrum that had become a nightmare? She might have been sharing sentiments with the Buzzcocks, 'Ever fallen in love with someone you shouldn't have fallen in love with'. I was probably sharing the lyrics too. If she was singing 'Every day I love you less and less' (Kaiser Chiefs), that wasn't on my playlist. More akin to my mind set at the time, Adele, 'Scars of your love, we almost had it all.'

Other's charms - she might have been more selective. Choosing someone who shared building sites with me, that made working very difficult. Someone who was also a hasher, that wrecked run nights. Someone she had baked and decorated a wedding cake for, I had helped, little thought for that ill-fated link up. May as well hitch up with a highwayman or the leader of Al Qaeda - oh, that was her choice, to dance with the devil. Traded a Rolex for a Timex. I wish she had sat down with Kate Bush 'Running up that road' instead.

Towards August Wendy and I were still together. We were due to go via

Bath for a weekend, pick up her mum and dad, onto Stoneleigh for a Guide Dog event. We were to get a thank you for our charity effort. As the weekend approached, I was told she would go on her own. Strange I thought. In the end we did go together. Afterwards, very tired it was suggested we stay overnight with her parents, rather than go straight back. She was less than keen, even more strange I pondered. On returning to Bovey Tracey, she told me she wasn't coming in, she was going back to her flat - her things had been secretly removed from my place. Breaking up is hard to do. Paul Simon penned his '50 ways to leave your lover' (1975), this wasn't listed, Train took a leaf out of that book, (2012) '50 ways to say goodbye'. What would I tell others when asked, she was 'fried getting suntan'.

We had both been involved in planning for and running a celebratory TVH3 weekend for 23rd August -1234 runs since its formation. We went together. I put up a tent for us earlier in the day on the Friday, by the time I returned it had been moved. In 2008, political correctness allowed 'Rear of the Year' awards, the hash would hold its own. Wendy entered and won, unsurprisingly, (she looked good in the 2005 calendar too) the sole self-appointed judge, that member of a terrorist cell. I think I was being made a fool of. (Jennifer Ellison won the celebrity 2008 Rear of the Year, the competition was banned in 2020.) Coincidently, Melon Picker spoke to me at the final disco as we watched his partner, Honeydew and Soapy (who I still thought was mine) on the dance floor,

"Aren't we lucky!" he said.

Wendy and I would share the tent that night, but the Eagles have it, 'You can't hide lying eyes.' My 50th birthday was a miserable time in my life, 14th September 2008, very different from Dunvegan a year previous.

What was needed was for Wendy to come right out, saying once and for all, it was all over. Perhaps she did, but I didn't want to hear it. I was smitten, beguiled. I had come to idolise, that is never good. What followed was a tussle with ever-growing acrimony. I would spend far too long driving alone past her street - I could have provided the words for Olivia Rodrigo. That was part of the problem, living so close. We had time together, time apart. Suspicion fueled jealousy; I stalked as much as I was stalked. I am certainly not proud of some of my behaviour, but I didn't have a third party to run back to.

The trouble with break ups is that other people get involved. For some in the hash, it meant taking sides. By now Wendy's children were pretty much against me, and I even at times had to be smuggled into her flat.

New meaning for Gordan Lightfoot's 'Creeping round my back stairs' (Sundown, 1974). I still went with her for some house sits, other times it was someone else. There were long periods apart, but we got back together for Christmas 2009. On New Year's Day morning, while I got up to take Havoc for an early morning 'busy', Wendy went through my phone to find two generic Happy New Year messages from harriets. By 9am I was back at my own house alone. I knew only too well, 'The female of the species, was deadlier than the male'. (Kipling or Space - take your pick.) I needed to 'get relative with the inevitable.' The trouble was I was too arrogant to think anyone would leave me.

I moved down the A38 for work and distance away. Another problem with break ups - there are always songs to provide reminders. Scouting for Girls were the worst. 'She's so lovely', 'Little bit lost without you, really big mess inside'. 'Your fault not mine, one foot down the line'. It was inescapable. Throw in a bit of Annie Lennox 'Walking on broken glass', Carol King 'Too late baby', advice from Maria in Sound of Music 'Cry a little and wait for the sun to come out', and Dolly Parton 'I will always love you - bittersweet memories' and you have a recipe for jumping off Chudleigh rocks, and I wasn't too far from that. For a long time, my world stood still. 'I sat and talked to God, tried to contact the living' (Robbie Williams). I was 'All cried out, someone else was sitting in my seat, a whole lot of loving for a handful of nothing' (Alison Moyet.)

Blackadon and SHH3 would be good Samaritans and liberators. My advice to anyone going through a messy break up - unplug the TV, tune the radio to Classic FM (no lyrics) and rip the knob off, break all records (vinyl), place all CDs to scare birds on the allotment, throw your smart phone off Chudleigh rocks rather than yourself. Avoid all contact with song lines as you would avoid acquaintances with Covid. Socially distance. This I did from TVH3, it was an unwritten agreement, Wendy would hash there, I would do my running with SHH3. The problem was, she conveniently forgot the agreement at times.

We still weren't finished killing each other. I had to listen to the elements, Earth, Wind and Fire – 'After the love has gone'. Eventually, I said to her it's time to move on, why don't you shack up with Melon Picker, who by now was single himself - she must have taken my advice. The next and last time I saw them they turned up in Ivybridge for a hash together. They never came into the pub. They later married. If they are still together, I wish them well. Mazel tov and Toda.

I hope Wendy has found true happiness. Something eventually came out of an ill-fated pub experience at Ilsington. Without it she would never have come upon puppy Havoc, unlikely found hashing or a new husband. That was my gift to her, as well as *trying* to provide memories of a lifetime, for a lifetime.

There it is then, on the bit you've been waiting for, suspected since chapter one, we didn't stay together. I've provided the detail Havoc skipped over. In summary, we had our adventure, discovered loads, achieved goals, had some fun but not as much as we should have done. Came home, should have lived happily ever after, instead Wendy goes off with another bloke, and I am left a quivering wreck. 'Take a look at me now, how can you just walk away?' (Phil Collins).

It hit me very hard, I felt furious and humiliated. Why was I so hurt? Lots of people experience a jilting, 'John did'. When it happens at 13 or 25, you have time to get over it. When it occurs at 50 it's somehow harder especially when you have sacrificed so much for that person. After an admittedly indecisive start, my commitment to her had been absolute and at no small cost.

I felt I had given up on a 20-year marriage, two children, a comfortable lifestyle and lost a career in the process too. The relationship with my children, if you can call it that, is certainly bludgeoned. The loss, monumental, and all for what? To have all that sacrifice wiped out was devastating. No different on reflection from millions of others, but few of those will have experienced something as immense and prodigious as Wendy and me. The walk of a lifetime. That would surely bond us for eternity. Unfortunately, you cannot force someone to love you. Would I really have wanted her to stay when the feeling had died? The tunes throughout really did resonate in my head, along with many others, sometimes they still do.

But what about other reflection. I am often asked questions. (When doing talks about the walk, come along, I can sign your book.)

What was the best bit?
Genuinely, meeting so many wonderful people. Kind, generous, trusting, full of inherent goodness. From all walks of life. People with wealth, others with little, often very willing to share what they had. There was the odd rogue, but they were outnumbered ten to one. It restored and embellished faith in mankind. As it turned out the friendships were fleeting, but I remember those people and hope I can emulate them. Thank you each and every one. We may have had to sing for our supper lots, but sharing our adventure was for many living it for themselves. For whatever reason, commitments, lack of courage, uncertainty about personal fitness many

were never going to embark on the likes of this for themselves, but to support us was truly sharing in the marathon without having to do the miles.

How many pairs of boots did you get through?

If not the most frequently asked question, certainly the second most asked. We had planned for three pairs each. 2000 miles per pair, we had our starting ones and two other pairs each were posted. All had some mileage on the clock, but not 500 miles as in the case of JM. If ours had 60, that was probably as much. Wendy was soon in need of a change, and we found Granny Vera.

We carried trainers, something to change into of an evening, and soon found we were walking in them. We walked some of these to total destruction as we did low ankle approach shoes. I don't think you need high ankle boots for support necessarily on much of the walk, if the high ankle is to keep your feet dry, forget it. Even with gaiters up to your knees, your feet will get wet, better off thinking of footwear you can dry out easily. I didn't wear rubber 'crocs' but if I were doing it again, I would take a pair.

What was the most scenic bit?

Always asked hard to answer. Every bit had its beauty and interest. Pin me down and I might be predictable, a toss-up between the Southwest, Pembrokeshire and Scotland. The country is full of places I want to return to, there is nowhere that would be off limits. Out on the cliff, or beach, periods of remote isolation, times to enjoy peace and solitude, just the two of us, we weren't always arguing. One could enjoy the scenery, if you didn't look up for too long and forget where you were putting your feet. Juxtaposed to these were places of settlement, from hamlets to cities, where we would encounter other people. The scenery here was just as thrilling, new acquaintances colouring, flavouring what was to be seen. My account is punctuated by place names. I make no apology for that. Name a town and my memory juices start to flow; Cromarty - Santa Claus, Wells in Norfolk- Popeye Frary, West Wales – Pencastell Pete! Everywhere holds a memory, I generally don't need much of a prompt and I can tell you a story.

What was the hardest bit?

Asking people for money, that was true for both of us, I just stuck at it more often. The charity bit I allowed to be all consuming. There were benefits to it, we would have never received the support we got without it, but it caused a disproportionate number of domestic problems. It began to feel as though I had to do it, because people were so good to us. Physically, carrying the rucksack was tough, we had too much gear, shoulders suffered, my knees still feel the pain. For Wendy, it was probably being with me.

How far did you walk?

Look up the distance around the coast and you will get a variety of answers. JM some 7000 miles, PH concludes England some 2,300 miles, Scotland 2,000, Wales 731. In all honesty our pathetic belt pedometers gave us little guidance. How long is your stride length? We didn't have a phone app in 2006, our GPS ran out of battery before we got to Wick. Our original estimate was to cover 5000 miles, on reflection we did all of that, me just catching up with Wendy! It would have been nice to know precisely, but we weren't setting any distance or time records. Judging by the thickness of skin that fell off the soles of my feet at the completion, 1mm for every 1000 miles, it was as good as we had predicted.

What was the most useful bit of equipment?

Surprisingly, for me walking poles. Probably for Wendy, anything which gave her some, even temporary foot relief. She really did suffer. I don't know if she ever tried the onion and chicken fat! The tent was fab, thank you to the manufacturers. My kit was probably of the order of 60lbs, Wendy's 40lbs. JM concluded the rucksack was not a strain. That is the most surprising thing to me. I found it a real burden, one reason to take a support vehicle. It got you noticed but did permanent damage to knees. I await the replacements.

What was the most embarrassing bit?

That loo in Liverpool and changing my pants in Kent were up there. Not staying together as a couple was far worse. I genuinely feel by not doing that we let down people who supported us. They gave us so much, we owed it to all of them to finish, succeed and enjoy memories of the experience together forever. Sitting down in front of the weather map on TV and sharing memories. It is quite like a sense of guilt about engagement and wedding presents when marriages go wrong. 'Dry your eyes mate' (The Streets.) Additionally, for me, being unable to stay in touch with people. My duplicate copy of contact details was never returned, left in Wendy's flat and consigned I was told to a BBQ. That is a big regret.

Do you feel the walk caused your breakup?
No. The relationship was probably in danger before we started. It did provide some extra fuel. I felt we were 'Two hearts, two hearts that beat as one' (Richie and Ross) I was wrong. At times we were a great team on the walk, but we couldn't sustain it subsequently. I tried and fought to make it work, my efforts in the end were insufficient. If you want to place the blame solely in one spot, it must be at my door.

Churches seemed to play an important part.
They did, all denominations. We met a good cross section of vicars and holy types, went to several services. The children at St Combs were the most heart stirring. I wouldn't say I was a religious fanatic. I don't go to church every Sunday. When I do, I enjoy the services. Put me on the spot and I would say I am believer and not the kind The Monkey's sang about. The walk strengthened my faith.

Did you lose weight?
Unlike the Hunts, no, more is the pity. Wendy's cooking was too good. Plus, we had too much Ecklefechan Tart and too many hot Welsh cakes. Food foraged always tasted great. I don't know how many pints of milk we drank. It wasn't 529 and we certainly didn't munch through 1,511 chocolate bars! It seems kind of OCD to even bother counting, JM. Ice creams - probably no more than ten each on the entire walk, PH you have that record.

If doing it again, what would you do differently?
Well, the lesson for me is self-evident - be nicer. Both before, during so you don't waste time and energy firefighting after. That way you might not be left as a single member of an elite club, instead you are half of a special couple within it.

I would still go clockwise; the other way just seems wrong. Our start and finish never really helped us, from a publicity point of view, probably choose London. I would go to Southampton as a change from the Isle of Wight, jump across the Severn rather than go to Gloucester only because it would be different. Stick to the mainland in western Scotland, I really want to go to Knoydart as well as other bits we missed. You really couldn't presume on CalMac again. Beg a ticket to Shetland instead. Somehow lighten the loads you carry, spending more on different kit to begin with. If doing it for charity I would also get the boundaries clear before starting. Get clarity from the charity as to what they can provide. It probably needs more people and greater liaison in all aspects of preparation, Spud had a walk committee. It is perhaps too much to do all on your own, we had the hash. Thank you for everything they did, just lock down your partner.

The fund raising/publicity bit might be easier now with social media, at least if you own an iPhone and am not a technophobe like me. A camera drone might enable some sublime, impressive image capture.

Coastal walker call ups.
I have mentioned in my bibliography a website listing many who have achieved this. I knew Havoc *'Wherever I hang my lead'* quite well, or so I thought. I have never met JM, corresponded briefly with JT and PH, was fortunate to meet Spud and SH/RH, would like to meet MW and RW. Others have bashed it out in more recent years. Alex Ellis-Roswell started in 2014 and amassed 9500 miles with RNLI being a large part of his trek. Ruth Livingstone gave up being a couch potato at 54 in 2016 to begin her achievement. Quinton Lake called his 'the Perimeter', covered something like 6600miles in 5 years I believe and took lots of photos. James Lloyd (2022) supported Mind. These are just the ones I have heard of. I point readers in their direction for comparison. Would love to meet you all on the beach sometime. Other listers; Bradbury, Green, Robinson, Crane, Humble, Bussell, Portillo, to name just a few all do their own bit of walking, not always on the coast path, followed by film crews. Many I have asked for a leg up by way of a review, achieving that more difficult than walking.

Good luck to you all, if nothing else it shows a widespread interest in walking and perhaps the coast too. After all, Susan Calman managed it with cameras in tow in an old van and living exclusively on cake.

Would you support the same charities again?
Charity selection is an individual choice. I would never be fit enough to be able to do it again. I might be able to cycle 5000 miles if I had a free year, but you couldn't stick by the sea. You would have to navigate, I would get lost, Wendy might hope down a Thai sewer! We did reach our £50,000 target, don't be tempted to set one. It was all raised from our own single-minded dedication. Some £12,000 before we started, over £38,000 from people en route - £1 here, 50p there. In 1977 JM raised £40,000, £3,000 from individuals en route. Spud raised £44,000 for Shelter in 1993/4. We could rightly be proud of our charity effort. If I ever manage to sell any of these books, the proceeds will go to Guide Dogs, in respect to Wendy and to my new partner who is a regular subscriber/supporter and has had her own eye issues.

That brings me nicely to 'What becomes of the broken hearted?' (Jimmy Ruffin). They respair, thanks Susie Dent - always handy knowing a lexicographer! It's a 15th century word meaning to recover from despair.

I met Liz, my new partner, it took me some years. We have been together now for over 10. She can put up with me. With great patience we return to places and see if they are winning at life, as I believe I am. Those observations appear in the next eight chapters. She has changed me. I am now equipped with light weight; breathable trousers and the legs detach to form shorts. Gone are the days of old rugby shorts, the crotch hanging out, make do and mend. Ai no corrida now every day.

We are a strong team, she is fantastic. I consider myself blessed to have met her. She is 'Simply the best' (Tina Turner), her 'Love is King' (Sade). We have our spats, but they are short lived. She hasn't, as yet, grown to despise me. Sorry, isn't the hardest word, we do talk it over, I don't need to turn triple somersaults to make her love me, we can both be heard. Wise advice, 'We all make mistakes, make amends, move on. You are the author of the book of your life, turn the page.'

Another of Elton's lyrics sums it up well, 'How wonderful life is while you're in my world'. 'More than a woman to me.' (Bee Gees).

In this section are eight chapters of varying length, written after re-visits following the walk. They attempt to describe a handful of places, with observations and experiences, to bring things up to date. Just as I evaluate if I am winning at life, are these places winning too? Not every inch of coastline is included for obvious reasons with apologies to places overlooked, especially those north of the border - too far to travel and time available dictates the length of what's been included. Each visit is dated, often the direction of visit was anti-clockwise contrasting with the walk. They are however presented in geographical order around the coast as the original walk was conducted.

Chapter 47 – East Coast Revisited

Beat me on the bottom with a Woman's Weekly

"Life is like a camera. Just focus on what's important, capture the good times, develop the negatives and if they don't turn out, take another shot."

IT WAS AUGUST 2021 before I could take a nostalgic look back on some of the east coast. That began in the form of a motorised touring holiday starting in Boston. What follows is therefore a limited whistle stop tour over ten nights, with only circumstantial observation.

JM admired Boston town with 'well preserved character, attractive warehouses and busy river,' and made a mental note to return and explore. Spud found estuarine sewage works, rubbish dumps and scrap on the banks of The Whitham and cabbage leaves, squashed tomatoes and burger wrappers in the market square. SH wrote 'Silos and steel terminals, transformers and pylons showed Boston's industrial systems were in good health,' but JT found them a muddle and confusing to navigate and The Haven anything but.

Australia's founders and other citizens from here established a cousin colony in Massachusetts, 1630, suggesting it has long been a place to depart rather than hang around. Cycling along the river we found some of the 'unloved and unkempt' areas PH discovered. It was reported in 2016 Boston was the 'most murderous' place in England and Wales. We made a hasty retreat down a path before we became a statistic or at least became unsaddled riding over a victim. It was plain to see high levels of social deprivation, an observation backed up by mid-2000s figures which showed Boston had the highest obesity rates of any town in the UK. A 2011 census put the population of the borough at 64,000 with 15% of the population born outside the UK, 11% born in EU accession countries. Near the Savoy cinema on West Street there was a large gathering of people. Loud music from the boot of an adapted car, raised voices, many not English. Between the shell suits, 'tracki' bottoms and leggings it looked like things were about to 'kick-off,' so we made another swift withdrawal.

Was Boston 'winning at life'? - perhaps not!

We descended on Skegness via motorhome on the A52. 20,000 visitors may have arrived for the 1882 August Bank Holiday and 1890-1945 have been described as the boom years for this archetypal seaside town that still relies heavily on tourism. The advent of the foreign package holidays in the 1970s may have had an impact but fortunes fluctuate, and it seemed with restrictions on international travel as a result of the pandemic things were looking up for Skeggie, affordable staycations being all the thing. Self-catering was clearly doing well, I didn't count them, but it was quoted there are well over 100,000 caravans and chalets stretching all the way to Ingoldmells, a largely linear seaside sprawl punctuated by every form of 'tacky' attraction imaginable.

Tourism seemed to dominate the town and one could envisage the economic challenge of low paid, low skilled seasonal work that goes with it. The town received considerable regeneration grants from the EU in 2001 but it didn't stop strong support for Brexit 15 or so years later with cries of give state funds direct to the town. Reuters labelled it Brexit-on-Sea. Others might still arrive on the Poacher Line, the 55 mile rail link to Grantham. The name stems from a traditional English folk song, an unofficial county anthem, expelling the joys of the pastime in Lincolnshire. It also explains the name of the lifeboat seen in 2007, which was actually retired in 2017. Her replacement I discovered was a Shannon class boat, The Joel and April Grinnell.

We stopped for a coffee and a bit of a walk at Sandilands. Somehow however, motorised touring didn't get you up close and connected to the coast and the sea like hiking on foot. Mablethorpe had more amusements than I remembered, other places seemed unchanged from 14 years earlier. At Cleethorpes the tide was out and the sea had retreated to Jutland. Ross Castle and the pier were just the same and Deli-Licious was still trading. There was no pilot boat waiting so we crossed The Humber on the A15 and journeyed north to Bridlington and Scarborough.

I was something of a renewable's sceptic back in 2007, seeing solar farms and wind turbines as something of eyesores. The technology has moved on in 14 years and wind farms now stretch further out to sea, where they can be more effective and generally less visible. The likes of Hull and Grimsby now manufacture and provide crews to service these turbines, skilled and well-paid jobs for Humberside workers. A necessary revolution in clean/green energy has opened my eyes. We will see if the UN Conference in Glasgow (COP26) brings a wider transformation, both in human consciousness and activity.

It was very apparent how quickly you could get to places but how little you could see compared with foot slogging. We had short walks and frankly that is all I can manage nowadays. I might be able to manage five miles, the occasional longer distance but not the 15/20 miles a day, every day continually, done back in 2006/07. Compressed cartilage, stiff and painful knees are now a legacy of a lifetime of sport, activity, mileage and bag carrying. I genuinely believe that carrying in excess of 60lbs daily for 11 months has contributed to arthritic knee problems and now an inability to run. Impact when attempted simply results in knee pain. Sport and hashing are a thing of the past. Walking football still requires you to kick a ball which hurts, walking basketball might be a possibility? I would enjoy cricket, but who wants an old fogie who can only field in the slips and never takes a quick single. Certainly, to repeat the coastal circumnavigation would be impossible, I am no longer fit for purpose. Would I do it all again now knowing the consequence? With no hesitation.

The fissure between two steep cliffs, which is Robin Hood's Bay is a darn sight easier to arrive in by foot than by six berth motorhome. Less conspicuous to residents also who defend their parking spaces with zeal. In a maze of tiny streets smuggling is now less evident than tourism, which is the main income source. Getting a table for lunch was a bit like a scramble in Sherwood Forest when a folklore hero handed out goodies to the poor. Add the odd film crew using the village as a set, (Phantom Thread, Daniel Day Lewis, 2017) and you have recipe for mayhem. 2021 however, RHB was winning at life. In fact, this whole stretch of coast may well benefit from Si and Dave's biker travels, 'Go North' (BBC 2021) which sees them waxing about the region's wine, seaweed, kippers, langoustine and all manner of gastronomic produce. Surely this sort of exposure can only add to an area's attractiveness and encourage others to romp, perhaps not on a motor bike.

On the Durham coast we stopped at Easington Colliery just off the A19. On the walk we hugged the coast closely here, never really venturing even more than a few metres away from the sea. The mine closed in 1993. I saw for the first time really the rows of miners terraced cottages, set at right angles to the sea. Scenes for the 2000 film Billy Elliot were shot here and locals filled extras roles. A 2021 walk will be remembered for a very blue sea and largely litter free surrounds with great colonies of Golden Rod, an attractive weed. Local people seemed to have a pride in their community, even though economically things looked stayed. One row of shops, all with metal shutters, all closed even though it was mid-afternoon. An old Victorian school that now looked as if it was starting to be developed - though the internet says things have been on hold since 2003. We found the old colliery pay office, the last evidence of a pit which still houses that northern fixture, a Colliery Band. Nearby 83 planted trees marking the lives lost in a colliery explosion in 1951.

At Newbiggin-by-the-Sea we didn't know whether to ring the Coastguard or Samaritans on seeing a man and women perched on a platform looking out to sea over the breakwater. It took a while to realise it was the 'Couples Statue' (Sean Henry) installed in 2007, but after we had walked by. It remains a local talking point. My earworm went straight to Victoria Wood, Ballad of Barry and Freda, 'Let's Do It.'

Twenty minutes north in a vehicle gets you to Amble, a day's walk on foot, 20 odd miles I had done, albeit in the opposite direction. It was nice to be back. Amble has a go slow, off life's treadmill feel about it. It's a place for a wander, listen to the local accent, you won't understand it, but it's fun to just take in. Folk are friendly, there are fewer fishing boats than there used to be, but you can buy a very fresh wet fish supper and there are any number of chippies. You may well have to queue.

It was on The Sunday Times pick list of UK coastal hot spots (2019) and it had lost none of its charm from 2007. If you find yourself bored count the number of model boats in shop windows, you will need more fingers than two hands. I tried to find Shelley who had put us up on the walk and called at the lifeboat station. I bumped into John, who we met then, still working. We reminisced, talked of other east coast stations staff, all of whom it seemed had now retired. Shelley had moved too, to Cornwall, to be near her dad. John was critical of some of the changes that had happened around the harbour, new 4/5 storey flats, an expensive new Harbour Master's office under construction - he was just like me, didn't accept change easily, probably a trait of aging. Just to see a face from 2007 and hear a Northumberland accent was however, invigorating and comforting at the same time.

More evidence that Amble is friendly - it is known as 'the friendliest port'. In 1935 the RMS Mauratania, the sister ship of RMS Lusitania, was on her last voyage to Rosyth to be broken up. Amble sent a telegram to her saying, 'still the finest ship on the sea'. The reply came,

'To the last and kindliest port in England'.

'Amble - the friendly port' is still seen on town signs.

We decided to cycle and went first to Warkworth for a paddle in the sea, a stunningly beautiful beach, which should be award winning, even if it isn't. Spacious, unspoilt and quiet, one of a number along this coast said to be collectively the finest in the UK. Then on to Alnmouth for soup and stottie bread. To be honest the stottie was not as good as I remembered it, so the challenge remained to find some better. My knees do allow cycling and we took a cycle path inland, to Alnwick, pronounced A-nuhk. We weren't in search of bread particularly but did find a castle, gardens and Barter secondhand bookshop in the former railway station. It is one of the largest in Europe, with cozy armchairs, a model railway, and great to just ramble through. It was lovely to see children just sitting quietly alone reading, buried in pages of Harry Potter or whatever. If it was 'Philosopher's Stone' or 'Chamber of Secrets' they couldn't be blamed, the films of both used scenes shot at Alnwick Castle.

Alnmouth would feature as a 'Village by the Sea'. Ben Robinson would explain that it was once a busy trading port, at its height in 1750. A storm in 1806 and a tidal surge saw the harbour channel change course. As ships got larger the port became too shallow and Alnmouth dwindled in importance. Guano, sea bird poo was once imported from Peru as a fertiliser. The valuable excrement made it to at least two episodes of the

Onedin Line, where James no doubt got his hands dirty and crew had to put up with the pong, 1972/76.

Our short tour was becoming a tasting trip as who could resist not trying a Craster kipper straight from the smokehouse especially when it came in a bap at a discount when you paid for parking. The walk to Dunstanburgh, again in the opposite direction, within my capabilities and filled with memories. The castle ruins have been falling into further decay since 1538 and one can sit and attempt to visualize Henry VIII's Navy anchoring at harbour. In search of that elusive stottie we returned to The Ship at Low Newton still by the sea. The square of former fishermen's cottages was unchanged, but soup now came with sough dough, something of a disappointment.

Seahouses was humming, clearly winning at life, with modern day religious mystics and wildlife watchers waddling like penguins to board ferries to the Farne Islands.

Catches in the covers on the cricket field shadowed by a castle colossus. Bamburgh's battlements, once a boarding school, stood like a defiant teenager towering above Budle Point. The Grace Darling Museum was still closed, so we revisited her grave to pay rescue respects. Our resting spot a lay-by overlooking Budle Bay with curious cows for company and Holy Island (Lindisfarne) in the distance. I dreamed I could play the harmonica and tambourine, I was in fact a dream seller, and someone was due to meet me on the corner. It was 1971, I had slightly longer hair, on The Old Grey Whistle Test with 'Whispering Bob' as an early Christian Abbot. I woke with a bit of a start as the Vikings arrived. Strange stuff doing a 180 and this coast backwards, at least I could empathise more with Spud and JT.

Both, on their walks had their vehicular supports. The 'Spudtruck' may not quite have been up to JT's camper van deal. PH had 'Snickers,' and now we had four wheels which seemed to need a name. Beluga I thought, after the whale, the over cab swelling resembled a melonhead. Having a backup van had its advantages while circumnavigating. You knew at the end of the day you would have somewhere to lay your head. It also came with drawbacks. The logistical nightmare of finding drivers. I imagined everyone would want to bag Cornwall in July, Hartlepool in February was not so popular. Then there were fuel costs, breakdowns, cry-offs and you might not meet quite so many people. Being gone for a year almost, we didn't have 52 friends, let alone that many who wanted to give up a week of their lives to drive a bus and be lumbered with me for a week.

The alternative was become a tortoise, carry your shelter and if you were lucky supplement that with offers of billets, be they private or commercial. Additionally, we found community buildings with kindly caretakers, something we had completely never planned for or imagined. Our experience in 2006/7 did bring us into contact with so many new, kind and generous people. Many had interesting back stories and meeting them enabled us to get a flavour of a place, over and above that of just parking up around the corner. We frequently had no idea as light was fading where we would stay. Scarier than having a mobile bedroom, but more exhilarating too, I wouldn't change that if I was doing it again.

We didn't have a TV to watch The Spinners, or tufted Wilton. My 'eavy breathing days had gone and the Y fronts were baggy with loose elastic'. With an avocado, the flameproof nighty buttons may have got slightly singed as we settled down to catch the moon fully up.

Chapter 48 - East Anglia Revisited - April 2022

Can music save your mortal soul?

"Open different doors, you may find a 'you' there that you never knew was yours. Anything can happen."

OUR EASTER BREAK should have taken us to Scotland, but Owain Wyn Evans had put paid to that. One might have thought sponsorship from the Welsh Tourist Board for all those suits, might have seen him drum up a bit of trade for The Valleys, but that didn't occur either. After Michael Fish in 1987, trust in weather forecasters remained suspect, but best give Owain the benefit of the doubt, bless him! Instead, we headed for Norfolk via an indirect route and ended up south of the river Waveney at Kessingland.

St Edmund's still had a thatched nave, though it was due a new toupee. The lady vicar told us Joan Oddy at 85 was still a dog lover, still something of a rebel, still receiving communion and I left her a message in the church visitors' book.

The beach down the cliff from The Hollies caravan park was quite inviting, much like I remembered the one at Benacre a bit further south. Lowestoft was less so. Oulten Broad was okay, the town centre more concrete carbuncle and not winning at life. A sign by the railway station outside the Tourist Information office read 'Cycle Route 1 to Great Yarmouth – 1 mile'! I mentioned it to the lady behind the desk who was decidedly uninterested and went back to filing her nails.

To check it out I drove to Corton and we walked with friends to Hopton on Sea. That bit alone was three miles, so rather like weather forecasters, never trust cycling signposts in Suffolk. Not the most attractive bit of coastline, the concrete promenade in one place completely destroyed. We had already seen the works involving the re-routing of a major pipeline due to coastal erosion. Now an enormous pile of giant rocks, hopefully not Russian, ready to be dropped in at the base of the cliff. Very numerous blue and yellow Ukrainian flags everywhere, supportive of the resistance to Mr Putin.

Later we ended up at Caister. The name thought to be derived from Latin meaning 'fortress'. That might have been incentive enough for the Romans to build a stronghold, some remains of which can still be seen.

In the Art Deco styling of the unpretentious Never Turn Back pub the landlord was very welcoming. Prices were equally inviting, I thought I was back in 2007, and he told us his business model was based on the 'grey' pound (£). I looked around, I think I got the meaning, I guess I was now one of them. (Good place to try selling the book!)

The pub sits slightly wearily behind the beach, neighbouring the proudly independent lifeboat sheds. Jet boats here remain the fastest in the country and I read a new all-weather boat was due later in the year. The 1901 disaster saw the lifeboat capsize when she tried to rescue a stricken boat on the Barber Sands, resulting in the loss of nine crew.

A village memorial remembers the event. Controversial conversations with some locals revealed the ethos of those now 'Never Turning Back' 'might' be guided as much by securing lucrative salvage rights as for saving lives.

Good Friday in Cromer revealed long queues for award winning fish and chips and a shortage of bottled camping gas, though the two were not related. Havoc would have been pleased to know there is now a 'Doggy' café where they can go and take their owners. The abundance of canines everywhere was it seemed resultant of pandemic lock downs. How soon before animal rescue shelters were overflowing when new owners decide they cannot go on holiday anymore? I chatted to one Doberman owner whose 11-year-old dog had been neutered two years earlier only to become arthritic as a result. I knew exactly how the old boy felt, should never have had that vasectomy!

One new thing was the Artspace Bigger Picture scheme which brought replicas of famous paintings to the streets. I liked the idea, and it seems locals valued it too. A second was the Deep History Trail encouraging explorers to visit 22 miles of coast here and with the aid of an app to discover something of pre-history and Doggerland, a land bridge that once linked the east coast to Europe. Such initiatives seemed to point in the direction of 'winning at life' to me.

Sheringham was busy on Easter Saturday. To avoid the crowds, I went for a haircut. My namesake reflected the sort of pace of life still to be found in Norfolk. Whenever he spoke, he turned off his clippers. He charged a tenner, at his rate of working he would earn £20 in a day, by the time he had finished the top of my head I had grown a beard. I now understood how so many people managed to become centenarians, I was at risk of becoming a dinosaur on the local app. As for my reflection, he never showed me a mirror, was that down to his clipper skills or my ever naturally emerging bald patch.

Seeing a sign for Upper Sheringham I just had to visit All Saints. Hedgerows leading inland were humming with bird song and verges blossomed with wildflowers, not least forget-me-nots. In fields rape, rows of commercial daffs and narcissi nearing their end and newly cultivated trenches, earthed up rows, soil cloches for potatoes, so perfect there was hardly a particle out of place. At the church I found the mermaid on a pew end, it brought a smile. As for the white witch's house, I think she had moved.

I took the next seven days revisiting north and west Norfolk's shoreline anticlockwise, all the way to Peter Scott's lighthouse at Sutton Bridge. Traditional flint and pebble houses proliferate. I wondered if so much hardcore was being purloined from the beaches what was going to hold back the tide. A five-storey windmill at Cley kept watch, it was sold in 1921 for £350, today you would have to put four noughts on the end of that.

At Blakeney local 'agricultural' accents amused. One old boy waxed lyrical about his 'carbureter,' at least that is what I think he was saying, rather strange since he was driving a wheeled Zimmer frame. It looked as if a pair of bumble bees had come to pollinate his ears, until I realised his tragi were a mass of whiskers! As us gentlemen of a certain age lose our hair so new growth sites emerge, we all suffer. If you visit a Turkish Barber, they will sometimes singe them with a flaming cotton wool bud. This guy would have caused a dual incendiary rousing. Other accents overheard were of miscellaneous international origin.

Nearly as entertaining were the antics of the waterfowl on the pond. Drake mallards squabbled for mating rights with outnumbered hens. One led her fluff ball offspring, the first seen this season, for an introductory paddle. Like clockwork bath toys they all disappeared in different directions. Keeping children under control, I knew all about those difficulties. A shell duck flew in. On landing with a neck extension, he raised his chest to air his wings, immediately the tail wiggled like a young John Travolta, and he stooped extending his bill to drink. I have seen this ritualistic behaviour from others, ducks that is, it is almost balletic. The capers of turkeys in a pen were just as showy. Aggressive and territorial, I named the biggest Bernard, but perhaps Vladimir might have been more appropriate.

On a strategically timed boat trip to the Point, terns took to the air in squadrons, alarmed by horsepower, and noisy oyster catchers skimmed the water surface like ornamental wall art trios. Atlantic grey seals lay on the sands, like Cuban smokes, occasionally raising a flipper to wave,

"Now please leave us alone".

As the tide retreated, all people trafficking franchises struggled to return to dry land, but we were in the 'Temple' not having to rely on 'Mr Bean'. (Some were disappointed it wasn't Sean!) As the sea fell back and disappeared it was just marked by vertical masts of wind turbines barely visible in the haze.

Evening sunshine and ruffles of clouds striped the huge sky, providing a nautical souvenir with pines silhouetted on the horizon at Holkham. At The House, home of the Coke family (pronounced Cook), Earls of Leicester, Holm oaks nibbled by the estate deer. The Cokes have had a lot to do with agriculture, historically their money helped push back the sea, create a seawall, establish new fields and extend the cultivatable acreage. A railway once ran from Holme to Wells but it was lost in the early 1950s when sea defences were breached, never to be replaced. Mankind might tinker, but the power of nature has the final say.

In fields hares played 'you can't see me', something they were really not very good at with winter wheat just a few centimetres tall and where they had done their worst, it was grazed to a cricket wicket. Scarecrows seem totally outmoded for 2022, pigeons and jackdaws were unphased and intrepid crows and gulls shared bird talk resting on straw filled shoulders. Nearby young pigs frolicked in dusty pens, while sows snoozed and sunbathed.

In Wells there were archers at The Buttlands, but they came via Radio 4. The harbour miniature railway marked on my AA 2022 road atlas had shunted off without trace. The ten inch inland one to Little Walsingham was serving those pilgrims wishing to visit the shrines. The gantry leading from apartments, once harbourside maltings, was as distinctive as I remembered. Seeing the name 'Frary' on a seafood stall, I asked if Alan was still around, but he had retired and moved to Scotland. Their gain, our loss.

We searched high and low for the artwork horse installed to commemorate equine lifeboat launching but it seemed to have bolted. Either enticed away to join Lloyds, still in a winter storage stable or repatriated by artist, Rachael Long. It wasn't until we requested a photo finish that wc spotted it, directly opposite that gantry and the Frary crab caravan. Close by a lobster hatchery, only set up in 2021 to improve sustainability in the area. 'Berried hens', egg laden females, are raised and young hatched for future release and ultimately table centre thermidor.

Stiffkey had a yard where wooden boats were brought back to their former glory. No G cramps are spared in replacing wooden gunwales on cockles, sailing dinghies. A 15-foot boat can easily employ around 70. In Morston harbour, the oldest local boat 'Mary', resembling a small Noah's ark sat on a mooring close to the former lifeboat station on Blakeney Point, closed 1935.

The six-storey windmill at Burnham Ovary Staithe was just as I remembered it. There were no yellow legs at Titchwell and they hadn't taken my advice and changed the name to 'Twitchwell'. Hunstanton's cliffs didn't seem quite so tall, and I couldn't really recall the distinctive zig-zag beach groynes, but we all have memory issues sometime. The 4000-year-old sea henge washed up at Holme in 1998 is now in a museum in Kings Lynn. The iconic Campbell's soup tower closed the same year we were there - 2007, was blown up in 2012, making way for a new business park.

As we made our way past three villages carrying the name Walpole (wall pool) I was reminded of Sir Robert, Whig, hard hitter in 1720s - 40s, who came from nearby at Houghton Hall and had a 20-year uninterrupted run as British Prime Minister. The key to this success, stay clear of too many parties and be careful who you give jobs to.

The twin lighthouses at the end of the Nene outfall hadn't changed. The proposed Snow Goose visitor centre hadn't hatched. The Sutton Bridge Hotel was in ruins, a sorry sight, but as we made our way through the fens at Wisbech I did spot a sign for Chris Boyall's chippy. Somehow, whatever he did, he would be winning at life.

'I can still remember' so much vividly from 2006/7. 'Music made me smile' during the walk. Come a breakup in 2008 I could 'hardly take one more step, hands clenched in fists of rage.' We can strip bare the lines of Don McLean's American Pie (1971) for his meaning in exasperation, but we find our own within lyrics too. Music moves through the fabric of our lives. Fourteen years on for me, I had found a perfect fusion, 'learned to dance real slow.' Music saved a mortal soul. It certainly helped to 'soothe a savage breast.' Winning at life? dunwalkin, but on the right path.

Chapter 49 - Reflections at Southend, September 2020

If I never loved, I never would have cried

"The future is you revisiting places you've once been, with a fresh set of eyes. It's the closest thing we can ever get to time travelling."

WE DECIDED TO overnight in the car park at Two Trees Island, just outside Leigh-on-Sea and spitting distance for any coastal walker from Southend. The Two Trees which presumably gave it its name were not obvious, chain sawed, just many bushes as we arrived in the dark, I had noted it in my 2007 diary. I was glad we didn't have to pitch a tent there. Arriving on Friday night 25 September 2020 in the dark I almost drove down the slipway to park, or to sink in the mud flats of the Thames. Thank God Liz stopped me. I wondered if it was a dogging venue, fly tippers' holy grail, teenage courting couples or boy racer haven. There is little worse than youths practicing their wheelies revving throbbing engines, puking out copious fumes from exhausts with stereos turned to full blast. We wouldn't be able to see them through their tinted windscreens and it was pitch black anyway. Liz chipped in,

"You do take me to some lovely places!"

Liz, was my 'new' partner, we had been together since 2012. In 2007 she was that mum doing the ironing and making packed lunches, the other side of the river, just outside Gravesend. We were in our second 'waggy'.

The night hours passed with very little racer disturbance and hardly any sex. Daylight brought signs of a little litter, but no heaps dumped by inconsiderate fly tippers. There were some discarded facemasks – a sign of the times, and a group of five boys playing football ... but not with a ball. They asked if I wanted to join in and I politely declined, muttering something about an old war wound but asked what they were kicking around.

"A pocket pussy" came the reply.

I had to ask "what?" and they repeated,

"A pocket pussy – you put your dick in it!"

Later, I had to Google it, 'toy for solo fun/artificial vagina' and my education was fuller, at least on the topic of male cravings.

Elsewhere the saltings and river-lets remained much as they had been in 2007. Eel grass which made the estuary such an important place for birdlife was prolific. In fact, 13 wild fowl species can commonly be seen. I know this because I saw it on an information board. I loved these, and read the Thames supports the fifth largest total of wintering waterfowl, you might even spot an Iolo Williams.

There were concrete filled 'sandbags' used as a seawall, and the railway hugs the coast. Another couple picnicked in their car; a mum led her wellie wearing toddler to splash in puddles. A sign read 'no dogs on the slipway' – I thought Havoc would have been inconsolable. It was also £39 for a summer motorboat launching. Goodness knows much I would have been charged if I had driven down the ramp the night before.

We cycled out to Old Leigh, passing the old golf driving range which I remembered. It had reminded me back in 2007 of the 1996 film Tin Cup starring Kevin Costner. It was thoughts like these that would stay with you as you walked, breaking down the miles as you trudged to the next punctuation point on a 5000-mile trek. Now the range looked rather ram shackled. Magpies dodged golf balls as they landed. They collected and hoarded them, ready for re sale to ball-less links men.

At Old Leigh we passed Osbornes supplying cockles and the like. The part cobbled street contrasted sharply with the rather shabby Two Trees Island. Large wooden posts hooped with old tyres fended off arriving and mooring boats. There were the remains of a very old water spring, with another illuminating information board. Ye Olde Smack pub owing its name to a type of fishing boat. Even the burnt-out Leigh Fishermen's Co-op building gave the place a certain charm. Helen Mirren was brought up here and went to school locally. I wondered if she visits for a 'smack' and a rendition in the style of Molly Malone.

A little further along we passed the Essex Yacht Club with its appealing headquarters; a ship – The Wilton. A former HMS minesweeper, the first ever glass fibre warship that was affectionately known by some as HMS Tupperware. I was reminded of The Egremont, an old Mersey ferry, once a sailing base in the Salcombe estuary in Devon. I visited it many times with groups of visually impaired school children from Exeter. Its future was in doubt in 2018. Up for sale in 2020 if you had a spare £100,000 and I am unsure if the iconic vessel survived the breakers?

Cockle pickers could be seen wading the mud flats and at low water any number of sea paddling pools became visible right along the front. There were no children in these today but a little further along kids pranced and skipped in the floor fountains and pools created at Southend. Oh, how I wished for that energy in 2007 and even more now. How quickly that youthful, physical exuberance disappears, but where does it go? A beach metal detectorist searched for a forsaken 20 pence piece - 13 years ago, I would have mugged them for it to put in my collecting tin.

The Oyster Creek Kitchen on the Western Esplanade and the eatery/cafes at The Arches, resourcefully created, were very inviting. The air was bracing, the wind ripping from the east and there were abundant amusements at Adventure Island. Nearby, the aquarium asked, 'who would like to be a little otter?' and there were long queues. We chose to eat at Ocean Beach on the Eastern Esplanade. £21 for two posh sandwiches – a lot more than the £10 daily budget we had in 2006/7 to feed two adults and a dog. They were actually very good and lip-smackingly tasty. A twin room at The Castle pub opposite for £42 seemed like a no brainer if you were a walking couple without a tent, campervan or hash backup. The Harvester at Shoeburyness presumably minus buffet at this time, and the Toby Carvery which frankly looked awful, were not so inviting.

Masks, one-way systems, hand sanitiser, disclosure of contact details, table service only, socially distancing footprints stencilled on the pavement and hand washing instructions for 20 seconds in the loos were further signs of the time. iPad ordering devices, payment apps even portable card reading machines – all now part of everyday life. I don't remember their existence in 2007 and I am fighting off possession of an iPhone myself with every sinew.

On the beach itself crows patrolled with a waddle of authority. I couldn't decide whether dunnets scurried and scampered or dashed and darted but whatever it was, it was bloomin' quick. A single sandling stood wondering what all the fuss was about, and seaweed and dry leaves tumbled straight out of a Western movie. With the tide out, boats listed – their keels on mud flats as if they were struggling to stand but failing after a heavy night at Wetherspoons.

We cycled as far as Shoeburyness Common and the prominent mast of the Coastguard station. This was as far as I had walked in 2007, beyond to the northeast the military ranges of Foulness. Cycle paths were very good, in places if you detoured you might risk a £100 fine as well as mowing down a local. Some walked, others jogged, many squeezed into rather unflattering hi viz Lycra while clinging to their hydration bottles.

At least there was no shortage of public loos if you happened to be caught short – there seemed enough for one each for the whole of southeast England. A road sign saying 'Caution Boats Crossing' made me chuckle. The boat park was inland from the main road, meaning launching would involve a trailer road crossing.

Now I know stereotypical views are over simplified and generalised which might lead to expectation, but they must originate somewhere, right! That of an Essex girl is widely known, JT referred to it. The number of girls with long straight blonde hair, suntanned (to the extent that they must have been under a sunlamp for the last six months), with fur lining protruding from their Ugg boots, phone at the horizontal in one hand and fag in the other was uncanny. Many having said this, were very attractive and Essex folk in general were very pleasant I found. They would make eye contact sometimes above their face mask and exuded a sense of well-being and self-confidence. When I was asked by the very pleasant waitress in the Ocean Beach if I wanted chips with my sandwich, I replied,

"No thank you, I'm saving myself".

The lady on the socially distanced table next to us smiled as if to say, "Why bother!"

What can only bc dcscribed as large see-through Perspex ice cubes could be found along the front. All the trappings of a consumer over-packaged society on display, showing what had been picked up in the last 24 hours

over (x-number) metres of seafront. Clearly these were designed to prick the conscience and deter careless littering. I wasn't sure of their value. It was a bit like the question 'do you have litter bins or not?'

If present, they are often so overflowing, rubbish spills out everywhere. If not, there is nowhere to dispose of litter so people just throw it down anyway- take it home, some hope. All that could really be concluded is that our throwaway society is shameful, trophy cabinets showing off our squander and ignominy. This is the on-street evidence of our wilful planet destruction, that such as micro plastics wholly as hideous and dangerous to marine life, just not so easily seen.

We could not leave without actually going on the pier. I did not remember the entrance, it seemed to have had a bit of a makeover since 2007. Posters informed fishermen what size of cod or lobster they caught could be taken home and dogs were still not allowed! I would point out that there is considerable RNLI infrastructure on the land end of this lengthy antennae. Between it and the boathouse, where Havoc had not been allowed, are housed an Atlantic (85) B class, two D class inshore boats and a hovercraft. All named Vera or Len, or William, or Julia and Agnes after subscribers. Legacy is of course one of the principal ways of funding, which the RNLI target.

The pier itself is one of some 42 around England with a further six or so in Wales. It has survived fires, partial destruction, rebuilding, and two World Wars since 1829. The Sir William Heygate train trundles past those who choose to walk its length as we did, passing the elaborate metal cast backs of resting benches and noting that the main hardwood plank decking is 13 boards wide. Not for the superstitious. You can sponsor a board if you care to do so.

We enjoyed tea and a bun at Jamie and Jimmy's Café at the far end but because of social distancing could not view all the celebrity photos hanging from the walls with the exception, and somewhat ironically, that of the vertically challenged Danny de Vito and Warwick Davies. Celebrity spotting over, we crawled back against the wind, retaining the entry ticket as a keepsake. The wonderfully eccentric late John Helsden, Wendy's father, who was not averse to collecting, notably bricks and tickets, would I am sure have viewed it for his collection. (Adults 17-59 – summer - £2 each. I was 62, did I need to pay?)

On returning to Two Trees car park our camper, looking like a beluga whale, lay alone and stranded on the tarmac. Fortunately, this melon headed monster did not need refloating. As I loaded the bikes on the carrying rack a fox appeared. It was not a grey/brown urban fox but a youngish red one. It remained no more than six feet away, not frightened by beluga or me. I even had to close the side door in case he decided to hop in for a lift or a spare chicken drumstick. Havoc, I couldn't help thinking, would have been loud, highly excited, overly curious and lunging so much he would have emulated a rearing Lipizzaner. It also made me think back to a snared fox in Scotland. Eventually we left this one alone to the Essex Wildlife Trust Nature Reserve.

The visit brought it home that taking one's time is important if you want to see anything. We had not rushed at all in 2006/7, just conscious of getting on to our next point/destination. JM averaging three miles per hour and covering 30 miles a day without breaks was indeed an extraordinary marathon walker, but he must have been an extraordinary observer also if he managed to see anything circumnavigating this sceptred isle.

Southend - 13 years on from the walk, winning at life? I think it was trying hard and generally succeeding, sounding like a pupil school report I used to write. PH had a view on this, he concluded nearness and commutability to London partly explained why it was outdoing other places more far flung. Would I be returning any time soon? I hoped so, if only on the off chance of bumping into Helen Mirren.

The master lyricist, Paul Simon's (1965) words resonated. 'Sleeping in my memory', 'books and poetry to protect me' - the rock hurdled, isolation and detachment over, the decision was made to write my story, with Liz's blessing and offers of support.

Chapter 50 - Gravesend revisited, to become a new home

Brushing off the dust, you hear my voice, I am a champion hear me roar

"It was an opportunity to honour, retaining just the right amount of memories to bring out flavour, and leaving plenty of room for new ones."

THIS ONE WAS MORE all-consuming. I moved there in late 2012, to be near a new partner and foster a fledgling relationship, distance ones never work, you must be prepared to commit.

Landmarks - well there were some new ones. HS1 had opened in November 2007, with a new station at Ebbsfleet, some said it sparked regeneration to the area. I found Windmill Hill and with it views east to London's skyline. I discovered Gravesend had a large Sikh community, 15,000, 15% of the population. I think the gurdwara (temple, residence of the Guru) was largely on its way back in 2007 but as far as I can discover it opened officially in 2010. The Guri Nanak Darbar is one of the largest outside India and cost £12 million. When Liz, my new partner, and I would cycle to the west its turrets and domes stood proud on the horizon and would transport you to Agra and the Taj Mahal.

On one of those cycle trips, we were returning as light was fading. I had been scrumping plums near Cliff, a carrier bag on my handlebars and neither of us any lights. We were making good time and from behind us a voice saying,

"Stop, Police!"

We turned to find a Policeman on a push bike, very out of breath, saying

"I could hardly keep up with you and where are your lights?"

We explained we were making haste to return home before it got any darker.

"I could give you an on-the-spot fine" was the reply!

This was in the middle of countryside, no houses, or streetlights, and it begs at least four questions. When was the last time you saw a Policeman on a bike? What was he doing in this location, there certainly wasn't much crime to deter? Covert surveillance on Kent's dogging activity? Was his uniform, and bike for that matter really Police issue? We never stopped for answers, apologised, got going again, I think he might have been hard pushed to catch us in a chase. As for the plums, he never asked, they were delicious!

In subsequent years new statues have popped up, landmarks, I loved them. A bronze of Elizabeth II near the river in 2018, showing the council's patriotism, minus traffic cones on my viewings. Not far away one of Squadron Leader Mahinder Singh Pujji 2014, distinguished RAF fighter pilot celebrating racial diversity and India's contribution to the British war effort. A little away from the river, old Queen Vic had her traffic cone, the question was it the same one as in 2007?

Other ambitious proposals have been formulated to rejuvenate the area. A lower Thames crossing. It soon becomes apparent when living there if you want to go anywhere to the north, you first must go to Dartford and endure the inevitable traffic jams. A Thames Hub airport on Grain, still some seven years off at least at the time of writing. A Swanscombe peninsula theme park, Kent's answer to Disneyland, still away with Tinkerbell. What is new is a crematorium at Chalk, Thames View, inescapable endings face us all.

Having shelved the walking boots, I dipped my toe back into education moving to Gravesend. Minibus drivers are always in demand and one such trip was to Reculver. Humanities field trip, combining all things SPQR with counting rocks on the beach. A favoured destination for all Kent's Year 10, the thing they learnt most was the phone signal was rubbish.

I got very close up with the river traffic, piloting the rescue boat for students learning to row. One eventful afternoon saw two teenage girls ram a large mooring buoy and capsize. I was there to haul them in and retrieve a shattered boat, but it didn't stop the Port Authority launching theirs to inspect the buoy and take a look at our damaged 'quinquereme'. The nursery rhyme 'Girls and 'buoys' come out to play' came to mind, 'come with a whoop, come with a life jacket, come with fibre glass resin or not at all!'

Was Gravesend winning at life? Not if you ask many about shops in the town centre. Not if you only look at PH's photo page 201. Yes, if you are into escape rooms, I don't remember them being around in 2007, unless you lived in Japan. Gravesend has a bit of a reputation for the Houdini-esque phenomena as well as regularly being one of the hottest places in the country. (Highs can reach 38 degrees C).

In the last 11 years I have seen quite a lot of Gravesend and the surrounding area. From being chased by policemen, to the inside of schools, fishing teenagers out of the river, breaking bread at the temple, viewing the public art works and attending funerals at the crematorium. The Katy Perry hit from 2013 struck a chord for me then. 'Rock the boat, I got up, shake the ground, a fighter' - my time to 'Roar'.

Chapter 51 - Westgate and Thanet revisited, July 2021

There are places I'll remember

"Reduce the spread, keep 2metres apart."

FOURTEEN YEARS ON it was time to revisit east Kent. On a July Friday evening we departed in our motorhome, arriving late with half an above cab window missing - ripped off on the A299. A Samaritan garage owner gave us a bin bag and very adhesive 'pandemic floor distancing stickers' for a temporary repair. We parked up on the seafront at St Mildred's Bay, Westgate by 11.30pm. In the morning circular discs with footprints made it look like half of Thanet had walked over our van in the night and we half expected the remainder to be orderly queuing for breakfasts. A memorable start to the weekend.

I looked again at the war memorial, now with time to ponder the names. Luck, Price and Champs. None of them had luck to be able to return to their homes, all paid the ultimate price, all were champs. The only 'Pointer' for humanity that was 50 less (29) died in WWII, (79) were lost in the Great War. Mankind was moving in the right direction.

We cycled west on route 15 to Minnis Bay and on to Reculver. The sea was a black headed gull bobbing one, with pongy pockets of rotting seaweed. Vibrant lanky Korean dandelions, purple thistles, teasels, ragwort and mallow. Off white cow parsley, hogweed, hemlock and Queen Anne's Lace. Pink pigmy bell flowers of field bind weed and blushing cultivated salt cedar with grasses by the dozen, and fun for all hay fever sufferers, made me think how different an outlook one gets seasonally and with life's years passing.

To the right, black cormorants socially distanced on groin end posts with their washing drying. To the left telescopes lay dormant on observation balconies fronting architect designed, nautically inspired dwellings on unimaginatively named streets like 'Sea Road' and 'Cliff Field'. Low chalk cliffs fractured and rounded, weathered crevasses home to some birds and bats. The mineral calcite limestone, once microscopic sea plankton, now made a perfect and readily available 'artists' material. Tic-tac-toe and hopscotch beneath our tyres, 'Boris is a poo bag', 'The Queen a drug baron', and 'Priti Patel eats babies', apparently, all while watching our progress.

As we retraced our cycle tracks, dodging 'pink flamingoes' and 'green crocodiles', a sign it was summer and the inflatables were out, I couldn't help thinking the Battle of Britain was fought above our heads 80 odd years ago and 25 before that sea planes from a base at Westgate patrolled the skies, then the Royal Navy Air Service (RNAS) which would become absorbed into the RAF. Offshore, a proliferation of wind turbines since 2007, now covering 35 square miles and providing renewable power for 200,000 homes. I would need to pedal hard to generate that much.

Clusters of people met in shelters, a dog walker, someone on a mobility scooter, groups of three or four all bird watching or chewing the fat and putting the world to right. Regular faces it seemed, this was home for some, their patch, we just like in 2007 were only passing through.

John Betjeman wrote a poem entitled 'Westgate-on-Sea'. We didn't see any 'prunes' or 'suet', 'wire on glasses or teeth' but we did see a bride rushing from her 'steeple' to a reception, in trainers rather than 'plimsolls', 'bursting' from her dress, perhaps the result of too much suet!

In Margate the awful tower block remained as did the more welcoming Yacht club from 2007. The clock tower with its sailor's time ball had seen some refurbishment and the Turner Contemporary had arrived at a cost of £17.5million along with a cast iron Gormley on his holidays from Crosby. A catalyst for regeneration - for me the jury was still out.

The sunken garden had not disappeared to Atlantis, low maintenance gardening techniques had saved it, sacrificing high maintenance immaculateness. Paint scorched terraces in the Old Town, tired pubs and takeaways and I wondered if the buffet at the Bull's Head, where Eric Morcombe had his wedding reception, still served sandwiches with curled up corners.

Broadstairs was still more 'easy footing'. We enjoyed an ice cream on a freshly re-painted bench and discussed what flavour green Clanger soup was? Oliver Postgate, the writer of the children's TV series lived here, according to the blue plaque and accompanying Clanger mouse mosaic. How do you write Clanger speak? They whistled! Rumour has it in one episode, when a door would not open, Postgate had written,

"Sod it, the bloody thing's stuck again!"

He was behind, Bagpuss, Ivor the Engine and Noggin the Nog, so we did our best to try whistling,

"Oh dear, the silly thing's not working again!"

I tried to imagine what Postgate and Dickens, a frequent visitor and who seemed to be keeping the town clear of 'Hard Times', would have made of offenders doing community service sanding, scraping and renewing paintwork. It seemed to me they were doing a good job, somewhat at Victorian pace, with childlike work naivety, but resulting in a Broadstairs that appeared winning at life and with 'Great Expectations'.

I had my memories from 2007- they had something to do with 'Rubber Souls' (soles). Liz, my now partner, had hers of Westgate from childhood. Walking donkeys on the beach, family holidays. Places to remember, all our lives, 'some not for better, some remain, some have changed.' (In My Life - The Beatles, 1965).

Chapter 52 - Southwest, living there 2008-2012 and revisiting October 2020

The only truth I know is you

"Hard to tell where Heaven stops, and the earth begins. Of all the paths you take in life - make sure one of them is to the Southwest."

HAVING FINISHED THE WALK at the back end of 2007, I lived in Bovey Tracy, the eastern gateway to Dartmoor and as time went on, I moved to the southern edge near Ivybridge for work and to distance myself from Wendy. Hashing almost exclusively with South Hams either running, laying trials or RA- ing! (Self-gratifying and feeding the ego - like Mel Brookes, 'I was a large admirer of my own work!') In many ways the hash was my saviour. The unwritten rule, I would hash with South Hams, Wendy would keep to Teign Valley.

However, I was on duty one night in Paignton when Wendy turned up and by coincidence, I had to award her a run badge, something like 100 or 200 runs achieved. Other times too, she might appear with a partner, dressed saucily at a halloween run (Charleton), or a special night canoeing/running in Exeter, or at the South Hams annual dinner (Berry Head) or South Brent to be nosey, or Dartington to rub my nose in it, (comments while I picked up dog mess from a pooch, 'Callie,' I had taken along for the run). All pretty much designed to build my distress and remind me I was no longer with her. I was left humming an old Tremeloes hit, 'Here comes my baby - and it comes as no surprise to me, with another guy'.

But I was getting out there, seeing the county and a day job would take me to Teignmouth and Torquay, Dartmouth and Dittisham, Bigbury and Plymouth. I loved seeing the coast and living there, I was never conscious of much changing. On one occasion while working and living at Blackadon Holiday Barns a group came down for a works weekend away from the Chinese embassy in London. I was charged with driving the minibus and showing them the delights. They never quite made it out of the bus at Princetown, stilettoes are not too useful on the moor but they loved collecting limpets from the rocks at Salcombe and BBQing back at the farm, (bit 'wubberwy' for me).

Steep and rugged slopes, a lonesome pine tree, deckchairs on a promenade change little over the years and in Devon the pace of change thankfully unhurried.

I moved to Kent in September 2012 leaving behind my beloved Devon and hashing. I have been back to the Southwest a few times since. A week's holiday in October 2020 took my partner Liz and I via carnival town Bridgwater to Minehead. Something didn't feel right, then I realized we were going the wrong way (anticlockwise). Exeter Chiefs were playing Wasps in the Premiership final (winning 19-13). That was different, back in 2007 I don't remember them being that successful and certainly not back in my playing days at Exeter. Flags and shirts, even though we were in Somerset showed Chiefs were now a regional elite. We watched the game at Minehead Barbarians RFC and that was different too, for the wrong reasons. There was no sense of a friendly welcome which I have always found at every other club I have visited. No opportunity to park our motorhome in their car park overnight, was that the pandemic? No opportunity to try out a child's hoverboard (Segway without handlebars) - I would have loved a go. These were new, developed 2013. We slept in the van, parked up in an industrial estate.

On the seafront Butlins was still tented with eight poles and wires. Where Wendy and I had 'fought', Liz and I are more like 'carrots and peas' which made watching Forest Gump all the more enjoyable. Conifer covered hills rolled down to the sea, cottages tucked down behind a seawall and an offshore wind constantly changed the colour of the bay and sky. Artists would have hated it; a half decent windsurfer would be in Barry in ten minutes. I checked out the Owen Cunningham hands and map sculpture, designed by Sarah Ward, marking 630miles to South Haven Point since 2001, and looked for MW witnessed graffiti in bus shelters 1982, but still didn't find any.

Outside the public loos a very strange aroma. I asked the bloke disappearing in a cloud, 'what's that?'

"Dinner Lady - Lemon Tart" came the reply.

I thought that's no way to talk about Victoria Wood and was none the wiser. It was a vape flavour, that was different from 2007, I don't remember passing any vaping shops, although apparently, they had been around a couple of years. Started as an antidote for smoking, it may have its place in fighting the irreversible consequences of tar, carbon monoxide and the like but vape still contains nicotine and that is addictive. In 2023 - it is reported as a growing problem with teenager use. How is it that mankind works on one problem only to create another? Action - consequence, almost as perennial as Newton's third law.

Inside the automated loos, claustrophobic chaos. Place hands under, press for soap, wash for 20 secs, the dryer to the right (a Somerset shrew rather than a Welsh dragon). Another press here, the black button had worn off, how to lock/open door left me totally bewildered. I found the whole experience so intimidating I wet myself. While toweling off my groin I noticed there were no braille signs, David Blunkett - stay clear of Minehead. Having worked through the instructions of how to open the door, I failed to find it for another ten minutes and was only rescued by a citrus smelling hombre himself now needing relief. He could have been a Mexican, but it might just have been what the vape had done to his skin.

Back in the van from Porlock we took the toll road through beautiful woods and views over Porlock Weir. It cost us £5 at the other end, I hadn't had to pay on foot, but then this time I didn't get ill from sleeping in dog poo.

The Exmoor coast is one of the highest, wildest and most scenic in the country. Between Porlock and Foreland Point is the longest stretch of coastal woodland in England and Wales.

Inland the Doone Valley, inspirational for RD Blackmore's, 1869, romance 'Lorna Doone'. I reminisced. First to 1978 when as 'three amigos' on summer camp from St Luke's, two mates and I got lost on Darlick moors (a skip and a jump west of Withypool). Secondly, to visiting with Wendy prior to the walk and exploring Blackmore's tale of 'Jan' and 'Lorna'. Poignantly, I found myself humming Stevie Wonder's 'part time lover - undercover passion on the run', auspiciously. On the radio Art Garfunkel's 'I believe when I fall in love, (this time) it will be forever'.

We dropped into Lynmouth and struggled to find anywhere to park; should have been walking. Surfers were providing revenue for the town council in parking fines if nothing else. The romantic poets liked to stay here, and I wondered what the rooms were like in the Shelley Hotel.

Now it was time to ride the funicular railway *up* to Lynton. George Newness paid for it and the ride was completed in 1890. We stepped into Guns Art Gallery and chatted to the owner about the pandemic lock down and how it had affected business. He described this half term opening as a tap with him collecting what he could before closing for the winter. I asked if he would survive and the stoic reply came,

"We have been here 127 years; this little blip will not stop us."

Outside and looking towards Countesbury the coast looked impossible with no path visible. It made it even more mind boggling how they got the Louisa up there in 1899, how had I managed it in 2007?

Combe Martin is arguably the longest village street in England. One and a half miles, the road name changes seven times along its length. RB mentions this saying it's the second, he goes on to name Stewkley in Bucks as the longest. In truth it is a very different village. (Any number of sideroads intersect with North and South High Street and at the triangular junction by the church one route shoots off to Soulbury. It has a far less linear feel about it.)

I remembered the Pack o Cards, 'the only noteworthy building in the village'. Still there, four storeys, 13 doors on each floor, and 52 stairs. Built in 1690 by a certain George Ley who apparently got quite lucky at the gambling table. I also remembered borrowing a swig of meths. I should have been bold, asked for two quid and gone next door to buy a bottle of White Lightening (other ciders are available but not nearly so cheap).

Ilfracombe had definitely upped its game from 2007 or at least it grabbed my attention more. Perhaps I wasn't smarting so much many years on, having not been given an interview (2004). Overlooking Hillborough period terraces and mansions that seemed to have been given a facelift. Even the 14th century chapel on top of Lantern Hill had seen a coat of paint.

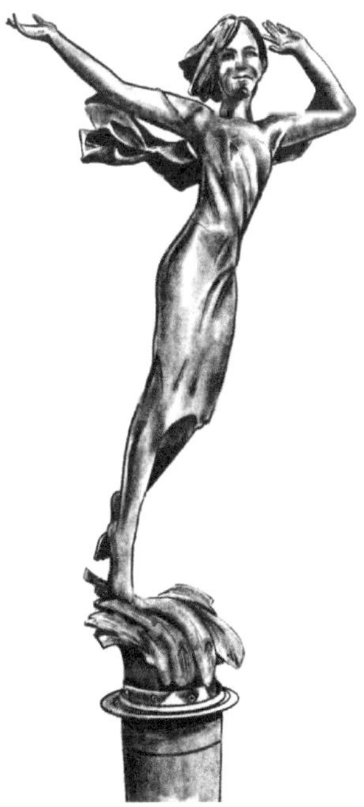

Nearby a nymph like statue, Ekaterine (Kate) remembering a 14-year-old Russian girl who fell to her death here in 2000. (It seemed right to give mention to this, a girl full of beauty and energy with a life ahead of her. At the time of writing Russia are a week into a war with Ukraine, may the smile of this girl open hearts of those who wage it. Who knows how things will unfold, the fate of the world seemingly in the hands of one man?)

Elsewhere tunnels and a Bath House, converted as a wedding venue. By 2020 covid had put paid to many bookings. Triple jumper Jonathan Edwards lived here 1976-87 and mosaics mark his achievements, 18.29m, still a world record since 1995, that's 60 feet. There was a 'Happy Bench' with an inscription, 'Nobody needs to feel lonely'. At the pier since 2012, Damian Hurst's 'Verity.' A 20m bronze, full of symbolism, which seems to have boosted tourism. Nearby, children catching crabs and filling their buckets.

The Admiral Collingwood, Wetherspoons, had taken on the 'Landmark' cone theme, but had suffered a mastectomy. The loo doors were covidly wedged open, I wouldn't have the same ensnared experience as Minehead. The numbered dining tables were busy for early evening Sunday meals. I looked for a menu but couldn't find one for the obesity. Deep fried everything didn't help. My mind went to Squeeze Gut Alley in Whitstable, JM's Mars Bars, SH/RH weight loss, and PH's ice creams. I was no lightweight, as a child always told to clear your plate, bread and dripping for Sunday tea. Always an eye for a bargain a sucker for 'buy one get one free,' but the ship's crew here had been on more than four square meals a day. Collingwood needed to discover plyometrics.

Beautiful Rockham Bay on the way to Woolacombe, the chosen view for June, in the 2021 coastline calendar.

We parked up at Blackmoor Gate. Exmoor was Europe's first International Dark Sky reserve, 2011, but we didn't see the Milky Way (or any other chocolate bars!) We cycled the next morning to allow me to revisit Paracombe, Heddon's Mouth, Hunter's Inn, Woody Bay, Lee Abbey and the Valley of the Rocks, but ended up pushing the bikes a lot of the way. Those thinking they might cycle around as opposed to walking, it's not as easy as it sounds.

We ate in Instow, the same place Wendy and I had stayed at in 2007, then drove to Bude. The car parks were full, half term, but people not going abroad. There was a line of 'Just Go' rented motor homes, everyone was after them. There were swimmers doing laps in the sea pool, the surf schools were handing out neoprene like the nit nurse used to give out lavender oil and vinegar, and grandparents juggled ice creams and clubs at the ornamental golf, the sparkle in their eyes not knowing to lick or putt. RNLI beach lifeguards were supposed to be on duty until 6pm; when I was sure it would be dark by 5pm! The cliff line stretched out to the south, and we headed that way with deja vu memories in Boscastle and Tintagel.

At Port Gaverne I looked for evidence of a once thriving slate shipping industry but found very little, sorry SH. There was also scant evidence of any fishing at Port Isaac. Wandering around the harbour we saw no boats, no fish, and no cats! I wondered if we might bump into MW's stammering, bloody aproned fffffffish operative, but he seemed to have fff"ked off too! The nooks, crannies and alleys were relatively quiet. I guess the fishermen had all 'gone fishing' or joined the shanty singers and were touring or a making a movie. I wondered what it is like to live there now. What was the depth of community spirit? Who could afford to live there? Second homes, without lights on, seemed popular. What was it like living with tourists and /or film crews? As for registering with a doctor, you may as well put your name down with the figurehead above the sweet shop.

As we travelled further south my simplistic general impression was that properties were looking better. There was more pride in the appearance of houses, perhaps a wealthier economy than I remembered, perhaps more holiday homeowners with more money to throw at their little piece of Cornwall. New builds weren't the carbuncles on the face of a much-loved friend that they used to be, or planners were reigning in architects. Wind and solar farms were proliferating, but we needed to get energy somehow.

We braved the rain south of Portreath for a walk, for me revisiting the razor-edged rocky cove at Ralph's Cupboard. At Hell's Mouth the sea was exploding at the base of black cliffs, it was aptly named. Inland there is a prominent monument on Cornwall's highest point, Carn Brea. A 27m high Celtic cross is dedicated to Francis Bassett, died 1835, a politician whose character featured in the Poldark novels. Redruth was also aptly named, it literally means 'ford red'. We were heading for the point where the Red River (Koner) meets the sea beyond Godrevy. Minerals released into it formerly turned the water red. This was mining country, Redruth and Camborne mining towns. They also used to play an interesting brand of rugby that I can testify to, the red might aptly have been the blood shed at Hell Fire Corner. Our walk was cut short as the air ambulance and rescue services sprang into action at Gwithian. I read later nine people were swept into the water by waves, fortunately they were all rescued (28/10/2020).

I got talking to a fisherman at Hayle as he salted a catch and stuffed it into tubs. There were winter mackerel to be had, as a result of warmer waters, and 'good money' to be made, larger fish sold, smaller ones kept for lobster bait. But there were also controversial new building projects happening and fishermen were feeling marginalised. Leisure and retail units and £1 million houses didn't want bait tubs as neighbours. House prices had rocketed and affordable housing for the likes of him and youngsters hard to find. The same was true at St Ives. If anything, it was worse there, and according to him anywhere near the sea in Cornwall was the same. He would feature in a BBC 2 documentary shown in

February 2021 highlighting the problems as harbours and towns like Hayle were dragged into the 21st century.

At Penzance we called into the Yacht Inn. Unfortunately, we heard Peter George from back in 2007 had passed away, RIP. We were told hundreds turned up to see him off. We also tried to get back in touch with Eddie Wood but were told he had health issues of his own and what with Covid was shielding. The Yacht Inn is an Art Deco building with a similarly styled lido, the Jubilee pool in front of it, the largest seawater pool in the country, surely a winner with all those who have taken up outdoor swimming.

Humphrey Davy, the chemist and inventor of the safety mining lamp (1815) was born here and about 20 years later a piece of architecture was put up that has caught eyes since - the Egyptian House. The brown and cream paintwork and styling took my eye this time around with a bit more time to explore. The Round House and Chocolate House were also fun to find.

The railway arrived, the station the most southerly in Britain saw the first passengers from London in the 1860s. Traditional industries used to send potatoes, broccoli, fruit, flowers and fish the other way but the decline of Cornwall's staples - mining, fishing, agriculture have led to a downturn economically.

Today it might take tourists just five and a bit hours, to do the 275 odd miles, six and a bit in a car. In 2007 it took us 50 days to walk from London to Penzance. In 2020, we could still see the signs of relatively expensive housing, low wages and high unemployment. There were also a wealth of eating places, galleries and antique shops. A Lloyds Bank building that any capital city in the world would have been proud of and a plethora of pubs. The Wetherspoons is named after John Tremenheere who was made Mayor in 1655. Nine more Tremenheeres followed him to wear the chain of office, the last one in 1797. Cornwall has its frequently occurring prefix 'Tre', Penzance its frequently occurring Mayor's 'menheere'.

The road to Lizard is narrow - I lost a door mirror! I could empathise with those who circumnavigated with a support vehicle and running repairs they might have needed to endure. There were seals at the old lifeboat station and crows above were practicing their 'Red Arrows' routine. In 1907 the Suevic rescue would see 456 lives saved. I further read that geology and climate create the landscape on Britain's most southerly point. Even in October, there were yellow flowers blooming on succulent hugging walls. In shop windows serpentine, uniquely coloured stone ornaments for tourists to take home, I preferred a pasty.

Cadgwith hadn't changed much, 50 or so houses in a picturesque setting, a little, blue painted timber and tin chapel. Seven boats scrabbled for space on the tiny beach and road, shared with nets and pots. Poltesco was the site of former serpentine works, and we managed as far as Kennack Sands in an attempt to walk to Coverack but realised I wasn't as fit or young as I used to be.

I re-read MW's account of St Mawes. Clearly, he had one eye on a 16-year-old Brigitte Bardot going on 25. I worked out she would now be 56. His Wellington wearing, fibreglass skipper was 'cantankerous, belligerent, obnoxious and unpleasant'. I thought he could be describing me.

Rather like we had graded village halls MW had a charm scale for places and Portloe on Roseland came out a six (out of 12.) I wondered what he would give Mevagissey as we stepped back into town.

It started life as 'Porthhilly' back in 1313. Narrow streets nestling, that's every Cornish village you've ever been to, but this one has two harbours, (inner and outer.) The village signs are charming, must be at least a '10', and do show a certain sense of community, which is replicated walking through. About 2000 people, 69 are fishermen, and 63 fishing boats are registered making it Cornwall's second largest fishing port. It was one of the first places in Cornwall to have street lighting - powered by pilchard oil. On the plus side the mussels we bought for tea were a '12', but the museum, closed in 2007 remained shut in 2020, longer lunch breaks than France, on a post Brexit scale only an '8'.

We couldn't go everywhere but I had to revisit Charlestown. I had been 'backalong', around 2010, to meet a date in the pub. She turned up with her son, I don't recall her name, but the son was called Rocky. After I paid for his dinosaur nuggets and chips, she left. Such are the perils of internet dating. I later changed my profile name to 'Gullible'. In the harbour, 'Anny', 'Kajsamoor', 'Iris', and the square rigged 'Phoenix'. Boats undergoing repairs and getting bit parts in TV and film; Dr Who, Poldark and Apocalypto.

The museum of shipwrecks was fascinating, eventually. The old lady who was in the queue ahead of us was totally oblivious to the public behind. Liz and I joked loudly, 'the tide will have gone out', 'our parents will have died before we get to see these wrecks', 'they're not dead, they're resting!' It made not an iota of difference.

At last, I didn't know that there were over 250,000 wrecks around Britain. In May 1913 two large ships were lost on the Lizard in eight days. SS Torrey Canyon (1967) devastated marine life and affected the environment for years. I also was able to put to bed a nagging incomplete memory. From school days (1967) I could recall bits of a poem, 'Sandalwood, cedarwood and sweet white wine.' On the walk I would try and remember more, 'Dirty British coaster' what was it? It would drive me insane. 'Firewood, iron-ware and cheap tin trays'. Then in the museum you get to see John Masefield's poem, 'Cargoes' and it wrapped up all those irritating anamneses.

Outside the path seems permanently diverted inland of Crinnis Cliff Battery. The barriers are more substantial, too many idiots had no doubt tried clambering over and the rear gardens of houses at Duporth were themselves being worn away. I could proudly claim I was one of those successful idiots.

We crossed the Tamar just ahead of storm Aden and were battered and jostled all night parked up at Mutton Cove. The ten miles around The Sound is best explored by bike. Famous 'Janners' have their names engraved on posts - Dawn French to Michael Foot to name just two. Boys on scooters attempted to mow down pigeons. Bikers posed by their chrome raised handlebars, hangers for helmets, shades and whiskers are a must. All manner of hen party outfits left little to the imagination. The biggest city on the Southwest Coast Path; there is lots to see.

This return to the Southwest taught me coastal locations were resilient. Things might change; pilchards disappear, and many shout fishing is on its knees. Mines close. Plymouth was heavily bombed in the early 1940s. The economy has its downs, pandemics and Brexit, but it seemed coastal towns had an ability to re-invent and transform themselves, to evolve, survive and grow.

Most places were winning at life. That must be in some part down to the fact that they are physically by the sea. It has the potential to provide food, a means of transport, a trade medium. With it comes wildlife, leisure pursuits, scenery which draw people to visit. Tourism therefore must sit large in the economy, something which must be embraced, providing goods and services for all those visitors.

I hope to visit often, if not return to live there again someday. So, with thoughts many miles away, I gaze beyond rain drenched streets, not to England, but to the Southwest, where a certain truth lingers. There, with the grace of God, go I. (Paraphrasing Paul Simon,1965, Kathy's Song.)

Chapter 53 - Clevedon, Bristol Channel and Severn Revisited October 2020

You can go the distance; you can walk straight through hell with a smile

"There is something about an English seaside town that conjures up the most romantic feeling of nostalgia and history. Paradise is at the pier."

NONE OF MY 'BOOK HEROES' gave poor old Clevedon much of a mention. SH described it as having 'nothing'. Partly because of this, plus it could be combined easily with a visit to see Liz's second newly arrived grandchild, we drove down on a Saturday afternoon.

True, the miniature railway (toy train) had closed for the season, the bouncy castles had been deflated beneath tarpaulins and the roundabout had been 'magicked' away by Florence, Dougal and Zebedee. In the cold park youths still played, some in shorts, with bikes, scooters and skateboards – getting a final few outings before winter bit. A couple exercised an ageing English bulldog traditionally while another tied it's master up like Houdini, with a long retractable lead. I thought to myself, at least somebody still loves bulldogs!

The front was actually busy with people for mid-October, donning bobble hats they had found out from the bottom drawer of bedroom cabinets. One dad, far too old to be giving demonstrations, refused to give the skateboard back and a miserable looking, helmet clad daughter sat glumly and scolded on a bench praying for him to fall off. Another kiddie gave his impression of an angry panther or perhaps it was a rabid coyote – either way, it wasn't going to make it onto Britain's Got Talent or 'Stand in any halls of fame.'

Any number of national flags streamed towards the town centre on a sharp exhalation from the Bristol Channel. Threadbare and frayed in varying degrees I couldn't help thinking we had defeated Argentina, fought off an attempt by the Scots to leave politically, even if Nicola Sturgeon hadn't gone away forever. Meanwhile other Commonwealth countries wanted to leave, and the other continentals represented we wanted a divorce from. Sheldon Cooper would have fun with these flags.

What used to be known as 'Stinky Corner' now smelt of pizza wafting from the Salthouse Bay pub. Marine Lake, a seawater pool for learning to sail, canoe and swim, lay waterless. A digger sat idle at the entrance. The detritus to be dredged, and a sign read that it was to be refilled the following Wednesday. Opened in 1929 it had had a chequered life, popular then often forgotten. Restored in 2014/15, bunches of flowers stuffed into a fence, marked a passing. I read online that a 66-year-old woman had injured herself falling from a raft banging her head on the 16 September 2012. Were these floral tributes paying respect to this poor soul? Unfortunate and tragic, it was still nice to imagine this open water leisure provision would provide much pleasure for others into the future.

From this point regal towers of the town shared the treeline. The Curzon Cinema, as shown on TV, having been running since 1912 was closed, at least temporarily. Flatholm and Steepholm provided incisors for the mouth of the Severn. Barry, Cardiff and Newport were distinguishable with the backdrop of black mountains. I couldn't help thinking I've walked there. What impact would a Severn barrage, depending on location, have on Clevedon and this stretch of coast, if ever built?

Gulls practising their hang-gliding skills did so with ease, but I had to laugh at some of their attempts to land on the seawall in the wind. Richard Adams' Kehaar was not alone! These birds were happier in the heavens than on terra firma.

A sign read Poets Walk to a local nature reserve, so we headed in the opposite direction on a looped stroll of our own to Ladye Bay.

Grey impasse – bathed in bright autumn sunshine, glaring off a mud ruffled, corrugated sea. Lamb's tongue ferns, seedy blackberries line a love tunnel part shaped by brow bending breeze. The sound of wind, ever present lapping of waves on kelp covered rocks visible at the cellar of this tidal drop. Best Western hosts a slimline economy joining. Flats and apartments, old and new-seeding sunflowers and bedraggled tomatoes in tired grow bags lined balconies, with colourful busy lizzy baskets swaying. Parking bays cordoned off creating extra wide walkways, lead back to a short pier resting on elegant iron legs, turreted at yonder end.

Okay, no poet but apparently John Betjeman thought it, the pier, the 'loveliest in England'. Was this on a par with St Pancras Station?

It was a Saturday and Rylan Clark-Neal was on Radio 2. Was Clevedon 'winning at life?' 'A champion, on the walls of the hall of fame'?

The jury was still out, for the time being it was as if Clevedon was going into hibernation. We drove north to Portishead, a marina surrounded with overspill housing from Bristol, roads meandering through dwellings snuggling in cul-de-sacs. Portishead it seemed, had won and mounted the victor's podium. JT described it as a 'boom town' in 2006. Now it had added 'bang-a-bang'.

We took in the industrial landscape of Avonmouth and Severnside before passing north under two Severn crossings arriving at Littleton-on-Severn and Whale Wharf. A beached whale here in 1885 was some 20 metres long, attracted 40,000 sightseers and apparently three men could stand in its mouth, at least before it was turned into fertiliser. Captain Bill Pegg did his own bit of crash landing on the mud flats here in 1954, 55 years before Captain 'Sully' thought about it on the Hudson, ('the greatest, the best').

Kypes and putchers in these parts were funnel shaped baskets for catching fish, especially salmon – surely two great contenders for Call My Bluff? This whole area provides a rich ecosystem for wildlife.

Clevedon's grade 1 listed Victorian pleasure pier may have its pull factor. However, just down the Bristol Channel, it needed to watch out. Started in March 2022 at Weston was See Monster, (a 'King Kong banging on your chest') right by where the 'T and c' of Tropicana had been lost. Nessie might need to be on her guard too! I loved these public artwork installations. Built from a former oil platform, at 35 metres high, including amphitheatre, waterfall, gardens and telescopes it is due to open in June 2022. (I imagined the swivel ones you put a coin in to gaze over the waves.) The 200,000 expected visitors will need to be quick; it will only be around for two months, phew, Loch Ness could breathe a sigh of relief. It is said it will showcase UK creativity and innovation. Okay, the telescope might be a bit more JWST.

This revisit was a fleeting one. With The Script (2012) reverberating. Around the corner the Principality deserving closer scrutiny.

Chapter 54 - Wales Re-visited. May 2019 and August 2020

Thought you were one in a million

"bom um cam, cer mla'n - *with each step, go forward.*"

THE BANK HOLIDAY weekend at the end of May 2019 allowed an opportunity to re visit some of Wales. Exploring in an old camper van (no1) I recorded the trip in a diary which here provides something of a snapshot of Britain's coast some 12 years on from when I walked it. This was also long before I decided to write something formally. That only started in earnest in October 2020.

We arrived at the gateway to the Gower. The Mumbles cycle path seemed even busier than a dozen years earlier almost to the day. Cycling figures surely show an increase in the activity. (Evidence from cycling shops and the shortage of bikes from the middle of 2020 as a result of Covid/lockdowns/etc would seem to support the fact that getting back on two wheels is booming.) Jeremy Vine, you are not the only one.

I did not remember the term *mamil* in 2007 - now lycra wearing middle-aged men, and for that matter women, abound everywhere. Surely our GPs are happy. On the edge of The Chilterns and in the flat Vale of Aylesbury cyclists swarm and new businesses thrive. Cafes and farm shops provide rest and refreshment. Special racks have been needed to stow bikes and, as well as tea and buns you can buy a puncture outfit or use the in-house compressor to re-inflate your tyres. In Buckinghamshire near Milton Keynes roadside bike service stations with more cables holding spanners than Squiddly Diddly had legs keep the concrete cows company. (2014 would see a move to The Chilterns, birthplace for me, new adventure for Liz.)

The hotel at Oxwich offered Brit Stop bookings where campers could stay on their car park overnight for free, the unwritten rule being you spend a bit over the bar. We were fast catching up with New Zealand. The hotel was also hosting a wedding, but to be honest we were not really sure about the look of the bride and groom. Wedding planners may have been around a decade or so ago but surely not in the numbers we now find. Pre-pandemic, all the trimmings and expense involved with getting hitched, even allowing for inflation, now far outstrip 2007 prices. Pandemic restrictions saw the average wedding spend fall but that has soared since to an average now of £18.5k.

We visited Three Cliffs Bay, Port Eynon and Rhossili. Early morning mist lifted, and a fine sunny day saw people paddling, enjoying water sports and admiring an almost unchanged coast. Purple foxgloves in abundance, waters still meandering across sands to the sea, less wind smashed tents at Three Cliffs campsite but a distinct lack of petrol stations on the Gower, far better enjoyed on foot. Liz and I sat overlooking glorious bays, with cotton wool clouds, the outline of Exmoor in the distance, practicing our words. Not Welsh, but for a forthcoming amateur dramatic performance we were involved with. We were about 80% perfect, The Gower - 100%.

The weather deteriorated and we drove east back to Penarth if for no other reason than we needed to find a petrol station. Penarth is still the wealthy side of Cardiff once promoted as 'The garden by the sea'. Commuters, a substantial retired population and the likes of us can still enjoy palm trees at the Italian Gardens and the well-kept Alexander Park, ponds, bandstand and topiary. We parked up on the cliff road, just up from the pier. They had spent £4 million on this since I was last in town, with the refurbishment opening in 2013.

From here Flat and Steep Holm and directly opposite, Weston Super-Mare. We were now able to cycle the Cardiff Bay barrage and went into Cardiff. The Eisteddford meant everywhere was buzzing but even on a Sunday evening we got an unexpected insight into local culture. Lots of teenage/young girls, very short dresses, often quite overweight through too many pizzas, chips, jugs of cocktails, revealing in all the wrong ways. Overseeing them all from his plinth, rather ironically, Nye Bevan, father of the Health Service. We enjoyed a slightly more restrained glance at Welsh culture the next day with festival singing and dancing before cycling the barrage again, unable to cross it in 2007, now we couldn't stop ourselves, four times on this trip.

With a newer van (no2) and following Covid restrictions we returned to Wales in August 2020. This time we drove to Burry Port and parked up just off the coastal path cycleway. We pedalled east back to Loughor Bridge. The café at the National Wetland Centre had not re opened after Covid and visitors were only being allowed on a booking system. With the increase in cycling perhaps the extravagance of the cycleway was insightful, I had been critical of it before.

We returned to Burry Port via Llanelli town, still looking very run down, found Strady Park developed with some goalposts from the ground now re positioned in the Sandy Water Park. They somehow didn't look as high as I remembered them. The harbour and marina also looked much developed with a new lifeboat station having opened in 2019.

It looked very different to me and certainly would have been unrecognisable to Amelia Earhart who in 1928 gained celebrity status as the first female passenger to cross the Atlantic, landing at nearby Pwll. Four years later she would achieve the first female non-stop solo transatlantic flight. She would disappear a further five years on and was declared dead in 1939. At a time when strides are being made for women's rights and gender equality perhaps it is correct to recognise a prominent woman and pioneering aviator, role model to others in 2023. The last 16 years witnessing many social changes in this respect.

Next stop for us was Carmarthen but we struggled to get there. On the walk we had crossed from Ferryside to Llansteffan avoiding the County town possibly the oldest in Wales. It was as if fate had determined I should not go there as the brakes failed on the new van, rear wheels making awful and expensive sounding groans. We eventually made it and parked by the concrete Tywi Bridge. Landmarks changeover time, this would have once been a medieval stone crossing. We then cycled to Llansteffan, had a good look around the castle, what else is there to do in Wales, a cider at The Castle Inn and met lovely friendly people. It was all very much like years earlier.

The mechanics the next day sorting out the van were equally friendly and could not have been more helpful. While they made us fit again for the road, we had a look around Carmarthen. A sign of the times were queues outside banks and the Post Office. Many shops had not re opened after Covid and the town had a very slow to energise feel about it. I had my first ever go on an outdoor velodrome, nearly just as slow.

As if to further illustrate the point of landmarks changing, like in many other places, the former buildings of a mental hospital now used by university and councils at St David's Parc. Old style institutions close, we now just have millions more with mental health issues that nobody knows what to do with.

Dominating one end of town Picton's monument, at least for the time being. Lieutenant General Picton died at Waterloo. The monument had been rebuilt a few times but now faced a removal drive. Picton's treatment of slaves was behind the campaign and followed on the back of the Colston statue removal in Bristol, June 2020. Ramifications of the George Floyd killing in the States in May had reached mid Wales and the Black Lives Matter movement of course continues.

Ferryside proudly operates an independent lifeboat station originating from 1835, the RNLI ran it until 1960, and it was re-established as an 'independent' in 1966. We came across a number on the walk, Caister in Norfolk and Sidmouth in Devon to name just two. They are often overshadowed for funding and publicity by RNLI stations but have proud histories and the volunteers we met around the coast on the walk were great to us, even though we were raising money for big brother. Some have been adopted by RNLI then lapsed depending on the review of service required, which changes keeping pace with coastal ebb and flow. Often these independents operate with retired RNLI equipment. One could imagine a mutual suspicion of one another, particularly if the long local history of a station is factored in, if after review a station is felt to be redundant. We however noticed no real animosity between operators during our journey, they coexist and get on fine.

I did know the RNLI operated 238 stations, all-weather and inshore boats plus hovercrafts, with the service area broken down into six regions and needing some six launch methods depending on location. Additionally, there are the beach patrols and lifeguard services. A running cost annually of some £177 million. On our walk we saw much of the charity's work, even witnessed some of the behind-the-scenes bits, scheduled deliveries of everything from boat fuel to ballpoint pens for sale in the fundraising shops.

What struck me on this return visit to Carmarthen Bay is that apart from the Ferryside Independent there were no stations between Burry Port and Tenby. All the way around Pembrey, rivers to Kidwelly, Carmarthen and St Clears, around Pendine and Saundersfoot before reaching Tenby. I estimated some 65/70 miles of coast. Normally the distance between stations seems to be 25/30 miles, some are much closer to each other, 8/10 miles. Clearly there must be all sorts of factors to be considered when reviewing where there is need for infrastructure, but I could not find criteria from RNLI literature. Suffice to say, if you are going near or on the water on this bit of coast, throw some money in the Ferryside collecting tin first.

We enjoyed a couple of walks, with less intent from Laugharne. One described as Dylan Thomas's birthday walk through woods to the south of the town, the other in the opposite direction up to his writing room and onto find his grave at St Martin's. The castle was open, but with restricted access, we were less than impressed by the online booking system due to Covid. The whitewashed clock tower with flagpole, bell and weathervane must have been enjoyed by the poet when he lived here. In fact, a mini tour, in his footsteps, taking in places he lived, drank and played in the area from here to Tenby and New Quay might be interesting and enlightening - perhaps another time. For now, local boys swam in the shallow ribbons of water at the castle foundations, far from going 'gently into the good night' and doing their own raging 'against the dying of the light'.

We looked for Cecil Davies and his small caravan, but they were nowhere to be found. There was no sign of JG Parry Thomas's car either, buried in Pendine Dunes after his death in 1927. In the three years prior to this the World's Land Speed Record was broken five times on the sands. Some 2020 boy racers were doing their best to match it on the road but were getting nowhere near the 174.88mph Malcolm Campbell reached. Thomas died trying to break Campbell's record (the current record is 763mph).

A constant thought, anxiety, frustration on the walk was where we were going to stay for the night. On reflection this uncertainty sometimes contributed to rows. In 2007, arrival at Tenby was a case in point.

Very occasionally we would know our daily destination in advance, which was helpful and would partly dictate our pace for the day. If we were in very remote terrain, the necessity was to find an open shop before we needed to camp to supplement whatever rations we were carrying, without overloading rucksacks for miles. These were heavy enough at the best of times.

A very known schedule, like SH/RH, might mean you knew where you would be staying but required much more planning and probably greater contacts than we had. It also denied quite a bit of flexibility. A support vehicle, as had Spud, JT and PH required a rota of drivers, pre-planning and probably more friends and working budget than we could manage. Reading their various accounts, one could scoff and be jealous of a

Spudtruck or Snickers but revisiting Wales in our own vehicle one gained a greater sense of the difficulties of getting it down coastal lanes and finding a parking spot. After a full day walking one might tie up with the van, crash and spend time with your support driver.

Our experience generally, I felt, meant we met more people. Either being offered impromptu accommodation, getting money out of them while collecting, or the necessity of walking into a shop or pub knocking everything and everyone over with a massive lump of backpack, which in itself was an immediate conversation starter.

Tenby, where I had wanted to go back to, could have proved such a difficult parking place. The fact that many places were closed, meant the car park at the leisure centre was empty. We explored on our bikes, popping into cafes and galleries to miss the worst of the rain. A sign outside the Coach and Horses boasted that Dylan Thomas in 1953 left his Under Milk Wood manuscript on a stool after a heavy drinking session. That future mini tour seemed even more inviting.

After a good while in the saddle, which I was much more suited to 13 years on, Liz was needing of a day where her 'undercarriage' could recover so we walked, for me revisiting lots of Stackpole, Broad Haven and St Govan's. I was reminded of the Castlemartin danger zone signs which read.

'Do not touch any military debris, it may explode and kill you.'

Underneath a Welsh poet had scribbled,

'If Covid doesn't get you first'.

This time on Barafundle Bay the ear worm was Beach Boys, 'Where I belong'. The Stackpole estate, now National Trust, covers about five square miles here, 100 acres of lake, 30 km of trails. Much created by the Cawdor family in the 18th and 19th centuries who had a grand vision for these parts, lands were requisitioned at the start of World War Two by the military, so forming Castlemartin Training Area. The plans were abandoned, and a large mansion demolished in 1963. About 11 miles of walking was enough for me for one day now.

School holidays meant we could park in a large car park at Henry Tudor's School, outskirts of Pembroke and cycle back in for a good look around his birthplace, Pembroke Castle. The walk would never allow this degree of exploration but the towers, curtain walls, keep and halls deserve visiting with one-way systems and hand sanitiser at every turn.

Everything in town was Tudor this or Tudor that, businesses trying very hard, but with a poor, run down look. One could only assume with an absence of national chain stores it was partly a victim of out-of-town retail parks, Haverfordwest, the internet or all three.

From St David's, camping on a site for two nights with friends, we could re-visit and enjoy Solva, clear views over St Brides Bay, Marlowes Head and Skomer. A great pasty from the cathedral refectory and an even better turf and surf meal with wine from a bistro were something we could not have managed on our daily walk budget. I could not help noticing the emergence of a St Elvis Brewery and Distillery, now making and distributing products. They must have taken my advice to use the name as a marketing tool or at least were reaping the benefits of the rise of gin since 2007.

St Justinian's now had three lifeboat houses. A very old shed, behind a semi-circular topped one and a wave topped new shed opened in 2017. Flocks of sparrows played in the hedgerows, a game that could only be described as 'all fly off and then come back again'. Chris Packham might be able to shed more light.

Whitesands Bay was busy with mainly wetsuit clad swimmers and bodyboarders. We did manage a very quick dip but Atlantic waters in August can be very chilly without the benefit of neoprene, another sign of aging. The beach made it to 'Miss May' in the Carousel Calendars Coastlines of Britain 2021. I collected Pembrokeshire potatoes from the field edges to remind me of doing similar during the walk. Bike brakes and gears did rather let us both down in the city of the patron saint, Liz going over the handlebars and me finding the river Alun as the only way of stopping, but it all added to the memories. We had potatoes for tea under a twinkling, starry sky, unaffected by bleaching from artificial lights.

The A487 runs almost parallel to the coast from St David's to Fishguard. The lanes to the sea are not large campervan friendly as I tried to get down to Abercastle. The local tourist magazine had recommended a walk from the village to Porthgain, about four and a half miles, a favourite with Loose Women and Pride of Britain's Carol Vorderman. Finishing with a drink in The Sloop, I thought we might bump into her, share a bit of Welsh as I understood she was learning it. Finding somewhere to park accompanied by heavy rain eventually put us off starting.

"I bet Alfred Johnson wasn't put off by a bit of rain" I said to Liz.

"Who's he?" she replied.

"A bloke who was the first to sail single handed from Massachusetts across the Atlantic." (He did it in 1876 and it took him 66 days.) "He landed here, and they've even got their own shipwreck from 1917."

Rain thudded against the windscreen like we were in a carwash. Liz really wasn't up for it. I convinced myself I was just listening to reason, I had discovered compromise, I had grown in 13 years. Truth be known, I didn't need a lot of further persuasion than the heavens were offering, I really had changed, I was getting soft. I consoled myself thinking it was an improbable occurrence for Carol Vorderman to be at The Sloop anyway, we would need to do our own mental arithmetic counting down from 501.

We motored up the coast on to Cardigan, Aberporth and New Quay stopping briefly in all three. I can't say they looked or seemed very different than I remembered them from 2007. Old black and white photos seem very similar to more recent coloured ones.

Driving the distance and covering it in just a few hours, as compared with several days on foot, did remind me however of the word-of-mouth information we would receive while walking. Spud received just the same. Peoples lack of perspective and mileage acumen was frustrating. 'Nice day for a walk' became infuriating.

'It's just up the road' one would say, 'take you about half an hour'. In reality it might be half a day's walk. Those not used to being on foot would vastly under estimate, sticking to their vehicular timer. Two miles might turn out to be 20. On other occasions people might say,

"You can't walk there it will take you forever, take the bus or we will give you a lift."

In reality, it turned out to be less than half an hour. Over estimation was just as prevalent as under estimation, shame on the like of parents, teachers, Duke of Edinburgh tutors and all charged with imparting these skills. National map reading skills are surely scandalous. I saw a group of D of E bronzers just the other day being escorted by police off a motorway hard shoulder. Local geography knowledge is just as bad, 'never heard of it', when places were a stone's throw away, at times even in view (Okay, so why did we need to ask?)

Aberystwyth offered the same difficulties of parking and brought it home that exploring the coast on foot might be the best means of transport after all. Bikes might have a place but also have limitations. Some have done it in a kayak, but I expect they have their own shortcomings. There was no way of replicating my 2007 experience, age and fitness would not allow it if I were totally honest, but it had been fun going back to Wales looking for similarities and differences in time. Wales 'winning at life'? I think so, but you might need to check with Roy Noble.

We sat enjoying a sandwich overlooking the Dyfi Valley as it opens approaching Cardigan Bay. Sandy dunes and beaches, greenery to answer anyone asking 'how green was my valley' without uttering a word, with mountains behind. Like JM and SH/RH it was time to turn in and find a mountain. Inland Lake Bala was warmer than the sea and although Aran Benllyn wasn't Snowdon, it was still a challenge. Poignantly, Billy Joel provided the entertainment, 'play me a memory' of when 'I wore a younger man's clothes'. However, this was Wales, not Madison Square Garden, so Stereophonics (2015) shared top billing, 'I wanna get lost with you.'

I would happily have 'got lost' with Liz, my new partner. Having bagged Aran B, 96 ft too short to be a 'Munro' and roughly 350miles from Scotland, which would take you the best part of seven hours in a car, avoiding teenagers on the hard shoulder, we sat in a small car park by the rugby club. However, we couldn't get lost there either. We had company. A guy who had been kicked out by his wife or girlfriend, sleeping in his car. I knew the feeling. He was on his phone quite a lot trying to make amends. I knew that feeling too. Later other cars came and went, probably quite a lot of north Wales drugs exchange was done in this car park. I didn't know that feeling but mention it as a tip off to the local constabulary. Time to dream of Phil Bennet, hands on his knees, behind his own goal posts, out of breath after conceding a fabulous St Luke's try. That was 'the greatest try of all time' not the Edwards effort for the Barbarian's 1973.

Chapter 55 – And breathe

Heaven holds a place for those who pray

"My mind is like my web browser, 19 tabs open, 3 are frozen, and I have no idea where the music is coming from."

SELF-REFLECTION, packaged wisdom, wellness. In for three, out for six. It is said we do not learn from experience... we learn from reflecting on it.

There was something exhilarating and liberating about writing this. It had become a memoir. Cathartic and seminal at the same time. All those poor souls who had suffered my procrastination about the walk can now buy a copy and save themselves an ear bashing. They will get an insight into what makes me tick as a bonus. Quiet introspection exposé.

Writing reminded me of that World in Action documentary – 'Seven Up.' Other poor souls were filmed at the age of seven, a cross section of society in 1964. The film crew would then revisit them every seven years for a catch up, I think it went on until the guinea pigs were in their fifties. An inherent premise was that the first seven years shaped the adult they would become.

I don't think my first seven years shaped me that much. Some fundamental beliefs and value systems may have been laid down. I was taught the difference between right and wrong. The second son, two very loving parents, perhaps a propensity to putting on pounds, some shaping. I was always told, eat it up, clear your plate, waste not want not. It was one sure fired way to avoid employing a 'Mara Gantry' (NF Simpson, One Way Pendulum). Bread and dripping, bacon dumpling, it's how I became one, while at the same time remaining fattist. Does my bum look big in this? If you need to ask the question, you almost certainly know the answer. (I followed Eric Sykes as 'Mr Groomkirby' in the school production,1976).

The 7-14, and 14-21 septennials were shaping in the sense that I discovered competitive sport, and others thought I was quite good at it. Secondary school was successful, many creditworthy role models encountered, reports universally exemplary. (There was the problem, the antithesis of what *Jezza* said, 16th July, 2006, 'Nobody who was successful at life ever had a good report.') It explained my failures. University was a blast. More exquisite mentors to model oneself on. Why didn't I learn from them? The only failing of my teacher training, a lack of preparedness for the changes in education which would materialise. In fairness, no one could have predicted the social changes that occurred, 1977 to the present day. Four years in Exeter however, were thoroughly enjoyable and very successful. They were very sculpting; I also met my future wife.

The following three septennials were all about making homes, moving up the ladder, career, sport and two children. Probably in that order chronologically and I am ashamed to say in importance. My children often became poor seconds. I was extremely selfish. The ironic thing now on writing, is that my parenting and caring is devoted to my own aging mother. Increasingly at touching 90, she needs more support. Fortunately, I had found an excellent mother for my offspring. One who I was less than fair to. She is the one to be credited for any successes of theirs. I am not sure how these 20 or so years shaped me. All I know is that my energies were often misdirected. What I can look back on with some credit, is a work ethic. (It is what earns me the title 'Taz' from Liz now). Pity more of that was not devoted to my children. I would urge all fathers to sit and listen to Harry Chapin, 'Cat's in the Cradle' 1974.

What did shape me was meeting Wendy. We should have stayed as successful work colleagues, even running partners, never turned it into a relationship. It was a '120-watt bulb that burns too hot to last'. That ultimately would very much change my life. It led to a marriage break up, two if you include hers. Her first husband asked me to look after her - guess that wasn't quite so successful either. It also led to a career meltdown and most tragically a distancing from my children as I repeat. Divorce, and my kids seeing my selfish actions as abandonment, has culminated in any relationship with them as almost impossible - despite best efforts. Currently my daughter refuses to speak at all, my son finds a bit more time, but both have themselves suffered mental trauma, perhaps their own relationship difficulties, as a result of perceived rejection. My punishment for not being there in their formative years. I have my personal regrets, missing out on reading them a bedtime story. My legacy in this sense, neglectful. They have successful lives, despite having me as a father. What will they do when I am gone, and they have no one else to blame?

My son, has expounded to me that coming to terms with the fact that his father is flawed, not a 'super dad', one he can torpedo from a pedestal, is helpful. He now just sees me as a person with human failings and just wishes they weren't so numerous. I don't recall consciously climbing a pedestal but somehow became elevated only to crash and burn. What might be said as my eulogy? I will write it for them, NOT a great father or husband. What I can add though is that my children are truly loved.

I know I have a propensity to be argumentative, which can result in me being loud. Some might say aggressive, that is because I am like a dog with a bone. When your appearance is short and squat, snarling, and like a bulldog, that builds the guise. There are lots who can vouch for that, Wendy and Havoc among them. However, when I was called a narcissist the other day I was stopped in my tracks. I had previously heard the same person confuse Alzheimer's with Asperger's, so perhaps shouldn't have taken it too seriously, but my need for knowledge gene was sparked. Amateur psychology detectorist, time for some self-psychoanalysis. I was further prompted by Blur who would have a song with the same title, 2023. I hadn't a clue what it meant, sounded sinister, a bit like Cape Wrath. It could have been a tendency to keep falling asleep for all I knew.

My quest for transcendence soon led me to other associated terms, sociopath and psychopath. They sounded even more ominous and alarming. Did I really possess an antisocial personality disorder? The characteristics needed ticking off. Arrogant - well, I have already admitted to that. Exploitative for one's own gain - Bill Johnson in Combwich on the river Parrett might agree with that. Entitled - ignoring restraining fencing and signs at Charlestown and the episode at Acheniver youth hostel evidenced this. Lack of care about the feelings of others - Wendy would be quick to add a voice to that. She might also want to throw in manipulative, deceitful and exhibits controlling behaviour. Liz would certainly confirm demanding and might also add low emotional intelligence and lack of empathy. There it is then, the diagnosis confirmed. In psychological terms her being with me might make her a 'flying monkey', (rewatch Wizard of Oz) an agent working for me, but I don't think she would agree.

I am not totally convinced by the identification narcissist. Need for admiration - not reflected in material things. I drive a Vauxhall Combo not a Buggati/Tesla hybrid. You are more likely to find me at the charity shop than in a Cesare Attolini. The experts say the cause of this personality disorder is often emotional abandonment in childhood. If that means from parents, that was never the case from my own. I will not have my parents blamed; fault lies on my shoulders. The case is rather different for my own poor kids. As for treatment, experts recommend more self-love as this motivates more positive behaviour and reduces harmful stuff. 'Learn to love oneself, the greatest love of all.' Now I am confused Whitney, 1985, but probably need to ask lyricist Linda Creed for guidance. I would have thought a narcissist wants to pull back on the self-love, self-importance bit, and cast an eye out for others more. I don't have to be the centre of attention - I can play second fiddle, although I have the musical ability of a central American bing frog, I can walk in others' shadows. Surely if the narcissist verification was wholly accurate,

I would have the latest smart phone and spend all my time on social media. What I can see is that many of the characteristics do poke their head up often, and to ignore is a sure-fire way to mortally wound a narcissist. What I need to personally attend to is not ignoring the behaviour. Here I think God can help. Whether you 'believe' or not, most world religions do offer a code to live by. 'Love you neighbour', be kind, respectful and care about others. It's the doing it consistently that's hard. Stop, think and show respect - be a 'STAR'. Mindfulness, surround yourself with nature, out on the coast path - alone.

One accuser would be horrified I am writing this book. Just magnifying my own self-importance, getting my own back at Wendy, with little thought for my current partner, Liz. Allow me to just reiterate, Liz has been supportive and encouraging in getting it to this point. Fully behind it. If I have one skill it is being able to pick a 'winner'. Either that or I am blessed with a lot of luck.

Because of my hesitancy about leaving my wife, family and a house that had just been completed, for another, that 'another' impulsively terminated her contract with our employer who in the days ahead soon showed me they valued me less than I did myself. I wasn't sacked, but pressure was applied for me to resign and to cut that story short, I found myself on the building site. Career stalled, from propriety to obscurity. My quest to be the world's best teacher ended, I always was something of a perfectionist. My dreams of becoming a Head misguided. In truth I taught some reasonable lessons, occasionally had ten out of ten days. I was never Head material. Perhaps more had 'negative' experiences as a result of me than 'positive'. Did I add to their world, change their lives for the better? Perhaps not.

That is why I think I found the split from Wendy so painful. It cast some very long shadows. There might have been a tough bulldog-like exterior, but the interior was from the soft centred Cadbury collection. (I am led to believe foil wrappers are a contender for 'Say yes to the dress'.) I had given up my world, for one with her. One year of that had seen us do something quite extraordinary, unique in its experiences, to have that betrayed with such superficiality and flippancy was hard to take. Was this a Shirley Valentine thing? An impulsive fling to put an end to trauma. A succumbing to advances all for a bit of 'making fuck!' Whatever happened to talking? 'How could something so right, go so wrong?' (Jermaine Jackson). Wendy had given up lots too, but it is certainly fair to say she didn't give up a comparable career or her relationship with her children. I read she now has grandchildren to love and enjoy, she is winning in that sense. Eulogy supplement - NOT a great partner or friend, but someone who once truly loved.

This, however, is beginning to sound like engrained hostility - a red light that stubbornly will not change. For cathartic cleansing I need to stay on 'Greenlights' (Matthew McConaughey) and remember it is the journey that is important, not the conclusion or destination. That is just one moment. What you do on the way shapes you.

Reflecting, my life has been rainbow coloured throughout, only occasionally drab, stupefyingly varied, a helter-skelter ride. Take jobs for a start. I've taught mainstream and special needs with extended stints with visually impaired and pupils exhibiting challenging behaviour. The latter is just like 'Clockwork Mice' (1995). Did I really do this just to gain admiration from others? Experience, skills and knowledge accrued, even taught Braille. But have I used these to the full? Have I added to the world? Not in any significant sense. Have I made friends? Not many. Not enough to take turns driving a support van on a weekly schedule around Britain. If your company brings more pain and grief than joy and pleasure, simply distance yourself. In defence, one thing I would add is that if you do seem to possess a generalised capability persona or disposition, coupled with dynamism and a 'giddy up' coding it can undermine others, make them feel ill at ease and limit friendships.

If no one cares or shows up at a funeral, I have only myself to blame. I know I am not infallible, and the day will arrive sometime. I am not in the high earner league with the capability to call upon artificial intelligence to keep me alive forever. When the sun goes down on me, if there is no one there, not even St Keverne - so be it.

I have earned a living in construction from groundwork to roofing, painted and decorated, property maintained, window cleaned, delivered topflight swimming instruction for specialised populations. Gardened - although I say it myself, I am at least half decent with a strimmer, cemeteries a specialty. When you fall through a cracked Victorian grave slab you can be forgiven for thinking Satan has come to get you. 'Where the devil don't go' (Elle King) competing with the engine drone. Spare a thought for the next grass cutter you see among the headstones. I have driven all sorts of vehicles, attended abattoirs, nearly as hot reversing a trailer as with a two-stroke brush cutter. Some even say I should use my artistic side to sell my skills as a flower arranger. Constance Spry look out.

One venture that was explored, 2000, I underwent training and selection for the youth development charity, Raleigh International. Following this I was offered the post of Deputy Expedition Leader (DEL) for the Devon and Cornwall millennium trip to Ghana. I could even fool selection panels. That in itself might be an accolade, but my employer would not release me to fulfill the role so there was no chance of building upon it. That's life, professional development opportunity missed, who knows I might have destabilised a continent.

Elsewhere I've played sports to the full, done every type of outdoor/adventurous activity you can think of, coached rugby, refereed basketball, driven a powerboat, led expeditions, instructed in life saving and first aid. I've trodden the amateur boards, even written for the very amateur stage, changed barrels, pulled pints, cooked chips and egg, all with accreditation certificates to testify. Even been Father Christmas! Okay the last one might be seasonal, but why have the others all been five-minute wonders? Am I constantly striving for newness and variety? Short lived success, or consistent persistent failure?

In the last decade I have dipped my toes back into education as a Cover Supervisor in Kent and Specialist Teacher in Buckinghamshire. Both brought thanks, honour, compliments and plaudits. I enjoyed the roles for a while, career reinvigorated, but I am too cynical to stay. I could not go for the quiet life, keep my head down, take the money and the holidays, proliferate the paperwork and the nonsense. I am not one for climbing aboard a fashionable bandwagon going around in ever decreasing circles. Certain aspects of education might be better now than they were. They must be, Ofsted says so. Other aspects are questionably not, some of the stuff I have recently observed is demented drivel. I decided to ditch the laptop, tear up the EHCPs, take a cut in wages for much longer days, less holiday and more physical graft. I work on a farm, with associated shop, my life reverberates around cow shit, silage, rape seed oil and 'eau d'woodshed'. Some of it is monotonous, repetitive, mind dulling, but at the same time no two days are the same. I love it, cannot see myself changing again. A proper job, primary sector.

I look with a very sceptical eye on the employment market even more so since lockdowns with the whole notion of working from home, virtual this and online that. Proper jobs! The sector model in economics divides work activity into three, sometimes four areas. Most proper jobs for me sit in the primary or secondary sectors, it is when you get to the tertiary sector my mind begins to boggle. Commerce, administration, financial and real estate actions, business and personal services, some aspects of education, health and social work. When you get to the quaternary sector - analysts, researchers, advisors, policymakers that my blood really starts to simmer. I am very much on side with anthropologist David Graeger, 'Bullshit jobs.' He argues that the productivity benefits of automation which were supposed to deliver a 15-hour working week have really seen the rise of all sorts of paid unnecessary, pointless and pernicious jobs - more than half of society's work is pointless. These are to be found in the private and public sectors.

If you watch the aptly named TV quiz show Pointless, you will get what I mean. When Alexander Armstrong asks the contestant what they do, if they reply with some assault on nomenclature that you like me have never heard of, it probably is 'Pointless!' Asset Management, PR, HR, consultancy, health and safety, civil service, local government, administration, probably box ticking and 'pointless'. Lexicographers vouchsafed!

Extend this under a heading of dubious to include all things working from home. For me Jacob Rees Mog is quite right putting post-it notes on desks saying are we likely to be seeing you again in the next five years! Teachers doing online lessons. Take it logically and you only need one 'shit hot' science teacher to deliver a lesson and all the others become redundant. Come to think of it we will not need schools, Ofsted or uniform makers and could solve our emissions/ greenhouse gas problem in an instance because there would be no need for mums doing the 200-metre school run in the SUV the size of a small country. I say science because talking to a Year 10 student recently he told me,

"We don't do experiments anymore because student behaviour is so bad!" All from a textbook. CDT has long just been paper and string.

Driving enables me to observe more frustration, and rant even more. I can't decide if I am turning into Jeremy Clarkson or one of Terry's Old Gits. When I am not stuck in jams at 8.50am and sometime shortly after 3pm, (in fairness that is only in term time,) I am pulling my hair out at roadworks. Firstly, it is the trundle wheel waving jobs worth and his assistant with aerosol paint - just fill the bloody potholes! Then it's the small army of hi- vis, hard hat wearing tea drinkers who congregate doing shovel repose. The 4-way traffic lights enable me to sit looking at the SUV drivers, who sit looking at me. There is no sign of a hole in the road, the lights will be there all week and into the weekend. No sign of any work being done but the traffic needs to be calmed. The wheels of the economy are at a standstill, but the not present workers will no doubt strike for a pay increase. Liz Truss will give us all tax cuts, and the economy will all be fine! While I've fallen asleep waiting for the lights to change, someone toots their horn at me, and my anger scale goes from 0 to 10 in an instant. Where's Matthew McConaughey's book now. I need to be back on the coast path, this time alone, with trainers.

Reduce, reuse, recycle, repair - will probably go on my tombstone. I will chisel it myself in advance, because I don't believe in spending anything on things you can do yourself. If we all did, those societal jobs would be 75% pointless, rather than half. No need for dog groomers for starters, though I am not brave enough to include dog sitters and walkers. Reduce expenditure, DIY, you don't need a wedding planner. B&Q my favourite store along with charity shops. Repair - a bit of gaffer tape on a BBQ handle, that has got to hold it. Come to think of it, I might be able to reuse that Victorian funeral stone I fell through, it was already inscribed 'World's Greatest Miser'.

I have concluded I need a physical outdoor job. I could never endure an office. At 64 I hope the body can hold together. We might be able to 'rent a cottage on the Isle of Wight, if it's not too dear!' In the summer, if somebody in Westminster gets a handle on inflation. Hopefully, Liz will still need me and feed me, I am not looking to do anything incendiary. I can't see me ever retiring, I've been divorced, the only winners the solicitors, once you do that retirement is a pipe dream. It is one glaring omission from Baz Luhrmann's rules for life. He says maybe you will divorce at 40, he doesn't say avoid it. He utters, floss, dance, travel, stretch, do one thing every day that scares you. He advises getting plenty of calcium, being kind to your knees, avoiding jealousy, friends will come and go, but above all, use sunscreen. I think Nivea should add it to their bottle, water resistant, ocean respect, protects and moisturises with quick absorption to prevent divorce!

A move from Devon effectively ended my hashing. At its height it was four times a week. Now it's a thing of the past. There are no groups very nearby, Bicester and High Wycombe are just a bit too far. I have contemplated starting a group but with knees that no longer allow running, I wouldn't be a great role model. If anyone reads this and fancies doing likewise – give me a call. My suggestion for a group name - Chiltern Edge, the terrain would be ideal. A comment from Groucho Marx worries me slightly, 'I refuse to join a club that would have me as a member!' I still see old hash mates occasionally, and we put the world to rights. A ten hour a day physical job doesn't leave a lot of time or energy for the gym, so I really do need to follow Baz's rule and s-t-r-e-t-c-h.

Winning at life? I think so, physical, emotional, social, spiritual and intellectual wellness are not bad. I look at Max Ehrmann's poem 'Desiderate' and know I am a child of the universe. A humble career, it is a beautiful world, I strive to be happy, I am at peace with God. We are a long way from the blue space of the ocean, but we have canals with dead bodies and reservoirs. Blue health is very fashionable, especially as a result of lockdowns. Brain imagery research indicates a proximity to water (the sea) gives a feel-good feeling. Apparently, dopamine and oxytocin hormones are released. It's the reason why Hawaii is repeatedly named as the States' happiest place. It reminds me SH commented about a recurrent theme in seaside towns, their ability to rise from falls. What better reason to see if they are winning at life – revisit. Armed with my AA book of the Seaside, one day we might up sticks and find a fresh spot to settle. A two-day heat wave in July 2022 saw beaches bunged, bring on those ice creams. Global warming and seaside town prosperity seem to go together like Cornwall and pasties, Blackpool and rock, Brighton and LGBTQ+ populations.

The living world in 2023 leaves me quite perplexed. We take core samples from it to find out if it really is warming up. On the same day we are told we have had the hottest July ever. We are lectured as to what we need to do. The geological period is now the Anthropocene, since about the 1950's when we really started unsetting the apple cart. Goodbye and farewell Cenozoic, we know the consequences of our actions are irreversible. I am told I am an 'environmental hypocrite' because I sell wood. In the shop boxes of charcoal, product of Malaysia - burnt wood, transported halfway around the world so you can light a barbeque. Used tyres which I must pay to get rid of are shipped, so I am reliably told by the garage, to China to be burned. The horse fraternity, having covered half of southern England with chewed up rubber, have no more calls for any additional meneges. I had to buy a new freezer the other day, I went for English Electric, when it arrived it was made in China, coming the other way on the boat sending them my tyres. One last rant, I prefer HP sauce to Daddies - it isn't my favourite. Where might you expect it to be made? Westminster, no, The Netherlands!

As a final reflection I look at lists of adjectives describing human qualities. From the positive one I see dependability, reliability, resourccfulness and willingness to go that extra mile as personal attributes. Others sit more readily in the negative list, I still wrestle with an ego. High sense of own importance, superior attitude, need for attention and admiration. Let's throw in bullies and intimidates for good measure. In 'keeping livin' perhaps I should strive to be an 'egotistical utilitarian'. How to break a man's ego, leave him for another guy. I'm not quite broken. I question, I grow, I am on my way. 'What have I done today to make me feel proud?' (Heather Small). I have put pen to the page. I have acknowledged the support and generosity of all those who made it possible to complete the walk and contribute to raising that charity sum. I have written honestly, a full and frank account, admitting my failings, warts and all. I have a record to hold myself accountable to. I continue to purge.

dunwalkin has mixed meanings, it's a kind of metaphor. In one sense it's clear, the walk was done. It also means I've told my story, mistakes - I've made a few, but now I've mentioned them. I have also done a lot of other things and I will strive not to repeat the misdemeanors. I am done stewing on insults and so very thankful for a new start with a companion and partner to grow old with, who also likes the nose. Now we are off to do something scary! Eurythmics have the final word, 'Sweet dreams are made of this'.

Acknowledgements

My sincere thanks to anyone and everyone involved in the making and telling of this story.

To Guide Dog and RNLI helpers and contacts and those from Slimming World. To hashers all over Britain. To the amazing, interesting and helpful people we met on the walk, many now untraceable but whose contributions will never be forgotten. To everyone who donated to the not unsignificant amount raised for charity at the time, from children giving pennies to the few larger sums we received from companies. For help, hospitality, friendship, encouragement and inspiration.

To Wendy and Havoc who put up with me.

To Lynne Allen, a good friend for copy-editing and to two astonishing talented and kind spirited illustrators - Aishling Lynch and Jill Griffin. It has been a pleasure to have met you and I cannot thank you enough. To those who have assisted and advised in self- publication.

To those who have shaped me through the septennials.

To Liz - ever kind, reliable, unwavering support, a believer in me and true love.

To you, who put your hand in your pocket to buy this and raise a bit more for charity.

Thank you.

Bibliography

1. Automobile Association. (1972): Book Of The Seaside. Drive Publications, GB.
2. Bathard, Havoc (Wendy). (2018): Wherever I Hang My Lead. Devon.
3. Bryson, B. (1996): Notes From A Small Island. Black Swan.
4. Bryson, B. (2015): The Road to Little Dribbling. Doubleday, an imprint of Transworld Publishers.
5. Bullock, R. (2016): Good Days & Great Days. Bullocks Publications, Manchester.
6. Clarkson, J (2008): Clarkson For Crying Out Loud! Penguin Books UK.
7. Dillon, P. (2016): Walking The South West Coast Path. Cicerone, Cumbria.
8. Freeman, J.(undated): The Coasts Of Britain. WH Smith.
9. Hill, P. (2016): I May Be Gone For Some Time. Pulsio, England.
10. Hunt, S. (1999): the sea on our left. Summersdale, Chichester.
11. Legg, D. (2001): Coastal Walkers (or how they walked and are walking, the coast of Britain. Web site.)
12. McConaughey, M. (2020): Greenlights. Headline Publishing Group, London.
13. Merrill, J. (1981): Turn Right At Land's End. Penguin Books Ltd, Middlesex
14. Reader's Digest. (undated): The most amazing places on Britain's coast. London.
15. Sale R, Evans B, McClean M. (1989): Walking Britain's Coast. Unwin Hyman, London.
16. Talbot-Ponsonby, Spud. (1999): two feet four paws. Summersdale, Chichester.
17. Treadwell, J. (2009): A Bit Far For You Dear. Ralph Allen Press, Bath.
18. Wallington, M. (1986): 500 Mile Walkies. Arrow Books, London.
19. Winn, R. (2018): The Salt Path. Penguin Random House, UK.

Post Script

January 2024

My mother didn't quite make her 90th birthday, passing away on 25 September 2023 aged 89 after a series of falls and pneumonia. That did, however, relieve me of some of the support she needed. Love you mum.

At about the same time I was diagnosed with diabetes, type 1 - insulin injections. The DVLA did their best to remove my driving licence (and livelihood) but 6/6 vision and no evidence of hypos seemed to have kept them in their box - but I might be back walking after all!

I am now told I need half my pancreas and my spleen removed in surgery scheduled for 5 February 2024. So begins a new adventure! Time to take a leaf out of Beyoncé's song book. "Put your hands-up - if you liked it you should have put a ring on it". The smile on a face lets me know I am needed, the touch of a hand says she'll catch me wherever I fall (Ronan Keating). Walk on!